GET OU

PLACES TO VISIT - THINGS TO DO IN NORTHAMPTONSHIRE

by
Ron Wilson

Illustrated by
Elizabeth Noble

JEMA PUBLICATIONS

Published 1998 by Jema Publications

© Ron Wilson 1998

ISBN   1-871468-68-X

Publisher's Note
Every care has been taken in the preparation of this book and all the information has been carefully checked and is believed to be correct at the time of publication, However, neither the author nor the publisher can accept responsibility for any errors or omissions or for any loss, damage, injury or inconvenience from the use of this book.
It is advisable to check opening times, dates, etc. when planning a visit, as these often change rapidly. Although we have tried to indicate where there is an admission charge, we have not included prices.

Jema Publications
40 Ashley Lane
Moulton
Northampton
NN3 7TJ

Printed and bound in Great Britain by Intype, Wimbledon, London

ACKNOWLEDGEMENTS

The production of this book has only been possible because of the help and cooperation of a large number of people. These include Helen Whitney (Development Officer, Countryside Services, Northamptonshire County Council), Lynn Bradshaw (Manager, Countryside Centre, Countryside Services, Northamptonshire County Council), other staff at the Countryside Centre, Brackley TIC, Corby TIC, Daventry TIC (and especial thanks to the staff at Daventry for all their patience), Northampton Visitor Centre, Kettering TIC, Wellingborough TIC, Ian Clarke (Daventry Library), Planning and Transportation Department, Northamptonshire County Council (including Tim Brock), Celia Deeley (Tourism and Conference Bureau, Northamptonshire Chamber of Commerce, Training and Enterprise), Dave Watkins, Malcolm Tyler, Sue Paice (Pocket Parks Officer, Northamptonshire County Council), Daventry District Council, South Northants Council - and all the other individuals who have answered my queries, provided information, etc.

I am sure that I have omitted the names of some people: please accept my apologies and any help you have given has been appreciated.

Ron Wilson
February 1998

FOREWORD

We have tried to make the book as comprehensive as possible, but realise that in doing so there are undoubtedly omissions. We have sent out a large number of questionnaires, many of which were not completed. We have also made many telephone calls, many of which have not been returned. In addition, we have had to rely on 'second-hand' sources. In other instances it has been difficult to trace up-to date information, and we have omitted a number of groups, organisations and activities for this reason.

We hope to revise the book at intervals. and would welcome details of omissions, material for inclusion, etc. The name and telephone number of a contact is all that we need.

Please send any correspondence to Ron Wilson, c/o Jema Books, 40 Ashley Lane, Moulton, Northampton, NN3 7TJ. We will do out best to include new material in any revised edition, but the final decision must remain with the compiler/publisher.

Ron Wilson
February 1998

HELP

Entries in a book like GET OUT! are likely to change rapidly. We need your help! Please let us have any errors or omissions, together with any possible new entries for inclusion in future editions - see cut out slip on page 343.
in the case of the latter, the name and telephone number of a contact is all that we need.

Thank you for your help.

Ron Wilson

CONTENTS

The contents contain all the categories listed. Spend a while browsing through the book to familiarise yourself with the vast number of entries and references. An index has not been included as this itself would have become a gazette and totally unhelpful!!

Ss Peter and Paul, Kings Sutton

Canal Tunnel, Cosgrove

ACTIVITY CENTRES AND GROUPS

See also Residential Centres

BEACON ACTIVITY GROUP FOR THE BLIND

FACILITIES: Arranges a variety of activities, including driving around Silverstone Circuit, dry ski activities, gliding, tandem marathons, canoeing and camping. Outings also arranged.
LOCATION: Activities take place at different venues.
OPEN: Varies.
ADMISSION: Ring for details.   **TEL:** 01327 876065.

WARDINGTON COURT ACTIVITY CENTRE FOR THE BLIND

Provides a wide range of activities for the blind and partially sighted. The variety of courses and activities varies and is constantly being extended, and includes cycling, rambling, cookery, dressmaking, yoga, keep fit, croquet, archery, gardening, cane work, drama, pottery - the list is almost endless. The Torch Trust is a religious group which meets once a month at the Centre. This is one of only a few Centres in the country offering such a wide range of activities. Volunteers are always needed to help with activities.
FACILITIES: Clubroom style atmosphere, where tea, coffee and drinks are available. There is also an information centre.
LOCATION: Wardington Crt, Welford Road, Northampton - the No 20 bus stops close by.
OPEN: Ring for details.
ADMISSION: Various costs for different activities.
TEL: 01604 791333 (Supervisor).

ADVENTURE PLAYGROUNDS/AREAS

See also Amusement Parks

ADVENTURE WORLD
FACILITIES: Swings, slides, climbing frames, ropes and coloured ball 'pond'.
LOCATION: Daventry Leisure Centre, Lodge Road, Daventry.
OPEN: Mon/Wed/Fri 1000-1900; Tues/Thurs 1300-1900; Sat/Sun 0900-1700.
ADMISSION: Charge.   **TEL:** 01327 871144.

DINO-MITES
FACILITIES: 12000 square feet of fun for the children up to 12. Includes giant pyramid, bouncy castles, ball ponds, zip slides, soft play area for under five's.
LOCATION: Unit 60, Burkitt Road, Earlstrees Industrial Estate, Corby.
OPEN: Tues-Sun 1000-1900; school holidays 1000-1900.
ADMISSION: Charge.   **TEL:** 01536 409881.

BERZERK
FACILITIES: Indoor adventure playground with frame, giant bouncy mountain, dead drop slide, net walks, ballponds, crawl tunnels and much more. Food.
LOCATION: 4 Clayfield Close, Moulton Park, Northampton. Turn at Levis and Bezerk is at the end of the Close.
OPEN: Every day 0930-1700.
ADMISSION: Charge.   **TEL:** 01604 647213.

GIDDING ACTIVITY TOYS CENTRE
FACILITIES: Swings, slides, sand and water toys, climbing frames, trampolines and more - on a 'try before you buy' scheme.
LOCATION: Manor Site Farm, Great Gidding.
OPEN: Fri/Sat/Bank Hols and by appointment.
ADMISSION: No charge.   **TEL:** 01832 293591.

GO BANNANAZ
FACILITIES: Indoor adventure playground for children, with bouncy castles, various slides, including drop slides, crawling tubes, ball pools, and rope bridges. Cafeteria area. Birthday party facilities.
LOCATION: Unit 4, Dennington Road Industrial Estate, Wellingborough.
OPEN: Mon 1030-1800; Tues/Wed/Thurs 0930-1800; Fri/Sat 0900-1900; Sun 1000-1800.

ADMISSION: Charges.   **TEL:** 01933 275558.

FUNSTATION

FACILITIES: Bouncy castle, tube slide, ball pond, aerial runway, and lots more. Coffee shop.
LOCATION: The Old Fire Station, Newton Road, Rushden.
OPEN: Term-time Tues-Fri 1030-1800; Sat 0930-1625; Sun 1000-1625. School hols Tues-Fri 1030-1630; Sat/Sun 1030-1625.
ADMISSION: Charge.   **TEL:** 01933 318721.

SONDES ARMS

FACILITIES: Children's play barn and inflatable jungle hut for patrons.
LOCATION: Main Street, Rockingham.
OPEN: All week until 2100.
ADMISSION: No charge.   **TEL:** 01536 770312.

AERIAL ACTIVITIES

ACORNE AIR SPORTS

FACILITIES: Offers a range of air sports vouchers for activities in various parts of the County. These include gliding, helicopters and ballooning.
LOCATION: Ring for details.
OPEN: Ring for details.
ADMISSION: Various prices for gift vouchers. **TEL:** 01494 451703.

AERIAL PROMOTIONS BALLOON FLIGHTS

FACILITIES: Group discounts, gift vouchers.
LOCATIO: Local launch sites.
OPEN: Pre-arranged flights.
ADMISSION: Charges.   **TEL:** 0800 435134.

AQUILA GLIDING CLUB

FACILITIES: Ring for details.
LOCATION: Hinton-in-the-Hedges.
OPEN: Ring for details.
ADMISSION: Membership fees.
TEL: 01295 811056 (weekends only) /01295 710385.

THE BALLOONING BUSINESS

FACILITIES: Arranges balloon flights for individuals or as gifts. Each flight lasts for around an hour.
LOCATION: Northamptonshire. Ring for details.

OPEN: Available at various times - weather permitting.
ADMISSION: Ring for costs.   **TEL:** 01604 768617.

BRACKLEY GLIDING CLUB
FACILITIES: Gliding for members.
LOCATION: Turweston Airfield.
OPEN: Ring for details.
ADMISSION: Membership fee.   **TEL:** 01280 704470.

CANDYTWIST BALLOONS
FACILITIES: Arranges personalised flights over Northamptonshire and surrounding counties. Champagne balloon flights for every occasion. Gift vouchers available. CAA operator.
LOCATION: Northampton.
OPEN: Flights arranged according to requests and weather.
ADMISSION: Charge.   **TEL:** 01604 760417 and 01908 542803.

CJ HELICOPTERS
FACILITIES: Training, trial lessons, gift vouchers and corporate days.
LOCATION: Sywell Aerodrome.
OPEN: Availability varies.
ADMISSION: Charge.   **TEL:** 01604 760760.

COVENTRY GLIDING CLUB
FACILITIES: Operates from the disused Sibbertoft airfield.
LOCATION: Sibbertoft is off the A5199 north west of Northampton.
OPEN: Ring for details.
ADMISSION: Fee.   **TEL:** 01858 880429.

FLYLIGHT AIRSPORTS (MICROLIGHT) LTD
FACILITIES: Microlight flights and training.
LOCATION: Sywell Aerodrome, Sywell, Near Northampton.
OPEN: Ring.
ADMISSION: Charge. **TEL:** 01604 494459.

FORTRESS FLYING CLUB
FACILITIES: Pilot training and trial flights.
LOCATION: Deenethorpe Airfield, Weldon, near Corby.
OPEN: Varies.
ADMISSION: Charges.   **TEL:** 01832 205365.

NORTHAMPTON HANG GLIDING CLUB
FACILITIES: Hang gliding for beginners and training available.

LOCATION: Ring.
OPEN: Ring.
ADMISSION: Membership fee.
TEL: 01788 569687.

NORTHAMPTON KITE FLIERS
FACILITIES: Offers opportunities for anyone interested in kite flying.
LOCATION: The Racecourse, Kettering Road, Northampton.
OPEN: Activities take place 1000-1600 on the first Sun of each month.
ADMISSION: Telephone for information.   **TEL:** 01604 843374.

NORTHAMPTONSHIRE AIR CHARTER
FACILITIES: Evening pleasure flights at certain times of the year.
LOCATION: Sywell Airport off the A43.
OPEN: Tuesday, Wednesday, Friday evenings - ring to check.
ADMISSION: Charge. **TEL:** 01604 644678 - for details and ticket sales.

NORTHAMPTONSHIRE SCHOOL OF FLYING LTD
FACILITIES: A range of services and lessons, etc. which make ideal Christmas and birthday presents. Trial flying lessons, in which the person is allowed to handle the controls. Pleasure flights are available (up to five passengers). Acrobatic flights in a Pitts S2A, when the world can be seen from upside down! Exhilarating experience.
LOCATION: Sywell Airport off the A43.
OPEN: Flights/lessons by arrangement.
ADMISSION: Varies depending on requirements. **TEL:** 01604 644678.

PARACHUTE JUMPING
FACILITIES: Training provided, with twenty years of unrivalled service.
LOCATION: Ring for details.
OPEN: Ring for details.
ADMISSION: Charge.   **TEL:** 01832 280490.

PARACHUTING
FACILITIES: Parachuting throughout the County.
LOCATION: Varies.
OPEN: Ring.
ADMISSION: Membership fee.   **TEL:** 01234 751866.

SLOANE HELICOPTERS LIMITED
FACILITIES: Trial lessons, training and some pleasure flights.
LOCATION: Sywell Aerodrome, Sywell, off the A43.
OPEN: Ring for availability.

ADMISSION: Charge.   *TEL:* 01604 790595.

WALKBURY FLYING CLUB
FACILITIES: Flying training for PPL, night instrument acrobatics, self fly aircraft available.
LOCATION: Sibson Airfield, Peterborough.
OPEN: Ring for details.
ADMISSION: Fees.   *TEL:* 01832 280289.

AMUSEMENT PARKS

BILLING AQUADROME
FACILITIES: Set in 270 acres of parkland, woods and lakes. A range of activities, including 'white 'knuckle' rides, and more gentle rides for younger children. Amusements, games and miniature train rides, together with strolls around the lake and by the river. Swimming, boating, fishing, pleasure park, amusements, shops and refreshments. Fishing - by permit.
LOCATION: Off the A45 near Cogenhoe village.
OPEN: Mar-Oct - ring for details - 24 hour access.
ADMISSION: Charge.   *TEL:* 01604 408181.

COSGROVE LEISURE PARK
FACILITIES: Eight lakes set in 160 acres of parkland, with water and jet skiing, swimming pool and play areas.
LOCATION: Cosgrove, near Stony Stratford.
OPEN: 1 April-end of Oct.
ADMISSION: Charge.   *TEL:* 01908 263615.

WICKSTEED PARK
FACILITIES: This 150 acre park includes a 30 acre boating lake, and 1.5 mile miniature railway. Paid-for rides include Cine 2000, cycle mono-rail, roller coaster, pirate ship, dodgems, etc. There is a large free playground with safety surfaces. Catering, craft shops, etc.
LOCATION: On A6 about a mile from Kettering town centre.
OPEN: Good Fri-end Sept.
ADMISSION: No admission charge, but car parking fee. Rides operate on a voucher-wristband system.
TEL: 01536 512475.

ANIMALS

See also Aquarists, Farms, Country Parks, Garden Centres etc.

DIANE'S PET STORE

FACILITIES: Range of small pets.
LOCATION: 159 Weedon Road, Northampton.
OPEN: Ring.
ADMISSION: No charge.   *TEL:* 01604 753823.

DUSTON PET SHOP

FACILITIES: Rare varieties of gerbils, specialist guinea pigs. Advice and treatment for guinea pig skin problems. Various services. Guinea pigs bought and rehoused.
LOCATION: 2 Windsor House, Limehurst Square, Duston.
OPEN: Ring.
ADMISSION: No charge.   *TEL:* 01604 586222.

THE MENAGERIE

FACILITIES: Has a wide range of animals for sale, including reptiles, invertebrates and birds - and from the 'usual' to the 'exotic'.
LOCATION: 5 Lorne Road, Northampton.
OPEN: Mon-Sat.
ADMISSION: Free.   *TEL:* 01604 632846.

NORTHAMPTON REPTILE CENTRE

FACILITIES: Wide range of reptiles, with advice about keeping, etc.
LOCATION: 159 Weedon Road, Northampton.
OPEN: Ring.
ADMISSION: No charge.   *TEL:* 01604 753823.

THE PARROT WAREHOUSE

FACILITIES: Specialises in the supply and advice on parrots and related species.
LOCATION: Unit 11, The Business Centre, Ross Road, Northampton.
OPEN: Mon-Sat 1000-1700, Sun 1000-1600.
ADMISSION: No charge.   *TEL:* 01604 759800.

PET SMART

FACILITIES: A superstore devoted to pets, from the common to the not-so-common - from mice to chinchillas - and a range of reptiles.
LOCATION: Riverside Retail Park, Valley Road off (A45), Northampton.

7

OPEN: Ring for details.
ADMISSION: No charge.   *TEL:* 01604 406306.

PETS AND PONIES

FACILITIES: Small pets, including rabbits, hamsters, guinea pigs, cold water fish, small number of exotics, together with pet and animal foods, horse food, etc.
LOCATION: 6 Church Street, Long Buckby.
OPEN: Mon-Sat 0900-1730; Wed 0900-1300; Sun 1000-1300.
ADMISSION: Free.   *TEL:* 01327 842852.

TOUCHWOOD PET AND REPTILE CENTRE

FACILITIES: Range of small pets and a variety of reptiles.
LOCATION: 35 Cambridge Street, Wellingborough.
OPEN: Ring.
ADMISSION: No charge.   *TEL:* 01933 272767.

ANNUAL EVENTS

APPLE DAY

FACILITIES: A national event - various activities are organised locally.
LOCATION: Sulgrave Manor involved. For details of others - ring TIC's.
OPEN: Late October.
ADMISSION: Charges may be made.
TEL: 01295 760205 (for details at Sulgrave) - others: contact TIC's.

BARNWELL COUNTRYSIDE DISCOVERY DAY

FACILITIES: Range of activities organised including pond dipping, adventure trails, arts, crafts, quizzes. Great Pooh Sticks Race!
LOCATION: Barnwell Country Park.
OPEN: Mid-June.
ADMISSION: Ring.   *TEL:* 01280 273435.

BARNWELL HALF MARATHON

FACILITIES: Half marathon.
LOCATION: Barnwell, Nr Oundle.
OPEN: Mid-Dec.
ADMISSION: Ring.   *TEL:* 01832 275685.

BBC RADIO NORTHAMPTON'S TEDDY BEAR'S PICNIC

FACILITIES: A chance for everyone to bring their teddies along! Entertainment provided.

LOCATION: Billing Aquadrome.
OPEN: Usually early August.
ADMISSION: Come with your teddy and you get in free.
TEL: 01604 239100 (BBC Northampton).

BLAKESLEY SHOW AND GYMKHANA

FACILITIES: Agricultural Show and gymkhana includes show jumping, children's jumping and livestock classes.
LOCATION: Seawell Ground, Blakesley off the A5 near Towcester.
OPEN: Early August.
ADMISSION: Charges.   *TEL:* 01327 857057.

BRACKLEY CARNIVAL

FACILITIES: This traditional town carnival is organised by the local Round Table. Usual floats and entertainments.
LOCATION: Various venues in Brackley.
OPEN: June.
ADMISSION: Charge for some events.
TEL: 01280 702008 or 700111 (TIC).

BRAUNSTON BOAT SHOW

FACILITIES: A fun day out for all the family. Historic boats, trade stands, music and entertainment. Free fireworks display.
LOCATION: British Waterways Office and Braunston Marina, 3 miles west of Daventry off A45.
OPEN: Late May Bank Holiday 1000-1800 Sat/Sun; 1000-1730 Mon.
ADMISSION: Car parking and entrance fee.   *TEL:* 01788 890666.

BRIGSTOCK HORSE TRIALS

FACILITIES: International riders usually competing.
LOCATION: Fermyn Woods Hall off A6116 near Brigstock and south east of Corby.
OPEN: Prior to Burghley Horse Trials - usually April or May.
ADMISSION: Charge.   *TEL:* 01536 407507 (Corby TIC).

BRITISH GRAND PRIX

FACILITIES: The UK round of the Formula One World Championship. Plenty of excitement.
LOCATION: Silverstone Grand Prix Circuit.
OPEN: Early July.
ADMISSION: Charge.   *TEL:* 01327 857271 (Press Office).

BRIXWORTH BICYCLE BONANZA

FACILITIES: On and off road reliability trial through the Brampton Valley. Also guided bike rides and self-guided tours. Displays on road safety, new bikes. etc.
LOCATION: Brampton Valley - starts from Brixworth Country Park.
OPEN: Mid-June,1000-1700.
ADMISSION: No charge.   **TEL:** 01604 882322.

BROUGHTON TIN CAN BAND

FACILITIES: Midnight parade which takes place on the first Sunday after 12 December to herald the Patronal Festival.
LOCATION: Broughton is off the A43 to the south of Kettering.
OPEN: See above.
ADMISSION: No charge.   **TEL:** 01536 410266 (Kettering TIC).

CASTLE ASHBY COUNTRY FAIR

FACILITIES: Wide range of stalls, activities, events.
LOCATION: Grounds of Castle Ashby House off the A428.
OPEN: June.
ADMISSION: Charge.   **TEL:** 01604 22677 (Northampton TIC).

CLOWNFEST

FACILITIES: Clowns from around the country get together in Woodnewton, where the great Coco is buried.
LOCATION: Woodnewton near Oundle.
OPEN: September - alternate years.
ADMISSION: Ring for details.
TEL: 01832 274333 (Oundle TIC).

CORBY CARNIVAL

FACILITIES: Carnival floats, clowns, and entertainment, including bands, children's amusements, etc.
LOCATION: Carnival goes through town, then entertainment at Boating Lake.
OPEN: Mid June.
ADMISSION: Maybe charges for some events.   **TEL:** 01536 402551.

COUNTRY FESTIVAL

FACILITIES: Includes Hannington Vintage Tractor Club's annual rally, with steam engines, heavy horses, old farm machinery, arena events, craft stalls, children's entertainment. etc.
LOCATION: Lamport Hall, Lamport on A508.
OPEN: Late May Bank Hol.
ADMISSION: Charge.   **TEL:** 01604 686272.

DAVENTRY ARTS FESTIVAL

FACILITIES: Varied activities usually including theatre, workshops, live music, exhibitions, writers activities, etc.
LOCATION: At various venues.
OPEN: Runs in May.
ADMISSION: Charge for some events.
TEL: 01327 871100 (Daventry District Council) 01327 300277 (TIC).

DAVENTRY COUNTRYSIDE DAY

FACILITIES: A variety of activities including pond dipping, birdwatching, walks, as well as a number of stalls associated with the countryside. Usually some crafts. The events and activities vary from year to year.
LOCATION: Daventry Country Park on the B4036 Daventry to Market Harborough road, about a mile from the town centre.
OPEN: Held in May - watch press for details.
ADMISSION: Free parking.   *TEL:* 01327 877193 (Country Park).

DESBOROUGH CARNIVAL

FACILITIES: Annual carnival with floats, stalls, attractions, etc.
LOCATION: In Desborough.
OPEN: Late June.
ADMISSION: Some charging. *TEL:* 01536 410266 (Kettering TIC).

EARLS BARTON CARNIVAL

FACILITIES: Different themes for the Carnival. Takes place in June.
LOCATION: Earls Barton Recreation Ground.
OPEN: Ring for information.
ADMISSION: May be charges for some events.   *TEL:* 01604 810989.

EAST CARLTON COUNTRY FAIR

FACILITIES: Market stalls, craft stands and trade stands.
LOCATION: East Carlton Countryside Park.
OPEN: Late May Bank Holiday.
ADMISSION: Ring for details.
TEL: 01536 770977 (Countryside Park) and 402551
x 8007 (Corby District Council).

EAST OF ENGLAND SHOW

FACILITIES: This show, which incorporates the Northamptonshire Agricultural Society, features a wide variety of activities. Although the farming aspect is still important, the show caters for a wide range of visitors.
LOCATION: East of England Showground, which is on the A605 on the edge of Peterborough.

OPEN: Mid July.　　**TEL:** 01733 234451.

EVERDON HORSE TRIALS

FACILITIES: Horse trials with riders from all over the country. Opportunities for spectators to observe the horses as they use local fields.

LOCATION: Everdon Hall is signposted for the event.　Everdon is reached off the A45, at the Dodford turn, and is about 2.5 miles from the main road.

OPEN: August - ring for date.

ADMISSION: Ring for details.　　**TEL:** 01327　300277 (Daventry TIC).

FLORE FLOWER FESTIVAL.

FACILITIES: This annual festival has exceptionally high standards, with displays in the church and chapel and some village gardens open.

LOCATION: Flore is on the A45 between the M1 junction 16 and Weedon.

OPEN: Mid-June.

ADMISSION: Charges for some aspects.　　**TEL:** 01327 341264.

GREBE

FACILITIES: Annual event for young people.

LOCATION: Daventry Country Park, on B4036 Daventry to Market Harborough road, 1 mile north east of Daventry.

OPEN: Held in August - ring for date.

ADMISSION: Small charge.　　**TEL:** 01327 877193.

HAUNTED HALLOWEEN

FACILITIES: A lantern walk around Irchester Country Park, followed by a barbecue. Ghost stories around the fire.

LOCATION: On the B570 Little Irchester to Irchester road, and off the A509 south east of Wellingborough.

OPEN: Halloween.

ADMISSION: Ring.　　**TEL:** 01933 276866.

HEDGEHOG

FACILITIES: Environmental playscheme run by Watch and the Wildlife Trust for Northamptonshire.

LOCATION: Lings House, Billing Lings, Northampton.

OPEN: May - ring for times.

ADMISSION: Charge. **TEL:** 01604 405285.

HIGHLAND GATHERING

FACILITIES: Highland dancers, pipe bands, drum major competitions. Stalls and refreshments.
LOCATION: West Glebe, Corby.
OPEN: Mid July.
ADMISSION: Ring for details.   **TEL:** 01536 402551 x 8007.

HOLLOWELL STEAM AND HEAVY HORSE SHOW

FACILITIES: Vintage vehicles, traction engines, heavy horses, fairground amusements, demonstrations, arena events, etc.
LOCATION: Hollowell.
OPEN: First clear Sat/Sun in July.
ADMISSION: Charge.   **TEL:** 01604 505422.

KETTERING CARNIVAL

FACILITIES: Floats, events, attractions.
LOCATION: At various venues in Kettering.
OPEN: Mid-August.
ADMISSION: Charge for some events.
TEL: 01536 521128 or 410266 (TIC).

KINGFISHER WILDZONE

FACILITIES: A variety of activities planned for youngsters.
LOCATION: Barnwell Country Park, Oundle Road, Barnwell.
OPEN: Held August - ring for details.
ADMISSION: Small charge.   **TEL:** 01832 273435.

MUMMERS (TRADITIONAL) PLAY AND MORRIS DANCING

FACILITIES: Performance of traditional mummers play, together with traditional Morris dancing.
LOCATION: Stocks Hill, Moulton, near Northampton.
OPEN: Usually Boxing Day.
ADMISSION: No charge.   **TEL:** 01604 646818.

NORTHAMPTON BALLOON FESTIVAL

FACILITIES: A three day event organised by Northampton Borough Council. It is now one of the country's leading ballooning events. Around 80 balloons from all over the country, together with a varied programme of entertainment. Balloons fly from 0600-1800 each day - weather permitting. Extensive trade fair.
LOCATION: The Racecourse, Northampton, which covers 100 acres, on the A43 Kettering road.

OPEN: Mid-August - ring for dates.
ADMISSION: Free entry: charge for parking.
TEL: 01604 233500 (Events Office - Northampton Borough Council).

NORTHAMPTON CARNIVAL

FACILITIES: A procession of floats starting at Midsummer Meadow and going through the town.
LOCATION: See above.
OPEN: Third week in June.
ADMISSION: No charge.   *TEL:* 01604 784534.

NORTHAMPTON COUNTRY FAYRE AND SHEEP DOG TRIALS

FACILITIES: Apart from the Sheep DogTrials, traditional country crafts, such as thatching, blacksmithing and weaving, are interspersed with a large craft marquee, trade stands and agricultural bygones. There is also a well planned programme of entertainment.
LOCATION: Held at Delapre Park on London Road.
OPEN: Early Sept - ring for dates.
ADMISSION: Free.
TEL: 01604 233500 (Events Office - Northampton Borough Council).

NORTHAMPTON MARKET SQUARE

FACILITIES: Traditional bank holiday markets with extra fun and games, together with street entertainers, children's rides, live music and much more.
LOCATION: Northampton Market Square at the lower end of Abington Street in the town centre.
OPEN: Various Bank Holiday weekends.
ADMISSION: No charge for markets - ring for details.
TEL: 01604 233500 (Northampton Borough Council).

NORTHAMPTON TOWN SHOW

FACILITIES: Runs for three days and is organised by Northampton Borough Council. A wide range of attractions, trade stands, live music, fireworks display, talent competitions, youth bands, NFU marquee with live farm animals. Wide range of catering facilities.
LOCATION: Abington Park, Northampton.
OPEN: Around mid-July - ring for details.
ADMISSION: Charge made.
TEL: 01604 233500 (Events Office - Northampton Borough Council).

OPERATION SPRING CLEAN

FACILITIES: Organises an annual week of spring cleaning events in the county. Aims to improve the environment when volunteers respond. They recieve litter picking kits and certificates; there is a competition for the best litterpick.
LOCATION: Around the County.
OPEN: Usually April - ring for details.
ADMISSION: No charge.   *TEL:* Co-ordinator - 01604 236613.

OUNDLE FESTIVAL OF MUSIC AND DRAMA

FACILITIES: A wide range of classes.
LOCATION: At venues in Oundle.
OPEN: March/April.
ADMISSION: Charges for some events.
TEL: 01832 274333 (Oundle TIC).

OUNDLE INTERNATIONAL MUSIC FESTIVAL

FACILITIES: The Festival has achieved international recognition. Includes. music and drama, including young organists.
LOCATION: At various venues in Oundle.
OPEN: July.
ADMISSION: Various prices.   *TEL:* 01832 274333 (Oundle TIC).

PEEWIT WILDZONE

FACILITIES: Activity playscheme for young people.
LOCATION: Brixwworth Country Park, just off the A508 at the southern end of the Brixworth bypass.
OPEN: End of July.
ADMISSION: Small charge. *TEL:* 01604 882322.

ROTHWELL CHARTER FAIR

FACILITIES: The original Charter for the Fair was granted by King John and survives in a later charter given by James I. Today the Lord of the Manor's Bailiff rides around the town on horseback reading out the charter at various points at 0600 on Trinity Monday. The Fair continues for a week.
LOCATION: Rothwell.
OPEN: From Trinity Monday.
ADMISSION: Charges.   *TEL:* 01536 710897.

ROTHWELL MUSIC FESTIVAL

FACILITIES: Varied programme of serious and light classical music, chamber orchestras and choral works.
LOCATION: Holy Trinity Church.

OPEN: Mid-May.
ADMISSION: Charge.   **TEL:** 01536 710268 and 01536 410266.

RUSHDEN FESTIVAL

FACILITIES: A wide range of indoor and outdoor activities held over a ten-day period, including the Carnival (last Sat in June), Rushden & District Art Society Exhibition, Rushden and District Historical Society Exhibition, and a range of musical events - from opera to rock n' roll.
LOCATION: Various venues, including Hall Park, Rushden Hall, etc.
OPEN: Mid June - beg July.
ADMISSION: Various prices - but discount ticket available.
TEL: 01832 742042 (East Northants District Council Leisure Officer).

SKYLARKING WILDZONE

FACILITIES: Annual playscheme for young children.
LOCATION: Brigstock Country Park, on the south side of Brigstock village off the A6116 Brigstock bypass.
OPEN: August.
ADMISSION: Small charge.   **TEL:** 01536 373625.

ST CRISPIN STREET FAIR AND MARKET

FACILITIES: A fair with a wide range of rides and stalls, together with a street market.
LOCATION: Abington Street, Northampton town centre.
OPEN: Late October.
ADMISSION: Charges for rides, etc.   **TEL:** 01604 233500 (NBC).

SYWELL FAMILY NATURE DAY

FACILITIES: An afternoon of activities, games, and local conservation stalls.
LOCATION: Sywell Country Park.
OPEN: Mid July.
ADMISSION: Free.   **TEL:** 01604 810970.

THRAPSTON CHARTER FAIR

FACILITIES: Celebrates the granting of a Charter to the town in 1205 by King John. Local people raise money and entertain.
LOCATION: High Street - which is closed to traffic.
OPEN: Late June.
ADMISSION: Ring.   **TEL:** 01832 734636 or 274333 (Oundle TIC).

TOWCESTER FESTIVAL

FACILITIES: Includes carnival procession, and other events - vintage cars, fun run, etc.

LOCATION: Easton Neston Estate.
OPEN: Early July.
ADMISSION: Ring.   *TEL:* 01327 350099.

WAENDAL WALK
FACILITIES: Established in 1979, walks of 15, 29 and 42 km on one or two days. Also incorporates the Friendship Walk (10km) and the Swim (300m).
LOCATION: Walks - The Castle, Castle Road, Wellingborough - start and finish. Swim - Wellingborough Pool.
OPEN: Mid-May.
ADMISSION: Entrance fee.
TEL: 01933 228101 (TIC)/229777 x 4425 (Borough Council.)

WAGTAIL WILDZONE
FACILITIES: Holiday playscheme for young children.
LOCATION: Sywell Country Park, reached from the A4500 at Earls Barton crossroads - and then signposted - 0.5 miles along the road.
OPEN: May.
ADMISSION: Small charge. *TEL:* 01604 810970.

WELLINGBOROUGH ARTS FESTIVAL
FACILITIES: A wide range of activities, including theatre, writers' readings, exhibitions, arts and crafts, etc.
LOCATION: In and around Wellingborough.
OPEN: Last two weeks in June.
ADMISSION: Various prices.
TEL: 01993 229777 (Borough Council)/01933 228101 (TIC).

WELLINGBOROUGH JAZZ FESTIVAL
FACILITIES: A variety of jazz forms.
LOCATION: Venues around town.
OPEN: Nearest weekend to 14 Feb.
ADMISSION: Charge. *TEL:* 01933 229777 (Borough Council).

WILD TIME
FACILITIES: An exciting programme of illustrated talks, which varies from year to year, but includes birds, mammals, insects, etc.
LOCATION: Sywell Country Park, reached from the A4500 at the Earls Barton crossroads, and signposted about 0.5 miles down the road.
OPEN: Monthly from Jan-Dec - Thursday at 19.30.
ADMISSION: Small charge - booking necessary.
TEL: 01604 810970 (Sywell Country Park) 237220 (Countryside Centre).

WOODPECKER WILDZONE
FACILITIES: Annual environmental playscheme for young children.
LOCATION: Irchester Country Park, Irchester to Little Irchester Road, and off the A509 south east of Wellingborough.
OPEN: August.
ADMISSION: Small charge.   **TEL:** 01933 276866.

WORLD CONKER CHAMPIONSHIPS
FACILITIES: Held annually on the village green in Ashton. The conker 'champions' from around the world get together to 'conker' each other. Includes men's, ladies, intermediate, team and children's knockout events. The event has been enlarged in recent years and now provides facilities for other entertainment, charity stalls, etc.
LOCATION: In the village of Ashton, near Oundle.
OPEN: Sun in October.
ADMISSION: Ring.
TEL: 01832 272735 or 274333 (Oundle TIC).

ANTIQUES

ABBEY ANTIQUES
FACILITIES: Antique and pre 1930's furniture, paintings, clocks, silver, pottery, and house clearance service.
LOCATION: 116 Towcester Road, Northampton.
OPEN: Ring.
ADMISSION: No charge.   **TEL:** 01604 764321.

ASPIDISTRA ANTIQUES
FACILITIES: Victorian Art Noveau and Art Deco, with Eichwald a speciality.
LOCATION: 51 High Street, Finedon.
OPEN: Ring.
ADMISSION: No charge.   **TEL:** 01933 680196.

SIMON BANKS ANTIQUES
FACILITIES: Georgian, William IV, Victorian, Edwardian and shipping furniture and effects.
LOCATION: Quaker Lodge, 28 Church Street, Finedon.
OPEN: Ring.
ADMISSION: No charge.   **TEL:** 01933 680371.

BRIXWORTH UPHOLSTERY

FACILITIES: Traditional re-upholstery of antique furniture, with French polishing and top quality hand crafted upholstered furniture, made to personal designs and specifications. Also has a home visit service.
LOCATION: Ring.
OPEN: Ring for details.
ADMISSION: No charge.   **TEL:** 01604 881488.

BULEY ANTIQUES

FACILITIES: Silver, brass, china, old dolls, antique jewellery, pre-1930 clothes, linen and lace, antique and pre-1930's furniture, including chairs, tables, bureau, etc.
LOCATION: 164 Kettering Road, Northampton.
OPEN: 1030-1600 - closed Thurs.
ADMISSION: No charge.   **TEL:** 01604 631588/491577.

MALCOLM CAMERON

FACILITIES: English furniture.
LOCATION: The Antique Galleries, Watling Street, Paulerspury.
OPEN: Mon-Sat 0900-1730.
ADMISSION: No charge.   **TEL:** 01327 811238.

CAVES

FACILITIES: An amazing selection of antiques, including furniture, etc.
LOCATION: In the basement at 111 Kettering Road, Northampton.
OPEN: Mon-Sat 0900-1730.
ADMISSION: No charge.   **TEL:** 01604 638278.

CB ANTIQUES

FACILITIES: Antique furniture, china, glass and collectable items.
LOCATION: 13 High Street, Finedon.
OPEN: 7 days.
ADMISSION: No charge. **TEL:** 01933 681048 (day)/ 680085 (evenings).

M C CHAPMAN ANTIQUES

FACILITIES: Furniture - including dining, kitchen occasional, garden - tables, chairs, chests, sideboards, bookcases. Clocks, prints and paintings.
LOCATION: 11-25 Bell Hill, Finedon.
OPEN: Ring.
ADMISSION: Free.   **TEL:** 01933 681260.

PETER AND LAURENCE COOKSLEY ANTIQUES

FACILITIES: Pre-1930's furniture, pianos, etc.
LOCATION: Poacher's Gap, Boughton, Northampton.
OPEN: Ring.
ADMISSION: No charge.   **TEL:** 01604 842705.

CORNER CUPBOARD

FACILITIES: Victorian iron and brass bedsteads, Victorian English and continental kitchens.
LOCATION: 14 & 18 Station Road, Woodford Halse, off the A361 south of Daventry.
OPEN: Mon-Wed, Thurs-Sun.
ADMISSION: Free.   **TEL:** 01327 260725.

THE COUNTRY PINE SHOP

FACILITIES: Antique pine furniture from this country and abroad.
LOCATION: The Nurseries, Northampton Road, West Haddon.
OPEN: Mon-Sat 0800-1700.
ADMISSION: No charge.   **TEL:** 01788 510430.

CROUGHTON ANTIQUES

FACILITIES: Oak and general antiques.
LOCATION: 29 High Street, Croughton.
OPEN: Wed-Sun 1000-1800.
ADMISSION: Free.   **TEL:** 01280 810203.

DALES OF FINEDON

FACILITIES: General antiques bought and sold.
LOCATION: 1 High Street, Finedon.
OPEN: Ring.
ADMISSION: No charge.   **TEL:** 01933 680973.

DOLLIES ANTIQUES

FACILITIES: Pre 60's toys and dolls, collectables, curios, antique furniture.
LOCATION: 288 Kettering Road, Northampton.
OPEN: Ring.
ADMISSION: Free.   **TEL:** 01604 720124.

DRAGON ANTIQUES

FACILITIES: General antiques.
LOCATION: 85 Rockingham Road, Kettering.
OPEN: Ring.

ADMISSION: No charge.   **TEL:** 01536 517071.

E K ANTIQUES

FACILITIES: Quality furniture bought and sold. Also furniture restoration, French polishing, traditional hand finishing, renovation of period interiors, etc.
LOCATION: 37 High Street, Finedon.
OPEN: Ring.
ADMISSION: No charge.   **TEL:** 01933 681882.

FINEDON ANTIQUES

FACILITIES: A collection of ten antique shops around a central courtyard, and covering 5000 square feet. Displays include Georgian and Victorian furniture, clocks, pottery and porcelain, soft furnishings, collectible and decorative items and a range of antique and reproduction garden statuary and ornaments. Valuation service.
LOCATION: Vicarage Farm, Bell Hill, Finedon.
OPEN: Mon-Sat 0900-1730; Sun 1100-1700.
ADMISSION: No charge.   **TEL:** 01933 681260.

RON GREEN ANTIQUES

FACILITIES: English and continental furniture, silver, porcelain, china, glass and paintings.
LOCATION: 209, 215, 227 & 239 Watling Street, Towcester.
OPEN: 0900-1800 - or ring for appointment.
ADMISSION: Free.   **TEL:** 01327 350387.

PAM AND TONY HARVARD

FACILITIES: Furniture, clocks, copper and brass, china, jewellery, etc.
LOCATION: 23 High Street, Harpole.
OPEN: Tues/Thurs/Fri/Sat - 1000-1900.
ADMISSION: No charge.   **TEL:** 01604 830007.

HEART OF ENGLAND ANTIQUES

FACILITIES: Quality furniture and clocks.
LOCATION: 23 High Street, Weedon.
OPEN: Every day - 0930-1730.
ADMISSION: Free.   **TEL:** 01327 341928.

HELIOS ANTIQUES

FACILITIES: Complete range, including furniture, mirrors, linen china - whatever.
LOCATION: 25-27 High Street, Weedon.
OPEN: Every day from 1030-1700.

ADMISSION: Free.   *TEL:* 01327 340264.

HEYFORD ANTIQUES
FACILITIES: Range of material.
LOCATION: Church Street, Heyford.
OPEN: Ring.
ADMISSION: No charge.   *TEL:* 01327 340749.

PETER AND HEATHER JACKSON
FACILITIES: English and continental porcelain and furniture.
LOCATION: 3 Market Place, Brackley.
OPEN: Ring for times.
ADMISSION: No charge.   *TEL:* 01280 703259.

CHRISTOPHER JONES ANTIQUES
FACILITIES: General antiques.
LOCATION: Flore House, The Avenue, Flore, off the A45.
OPEN: Mon-Fri 1000-1700.
ADMISSION: No charge.   *TEL:* 01327 342165.

JOHN & JENNIFER JONES
FACILITIES: Paintings, furniture, china.
LOCATION: 2 Watling Street East, Towcester.
OPEN: Mon-Fri 0900-1800; Sat 0900-1700.
ADMISSION: No charge.   *TEL:* 01327 351898.

JUNO ANTIQUES
FACILITIES: Good range of furniture and collectors items.
LOCATION: 4 Bridge Street West, Brackley.
OPEN: Mon/Tues/Thurs/Fri/ Sat 1000-1300 & 1400-1700.
ADMISSION: Free.   *TEL:* 01280 700639.

KETTERING ANTIQUES AND HOUSE CLEARANCE
FACILITIES: Wide range of antiques.
LOCATION: 67 Montagu Street.
OPEN: Ring.   *ADMISSION:* No charge.   *TEL:* 01536 415612.

LAILA GRAY ANTIQUES
FACILITIES: General antiques, including brass beds, dressers, chest of drawers, tables, chairs, fireplaces, pine stripping and restoration service.
LOCATION: 25 Welford Road, Kingsthorpe, Northampton.
OPEN: Ring.
ADMISSION: No charge.   *TEL:* 01604 715277/720492.

MCFADDENS

FACILITIES: Antiques, gold, silver, jewellery, etc.
LOCATION: 324 Wellingborough Road.
OPEN: Ring.   **ADMISSION:** Free.   **TEL:** 01604 21543.

WILLIAM MARTIN ANTIQUES

FACILITIES: Antique clocks and barometers, furniture, jewellery, silver, china.
LOCATION: 16 Overend, Elton.
OPEN: Ring.   **ADMISSION:** Free.   **TEL:** 01832 280859.

MEMORIES

FACILITIES: All periods of furniture and collectables.
LOCATION: Heart of the Shires Shopping Village, on A5 2miles north of Weedon.
OPEN: Ring.
ADMISSION: No charge.   **TEL:** 01327 879837 (evenings).

R K J NICHOLAS

FACILITIES: Silver, glass, porcelain.
LOCATION: 161 Watling Street, Towcester.
OPEN: 0930-1800.
ADMISSION: No charge.   **TEL:** 01327 350639.

BRENDA NUTTING

FACILITIES: Ceramics and furniture.
LOCATION: 69 High Street, Brackley.
OPEN: Mon-Sat 1000-1800; Wed 1000-1200; Sun by appointment.
ADMISSION: No charge.   **TEL:** 01280 703362.

THE OLD BRIGADE

FACILITIES: Military antiques - medals, weapons, headresses, etc.
LOCATION: 10a Harborough Road, Kingsthorpe, Northampton.
OPEN: Ring.   **ADMISSION:** Free.   **TEL:** 01604 719389.

THE OLD DAIRY FARM CENTRE

FACILITIES: A continually changing collection of antiques, including bric-a-brac and collectables.
LOCATION: 0.5 miles from the A5 south of Weedon.
OPEN: 9 Jan-28 Feb 1000-1630; 1 Mar-24 Dec 1000-1730.
ADMISSION: No charge.   **TEL:** 01327 340525.

THE OLD HALL BOOKSHOP
FACILITIES: Antiquarian books, second hand books, also new ones.
LOCATION: Market Square, Brackley.
OPEN: Weekdays 0930-1300 & 1400-1730.   *TEL:* 01280 704146.

OLD TIMBERS
FACILITIES: Antique pine furniture, Victorian fireplaces, door stripping services.
LOCATION: 172 St Andrews Road, Northampton.
OPEN: Ring.   *ADMISSION:* Free.   *TEL:* 01604 720203.

OUNDLE ANTIQUES
FACILITIES: Collectables, glassware, china, stripped pine, etc.
LOCATION: 53 West Street.
OPEN: Ring.   *ADMISSION:* Free.   *TEL:* 01832 274132.

BRYAN PERKINS ANTIQUES
FACILITIES: Quality antiques bought and sold. French polishing and restoration by skilled craftsmen.
LOCATION: 52 Cannon Street, Wellingborough.
OPEN: Ring.
ADMISSION: Free.   *TEL:* 01933 228812.

REINDEER ANTIQUES LTD
FACILITIES: English furniture and clocks.
LOCATION: 43 Watling St. Potterspury.
OPEN: Ring for details.
ADMISSION: No charge.   *TEL:* 01908 542407/542200.

RESTALL BROWN AND CLENNEL LTD
FACILITIES: English furniture from the 17th-19th centuries.
LOCATION: Cosgrove Hall, Cosgrove.
OPEN: Ring for appointment.
ADMISSION: Free.   *TEL:* 01908 565888.

ROCOCO ANTIQUES
FACILITIES: Antiques and architectural furnishings, iron, etc.
LOCATION: 5 New Street, Lower Weedon.
OPEN: 7 days.
ADMISSION: Free.   *TEL:* 01327 341288.

JOHN ROE ANTIQUES
FACILITIES: Antique and pre-1950's furniture, wooden office equipment, old shop fittings, bookcases, sets of chairs.
LOCATION: Unit 14, Cottingham Way, Thrapston.

OPEN: Ring.
ADMISSION: Free.   *TEL:* 01832 732937.

SELBY SHOWJUMPS AND GARDEN FURNITURE

FACILITIES: Antiques, collectables and bric-a-brac bought and sold.
LOCATION: The Bungalow, Littleworth, Duncote, off A5 between Weedon and Towcester.
OPEN: Daily - 0930-1900.
ADMISSION: No charge.   *TEL:* 01327 350345.

D W SHERWOOD (ANTIQUES) LTD

FACILITIES: General antiques.
LOCATION: 59 Little Street, Rushden.
OPEN: Ring.   *ADMISSION:* Free.   *TEL:* 01933 353265.

THIRTY-EIGHT ANTIQUES

FACILITIES: English furniture.
LOCATION: The Royal Ordnance Depot, Weedon.
OPEN: By appointment.
ADMISSION: Free.   *TEL:* 01327 340766.

THE VILLAGE ANTIQUE MARKET

FACILITIES: General antiques.
LOCATION: 62 High Street, Weedon.
OPEN: Mon-Fri 0930-1730; Sat 1030-1730.
ADMISSION: Free.   *TEL:* 01327 342015.

LEE ANTHONY WRIGHT

FACILITIES: Antiques and fine arts.
LOCATION: Heart of the Shires Shopping Village, A5 2 miles north of Weedon.
OPEN: Ring.
ADMISSION: No charge.   *TEL:* 01973 552320.

AQUARISTS AND AQUATIC CENTRES

AQUAPET

FACILITIES: 120 tanks containing a wide range of both cold water and tropical fish, including 60cm koi carp. Tanks and aquatic kits. Pre-formed ponds and liners. There is also a bird section.
LOCATION: Causeway Park. 4 miles east of Northampton, 0.5 miles from the Great Billing exit on A45.
OPEN: Mon-Sat - 0900-1800; Sun 1100-1700.

ADMISSION: No charge.   **TEL:** 01604 786666.

AQUATIC ENTERPRISES

FACILITIES: Tropical and cold water fish, and aquatic accessories, including tanks.
LOCATION: 6/8 Sheaf St., Daventry.
OPEN: Mon-Sat (half day Wed).
ADMISSION: No charge.   **TEL:** 01327 705069.

BRYAN'S TROPICAL FISH CENTRE

FACILITIES: Has a range of fish from the common guppy to more exotic species.
LOCATION: 198 Studfall Avenue. (inside Pam's), Corby.
OPEN: Ring for times.
ADMISSION: No charge.   **TEL:** 01536 203656.

CRANFORD KOI

FACILITIES: Northamptonshire's Koi specialist. There are also tropical and coldwater sections, crystal clear ponds, tanks, and air stones to complete aquaria.
LOCATION: The Old Pump House, Unit 6, The Embankment, Wellingborough.
OPEN: Tues-Sun from 1000.
ADMISSION: Free.   **TEL:** 01933 271870.

DUSTON AQUATIC CENTRE

FACILITIES: Range of fish and accessories.
LOCATION: Duston Garden Centre, Millway, Duston.
OPEN: Every day.
ADMISSION: No charge.   **TEL:** 01604 758119.

FISH ARE US

FACILITIES: Tropical and cold water fish, plants, wide range of aquatic supplies and equipment. Free parking.
LOCATION: Kennedy's Garden Centre, Millers Lane, Wellingborough.
OPEN: 1000-1800 daily.
ADMISSION: Free.   **TEL:** 01933 442384.

FRIENDS IN SOGGY HOMES

FACILITIES: Aquatic superstore with a large number of aquaria holding thousands of fish. Also sells a range of aquatic equipment.
LOCATION: Harlestone Heath Garden Centre, Harlestone Road on the A428 Northampton - Rugby road.
OPEN: 7 days.

ADMISSION: No charge.   *TEL:* 01604 759503.

GM AQUATICS

FACILITIES: Range of cold water fish and accessories, including plants, tanks, etc., suitable for beginner or more advanced aquarist.
LOCATION: 66-70 Kingsthorpe Road, Northampton.
OPEN: Mon-Sat 0830-1730; Apr-Aug - Sun 1000-1700.
ADMISSION: Free.   *TEL:* 01604 716222.

THE GROWING GARDEN

FACILITIES: Aquatic (and pets) Centre.
LOCATION\: Barnwell Road, Oundle, just off A605, follow the signs for Barnwell Country Park.
OPEN: Ring for details.
ADMISSION: No charge.   *TEL:* 01832 273478.

HOBBYFISH AQUARIUM

FACILITIES: 20 years of experience of water gardening, and advice is freely given. Has a wide range of fish, including goldfish and koi, as well as lilies, marginal plants, ponds, liners, pumps, filters, ornaments, statues, etc.
LOCATION: Towcester Road, on A5, 0.2 miles north of the Old Stratford roundabout towards Potterspury.
OPEN: Ring.
ADMISSION: No charge.   *TEL:* 01908 542801/543330.

HOWITTS HOME AND GARDEN VILLAGE

FACILITIES: Tropical fish, coldwater fish for pond and tank and supplies.
LOCATION: 291 Rockingham Road, Corby.
OPEN: Mon-Sat 0900-1800; Sun 1000-1700.
ADMISSION: No charge.   *TEL:* 01536 262078.

KETTERING AQUARIUM CENTRE

FACILITIES: Wide range of fish, and accessories.
LOCATION: 63/65 Field Street.
OPEN: Ring.
ADMISSION: Free.   *TEL:* 01536 515304.

MEININGER TROPICAL FISH CENTRE

FACILITIES: Tropical fish from all over the world. Plants, food treatments. lights, tanks, cabinets and sole UK supplier of Maximal Biological Filter Systems.
LOCATION: 103 Welland Vale Road, Corby.

OPEN: Ring.
ADMISSION: Free.   *TEL:* 01536 460919.

NICKY'S FISH

FACILITIES: Tropical and coldwater fish, plus accessories, including tanks (can be made to measure), glass boxes, plants, etc.
LOCATION: 45 Overstone Road, Moulton.
OPEN: Ring.
ADMISSION: No charge.   *TEL:* 01604 644394.

PODDINGTON AQUATIC AND PET CENTRE

FACILITIES: Large selection of coldwater fish, pond plants, pumps, etc. Preformed pond and pond liners.
LOCATION: In Poddington Garden Centre, High Street, and signed of the A509 from Bozeat.
OPEN: Seven days a week.
ADMISSION: Free.   *TEL:* 01933 53656.

WHILTON AQUATICS

FACILITIES: Has a wide selection of cold water tropical fish and aquatic plants.
LOCATION: Whilton Locks, reached about 0.5 miles off the A5 and 3 miles north of Weedon, signposted Whilton Locks.
OPEN: Ring for details.   *TEL:* 01327 842727.

WOODMEADOW GARDEN WORLD

FACILITIES: Has a wide range of fish and aquatic plants.
LOCATION: Next to the Hardwick turn on the A45 between Northampton and Kettering.
OPEN: Every day.
ADMISSION: Free.   *TEL:* 01604 781260.

ART GALLERIES

See also Craft Workshops and Centres

ABINGTON GALLERIES

FACILITIES: A wide range of original oils and water colours, together with engravings. Picture framing also available.
LOCATION: 144 Abington Avenue, Northampton.
OPEN: Ring for details.
ADMISSION: Free.   *TEL:* 01604 27550.

ALFRED EAST GALLERY

FACILITIES: A wide range of exhibitions which include prints, creative textiles and portraits. Activity days and craft fairs are also held. Anyone interested in exhibiting should contact the Gallery.
LOCATION: Sheep Street, Kettering on A43 in centre of town.
OPEN: All year Mon-Sat 1000-1700. Closed Suns and Bank Holidays.
ADMISSION: Ring for details.   *TEL:* 01536 410333.

ALTHORP ART GALLERY

FACILITIES: Specialises in the work of local artists.
LOCATION: 17e Silver Street, Wellingborough.
OPEN: Ring.
ADMISSION: Free.   *TEL:* 01933 271977.

AXTEL HAIG GALLERY

FACILITIES: Differing exhibitions.
LOCATION: Homestead Farm, Back Lane, Holcot.
OPEN: Ring.
ADMISSION: Ring.   *TEL:* 01604 781180.

DOROTHY BLAKEMAN AND RICHARD AGER

FACILITIES: Artists producing a wide range of subject matter from horses to galleons, birds and pets from photographs. Paper weights also produced.
LOCATION: 31 Gordon Road, Oundle.
OPEN: Ring.
ADMISSION: N/A.   *TEL:* 01832 273345.

BLAKESLEY GALLERY

FACILITIES: Housed in a 400 year old barn behind Barton House. Wide selection of high quality watercolours, oils and prints, including some local landscapes. Has on display works by some of the finest artists and craftsmen in the country. Beautiful ceramics, glass, sculpture, prints, textiles and jewellery.
LOCATION: The Green, Blakesley, reached off the A5 or A361.
OPEN: Ring for details.
ADMISSION: Free.   *TEL:* 01327 860274.

CASTLE ASHBY GALLERY

FACILITIES: 19th and 20th century British oils, watercolours, together with contemporary art, sculptures, and prints, as well as gifts and decorative furniture. Interior design service also available.
LOCATION: The Old Farm Yard, Castle Ashby.
OPEN: Tues-Sat 1000-1700; Sun 1100-1700; Bank Hol Mon.

ADMISSION: Free. *TEL:* 01604 696787.

CENTRAL MUSEUM AND ART GALLERY
FACILITIES: A fine collection of Italian paintings from the 15th-18th centuries, and British art, comprising old masters, watercolours and oil paintings. Limited street parking. Car and coach parking nearby.
LOCATION: Guildhall Road, Northampton, close to town centre.
OPEN: Mon-Sat 1000-1700; Sun 1400-1700; closed 25/26 Dec.
ADMISSION: Free. *TEL:* 01604 639415.

CLARK GALLERIES
FACILITIES: Fine art dealers, restoration, picture framing.
LOCATION: 215 Watling Street, Towcester.
OPEN: Ring.
ADMISSION: Free. *TEL:* 01327 352957.

PETER CLARKE
FACILITIES: Always a superb selection of pictures, including oils, limited editions, framed and unframed prints and posters, together with sculptures, quality gifts, greetings cards. There are heat sealing, block mounting and picture framing services.
LOCATION: Watling Street Galleries, 199 Watling Street, Towcester.
OPEN: Ring for details.
ADMISSION: No charge. *TEL:* 01327 351595.

DAVID CLOSE PHOTOGRAPHIC GALLERY
FACILITIES: Wide variety of prints, including seascapes and local landscapes.
LOCATION: 27 High St, Collyweston.
OPEN: Ring. *ADMISSION:* Free. *TEL:* 01780 444245.

COUGHTON GALLERIES
FACILITIES: Wide range of 20th century British and Irish painters. The gardens are open from May.
LOCATION: The Old Manor, Arthingworth.
OPEN: Wed, Thurs, Sat and Sun - all day, but closed for lunch. All year - ring for times.
ADMISSION: Ring. *TEL:* 01858 525436.

F L DINSDALE LTD
FACILITIES: Original paintings, limited edition prints, artists materials, picture framing, restoration.
LOCATION: 3 Horsemarket, Kettering.

OPEN: Ring.
ADMISSION: No charge.   TEL: 01536 513046.

EQUINOX
FACILITIES: Gallery is a shop within a shop. Limited edition prints and cigarette cards.
LOCATION: Sheaf Street, Daventry.
OPEN: Mon-Sat 0930-1700.
ADMISSION: No charge.   TEL: 01327 312150.

EVERGREEN GALLERY
FACILITIES: Fine English watercolours and oil paintings by contemporary and traditional artists. Signed limited editions by well known artists like David Shepherd, LS Lowery and Robert Taylor. Signed etchings, engravings and graphics, antique maps and engravings. The major dealer for Paul James originals. Dealer for American limited editions, specialising in wildlife. Picture cleaners and restorers.
LOCATION: 12 Sheaf Street, Daventry.
OPEN: Mon/Tues/Thurs/Fri Sat 0930-1730 - closed Wed.
ADMISSION: Free - visitors are encouraged to look around without being pressurised.   TEL: 01327 878117.

FOUR SEASONS GALLERY
FACILITIES: Picture gallery which specialises in contemporary original prints. Framing service available, including paintings, photographs, tapestries.
LOCATION: 39 St Giles St, Northampton.
OPEN: Mon-Fri 0930-1730; Sat 0915-1700.
ADMISSION: No charge.   TEL: 01604 632287.

FRAMEWORKS
FACILITIES: Selection of pictures, prints, etc. and framing service.
LOCATION: 5 St Leonard's Road, Far Cotton, Northampton.
OPEN: Ring for times.
ADMISSION: Free.   TEL: 01604 709050.

FRESHWATER GALLERY
FACILITIES: Gallery with a good display of original prints, covering wildlife, sports, aviation, landscapes, classical, trains, abstract, American and sailing.
LOCATION: 2-3 Market Square, Northampton, in the centre of town.
OPEN: Ring for details.
ADMISSION: Free.   TEL: 01604 604092.

GALLERY 177

FACILITIES: A range of prints, and also framing.
LOCATION: 177 Wellingborough Road, Northampton.
OPEN: Ring for times.
ADMISSION: No charge.   *TEL:* 01604 601531.

THE GALLERY

FACILITIES: Changing exhibitions.
LOCATION: Towcester Leisure Centre - Springfields off the A43 roundabout.
OPEN: Ring.
ADMISSION: No Charge.   *TEL:* 01327 350211 ext 207.

GAYTON MANOR GALLERY

FACILITIES: Wide range of material.
LOCATION: 1 Milton Road, Gayton.
OPEN: Ring for times.
ADMISSION: No charge.   *TEL:* 01604 858667.

KEITH HILL STUDIOS AND GALLERY

FACILITIES: A range of styles of painting.
LOCATION: 15 Church Street, Rushden.
OPEN: Ring.
ADMISSION: No charge.   *TEL:* 01933 418959.

KINGFISHER GALLERY

FACILITIES: Has a good selection of oil paintings, watercolours, acrylics, pen and ink drawings, prints, decoupage pictures, quality ceramics, jewellery. First edition and limited edition prints. Woven silk pictures, cards and bookmarks. Beautiful paintings on pure silk. Some furniture. Gallery, coffee shop, parking, facilities for the disabled. Group evenings can be arranged.
LOCATION: Beech Lane, Kislingbury, reached from the A45 at the Kislingbury roundabout.
OPEN: Wed-Sun from 11.00 to 1700.
ADMISSION: Free.   *TEL:* 01604 830638.

BARRIE LAMBERT - KILSBY FRAMES

FACILITIES: Framed racing prints, including limited editions, interesting scenes, cats, dogs, framed sets of cigarette cards.
LOCATION: 6 Fisher Close, Kilsby.
OPEN: Ring.
ADMISSION: N/A.   *TEL:* 01788 823857.

MAESTRO GALLERY

FACILITIES: Occasional exhibitions of paintings/sculptures.
LOCATION: Arts and Crafts Shop, Abington Square, Northampton.
OPEN: Ring.
ADMISSION: Ring.   *TEL:* 01604 636521.

ALLAN MARKHAM

FACILITIES: Original works of art, framing, tapestries stretched, accessories.
LOCATION: 26 High Street, Wellingborough.
OPEN: Ring.
ADMISSION: No charge.   *TEL:* 01933 223894.

THE OLD BREWERY STUDIOS

FACILITIES: Wide range of prints. Also runs art courses.
LOCATION: The Manor House, Kings Cliffe.
OPEN: Ring.
ADMISSION: No charge to studio; charge for art courses.
TEL: 01780 470247.

THE OLD CHAPEL TEA ROOMS AND CRAFT WORKSHOPS

FACILITIES: Exhibition of paintings in the studios, gallery and tea room. Work on show covers a variety of mediums including oil, water colour, sculpture (in stone and wood), textile and pottery.
LOCATION: Chapel Lane, Stoke Bruerne.
OPEN: Summer - April-Sept every day 1000-1800: Winter - Oct-March 1100-dusk.
ADMISSION: Free.   *TEL:* 01604 863284.

OLD DUSTON FRAMING AND WOODCRAFTS

FACILITIES: Gallery of watercolours and oils. Prints and framing service. Tapestry and embroidery specialist. Repair and restoration service.
LOCATION: 46a Main Road.
OPEN: Ring.
ADMISSION: Ring.   *TEL:* 01604 584934.

ONSIGHT GALLERY

FACILITIES: Changing exhibitions of paintings.
LOCATION: Roadmender Club, 1 Lady's Lane, Northampton.
OPEN: Ring.
ADMISSION: Ring.   *TEL:* 01604 604603.

PEEP HOLE CRAFTS AND GALLERY
FACILITIES: Changing exhibitions of paintings by a wide range of artists.
LOCATION: 5a High Street, Long Buckby.
OPEN: Mon-Sat 0900-1300 & 1400-1700.
ADMISSION: No charge.   *TEL:* 01327 843638.

PHOENIX GALLERY
FACILITIES: Ring for details of displays, etc.
LOCATION: 10 Courtenhall.
OPEN: Ring.
ADMISSION: Ring.   *TEL:* 01604 863267.

PICCOLA GALLERY
FACILITIES: Occasional exhibitions of paintings by local artists.
LOCATION: Arts and Crafts Shop, Abington Square, Northampton.
OPEN: Ring.
ADMISSION: Ring.   *TEL:* 01604 636521.

DUDLEY RAVEN
FACILITIES: Paintings by local artists.
LOCATION: 34 Bliss Lane, Flore.
OPEN: Mon/Tues/Wed/Fri 1000-1700.
ADMISSION: No charge.   *TEL:* 01327 349012.

RIGHT ANGLE
FACILITIES: Specialises in antique water colours, prints and maps. Also stocks contemporary pictures and has a picture framing service. The only supplier of water-gilded and veneered frames in the area. Also hand made frames.
LOCATION: 24 Manor Road, Brackley.
OPEN: Mon/Tues/Thurs/Fri 0930-1300/1400-1730; Wed 0930-1300; Sat 0930-1300/1400-1600.
ADMISSION: No charge.   *TEL:* 01280 702462.

SAVAGE FINE ART
FACILITIES: A wide range of material, including pictures by local artists. Picture framing and restoration.
LOCATION: Alfred St. Northampton.
OPEN: Ring for details.
ADMISSION: No charge.   *TEL:* 01604 20327.

THE SPRING AND AUTUMN STUDIO

FACILITIES: A number of studios used for drawing and painting, ceramics and other workshops. These cover a range of art forms. There are art workshops from May to September, and regular open studios throughout the year showing the work of Ying Yeung Li and invited artists. Talks on art, etc.

LOCATION: Studios situated at Danvers House East, High Street, Culworth, just off the Banbury-Northampton road.

OPEN: By arrangement. For details of talks, etc., send an sae to Danvers House East, High Street, Culworth, Banbury, OX17 2BD.

ADMISSION: Exhibitions free (by prior arrangement); small charge for talks, etc.

TEL: 01295 760136

PHIL STENNING FINE ARTS

FACILITIES: High quality reproduction prints, limited editions, which can be framed, mounted or loose.

LOCATION: The Granary, Shotwell Mill Lane, Rothwell.

OPEN: Ring.

ADMISSION: No charge.   *TEL:* 01536 710573.

ROSALIND STODDART

FACILITIES: Painter and printmaker.

LOCATION: Artworks, 2 Bridge Street, Thrapston.

OPEN: Ring.

ADMISSION: No charge.   *TEL:* 01832 735215.

GEOFF TINEY

FACILITIES: Sculptor, designing and originating work from 2 inches to 30 feet. Landscape, monumental, architectural, theatrical, museum, special design for awards and trophies.

LOCATION: Castle Cottage, Braybrooke, Market Harborough, Leics, LE16 8LS.

OPEN: Ring.

ADMISSION: No charge.   *TEL:* 01858 464386.

WATLING STREET GALLERIES

FACILITIES: Originals, prints, sculptures. Picture framing.

LOCATION: 116 Watling Street East, Towcester.

OPEN: Ring.

ADMISSION: No charge.   *TEL:* 01327 351595.

GEOFFREY S WRIGHT

FACILITIES: A range of pictures.

LOCATION: The Old Farmyard, Castle Ashby.
OPEN: Ring.
ADMISSION: Free.   *TEL:* 01604 696787.

YARROW GALLERY
FACILITIES: Has a range of exhibitions on a temporary basis, including works from Oundle School.
LOCATION: Glapthorn Road, Oundle.
OPEN: Ring for details.
ADMISSION: Free.   *TEL:* 01832 274333 (Oundle TIC).

AUCTIONS

HEATHCOTE BALL AND CO
FACILITIES: Has a wide range of items for sale at regular auctions.
LOCATION: Albion Auction Rooms, Commercial Street, Northampton.
OPEN: Varies, ring for details.
ADMISSION: No charge.   *TEL:* 01604 22735.

KETTERING AUCTIONS LTD
FACILITIES: Furniture and effects, antiques, fine art, collectables.
LOCATION: Old Cattle Market, Northfield Avenue.
OPEN: Tues - 1800.
ADMISSION: No charge.   *TEL:* 01536 417533/519576.

MERRYS
FACILITIES: Antiques and later furniture and effects, jewellery, silver, ceramics, glass, pictures, clocks, books, collectables and bygones.
LOCATION: 14 Bridge Street, Northampton.
OPEN: Monthly.
ADMISSION: No charge.   *TEL:* 01604 322666.

SPENCERS (AUCTIONEERS)
FACILITIES: Wide range.
LOCATION: Unit 3a, Southfield Road, Corby.
OPEN: Ring.
ADMISSION: Free.   *TEL:* 01536 743755.

TRADE AUCTIONS
FACILITIES: Wide range of materials.
LOCATION: Unit 3, Queen Street, Kettering.
OPEN: Ring.

ADMISSION: No charge.   *TEL:* 01536 410383.

UNDER THE HAMMER

FACILITIES: Wide range of items.
LOCATION: 25 Craven Street, Northampton.
OPEN: Ring.
ADMISSION: Free.   *TEL:* 01604 602812.

WILFORDS

FACILITIES: Antiques, collectables, silver, jewellery, period and modern furniture.
LOCATION: The Salerooms, 76 Midland Road, Wellingborough.
OPEN: 0930 Thurs - viewing Wed 0800-1800.
ADMISSION: Free.   *TEL:* 01933 222760/2.

BIRDWATCHING

See also Country Parks, Nature Reserves, Woods.

EYEBROOK RESERVOIR

FACILITIES: The area was flooded in 1940 and it rivals the nearby Rutland Water. A number of birds can be seen on passage, including redshank, greenshank, ruff, curlew sandpiper and common tern. Winter birds include great crested grebe, Canada goose, mallard, wigeon, shoveler, teal, tufted duck and goldeneye.

LOCATION: Take the A6003 to Caldicote, or from Kettering and then to Stoke Dry.

OPEN: Access at most times.

ADMISSION: Free.   *TEL:* 01536 407507 (Corby TIC).

HOLLOWELL RESERVOIR

FACILITIES: A good number of common duck with some scarcer species. Winter wildfowl include Canada geese, mallard, wigeon, teal, tufted duck, shoveler, pochards, pintail and goldeneye. Birds on summer passage include sedge warblers, curlew sandpiper, ruff, greenshank and black tern.

LOCATION: Off the A5199 to the north west of Northampton.

OPEN: Access at most times.

ADMISSION: Ring for details.   *TEL:* 01604 781350 (Anglian Water).

NORTHAMPTONSHIRE BIRD CLUB

FACILITIES: Indoor meetings and two outdoor visits in May and July. Regular newsletter.

LOCATION: The New Village Hall, Moulton.

OPEN: First Wed of the month.

ADMISSION: Membership fee.   *TEL:* 01604 880009.

PITSFORD NATURE RESERVE AND RESERVOIR

FACILITIES: The Reservoir is one of the country's top bird sites. A number of hides have been put up under the auspices of Anglian Water and the Wildlife Trust. Bird life varies throughout the year, but includes large numbers of wintering duck and summer passage migrants.

LOCATION: Reached from the A508 Market Harborough Road, heading for Holcot.

OPEN: Certain areas of the reservoir are accessible at most times. Hides available by permit only. Ring before visiting. Permit needed for nature reserve, available from Fishing Lodge, Brixworth Road, Holcot.
ADMISSION: Fee for permit.
TEL: 01604 405285 (Wildlife Trust)/781350 (Anglian Water).

RAVENSTHORPE RESERVOIR
FACILITIES: Produces a good number of common duck, with the occasional rare species.
LOCATION: Off the A428 Northampton to Rugby road. Follow signs for Ravensthorpe. In the village follow signs for Teeton. The Reservoir is on the left outside the village of Ravensthorpe.
OPEN: Ring.
ADMISSION: Ring.   **TEL:** 01604 781350 (Anglian Water).

RSPB - MID NENE GROUP
FACILITIES: Regular meetings, outings, etc.
LOCATION: Ring.
OPEN: Ring.
ADMISSION: Membership fee.
TEL: 01933 355544

RSPB NORTHAMPTON MEMBERS GROUP
FACILITIES: Regular meetings, outings, etc.
LOCATION: Ring.
OPEN: Ring.
ADMISSION: Membership fee.   **TEL:** 01604 505607.

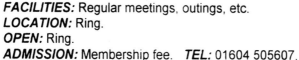

BALLOONING
See Aerial Activities

BOAT TRIPS

ADVENTURE FLEET (Union Canal Carriers)
FACILITIES: A wide range of boats available for groups for holidays on the canals.
LOCATION: Based at the Bottom Lock at Braunston, and reached off the A45 Daventry to Dunchurch road.
OPEN: Hiring available from spring through to autumn - ring for brochure.
ADMISSION: Charges made.   **TEL:** 01788 890784.

ALVECHURCH BOAT CENTRE

FACILITIES: Has boats for hire for holidays on the Grand Union Canal, and also for short breaks.
LOCATION: Gayton Marina, Blisworth Arm, off A43 south of Northampton.
OPEN: All year.
ADMISSION: Hire charges. *TEL:* 01604 858685.

ANGLO-WELSH WATERWAYS HOLIDAYS

FACILITIES: Narrowboats for hire, with one suitable for disabled use.
LOCATION: Canal Wharf, Aynho.
OPEN: Mar-Oct.
ADMISSION: Hire charge. *TEL:* 01858 466910.

BLISWORTH TUNNEL BOATS LTD

FACILITIES: Half day/day/weekend hire together with weekly holiday hire of canal boats.
LOCATION: Mill Wharf, Gayton Road, Blisworth, 3 miles from J11 of M1 and just off the A43.
OPEN: All year.
ADMISSION: Hire charge. *TEL:* 01604 858868.

BRACKEN - THE CRUISING RESTAURANT

FACILITIES: The narrowboat cruises the Grand Union Canal at the same time serving evening meals and Sunday lunches. The trip includes a three hour canal cruise. Parties of 4, 8 and 12 people catered for. Food is home-made and there is an imaginative menu.
LOCATION: Based at Braunston Marina, on the A45 between Daventry and Dunchurch, and just before the turn to Braunston village.
OPEN: Ring for details.
ADMISSION: Food and drinks on sale. *TEL:* 01788 891710.

BRAUNSTON BOAT HIRE

FACILITIES: Weekly hire, self drive boats.
LOCATION: Bottom Lock, Braunston, off the A45 Daventry-Dunchurch road.
OPEN: Easter to Oct.
ADMISSION: Hire charge. *TEL:* 01788 891079.

CONCOFORM MARINE

FACILITIES: Narrow boats for holiday hire. Also electric day boat.
LOCATION: Just off the A45 on the Daventry side of the Weedon crossroads, and 800 metres from the traffic lights.
OPEN: Ring for details.

ADMISSION: Hire charge.   *TEL:* 01327 340739.

FAMILY CANAL EXPEDITIONS

FACILITIES: A variety of canal based expeditions which take place during the summer. Booking is essential.
LOCATION: Various venues along the County's canals.
OPEN: Ring.
ADMISIION: Charges.   *TEL:* 01604 237220 (Northamptonshire Countryside Centre).

HEART OF ENGLAND HOTEL NARROWBOATS

FACILITIES: Hotel boats with crew and meals provided.
LOCATION: Based at Yardley Gobion.
OPEN: Ring for information.
ADMISSION: Hire charge.   *TEL:* 01831 556373.

INDIAN CHIEF

FACILITIES: Offers cruises along the Grand Canal from Stoke Bruerne.
LOCATION: Stoke Bruerne.
OPEN: Ring for details.
ADMISSION: Charge made.   *TEL:* 01604 862428.

INLAND WATERWAS HOLIDAY CRUISES

FACILITIES: Offers hotel boats, which include crews with meals provided, in fully equipped boats.
LOCATION: Ring.
OPEN: Ring for information.
ADMISSION: Hire charge.   *TEL:* 01604 407627.

JUST BOATS

FACILITIES: Boats for hire.
LOCATION: Crick.
OPEN: Ring.
ADMISSION: Hire charge.   *TEL:* 01788 822793.

LINDA CRUISES

FACILITIES: Cruises along the Grand Union Canal from Stoke Bruerne. 'Charlie' is available for 25 minute trips from outside the Canal Museum at Stoke Bruerne, and into the mouth of the Blisworth Tunnel. 'Linda' is used for one hour trips from Cosgrove Lock, which includes the Iron Trunk Aqueduct. Charter, public and school trips. Both boats can be booked for private parties on a variety of cruises from 25 mins to a whole day. 'Linda' has a fully stocked bar and affordable souvenirs. Children's birthday parties also available. Day boat hire on the 'Skylark'.

LOCATION: Orchard Lodge, Stoke Bruerne, reached off the A5.
OPEN: 'Charlie' is available daily from Easter to October and every weekend throughout the year - subject to demand and weather. 'Linda' operates Sun from 14.30-1545 - July-Sept/Bank hols.
ADMISSION: Various charges.   *TEL:* 01604 862107.

MILL MARINA
FACILITIES: River cruises, also fishing, toilets and bar.
LOCATION: Midland Road, Thrapston.
OPEN: April-Dec.
ADMISSION: Charge for some activities.   *TEL:* 01832 732850.

OUNDLE MARINA
FACILITIES: Hire of boats and cruisers on the River Nene.
LOCATION: Barnwell Road.
OPEN: Ring.
ADMISSION: Charge.   *TEL:* 01832 272762.

UNION CANAL CARRIERS
See Adventure Fleet

SAUCY SUE
FACILITIES: A narrow boat operated by Waterways Services, which can be chartered. Covered so suitable in all weather, and available for wedding receptions, OAP's, office parties, outings. Food - from a filled roll to a four course meal available.
LOCATION: High House Wharf, Heyford Lane, just off the A5 by the Narrow Boat a mile south of Weedon crossroads.
OPEN: Ring for details.
ADMISSION: Charge.   *TEL:* 01327 342300.

WATER OUZEL CRUISES
FACILITIES: Offers charter cruises for staff, schools, institutes, club outings, weddings, universities and private parties. Cruises to suit individuals and can include day, morning, afternoon, tea time and evening. The boat is licensed for music and the performing arts. Meals can be provided, with a choice of menu; bar service available throughout the cruise. Tea, coffee and light refreshments also served.
LOCATION: Water Ouzel is based at Union Canal Carriers, Bottom Lock, Braunston, reached from the A45.
OPEN: Ring for details.   *TEL:* 01788 890784.

WELFORD MARINA
FACILITIES: Ring.

LOCATION: Canal Wharf.
OPEN: Ring for information.
ADMISSION: Charge for hire.   *TEL:* 01858 575995.

WELTONFIELD NARROW BOATS
FACILITIES: Boat hire with a variety of narrowboats. Weekly and weekend periods. Also builds boats.
LOCATION: Weltonfield Farm on the A5 between Weedon and Kilsby, 0.5 miles north of the New Inn canalside pub.
OPEN: Easter to Oct.
ADMISSION: Charges for hire.   *TEL:* 01327 842282.

WHILTON MARINA
FACILITIES: Sells a wide variety of cruisers and power boats: moorings available.
LOCATION: Just off the A5 north of Weedon.
OPEN: Ring.
ADMISSION: Free.   *TEL:* 01327 842577.

YARWELL MILL
FACILITIES: Boating on the lakeside
LOCATION: Yarwell, near Wansford.
OPEN: Apr-Oct.
ADMISSION: Charge for some activities.   *TEL:* 01780 782344.

KEN YATES
FACILITIES: Boats for hire and sale.
LOCATION: Billing Aquadrome.
OPEN: Ring for details.
ADMISSION: Charges. *TEL:* 01604 408312.

CAMPING AND CARAVAN SITES

BILLING AQUADROME
FACILITIES: Pitches for more than 700 touring caravans and tents. Facilities for disabled.
LOCATION: Crow Lane, Great Billing, Northampton.
OPEN: Mar-Oct.
ADMISSION: Ring.   *TEL:* 01604 408181.

CHERRY TREE FARM
FACILITIES: Small number of touring caravan and tent pitches.
LOCATION: Woodford Hill, Woodford Halse, off A361 south of Daventry
OPEN: All year.

ADMISSION: Charge.   *TEL:* 01327 361351.

COSGROVE PARK
FACILITIES: 300 touring caravan pitches and over 100 tent pitches
LOCATION: Cosgrove, on the A508, near Milton Keynes.
OPEN: Apr-Oct.
ADMISSION: Ring.   *TEL:* 01908 563360.

KESTREL CARAVAN CLUB
FACILITIES: Touring pitches for 25 caravans and 3 tent pitches.
LOCATION: Windy Ridge, Warkton Lane, Kettering.
OPEN: All year.   *TEL:* 01536 514301.

MILL MARINA
FACILITIES: 30 touring caravan pitches and 12 tent pitches by the River Nene. Caravans for hire. Bar, fishing, toilets, showers and river cruises.
LOCATION: Mill Marina, Midland Road, Thrapston.
OPEN: Apr-Dec.
ADMISSION: Ring.   *TEL:* 01832 732850.

NORTHFIELD FARM AND COUNTRY CENTRE
FACILITIES: Has excellent camping facilities, including chemical disposal point. Access to study room if prior booking made.
LOCATION: Cransley, near Kettering.
OPEN: Ring for availability of facilities.
ADMISSION: Charges.   *TEL:* 01536 512305/510622.

OVERSTONE SOLARIUM
FACILITIES: 100 touring caravan pitches; 65 pitches with electrical hook-ups.
LOCATION: Ecton Lane, Sywell, Northampton.
OPEN: Apr-Oct.
ADMISSION: Ring.   *TEL:* 01604 645255.

STOWE HILL WHARF
FACILITIES: 5 touring caravans and 5 tent pitches. Facilities for the disabled.
LOCATION: Stowe Wharf, just off the A5, 2 miles south of Weedon.
OPEN: All year.
ADMISSION: Ring.   *TEL:* 01327 342231.

TOP LODGE CARAVAN CLUB SITE
FACILITIES: 80 touring caravan pitches. Bookings essential for weekends and Bank Holidays.
LOCATION: Fineshades, Duddington near Stamford, and off the A43 between Kettering and Stamford.

OPEN: Mar-Oct.
ADMISSION: Charge. *TEL:* 01780 444617.

THE WRONGS

FACILITIES: 5 touring caravans and 5 tent pitches.
LOCATION: Welford Road, Sibbertoft.
OPEN: All year.
ADMISSION: Ring. *TEL:* 01858 880886.

YARWELL MILL CARAVAN PARK

FACILITIES: 33 touring pitches. Lakeside picnic areas, fishing, boating, rally field.
LOCATION: Yarwell, near Wansford.
OPEN: Apr-Oct.
ADMISSION: Fee. *TEL:* 01780 782344.

CAMPING EQUIPMENT

BEST BUYS

FACILITIES: Tents - ridge and dome - and a range of accessories, including boots and watersports.
LOCATION: Nene Court, The Embankment, Wellingborough.
OPEN: Ring.
ADMISSION: No charge. *TEL:* 01933 272699.

BILLING AQUADROME CARAVAN AND CAMPING

FACILITIES: Wide range of quality camping accessories.
LOCATION: Billing Aquadrome, Little Billing, near Northampton.
OPEN: Ring.
ADMISSION: No charge. *TEL:* 01604 410197.

CIVILISED CAMPING AND LEISURE LTD

FACILITIES: Wide range of tents and accessories.
LOCATION: Wyevale Garden Centre, Newport Pagnell Road, Northampton.
OPEN: Ring.
ADMISSION: No charge. *TEL:* 01604 765061.

GMK CAMPING AND LEISURE

FACILITIES: Ridge, frame and trailer tents. Tent hire.
LOCATION: Billing Aquadrome, Little Billing, Northampton.
OPEN: Ring.

ADMISSION: No charge.   *TEL:* 01604 410838.

TRADEWINDS

FACILITIES: Wide range of tents, together with rambling, water sports, climbing, cycling andf trekking equipment.
LOCATION: 4 Park Road, Wellingborough.
OPEN: Tues-Fri 0930-1730; Sat 0900-1700.
ADMISSION: No charge.   *TEL:* 01933 276632.

CANALS AND WATERWAYS

BRAUNSTON JUNCTION

FACILITIES: The Junction occurs where the Grand Union and Oxford Canals meet. A walk along the towing path takes in the flight of six locks, entrance to Braunston Tunnel, a marina, boatyard and - in season - boat trips.
LOCATION: Braunston is just off the A45 between Daventry and Dunchurch. The towing path can be reached at various points.
OPEN: Can be walked at all times, although some facilities (like canal trips) may not be available.
ADMISSION: Free. *TEL:* 01788 890666 (British Waterways).

BRAUNSTON MARINA

FACILITIES: One of the largest marinas in the country with berths for 250 boats, there is a wide range of services, including a well stocked chandlery and signwriting and decorative painting. Moorings and boat hire.
LOCATION: On the A45 Daventry to Dunchurch road just before the Braunston turn.
OPEN: Ring for details.
ADMISSION: No charge. *TEL:* 01988 891373.

BRITISH WATERWAYS
EXHIBITION/INFORMATION CENTRE

FACILITIES: Wide selection of canal information. Changing displays on canal subjects/opportunities throughout the year. Small number of books/souvenirs for sale.
LOCATION: British Waterways, Stop House on the canal towing path at Braunston, 3 miles west of Daventry just off A45.
OPEN: Mon-Fri 0900-1630; 1300-1700 Summer Suns and Bank Hols.
ADMISSION: No charge to view exhibition.   *TEL:* 01788 890666.

CANAL MUSEUM
See under Museums

ENGINEERING OPEN DAYS

FACILITIES: A series of events, including guided walks and talks to enable people to discover the work involved in maintaining the canals.
LOCATION: Various places along the GU canal.
OPEN: Ring for details.
ADMISSION: Ring.   *TEL:* 01788 890666.

EXPLORING THE GRAND UNION CANAL IN LEICESTERSHIRE AND NORTHAMPTONSHIRE

FACILITIES: Leaflet detailing 18 walks with maps, along and around the canal. Split into Walks A to Q - of varying distances.
LOCATION: Covers the GU canal from Weedon to Belgrave.
OPEN: Can be walked at any time.
ADMISSION: Free.
TEL: 01327 300277 (Daventry TIC); 01604 22677 (Northampton TIC); 01788 890666 (British Waterways).

GRAND UNION CANAL WALK

FACILITIES: It is now possible to walk from London ((Paddington) to Birmingham (Gas Street Basin). Towpath accessible along the complete length, and there are possibilities for circular walks. A book 'The Grand Union Canal Walk', complete with Ordnance Survey maps, covers the 200 miles from London to Birmingham (or vice versa!), and includes history, places to visit, etc. It is published by Arum Press at £9.99, and available from bookshops or BW, The Stop House, Braunston, Daventry, Northants.
LOCATION: The towpath between Paddington (London) and the Gas Street Basin (Birmingham).
OPEN: It is possible to walk the towpath at any time.
ADMISSION: No charge.   *TEL:* 01788 890666 (British Waterways).

MARINE SECOL TRADING CO LTD

FACILITIES: Chandlery.
LOCATION: Billing Wharf, Brafield Road, Cogenhoe.
OPEN: Ring.
ADMISSION: Free.   *TEL:* 01604 890559.

MILLAR MARINE

FACILITIES: Provides canal art gifts, chandlery, pump out, as well as camping and touring caravan sites and moorings.

LOCATION: Just off the A5 behind the Narrowboat Public House, about 1m south of Weedon.
OPEN: All year round.
ADMISSION: Free.   *TEL:* 01327 349188.

OXFORD CANAL WALK

FACILITIES: Long distance walk between Oxford and Coventry along the Oxford Canal.
LOCATION: See leaflet.
OPEN: Can be walked at most times.
ADMISSION: Free.   *TEL:* 01788 890666 (British Waterways).

THE STOP HOUSE
See British Waterways Exhibition/Information Centre

WATFORD LOCKS

FACILITIES: There is a staircase of four locks, together with three other locks. It is also the entrance to Crick tunnel. Walks along the canal towing path.
LOCATION: Watford is reached off the A5.
OPEN: Can be walked at all times.
ADMISSION: Free.   *TEL:* 01788 890666 (British Waterways).

WEEDON

FACILITIES: An interesting aqueduct over the village street There is also a boatyard, and canal walks.   The main north-south railway line passes close by.
LOCATION: There are various access points to the canal towpath in and around the village, including steps onto the aqueduct in High Street. Boat trips from Stowe Wharf at certain times (see under Saucy Sue).
OPEN: All times.
ADMISSION: Free.   *TEL:* N/A.

WHILTON LOCKS

FACILITIES: The locks are interesting and busy during the summer and early autumn. The M1 is nearby, as is the main London-North railway line. The path forms part of the Grand Union Canal Walk. Large car park close by.
LOCATION: Whilton is just off the A5, north of Weedon.
OPEN: Always.
ADMISSION: No charge.   *TEL:* N/A.

CAR TRAILS

See Leisure Drives

CHILDREN'S ACTIVITIES

AFTER SCHOOL CLUBS FOR 8-13 YEAR OLDS
FACILITIES: Range of activities, including crafts and sports. There is also a quiet room for study and homework - and much, much more Registration essential.
LOCATION: YMCA, 4-5 Cheyne Walk, Northampton.
OPEN: 1530-1800.
ADMISSION: Charge.   *TEL:* 01604 638834.

ALLSORTS
FACILITIES: Leisure Club for children with special needs.
LOCATION: Abbey Centre, Market Square, Daventry.
OPEN: Sat 1500-1700 fortnightly.
TEL: 01327 872466.

CURIOUS CATS CLUB
FACILITIES: Various workshops for 8-12 year olds.
LOCATION: Daventry Museum, Moot Hall, Market Square, Daventry.
OPEN: Ring.
ADMISSION: Charge.   *TEL:* 01327 302463.

EXPLORERS' CLUB (NATIONAL ASSOCIATION OF GIFTED CHILDREN)
FACILITIES: Meets regularly with activities for gifted children.
LOCATION: Ring.
OPEN: Ring for information.
ADMISSION: Ring.   *TEL:* 01933 401334.

GRASSHOPPERS
FACILITIES: Four-wheeled motor bikes for children (from 5 years) to teenagers (17 years). Full tuition and supervision around a one mile circuit. Frisbee golf for all ages. Paintball range and games for the over 10's.
LOCATION: Horwell Farm, Banyards Green, 5 miles south of Brackley on the B4100 towards Aynho from the B4100/A43.
OPEN: Sat/Sun 0900-dark (1800 in summer), School hols, half term and Bank Hols.
ADMISSION: Charges.   *TEL:* 01869 345902.

NORTHAMPTON MOTOR PROJECTS

FACILITIES: Motorcycle training and activities. Bikes and equipment supplied for young people over 12 years of age. Group bookings available.
LOCATION: 13 Hazelwood Road, Northampton (Office).
OPEN: Ring for details.
ADMISSION: Charge.   *TEL:* 01604 760069/760496.

PLAZA SOCIAL

FACILITIES: Offers a range of roller disco skating sessions. Private hire for children's parties.
LOCATION: 2-4 Grove Road, Northampton.
OPEN: Most evenings and Sun afternoons, together with special holiday sessions.
ADMISSION: Varies, special rates for school groups and youth clubs.
TEL: 01604 633221 (during sessions).

RADLANDS SKATE BOARD PARK

FACILITIES: Park for skateboarding.
LOCATION: Studland Road, Kingsthorpe, Northampton.
OPEN: Ring for details.
ADMISSION: Ring.   *TEL:* 01604 792060.

TEETON ACTIVITY CENTRE

FACILITIES: Has a range of climbing frames, swings, slides, trampolines, etc on display.
LOCATION: In Teeton, 6 miles north west of Northampton and off the A5199.
OPEN: Ring.
ADMISSION: No charge.   *TEL:* 01604 505739.

WICKEN ACTIVITY TOY CENTRE

FACILITIES: Has a range of toys for all ages, including tree houses, climbing frames, garden swings, garden slides, roller coasters, paddling pools, football goals, dolls houses, forts, sprung trampolines, etc. More than 30 items erected for visitors to see, Catalogue available.
LOCATION: Hurst Farm, Whittlebury Road, one mile from Deanshanger - follow the signs for Whittlebury.
OPEN: Weekends/Bank Hols. from 1000-1800.
ADMISSION: Free.
TEL: 01908 571233.

WILDLIFE WATCH

FACILITIES: Junior arm of the Wildlife Trust.
LOCATION: Groups based in the following areas - Barnwell Country Park, Daventry Country Park, Farthinghoe, Irchester Country Park, Long Buckby, Northampton (Lings House) and Sywell Country Park.
OPEN: Ring.
TEL: 01604 405285.

YOUNG ORNITHOLOGISTS CLUB (YOC)

FACILITIES: Indoor and outdoor meetings.
LOCATION: Visitor Centre, Sywell Country Park.
OPEN: 2nd Sat of month.
ADMISSION: Small charge.   **TEL:** 01604 718576/647070/715749.

YMCA

FACILITIES: Provides a wide range of opportunities for youngsters, including fencing, junior weight-training, afternoon club. Children's parties catered for.
LOCATION: 4-5 Cheyne Wk, Northampton.
OPEN: Varies, depending on the activity - ring for details.
ADMISSION: Charge.   **TEL:** 01604 638834.

CHURCHES

Because of the increasing amount of vandalism, many churches are now locked. In most cases information is contained either in the porch or nearby giving the names of keyholders. We have only included an arbitary selection of interesting churches in this section.

Jema Publications is in the process of producing a Millennium book on all the Northamptonshire Churches.

ASHBY ST LEDGER - The Blessed Virgin Mary and St Leodegarius

FACILITIES: One of the few churches dedicated to the Saint - otherwise known as St Ledger. He lived from about 616 to 679, and was Bishop of

Sutun. There are many features of interest, including Jacobean pews, three decker pulpit, early brasses and some faded wall paintings from the 14th and 16th centuries. Some 18 scenes are depicted showing Christ's Passion, and they form one of the most complete sets anywhere in the country.

LOCATION: Ashby St Ledger can be reached from the A361 or the A5.
OPEN: Usually open.
ADMISSION: Free.   *TEL:* 01327 300277 (Daventry TIC).

BARTON SEAGRAVE - St Botolph

FACILITIES: Norman building with some Norman interior carvings. John Bridges author of 'The History and Antiquities of Northamptonshire' was buried here (1724) before the book was published in 1791. Guided tours may be available if enough notice given.

LOCATION: Ring.
OPEN: Ring.
ADMISSION: Donations.   *TEL:* 01536 513629.

BLISWORTH - St John The Baptist

FACILITIES: Built from coursed limestone with some ironstone in the tower. It was restored in the mid 19th century, and the South aisle rebuilt in 1926. The table-top tomb of Roger Wake who died in 1503 and his wife Elizabeth Catesby is prominent. He was a supporter of Richard III who died at Bosworth. There is some medieval glass in the north-west chancel window, and an old font.

LOCATION: In the village.
OPEN: See details at church. *ADMISSION:* Donations. *TEL:* N/A.

BRAUNSTON - All Saints

FACILITIES: Built in 1849 by William Butterfield, there have been at least two other churches on the same site since Norman times. Built in the original red sandstone, it has a prominent position on high land in the village. The 150ft high tower is a notable landmark. Wayfarers 14th century cross, Norman font, effigy of William de Ros, a contender for the Scottish throne, who died on a pilgrimage to the Holy Land in 1352, and was an ancestor of George Washington. An old parish chest.

LOCATION: Reached off the A45 and in the main street.
OPEN: Usually during daylight hours.
ADMISSION: No charge.   *TEL:* N/A.

BRAYBROOKE - All Saints

FACILITIES: Features include a rare oak effigy which is thought to be of Sir Thomas de Latymer, and a monument of 1566 to Sir Thomas Griffin.

The Norman font, with its mermaid eating a fish and intertwined snakes is a particularly interesting feature.

LOCATION: Centre of village.
OPEN: For services.
ADMISSION: No charge - donations welcome.   *TEL:* N/A.

BRIGSTOCK - St Andrews

FACILITIES: The church was originally within the boundaries of Rockingham Forest. The earliest parts of the building date from 850-900AD, and has some good examples of Saxon work, which includes the tower and a rare example of a stair-turret. The North Aisle was added during Norman times, and the South Aisle in the 12th century. Various additions were made during the following centuries. There is a room above the south door where the priest monk used to live.

LOCATION: Village.
OPEN: See information.
ADMISSION: Donations.   *TEL:* N/A.

BRIXWORTH - All Saints

FACILITIES: The largest of the surviving Anglo-Saxon churches in Britain. Built on a hilltop, it is not only of interest to the many visitors which come to the area, but also to historians and geographers as well. Although dating from the Anglo-Saxon period, there are many Roman tiles which came from an earlier building. The present church is smaller, and has lost two side chapels. There is a external stair turret to the tower, one of only four in England. Other unusual features include the ring crypt around the apse. There are only three in the whole of Europe. Services are held regularly on Sundays and during the week. A free car park adjoins the church.

LOCATION: The church is in Church Street, and is well signposted from the A508 Northampton to Market Harborough road.
OPEN: Can be visited at most times. Check for service times.
ADMISSION: No charge - donations welcome.
TEL: 01604 22677 (Northampton TIC).

BURTON LATIMER - St Mary The Virgin

FACILITIES: A great deal of external renovation, with a superb interior. There are nine paintings of the 12 patriarchs over the nave arcades, dating from the beginning of the 17th century. The North Wall shows the martyrdom of St Catherine. Other features include a 16th century studded North Door and Perpendicular chancel screen, poor box and some brasses.

LOCATION: Ring.

OPEN: For services - at other times by arrangement.
ADMISSION: No charge - donations welcome.   TEL: 01536 724491.

CANONS ASHBY - St Mary

FACILITIES: Privately owned by the Lord of the Manor since the Reformation (only one of four in England). It is unique in that the fabric is the only part of a monastic building surviving in the County. Renovation work in the 1970's ensured the survival of the church, part of the priory of Augustinian Canons founded in 1150. Although only parts remain it is still an excellent example of a surviving church of this order - probably only surpassed by one at Dunstable.
LOCATION: On an unclassified road halfway between Northampton and Middleton Cheney.
OPEN: When Canons Ashby House is open.
ADMISSION: Ring.   TEL: 01327 860044 (Canons Ashby House - NT).

CASTLE ASHBY - St Mary Magdalene

FACILITIES: Mainly of the Decorated style, with a recumbent marble effigy thought to be Sir David de Easeby (of Ashby) after whom the village is named - originally known as Ashby David. Fine example of a brass to William Ermyn (Rector, died 1401), and memorial to the Compton family.
LOCATION: In the grounds of Castle Ashby House. A public footpath leads to the church.
OPEN: Daylight hours.
ADMISSION: No charge.   TEL: N/A.

CHURCH STOWE - St Michael and All Angels

FACILITIES: Has parts dating back to Saxon times, but it has been altered and added to over the succeeding centuries. There is a Saxon Tower, and Norman north doorway. Several interesting monuments dating from the 17th and 18th centuries, and a Turner memorial from 1714.
LOCATION: Reached off A5, south of Weedon.
ADMISSION: No charge.
OPEN: Usually during the morning and afternoon.   TEL: N/A.

CRANFORD - St John The Baptist

FACILITIES: The 12th century church still has much Norman work to be seen, together with some fine 15th and 16th century Flemish glass and carved panels.
LOCATION: Ring.
OPEN: Second Sunday in July. At other times by arrangement.

54

ADMISSION: Ring.   TEL: See porch for keyholders.

CRANSLEY (GREAT) - St Andrews
FACILITIES: Originally built in the 13th century there was some remodelling in the 15th century, which included the spire and tower - of limestone compared to the ironstone of the rest of the building. The window in the tower was given by the American airmen who were stationed nearby during the Second World War. Musical events take place from time to time.
LOCATION: Village.
OPEN: By arrangement.
ADMISSION: Ring.   TEL: 01536 790253.

CRICK - St Margaret Of Antioch
FACILITIES: Has some Norman remains, together with some from the 8th century, although most of the building can be traced back to the 14th and 15th centuries. The tower almost glistens on a sunny day due to the property of the Hartshill stone. One former rector - Laud - later became Archbishop of Canterbury. Another notable grave belongs to Dr Smith who was involved with the abolishing of slavery and was concerned about the welfare of children employed at the nearby canal wharf. There is a font of Norman origin, and coats of arms, including those of the Beauchamp and Astley families.
LOCATION: On the A428 Northampton to Rugby road.
OPEN: Sometimes open, and list of keyholders displayed.
ADMISSION: No charge.   TEL: N/A.

CROUGHTON - All Saints
FACILITIES: Built about 1080, with additions made during the following centuries, with most of the present building completed by the 14 century. The most significant features of the church are the wall paintings which are thought to date from the 13th and 14th centuries, and are superb examples of medieval art. They depict various scenes, including the Flight into Egypt, the life of the Virgin Mary, and the Story of Holy Week.
LOCATION: In the village of Croughton.
OPEN: See details at church.
ADMISSION: Donations to upkeep welcome.   TEL: N/A.

DAVENTRY - Holy Cross
FACILITIES: Built between 1752-8 it is the only 18th century town church in the county. It is on a rise and can be seen on most approaches to the town. The obelisk spire gives it a distinctive

appearance. Built of Northamptonshire sandstone, renovation work has been carried out recently.

LOCATION: Market Square.
OPEN: Daylight hours.
ADMISSION: No charge.   *TEL:* 01327 300277 (TIC).

DAVENTRY - United Reformed Church

FACILITIES: Dates from 1722, and is Daventry's oldest building used for continuous worship. There is a nearby garden which is peaceful and secluded.

LOCATION: Off Sheaf Street.
OPEN: During services and at some other times.
ADMISSION: No charge.   *TEL:* 01327 300177 (TIC).

DESBOROUGH - St Giles

FACILITIES: Built around 1225 it is on the site of a former Saxon building. The decorated Tudor canopy above the Rood screen staircase is of great interest, and shows Tudor roses with the 'Stanford Knot', the emblem of the Stafford family who owned a great deal of land around the town.

LOCATION: Desborough is on the A6 to the north of Kettering.
OPEN: Ring for details.
ADMISSION: Donations. *TEL:* 01536 760324.

DINGLEY - All Saints

FACILITIES: Dating from Norman times, the church was changed in the 1600's. Inside memorials to the 8th and 9th Viscounts Downe can be seen. There is a fine brass to Countess Beatty. Musical events held during the winter months and at the end of July.

LOCATION: Village.
OPEN: Locked except during services.
ADMISSION: No charge.   *TEL:* See keyholders listed in porch.

DODFORD - St Mary

FACILITIES: A small church full of interest, having a Norman font, Jacobean pulpit and several medieval memorials, one of which is an effigy of a cross-legged knight (14th century). There is also an oak carving of a lady with angels at her pillow - thought to be Wentiliana Keynes (died in 1376), and an alabaster monument to Sir John Cressy (dated 1444) together with some 15th century brasses.

LOCATION: Off the A45, 3 miles from Daventry, 2 miles from Weedon.
OPEN: See details at church.
ADMISSION: No charge.   *TEL:* N/A.

EARLS BARTON - All Saints

FACILITIES: An interesting village church, with parts dating from Norman and later medieval times. It is considered to have the best preserved Saxon tower in England, and is especially noted for its ornamentation. The entrance is Norman. A superbly restored 15th century rood screen, shows the saints in 'modern' costume, with some brilliantly coloured butterflies above their heads. Other features include 14th century aisle windows of the decorated period and a 16th century Jacobean carved pulpit,

LOCATION: The Square; the village is signposted off the A45 or A4500.

OPEN: Certain times.

ADMISSION: See porch noticeboard.   *TEL:* N/A.

FAWSLEY - St Mary

FACILITIES: This small 13th century building stands in the middle of parkland, and once served the Knightley family who lived in nearby Fawsley Hall. There are delightful stained glass windows, with heraldic shields featuring both Knightley and Washington coats of arms. Old brasses and innumerable monuments - of a variety of shapes and sizes - to the Knightley family. Postcards and a history of the church available inside the building.

LOCATION: Fawsley is reached from a number of directions on unclassified roads, either from the A361 or the Newnham to Preston Capes road.

OPEN: Usually during the summer daylight hours.

ADMISSION: There is no charge, but donations for the upkeep appreciated.   *TEL:* N/A.

FOTHERINGHAY - St Mary And All Saints

FACILITIES: Dates back to the 15th century, and is distinguished by its magnificent tower and elegant octagonal lantern. It is set in a delightful and prominent position overlooking traditional water meadows in the Nene Valley. A model inside the church shows the Chantry Chapel as it probably was, which included library, dormitories, cloisters, chapter house, hall, kitchen and master's lodge.

LOCATION: Fotheringhay is reached off the A605.

OPEN: Ring for details.

ADMISSION: Donations.   *TEL:* 01832 226243.

GEDDINGTON - St Mary Magdalene

FACILITIES: Some Saxon remains, and also Norman windows in the north aisle, and the line of arcading above these points to a church here prior to the Norman Conquest (1066). The Saxons used this form of decoration on the outside of their churches, and is likely that it marked the exterior, before it was enlarged. Tours available.

LOCATION: In the centre of the village.

OPEN: If locked, keyholders names can be found in the porch.

ADMISSION: Donations for upkeep welcome.   *TEL:* 01536 742200.

GRAFTON UNDERWOOD - St James

FACILITIES: The tower and the nave are of Norman origin, and a notable feature is a superb stained glass window which was installed to commemorate the lives of the 1579 locally based members of the American Eighth Air Force who died in World War II. Annual Flower Festival in July.

LOCATION: Grafton Underwood.

OPEN: Can be visited at times when the local post office is open.

ADMISSION: Free.

TEL: 01536 410266 (Kettering TIC) - for more information.

GREAT BRINGTON- St Mary The Virgin

FACILITIES: The tower dates back to about 1200, with other features from the same period, including chancel, nave and aisles. Further additions were made in the following two centuries. Interesting features include an ancient font, caved poppy head pews, and the Spencer Chapel, which is the resting place for the Earls Spencer who have used it as their place of worship since the beginning of the 16th century. Tomb of Lawrence Washington, ancestor of the first President of the United States. Afternoon tea served on Suns from May-September. Refreshments if previously arranged.

LOCATION: Off the A428 Northampton to Rugby road.

OPEN: Daily 0900-1800.

ADMISSION: No charge, but donations to upkeep welcome.

TEL: 01327 300277 (Daventry TIC)/01604 770412.

GREAT GIDDING Baptist Church

FACILITIES: Built in 1790 it has its own peaceful churchyard. Most of the original furnishings remain, including a tall pulpit, box pews, gallery and brass lamp holders. This building replaces one which was on the same site and probably built in the late 1600's.

LOCATION: On the B660, 7 miles from Oundle.

OPEN: For services on Sundays.

ADMISSION: No charge.   *TEL:* N/A.

GUILSBOROUGH - St Ethelreda

FACILITIES: Notable features include the magnificent spire built in 1618, and superb stained glass by Burne-Jones and William Morris, which dates from 1877.

LOCATION: Guilborough is on an unclassified road off the A5199 or B4036.

OPEN: Usually open.

ADMISSION: Free.   *TEL:* N/A.

HARRINGTON - St Peter and St Paul

FACILITIES: Monuments to the Saunders family, 15th century screen and a rare example of a 17th century vamping horn - about 1.5m long the sound carried for more than a mile, and was used to call parishioners to worship.

LOCATION: In village.

OPEN: Services, or by contacting keyholders shown in porch.

ADMISSION: Donations.   *TEL:* N/A.

HIGHAM FERRERS - St Mary

FACILITIES: This 13th century church has a fine spire, noticeable from any approach to the town. The church, together with the Chantry and bede houses forms a unique collection of ecclesiastical buildings. Chichele College (see separate entry) is also linked to the development.

LOCATION: Off the A5/A6.

OPEN: During 'shopping' hours - Mon-Sat.

ADMISSION: No charge.

TEL: Key can be obtained from Higham Ferrers Bookshop.

IRTHLINGBOROUGH - St Peter

FACILITIES: Dates mainly from the 13th century. It has a remarkable 'strainer arch', which is thought to be only one of three in the country. The church has some of the finest 15th century glass.

LOCATION: High Street.

OPEN: See notice at church.

ADMISSION: Free - but donation to upkeep welcome.   *TEL:* N/A.

KETTERING - Fuller Baptist Church

FACILITIES: Built by Sir Morton Peto, one of the finest Victorian railway contractors, the building was erected between 1861-62 and is noted for its late classical ashlar facade.

LOCATION: Gold Street.

OPEN: Ring.

ADMISSION: No charge.   *TEL:* 01536 410266 (TIC).

KETTERING - St Peter and St Paul

FACILITIES: The majority of the building is in Perpendicular style, and the excellent crocketted spire is recessed and rises 55 metres. The tower of Barnack Stone contains a unique peal of 12 bells, and is darker than the spire. Interior features include a good example of a parish chest with records going back to the mid 17th century. A brass to Edward Sawyer, who was probably responsible for the south (Sawyer's) aisle early in the 17th century.

LOCATION: Centre of Kettering.

OPEN: Only after services, or by appointment.

ADMISSION: No charge.   *TEL:* 01536 410266 (TIC) for information.

KINGS SUTTON - St Peter and St Paul

FACILITIES: On the edge of the County, the church has a superb 60 metre tower, which is crocketted and recessed. The interior has many interesting features including a Norman font and a screen by Sir Gilbert Scott (responsible for restoring the church in 1866).

LOCATION: In village.

ADMISSION: No charge.   *TEL:* N/A.

LAMPORT - All Saints

FACILITIES: The tower is Norman, and a chapel dates from 1672, with a chancel and nave from the 18th century. There is a early 16th century processional cross, a Royal Arms of George II and some beautiful stained glass.

LOCATION: Lamport is just off the A508 between Northampton and Market Harborough.

OPEN: Ring for details.

ADMISSION: Free.   *TEL:* N/A.

LOWER HARLESTONE - St Andrew

FACILITIES: Some parts date back to the 13th century and the building has remained virtually unchanged since its construction. There is a 14th century font, and monuments covering 700 years to the local Lords of the Manor. It contains interesting carved stone decorations, featuring some of the original founders. There is a Flemish pulpit from 1500, and an east window by Sir Gilbert Scott, a 13th century font and an unusual vaulted crypt. The Earl Spencer of Althorp is the church's patron.

LOCATION: Off the A428 Rugby to Northampton road.

OPEN: Locked, but keys can be obtained from keyholders.

ADMISSION: No charge, but donations to the upkeep welcomed.
TEL: 01327 300277 (Daventry TIC).

LOWICK - St Peter

FACILITIES: Only one of a handful of Perpendicular churches in Northamptonshire, it owes its existence mainly to three members of the Greene family of Drayton, and the tower dates from 1667-8, and a contract dated 1415 still exists for the marble which was used for the tomb of a male and female with dogs at their side, and this is still in the church.
LOCATION: Lowick.
OPEN: See noticeboard.
ADMISSION: No charge.   TEL: N/A.

MIDDLETON CHENEY - All Saints

FACILITIES: The main features of the church are the stained glass windows, which date from the 19th century. These are considered to be some of the best examples of the work of William Morris and Burne-Jones.
LOCATION: Off the A422.
OPEN: See details at church.
ADMISSION: Free.   TEL: N/A.

MOULTON - St Peter and St Paul

FACILITIES: Dates mainly from the 13th century. There are fragments of a Saxon cross shaft, which shows an animal biting its tail.
LOCATION: In the village.
OPEN: See church noticeboard.   ADMISSION: Free.   TEL: N/A.

NORTHAMPTON - All Saints

FACILITIES: The medieval church was shaped like a cross, and the nave was so large that it originally stretched across the Drapery to the top of Gold Street, but much was destroyed by the Great Fire of 1675. All the important civic services are held in All Saints. Largely medieval tower and some Norman stonework within the four pillars. The chancel is mainly 17th century. There is a carved and gilded Mayor's Seat dating from 1680. The gallery gives a good impression of the dome, which is supported by the four great columns and the lovely ceiling plasterwork. The portico was added in 1710.
LOCATION: At the top of Bridge Street, Mercers Row and the bottom of the Drapery.
OPEN: Ring for times.
ADMISSION: No charge.   TEL: 01604 22677 (TIC).

NORTHAMPTON - Doddridge and Commercial Street United Reformed Church

FACILITIES: This is Northampton's oldest non-conformist church, built on part of the site of a former Norman castle. It was originally the Castle Hill Meeting Place, dating from 1695. It was here that Philip Doddridge ministered, and William Carey was baptised. There is a bust of Philip Doddridge above the pulpit, and the church still has a number of the preacher's books. Doddridge was influential in the formation of the Baptist Missionary Society. Car parking nearby.

LOCATION: Doddridge Street, Northampton.

OPEN: Wed 1000-1200; Sun 1100-1830. Other times by appointment.

ADMISSION: No charge.   *TEL:* N/A.

NORTHAMPTON - Holy Sepulchre

FACILITIES: The oldest standing building in Northampton, it is known as a Crusader Round, being built about 1100 by Simon de Senlis, who was the 1st Earl of Northampton. He constructed the building as a thank you for his safe return from the first crusades. It is meant to be a replica of the original Holy Sepulchre in Jerusalem. It is only one of four remaining round churches in the country, and is thought to be the largest and best preserved. Tour Guides available, parties welcome, souvenirs on sale.

LOCATION: Sheep Street, Northampton, not far from the town centre.

OPEN: Daylight hours.

ADMISSION: No charge - except during special events.

TEL: 01604 22677 (TIC).

NORTHAMPTON - St Giles

FACILITIES: The church was partially rebuilt in 1616, after the Tower had collapsed in a storm in 1613 which damaged the nave and left most of the church in a dangerous state.

LOCATION: St Giles Terrace, Spencer Parade.

OPEN: Daylight hours.

ADMISSION: No charge.   *TEL:* 01604 26677 (TIC).

NORTHAMPTON - St Matthews

FACILITIES: Built in Victorian times when the town expanded, it has a 52 metre spire which has been dubbed 'Phipp's fire escape' because it was paid for by a member of a well known brewing family. Canon Hussey commissioned Henry Moore to produce Madonna which was sculpted from Horton stone, and shortly afterwards the Crucifixion by Graham Sutherland was also commissioned.

LOCATION: St Matthews Parade, Kettering Road.

OPEN: Daylight hours.
ADMISSION: No charge - donations welcome. *TEL:* 01604 22677 (TIC).

NORTHAMPTON - St Peter
FACILITIES: On the site of a former Saxon church it has a Norman tower, with an 'unusual' pointed pyramid-shaped 'cap'. There is superb carving on the nave arches and the pier. The capitals of the columns show a variety of carved heads, animals, winged creatures, and foliage. There is an octagonal 14th century font. Outside, the round buttresses supporting the tower are arranged in threes, which is unusual.
LOCATION: Marefair.
OPEN: Ring for times.
ADMISSION: No charge - donations welcome. *TEL:* 01604 22677 (TIC).

OUNDLE - St Peter
FACILITIES: Has a 203ft crocketed spire, which can be seen for miles around. Most of the church was built in the 13th century, and particularly noticeable is the tall Decorated tower with a slim pointed spire. The interior has a brass chandelier from 1685, and a superb 15th century brass lectern shaped like an eagle.
LOCATION: Centre of town.
OPEN: See noticeboard.
ADMISSION: No charge.   *TEL:* 01832 274333 (Oundle TIC).

POLEBROOK - All Saints
FACILITIES: Mainly Early English with some Norman - 1175-1250. Good stained glass windows and E window of modern glass to Victor Ferguson killed in First World War. Roll of honour to American servicemen from Polebrook 351 Bombardment Group.
LOCATION: Church Street.
OPEN: See noticeboard.
ADMISSION: No charge.   *TEL:* N/A

RAUNDS - St Mary
FACILITIES: An early English building, which some historians regard as one of the finest - if not the finest - church in England. A 13th century elaborate six-light east window is a strikling feature. During restoration in 1874 some remarkable examples of wall paintings dating from the 15th century were uncovered.
LOCATION: Near centre of town.
OPEN: Visitors are welcome - details of keyholders on noticeboards.
ADMISSION: No charge, but donations to upkeep welcome.
TEL: 01933 228101 (Wellingborough TIC)/01832 274333 (Oundle TIC)

ROTHWELL - Holy Trinity

FACILITIES: The church is best known for the charnel house - or bone crypt - but this should not detract from many other interesting features. The 53 metre church is the longest in Northamptonshire, and was probably longer at one time. The tower, struck by lightning in 1660, has been renovated. Other features are poppy-head stalls, brasses, 13th century sedilia and piscina. The excellent acoustics have attracted many well known orchestras. Tours available.

LOCATION: Squires Hill.

OPEN: Most mornings from 1000-1200; Thurs 0915-1200; Sun 0745-1200. Bone Crypt open Summer Suns 1400-1600.

ADMISSION: No charge.   *TEL:* 01536 710268.

RUSHDEN - St Mary

FACILITIES: The recessed crocketted 50 metre spire is a distinctive feature of this mainly Perpendicular church. Internally there is a strainer arch which stretches across the nave, and has intricate tracery.

LOCATION: Centre of town.

OPEN: See notice board.

ADMISSION: No charge.   *TEL:* N/A.

RUSHTON - All Saints

FACILITIES: Originally built in Norman times only one wall now dates from this period, with the rest of 14th century origin. Inside there are some interesting effigies, including one to William of Goldingham (1296). The craftsmanship is superb, and it is considered the best example of chain mail in the country. The other effigy is to Sir Thomas Tresham, whose grandfather was responsible for the nearby Triangular Lodge.

LOCATION: Close to the River Ise.

OPEN: Sun 0830-1100; at other times - see keyholders on notice board.

ADMISSION: No charge.   *TEL:* 01536 713260.

SLAPTON - St Botolph

FACILITIES: This small church was started in Norman times and completed in the early English period. The small chancel has restored medieval paintings, including those of St Christopher. Other paintings include those of St Eliol (Patron Saint of Blacksmiths) and St George and the Dragon.

LOCATION: In centre of village.

OPEN: See noticeboard.

ADMISSION: Donations for upkeep welcome.   *TEL:* N/A

STOKE BRUERNE - St Mary

FACILITIES: On a hill overlooking the Grand Union Canal, the bulding had an interesting 'use' in the past, because the canal builders used it as a marker to ensure that the Blisworth Tunnel would be in a true line. There is a Norman base to the tower. There is a marble war memorial which is unusual because it bears the name of Elsie Bull, who was the daughter of the coachman at Stoke Park. She nursed victims of the First World War.

LOCATION: Reached from the A43 or A5.

OPEN: See noticeboard.

ADMISSION: No charge - donations to upkeep welcome.   *TEL:* N/A.

THRAPSTON - St James

FACILITIES: Is the oldest remaining building in the town, and dates from the 13th century. In the west nave the Washington coat of arms can be seen. John Washington, who was Lord of the Manor in the 17th century, was the great, great, great uncle of the first President of the United States.

LOCATION: Near the centre.

OPEN: See noticeboard for details.

ADMISSION: No charge.   *TEL:* N/A.

TOWCESTER - St Lawrence

FACILITIES: The most striking feature is the Perpendicular tower. The interior has an interesting table tomb to a former rector (1442-48). The organ was brought from Fonthill Abbey, and a 'Treacle Bible' features in the collection of old books.

LOCATION: Church Lane, off the A5.

OPEN: See noticeboard.

ADMISSION: No charge.   *TEL:* N/A.

WELFORD - St Mary

FACILITIES: This was a Chapel of Ease of the once important Sulby Abbey. The west tower is Perpendicular. There is an interesting south arcade which is early English, having circular and octagonal piers. A Calgary of granite and bronze in the churchyard, was erected as a memorial to the men of Welford and Sulby who lost their lives in the First World War.

LOCATION: The church is off the A5199 Northampton to Leicester road.

OPEN: See noticeboard.

ADMISSION: No charge.   *TEL:* N/A.

WELLINGBOROUGH - All Hallows

FACILITIES: The Parish Church of Wellingborough, the present structure replaces a wooden Saxon building which was close by. The south door is the earliest part of the building dating from Norman times, and has 15th century additions. Stained glass from the same period can be seen in the east window. Most of the church dates from the Perpendicular period. Other interesting features include the nave, font, chancel and Lady Chapel.
LOCATION: Church Street.
OPEN: Daylight hours.
ADMISSION: No charge.   *TEL:* 01933 228101 (TIC).

WEST HADDON - All Saints

FACILITIES: A superb font carved from a massive block of stone, has been dated as of 12th century origin and shows scenes of Christ's life, including the nativity, baptism, entrance into Jerusalem and His Ascension into heaven.
LOCATION: Centre of village.
OPEN: See keyholders list.
ADMISSION: Restricted.   *TEL:* N/A.

WHISTON - St Mary

FACILITIES: Built by Anthony Catesby, a descendent of the Ashby St Ledger family, it was the work of one man, and was completed over a 20 year period in the 16th century. It has never been altered. There is a tower constructed from brown and grey ashlar courses.
LOCATION: Reached on foot from the village.
OPEN: See noticeboard.
ADMISSION: No charge.   *TEL:* N/A.

WOODNEWTON - St Mary

FACILITIES: Coco the Clown is buried in the churchyard.
LOCATION: Near centre of village.
OPEN: Can be seen at most times.
ADMISSION: No charge.   *TEL:* 01832 274333 (Oundle TIC).

YELVERTOFT - All Saints

FACILITIES: Was begun in the 12th century, although most of the building took place in the 15th and 16th centuries. There are both Decorated and Perpendicular styles of architecture.   Distinctive monument to John Dyeson, who was the rector between 1439-1145, is inside and outside the north chancel wall. The bells were cast by Hugh Watts in 1635. The oak pews have some fine carvings.
LOCATION: Off the A428 Northampton to Rugby road.

OPEN: Usually between 1000-1600.
ADMISSION: See noticeboard.   *TEL:* N/A.

CINEMAS

FORUM CINEMA

FACILITIES: One screen cinema which provides a programme of interesting and unusual films. The Lings Forum Bar is open from 7pm each evening.   No advance booking except for special events as advertised.
LOCATION: Lings Forum Sports Centre, off the A4500 Northampton-Wellingborough Road, and opposite Weston Favell Shopping Centre.
OPEN: Mostly evenings, although some matinees in school holidays.
ADMISSION: Charge.
TEL: 01604 401006 (recorded information) /402833 (Admin).

ODEON CINEMA

FACILITIES: Multiple Screen Cinema. Regular changing programme of feature films.
LOCATION: A509 close to A14 junction, Kettering.
OPEN: Varying times.
ADMISSION: Ring.   *TEL:* 01536 514888.

PALACE CINEMA

FACILITIES: Has a regular changing programme of top films.
LOCATION: Gloucester Place, Wellingborough.
OPEN: Ring for details.
ADMISSION: Charge made.   *TEL:* 01933 222184/273733.

TALKIES CINEMA

FACILITIES: Changing programme of feature films.
LOCATION: 24 Market Walk, Queens Square, Corby.
OPEN: Varying times.
ADMISSION: Charges.   *TEL:* 01536 401026.

VIRGIN CINEMA

FACILITIES: This nine screen cinema has specially tiered auditoriums, ensuring that everyone sees the screen.
LOCATION: Sixfields, on the A45 Upton Way, Northampton ring road.
OPEN: Ring for details.
ADMISSION: Various prices.

TEL: 01604 583535 (programme information) and 580700 (credit card bookings).

COUNTRY PARKS

BARNWELL COUNTRY PARK

FACILITIES: Barnwell claims to be the first country park in Northamptonshire, but at the time of opening it was only large enough to be called a 'picnic park'. It has since attained country park status. The smallest of the county's country parks it covers 37 acres, which includes former gravel pits, together with picnic meadows, waterside walks and plenty of wildlife. Nature trail and audio cassette. Coarse fishing is available, including access for the disabled angler. There is a Visitor Centre and Ranger service. Toilets (including disabled), picnic area, car parking. Leaflets/booklets on sale.
LOCATION: Off the A605, 800 yards south of Oundle.
OPEN: All year round.
ADMISSION: No charge.   *TEL:* (Oundle) 01832 273435.

BOROUGH HILL COUNTRY PARK

FACILITIES: The site where earlier settlers first made their homes, and which was formerly renowned as the site of the BBC masts. Dramatic views over the local countryside with easy walks across open grassland.
LOCATION: Off Admirals Way, Daventry.
OPEN: All year.
ADMISSION: Free - and free parking. *TEL:* 01327 877193.

BRAMPTON VALLEY WAY

FACILITIES: BVW is different to Northamptonshire's other country parks, since it is 14 miles long, and based on the former Northampton to Market Harborough railway line. The route is suitable for a wide range of activities from pony trekking (at certain points) to cycling and walking. Disabled visitors will find the area accessible. There are car parks at Boughton Crossing (on the road between Boughton and Church Brampton), Pitsford-Chapel Brampton, Brixworth-Spratton, Maidwell-Draughton and Arthingworth-Kelmarsh. For details of exact locations contact the Rangers. There are displays at Brixworth Country Park, where walks leaflets can also be obtained.
LOCATION: The BVW starts near the Boughton level crossing on the edge of Northampton and completes its 14 mile route close to Market Harborough.

OPEN: All year round.
ADMISSION: Free.   *TEL:* 01604 686327.

BRIGSTOCK COUNTRY PARK

FACILITIES: The area was formerly worked for sand, and has been developed to include trails, with an adjoining trail through the adjacent Fermyn Wood. Picnic meadows, car parking, toilets (including disabled), Ranger service.
LOCATION: At Brigstock on he A6116 south east of Corby.
OPEN: All year round.
ADMISSION: Free.   *TEL:* 01536 373625.

BRIXWORTH COUNTRY PARK

FACILITIES: The newest of the eight country parks in Northamptonshire, Brixworth CP overlooks Pitsford Water and was established at a time when the Brixworth bypass was being built. There are waterside walks, as well as superb views over Pitsford Water. Work is in hand to enhance tree planting and to set up a wild flower garden. Ample car parking, picnic areas, new visitor centre, residential block, cycle hire, etc.Toilets (including disabled).
LOCATION: Off the A508 south of Brixworth.
OPEN: All year.
ADMISSION: Free.   *TEL:* 01604 882322.

DAVENTRY COUNTRY PARK

FACILITIES: The country park is centred around a British Waterways canal feeder reservoir, and as such is of interest for its bird life. Observation hides enable the birdwatcher to gain a better view of the waterbirds. There are also walks along the reservoir dam, through woodland and meadow areas. A new area of the park incorporates a freshly constructed pond. There is an Interpretation Centre, picnic areas, adventure playground, toilets (including disabled) refreshments at certain times of the year, day permits for fishing. Ranger service. Free car parking. A wide range of activities is organised during the year including walks, guided bird watching, an annual countryside day, etc.
LOCATION: On B4036 Daventry to Market Harborough road, and about a mile from the town centre.
OPEN: All year.
ADMISSION: Free.   *TEL:* 01327 877193.

EAST CARLTON COUNTRYSIDE PARK

FACILITIES: The area covers 100 acres of parkland with superb views into the Welland Valley. There are ponds and nature trails. Car parking, Heritage Centre with craft workshops, Museum, cafeteria, toilets (including disabled), shop, Ranger service.

LOCATION: East Carlton off the A427, 5 miles west of Corby.

OPEN: All year.

ADMISSION: Free.   *TEL:* 01536 770977.

IRCHESTER COUNTRY PARK

FACILITIES: The park covers an area of around 200 acres. There is extensive woodland with walks, an orienteering course, nature trails and picnic meadows. An audio trail is available for sighted and visually impaired people. Car parking, picnic sites, interpretation centre, Ranger service, toilets, including facilities for the disabled. Items for sale.

LOCATION: In Gypsy Lane, on the B570 south of Wellingborough.

OPEN: All year.

ADMISSION: Free.   *TEL:* 01933 276866.

SYWELL COUNTRY PARK

FACILITIES: The park centres around the now redundant Sywell reservoir, and the whole area covers 143 acres. The old filter beds have been turned into a butterfly garden, amphibian area and adventure play area. There is an arboretum and tree trail, as well as walks around the area, and a bird hide. Car parking, picnic areas, nature trails, toilets, including facilities for disabled. Ranger service and shop. Refreshments available at weekend. Fishing. Audio trail.

LOCATION: In Washbrook Lane, about a mile from the A4500 at the Earls Barton Crossroads.

OPEN: All year - 'overspill' car park when gates locked.

ADMISSION: Free.   *TEL:* 01604 810970.

SYWELL / OVERSTON

COUNTRYSIDE WALKS

The Countryside Walks leaflets marked by an * are published by Northamptonshire County Council Services, and can be obtained from Tourist Information Centres, some libraries, country parks and the Countryside Centre. Each leaflet contains a map showing the route, together with other interesting information. *Check which leaflets are in print.* The walks can be taken at most times. The list below gives an indication of those walks leaflets. There is a charge for the leaflets. For copies, or further information, contact the Countryside Centre on 01604 237220.

ALDWINCKLE AND WADENHOE*
FACILITIES: Includes an interesting circular limestone dovecote, various churches and a well with an impressive oak canopy.
LOCATION: Takes in Wadenhoe, Aldwinckle and Lilford, Thorpe Waterville and Thorpe Achurch.

APETHORPE*
FACILITIES: The village mainly consists of old stone cottages, with an interesting church in Perpendicular style.
LOCATION: Between Kings Cliffe and Woodnewton.

BLISWORTH*
FACILITIES: Takes in the area around Blisworth, including the canal tunnels, and views from the surrounding countryside.
LOCATION: Blisworth is off the A43 - see map in leaflet.

BRAUNSTON*
FACILITIES: Takes in the canal towing path, and various canalside features including locks and the now disused pumphouse. Includes an area outside the village boundary which give good views of the surrounding countryside.
LOCATION: Braunston is off the A45 between Daventry and Dunchurch - see map for details of walk.

BRIGSTOCK*
FACILITIES: An interesting village with a name, whose meaning still gives rise to contradictions. The walk takes in Brigstock Country Park, Mounterley Wood and the Fermyn Forest woodland walk, as well as the village. Includes the legend of the Bocase Tree.
LOCATION: Brigstock is just off the A6116 - see leaflet for details.

BRIXWORTH BRAMPTON VALLEY*
FACILITIES: Covers a small area of the village and the surrounding countryside. Interesting footpaths, including a double-hedged green lane and Senecio Lane, where Senecio (Latin for groundsel) was grown in medieval times to treat toothache and sores. It also goes to the former Brixworth station site.
LOCATION: Brixworth is off the A508 - see leaflet.

BUGBROOKE*

FACILITIES: The village is mentioned in the Domesday Book, and it means either 'brook of the ducks' or 'brook of the goats' - but maybe it refers to Bucca's dyke. The walk takes in Hoarstone Brook with its clapper bridge, the church and the chapel, knitter's grave and the canal.
LOCATION: Bugbrooke is on the B4525 - see leaflet.

BULWICK*

FACILITIES: The name for the village means 'bull' or 'bullock farm'. Interesting features encountered include the village pound, St Peter's Church, Deene, St Nicholas Church, Bulwick, and a tour outside the village boundary.
LOCATION: The village is on and off the A43 - see leaflet.

BYFIELD*

FACILITIES: An interesting village in a valley in the Northamptonshire uplands, Byfield is 550ft above sea level. There are many ironstone houses and the same material has been used for the local church of Holy Cross, thought to have been built around 1340. Also takes in the nearby Boddington Reservoir.
LOCATION: On the A361 Daventry to Banbury Road, some five miles from Daventry - see leaflet.

EASTON-ON-THE-HILL, COLLYWESTON AND DUDDINGTON*

FACILITIES: Three interesting villages in the North of the County. Takes in Collyweston Quarries, a Wildlife Trust reserve, Priest's House, All Saints Church (Easton), St Andrews (Collyweston).
LOCATION: Easton-on-the-Hill is on the A43 Corby-Stamford road - see leaflet.

EYDON*

FACILITIES: Eydon is situated on the south slope of a 580ft hill, and the settlement was undoubtedly already in existence for some time when it was noted in the Domesday Book. The walk takes in part of the village, together with the surrounding countryside, including Burnt Hill (mentioned in Domesday) and along the former railway - now dismantled.
LOCATION: Eydon can be reached from either the A361 or the former B40525 - see leaflet.

FOTHERINGHAY AND ELTON*

FACILITIES: Passes along part of the Nene Way, and takes in Fotheringhay, including the bridge over the River Nene, and into Cambridgeshire to visit Elton.

LOCATION: Fotheringhay is off the A605; Elton is also on the A605 - see leaflet.

GREAT OXENDEN BRAMPTON VALLEY*

FACILITIES: The walks take in the site of the Oxenden tunnels (not open), the church here, at Arthingworth and Braybrooke.

LOCATION: Great Oxenden is off the A508 - see leaflet.

GREATWORTH*

FACILITIES: One of George Washington's ancestors - Laurence Washington - was married to Amy Tomson, who was born in Greatworth. Until 1935 there were 'two' villages, divided by the Helmdon Road. The walk takes in the Church, and a viewpoint which gives a good 'picture' of church and village, and also part of the former green lane which is double hedged.

LOCATION: See leaflet.

GRENDON*

FACILITIES: The village gets its name from "green" and 'dun' - meaning green hill, and at one time depended very much on the shoe trade, which was a major industry in the village. Takes in Grendon Hall (now a residential centre), the church, and areas of medieval ridge and furrow, as well as what is thought to be the site of the Battle of Grendon.

LOCATION: Reached from minor roads off the A45 Northampton to Wellingborough at the Earls Barton flyover.

HARTWELL*

FACILITIES: The village gets its name from harts spring and the first people probably lived where Chapel Farm is now. There are two war memorials (possibly unique), medieval ridge and furrow, Church of St John The Baptist, and also takes in the nearby village of Ashton.

LOCATION: On a minor road from the A508 south of Roade.

HELMDON*

FACILITIES: The village owes its name to Anglo-Saxon times when it was called Helma's 'den' or valley. Ridge and furrow, parish church, medieval fishponds, and the former Great Central railway line.

LOCATION: Reached on a minor road off the former B4525 see leaflet.

IRCHESTER*

FACILITIES: Perhaps best known because of the remains of the former walled town, although Iron Age remains have also been found. Takes in Irchester Country Park, Irchester and Little Irchester, the Wellingborough viaduct, site of deserted hamlet of Chester-on-the-Water, River Nene and parish churches.

LOCATION: On B569 - see leaflet.

LAMPORT/BRAMPTON VALLEY*

FACILITIES: Lamport means 'long town', and has had connections with the Isham family at Lamport Hall since 1560, when John Isham bought the Manor. Takes in Hanging Houghton, Scaldwell, Old, the 'monument' to the now deserted village of Foxton, and Lamport.

LOCATION: Lamport is just off the A508.

LONG BUCKBY*

FACILITIES: This was possibly the homestead of Bucca, and was once known as Buchebi, and the word 'Long' was added towards the end of the Middle Ages, because evicted people from nearby villages established their homes on the roads leading into the village. Takes in Buckby Castle (recently 'renovated') where there are information panels, the parish Church of St Lawrence, the United Reformed and Baptist Chapels.

LOCATION: Long Buckby is on the B5385 - off the A5 or A428.

MOULTON*

FACILITIES: Local folk cannot agree about the derivation of the name for the village. It is variously thought to come from Mele-ton - a pre-Roman embankment and protected enclosure - or mule - meaning a stream - or even mola - a mill. The walk takes in the ruined church of St John, Moulton Parish church, The Spectacle, a folly built by the 2nd Earl of Strafford, etc.

LOCATION: Reached off the A43 - see leaflet.

NASSINGTON*

FACILITIES: The village still carries on the May Day traditions, and has its own hobby horse. A detour on the walk takes in the church and the Prebendal Manor House, thought to be the oldest building in the county. Other features include views of surrounding villages, green lane and the old clay pits.

LOCATION: The village is on a minor road north of Oundle, and reached from the A605, A1 or A47 - see leaflet.

NETHER HEYFORD*
FACILITIES: The village gets its name from the old English word for a hedge - meaning 'ford by the hedge' - and it was once known as Lower Heyford - its proper name was reinstated when it was discovered in various deeds. The walk takes in Church of St Peter and St Paul, Stowe Nine Churches, Watling Street (now the A5), the Baptist Chapel, etc.
LOCATION: Nether Heyford can be reached off the A45 or A5 - see leaflet.

NEWNHAM AND DODFORD*
FACILITIES: Both are mentioned in old documents which are thought to pre-date the Badby Charter of 944. Poets Way gets its name from a lesser known 17th century poet Thomas Randolph, who was born in a house in this part of the village. It also takes in Little Everdon (view of Hall), Dodford, including the church, and Newnham - church and Nuttery, as well as a track across medieval ridge and furrow.
LOCATION: Newnham is on the B4037, reached off the A45 or A361 to the south of Daventry - see leaflet.

OUNDLE*
FACILITIES: One of the most delightful towns in the County, the centre of which has probably changed very little for several hundred years. The area has been occupied since the Iron Age. The market bell is still rung at midday on Market Day (Thurs). The walk takes in the Parish Church of St Peter, Barnwell Mill, Ashton and Cotterstock - with a detour enabling a visit to Barnwell Country Park.
LOCATION: Oundle is just off the A605 - see leaflet.

PIDDINGTON - OLD DEER PARK TRAIL
FACILITIES: The village is just to the south of the old coaching route to London, and close to Salcey Forest. Takes in the parish church, the site of a Roman villa, and also goes around the deer park founded by Walter de Preston in 1128.
LOCATION: Off the B526 to the south east of Northampton - see leaflet.

POLEBROOK*
FACILITIES: The village was recorded during he Domesday Survey as Pochebroc, which means Goblin Brook, and the present village lies north of this brook. The walk includes the Church of All Saints, Armston, Polebrook Hall (not interior), the deserted village of Kingsthorpe. The villages of Armston and Kingsthorpe were small at the Domesday Survey - the total population being 18!

LOCATION: Polebrook is on an unclassified road off the A605 to the south east of Oundle - see leaflet.

ROADE*

FACILITIES: The settlement gets its name from earlier words which mean 'cleared land'. Takes in a ruined dovecote, air shaft from the Blisworth tunnel, view of St Mary's Church.
LOCATION: Roade is off the A508 to the south of Northampton - see leaflet.

STOKE BRUERNE AND SHUTLANGER*

FACILITIES: The walk takes in interesting features, including Blisworth Tunnel, The Grand Union canal and Shutlanger.
LOCATION: On unclassified roads off the A508 south of Northampton - see leaflet or from A5.

SULGRAVE*

FACILITIES: The village has been in existence for at least a thousand years, and is best known for its Manor. A number of walks are suggested which take in ridge and furrow, the many watercourses, the tumulus on Barton Hill, and Sulgrave Manor (not always open - charge for admission) and Church of St James the Less.
LOCATION: On an unclassified road off either the A361 or A5 - see leaflet.

THRAPSTON AND ISLIP*

FACILITIES: Thrapston, the larger of the two settlements, takes its name from Draefstestun, which means the 'farm of Draefst', and is pre-Christian. The tour takes in Titchmarsh Local Nature Reserve and the nearby Thrapston Lake, as well as St James Church, and Islip Church
LOCATION: Thrapston is off the A605 - see leaflet.

WEEDON BEC AND EVERDON*

FACILITIES: Both villages have interesting histories. Weedon means 'Hill with the temple' or 'Sacred place' and Everdon 'boar's hill'. The walk takes in the hamlet of Little Everdon and the village of Weedon, including ridge and furrow, the Depot at Weedon and the Grand Union Canal.
LOCATION: Weedon and Everdon can be reached from the A45, Weedon also from the A5 - see leaflet.

WOLLASTON*

FACILITIES: A number of walks is featured, including a village walk, Farndish Loop Walk, Three Lakes Walk, and Strixton Walk.

LOCATION: Wollaston is on the A509 south east of Wellingborough - see leaflet.

WOODFORD, DENFORD AND RINGSTEAD*

FACILITIES: The walk takes in Kinewell Lake Park in Ringstead, the medieval Three Hills Barrow in Woodford, and the Church of St Mary, Ringstead.

LOCATION: All three villages can be reached off the A14, and Denford and Ringstead from the A45. Woodford is south east of Kettering and Denford and Ringstead north east of Rushden - see leaflet.

YARWELL*

FACILITIES: A picturesque village which lies to the west of the River Nene. The walk includes a visit to Wansford Pasture Nature Reserve (Wildlife Trust), the Parish Church of St Mary Magdalene and Yarwell Mill.

LOCATION: On an unclassified road off the B671 to the north east of Oundle - see leaflet.

COURSES

ANGLIAN WATER

FACILITIES: Fishing at Pitsford and Ravensthorpe Reservoirs. One day 'Learn to Fly Fish for Trout' courses.
LOCATION: Pitsford and Ravensthorpe Reservoirs.
OPEN: Ring for details.
ADMISSION: Fee charged. *TEL:* 01604 781350.

BTCV
(British Trust for Conservation Volunteers)

FACILITIES: Runs a variety of courses on practical conservation topics, linked to countryside management.
LOCATION: Around the County - programme published regularly.
ADMISSION: Ring for details.
OPEN: Various times.   *TEL:* 01604 643653.

THE BRAMBLE PATCH

FACILITIES: Runs a range of courses covering patchwork and embroidery. Ring for a programme.
LOCATION: West Street, Weedon, reached off the A5/A45 crossroads.
OPEN: The courses run at various times.
ADMISSION: Tuition fees in programme.   *TEL:* 01327 342212.

DAVENTRY TERTIARY COLLEGE

FACILITIES: A wide range of leisure courses, as well those suitable for applicants who want to pursue academic studies. On site leisure and recreation activities.

LOCATION: Badby Road West, Daventry.

OPEN: Courses held at various times.

ADMISSION: Fees charged.   *TEL:* 01327 300232.

THE FALCON ACTIVITY BREAKS

FACILITIES: A number of specialist breaks is organised and includes falconry, ballooning, horse riding, flying, etc.

LOCATION: Centred on The Falcon Inn, Castle Ashby, off the A428, 8 miles from Northampton.

OPEN: Ring for programme.

ADMISSION: Charges.   *TEL:* 01604 696200.

FLOWER CRAFT WORKSHOPS

FACILITIES: Techniques for creating beautiful and unusual flower displays.

LOCATION: Off the High Street, Daventry.

OPEN: Ring.

ADMISSION: Charge. *TEL:* 01788 561065 & 01327 706066.

THE GARDENER'S ACADEMY

FACILITIES: Arranges a variety of events each year. Top lectures and small groups.

LOCATION: Coton Manor Gardens.

OPEN: Ring for programme details.

ADMISSION: Charge.   *TEL:* 01604 826077.

HILL FARM HERBS

FACILITIES: Arranges a series of practical workshops using herbs and other plants.

LOCATION: Park Walk, Brigstock.

OPEN: Ring for details.

ADMISSION: Charge.   *TEL:* 01536 373694.

KETTERING HERITAGE QUARTER - HANDS ON HERITAGE

FACILITIES: Arranges a variety of events and activities, including lectures, concerts, living history, etc. Courses for all ages during holidays.

LOCATION: Manor House Museum and Alfred East Art Gallery, Sheep Street.

OPEN: Activity days held every second Saturday of month and during holidays.
ADMISSION: No charge.
TEL: 01536 410333 ex 381 (Mon-Fri)/ 534219(Sat).

KNUSTON HALL

FACILITIES: Runs a wide range of residential courses, including soft furnishings, computing, retiring with confidence, wine tasting, bridge for improvers, lacemaking, hypnosis and relaxation, portrait painting, natural history, etc.
LOCATION: On the B569 just outside Irchester between Wellingborough and Rushden.
OPEN: Ring for programme.
ADMISSION: Charges.   **TEL:** 01933 312104.

MIDDLE NENE SAILING CLUB

FACILITIES: Provides a variety of courses for both adult and junior members, aimed at every level from the novice to the accomplished sailor who want to improve their race techniques. There is a special introductory session which can be used by temporary members. A leaflet is available giving further information.
LOCATION: Reached from Chancery Lane or from the middle of Thrapston.
OPEN: Ring for details.
ADMISSION: Charge.   **TEL:** 01933 460220 (Sec).

MOULTON COLLEGE

FACILITIES: Wide range of courses, including those in countryside management, agriculture, horticulture, equestrian studies, business studies, construction engineering, food studies, animal care, floristry and furniture crafts.
LOCATION: Moulton College, near Northampton.
OPEN: Varies - ring for prospectus.
ADMISSION: Charge for courses.   **TEL:** 01604 491131.

NENE COLLEGE

FACILITIES: The College runs a wide range of courses, and has a well-established school of art, as well as offering degrees and diplomas.
LOCATION: Boughton Green Road (Higher Education); St Georges Avenue (Further Education).
OPEN: Ring for information.
ADMISSION: Charges.
TEL: 01604 715000 (Park Campus); 403322 (St Georges Avenue).

NENE VALLEY ADULT EDUCATION

FACILITIES: Provides a wide range of courses in Wollaston, Earls Barton, Knuston Hall, Rushden, Higham Ferrers, Irthlingborough, Raunds, Thrapston, Oundle and Kings Cliffe, as well as many of the villages in the area. Courses vary from year to year, but cover topics like office and business skills, computing, flowers, gardening, nature, food, visual arts, GCSE, handicrafts, history, dance, literature, languages, etc. Brochure available.

LOCATION: At various venues covered by Nene Valley Adult Education.

OPEN: Refer to brochure.

ADMISSION: Charge.

TEL: Raunds and Thrapston area 01933 624138; Rushden and Higham Ferrers/ Irthlingborough area 01933 53231; Oundle area 01832 273550; Wollaston area 01933 664030.

NEWTON FIELD STUDIES CENTRE

FACILITIES: Runs a variety of adult/children courses on day/weekend basis. The courses organised by the centre are tutored.

LOCATION: Newton, reached on unclassified roads from Geddington, on the A43, and to the north west of Kettering.

OPEN: Courses arranged at various times; ring for information.

ADMISSION: Course fees vary.   *TEL:* 01536 741643.

NORTHAMPTONSHIRE BEEKEEPERS ASSOCIATION

FACILITIES: A member of the Beekeepers Association, the local Association runs courses in beekeeping for beginners and more advanced members. Possibility of taking various examinations of the British Beekeepers Association.

LOCATION: Varies.

OPEN: Meetings as arranged.

ADMISSION: Membership fee.

TEL: 01536 512500/01604 765454.

THE OLD BAKEHOUSE STUDIOS

FACILITIES: Housed in the former village bakehouse, Frances Lowe, a professional artist, runs a series of Batik workshops. The numbers are limited, so that individual tuition is possible, and the courses are suitable for novice and expert. There are lots of demonstrations, with all equipment and meals and refreshments provided. Pictures can be stretched and mounted ready to take away. An optional framing service is also available.

LOCATION: 7 Rushton Road Wilbarston, and the village is reached off the A427, which bypasses it.

OPEN: Ring for leaflet giving details of courses.

ADMISSION: Fee charged.   *TEL:* 01536 771484.

ORTON TRUST

FACILITIES: Arranges courses for stonemasons, including weekend courses on all aspects of the stonemason's craft.

LOCATION: 6m West of Kettering, on an unclassified road off the A14.

OPEN: Ring for details.

ADMISSION: Charge.   *TEL:* 01536 761303/710692.

SHIRE FALCONRY CENTRE

FACILITIES: Range of birds of prey, including barn, European, Bengali and eagle owls, together with falcons, red-tailed hawk and breeding aviaries. Three flying displays daily - 1200, 1400 and 1545. Non-residential courses also organised, including introductory (2 days) and beginner's (5 days).

LOCATION: West Lodge Rural Centre, Pipewell Lane, Desborough.

OPEN: Every day during spring and summer, weekends in autumn and winter..

ADMISSION: Charge for West Lodge, additional charge for Falconry Centre.

TEL: 01536 76066 (Centre)/01604 414155 (Out of hours)..

TRESHAM INSTITUTE

FACILITIES: Arranges a wide range of courses at the Institute and at centres in Corby, Kettering, Wellingborough, East Northamptonshire, Northampton and many of the surrounding areas.

LOCATION: Details in Tresham Times published termly.

OPEN: See literature.

ADMISSION: Charges.

TEL: 01536 402152 (Kettering Campus); 01536 402252 (Corby Campus); 01933 224165 (Wellingborough College Campus).

UNIVERSITY OF LEICESTER

FACILITIES: Runs a variety of courses for adults. The prospectus covers a wide range of subjects, incuding many which lead to certificates, diplomas and degrees.

LOCATION: University Centre, Barrack Road, Northampton.

ADMISSION: Varies.

OPEN: Courses held at various times.   *TEL:* 01604 251801

WILDER DREAMS HOBBY SHOP
See Crafts

WORKERS EDUCATIONAL ASSOCIATION
FACILITIES: Arranges a variety of courses and can usually provide a tutor for a specific subject.
LOCATION: At various centres.
OPEN: Varies.
ADMISSION: Charge.   *TEL:* 01604 811683.

CRAFT WORKSHOPS AND CENTRES

CLARE ABBATT
FACILITIES: A sculptor who produces portraits and other pieces in terracota and mixed media
LOCATION: Ring.
OPEN: Ring.
ADMISSION: No charge.   *TEL:* 01933 664506.

CARRY ACKROYD
FACILITIES: Printmaker and painter, specialising in agricultural landscapes and related images.
LOCATION: 4 Luddington-in-the-Brook, near Oundle.
OPEN: Ring for details.
ADMISSION: Ring.   *TEL:* 01832 293505.

S J ADAMS
FACILITIES: Wood turner producing items like tulip bowls, trinket boxes, lamp stands, bud vases, etc.
LOCATION: 46 Willow Way, Kislingbury.
OPEN: Ring for details.
ADMISSION: No charge.   *TEL:* 01604 830899.

ABINGTON HANDICRAFTS
FACILITIES: Needlework, tapestry, fine art and crafts. Wide range of kits. Oils, water colours, paper, pads - and almost everything for just about every craft.
LOCATION: 140 Abington Avenue, Northampton.
OPEN: Mon-Fri 0930-1730 (closed 1245-1315), Sat 0930-1630.
ADMISSION: No charge.   *TEL:* 01604 633305.

ANCHOR COTTAGE

FACILITIES: Sells lace, canal prints, needlecrafts and a variety of items made by local crafts people.

LOCATION: On the canal towpath off the A5 at Long Buckby Wharf.

OPEN: Ring.

ADMISSION: Free.   *TEL:* 01327 842140.

ANNA'S LACE CHEST

FACILITIES: Finished hand made lace and machine blouse linen, etc. Supplies all requirements for lace-making.

LOCATION: The Old Farm Yard, Castle Ashby.

OPEN: Tues-Sat 1000-1700; Sun 1100-1700; open Bank Hol Mon.

ADMISSION: Free.   *TEL:* 01604 696250.

ARCHITECTURAL HERITAGE

FACILITIES: Architectural antiques and reclamation, with a wide range of unusual materials - from old fireplaces to shop fronts - and everything from a bell tower to a door - continually changing displays.

LOCATION: Heart of The Shires Shopping Village, The Woodyard on the A5, 2 miles north of Weedon crossroads.

OPEN: Ring.

ADMISSION: Free.   *TEL:* 01327 349242.

ART AND CRAFT SHOP

FACILITIES: Art and craft supplies, handicraft materials, needlework and full picture framing service.

LOCATION: Abington Square, Northampton.

OPEN: Ring.

ADMISSION: Free.   *TEL:* 01604 636521.

ALISON AUBURN

FACILITIES: Produces water colours, oils and black and white drawings from photos.

LOCATION: Ring.

OPEN: Ring.

ADMISSION: Charges for work.   *TEL:* 01604 811079.

BALLOON ARTS

FACILITIES: Bouquets of balloons delivered or posted.

LOCATION: N/A.

OPEN: Office hours.

ADMISSION: N/A.

TEL: 01327 879806 (office hours): 01788 816591 (evenings).

RONALD BATEMAN

FACILITIES: Changing exhibitions. Also framing and picture restoration service. An artist who specialises in realism, the output usually allied to anecdotes and stories.
LOCATION: The Gallery, West Street, Oundle.
OP[EN: Mon-Sat 1000-1700.
ADMISSION: Ring.   **TEL:** 01852 274744.

ANN BECKWITH

FACILITIES: Pressed flowers for making your own pictures and personalised cards. Mail order. All flowers sent by return. Sae for list and samples.
LOCATION: 120 Main Road, Duston, Northampton.
OPEN: N/A.
ADMISSION: N/A.   **TEL:** 01604 582378.

MARGO BELL

FACILITIES: A printer and painter producing etchings, collographs, paintings and pastels. Includes both abstract and figurative.
LOCATION: The Manor House Studio, Overthorpe, near Banbury.
OPEN: Ring for details.
ADMISSION: Ring.   **TEL:** 01295 710005.

MIKE BENTON

FACILITIES: Picture framer, and can frame anything. Picture gallery with a range of prints and pictures for sale.
LOCATION: The Old Dairy Farm Centre, Upper Stowe, signposted off the A5 about 2 miles south of Weedon.
OPEN: Ring for information.
ADMISSION: Free.   **TEL:** 01327 340525.

ERNEST BERWICK LTD

FACILITIES: Crafts including models and kits.
LOCATION: 55 Upper Benefield.
OPEN: Ring.
ADMISSION: Free.   **TEL:** 01832 205272.

ROB BIBBY

FACILITIES: Thrown decorative maiolica pottery, which includes plaques, clocks and dinner sets. Also runs courses.
LOCATION: The Craft Studios, 43 Main Street, Woodnewton, near Oundle.
OPEN: Ring for details.
ADMISSION: Ring.   **TEL:** 01780 470866.

BILLING GARDEN CENTRE GIFT SHOP

FACILITIES: Wide range of craftsmen-made wooden toys, Caithness lead crystal, Millbook and Conwy pottery, potpourris.
LOCATION: Causeway Park, 4 miles from Northampton and 0.5 miles from the Great Billing turn off the A45.
OPEN: Ring.
ADMISSION: No charge.   *TEL:* 01604 786666.

JAMES P BIRD

FACILITIES: Old pine furniture. Uses antique reclaimed pine to produce hand-crafted furniture. Quotations for designs. Repair service available.
LOCATION: Showroom rear of 14 West Street, Weedon.
OPEN: Ring.
ADMISSION: No charge.   *TEL:* 01327 349509.

GRAHAM BLACKMAN

FACILITIES: Stained glass.
LOCATION: The Gables, Polebrook.
OPEN: Ring.
ADMISSION: Ring.   *TEL:* 01832 272755.

BLAKEMAR BRIARS

FACILITIES: Manufacture briar pipes on the premises.
LOCATION: Unit 10, Litchborough Industrial Estate, Litchborough, which is off the A5.
OPEN: Ring for details.
ADMISSION: Free.   *TEL:* 01327 830213.

BOAT SHOP

FACILITIES: Has a range of locally produced crafts, including teapots, Buckby Cans, old lace plates, brassware, etc. Also stocks a range of books, maps, etc for use on the canal, as well as provisions, sweets and ice creams.
LOCATION: Dark Lane, near Braunston Bottom Lock, along the towpath.
OPEN: All year round.
ADMISSION: No charge.   *TEL:* 01788 891310.

BOHEMIA

FACILITIES: Ethnic clothes, giftware, sculptures, art, prints and cards.
LOCATION: 15a Peacock Place, Northampton.
OPEN: Mon-Sat 0900-1730.
ADMISSION: No charge.   *TEL:* 01604 601418.

ELIZABETH BOND

FACILITIES: Potter producing a range of thrown domestic stoneware, earthenware vessels and garden pots. Sculptor - commissions taken.
LOCATION: Potshad Pottery Units 18-21, The Workshops, Barnwell.
OPEN: Visitors by appointment.
ADMISSION: No charge.   *TEL:* 01832 274274.

G BOOKER

FACILITIES: Makes patio and garden tubs.
LOCATION: Ring for details.
OPEN: Ring for details.
ADMISSION: N/A.   *TEL:* 01604 412642.

BRACKLEY CRAFT CENTRE

FACILITIES: Aladdin's Cave of craft kits, together with a wide range of artists materials, tapestry wools, etc. Help and advice freely given.
LOCATION: 4 Bridge Street, Brackley.
OPEN: Mon, Tues, Thurs, Fri, Sat 0900-1630.
ADMISSION: No charge.   *TEL:* 01280 700880.

THE BRAMBLE PATCH

FACILITIES: The patchwork and embroidery shop and a wide range of kits, fabrics, wools and canvas.
LOCATION: West Street, Weedon, just off the A5/A45 crossroads.
OPEN: Wed, Thurs, Fri, Sat 1000-1700.
ADMISSION: Free.   *TEL:* 01327 342212.

BRIDGE 28

FACILITIES: Unique crafts made by local people, including cards, candles, canal art, paintings, pottery, patchwork, jewellery, decoupage, etc.
LOCATION: Bridge 28, Heyford Lane, Nether Heyford, reached off the A5 at the Narrow Boat Inn, approx 1 mile south of Weedon crossroads. Bridge 28 is half a mile along on the left
OPEN: Every day 1000-1800.
ADMISSION: Free.   *TEL:* 01327 349171.

BRONTE FURNITURE CO

FACILITIES: Custom-built kitchens, fine furniture, bedroom, bathrooms, natural floor coverings, free standing furniture, panelling and libraries.
LOCATION: Old Granary, Castle Ashby, off the A428 east of Northampton.
OPEN: Tues-Sat 1000-1700; Sun 1100-1700; Bank Hol Mon.
ADMISSION: No Charge.   *TEL:* 01604 696772.

BUGLASS GALLERY

FACILITIES: Metalwork showroom with unique designs - from gifts to household furniture. Interior design metalwork from candleholders to individually made beds. Coffee shop serving morning coffee, light refreshments, cream teas.
LOCATION: Clifford Mill House, Little Houghton.
OPEN: Ring.
ADMISSION: No charge.   *TEL:* 01604 890366.

CALLAGHAN GARDEN ORNAMENTS

FACILITIES: Manufactures a wide range of garden ornaments, including pots, troughs, statues, animals, bird baths, etc.
LOCATION: 41 Nielson Road, Finedon Road Industry, Wellingborough.
OPEN: Ring for details.
ADMISSION: No charge.   *TEL:* 01933 440059.

CANAL MUSEUM

FACILITIES: Sells a range of gifts connected with the canal, together with painted canalware.
LOCATION: Canal Museum, Stoke Bruerne.
OPEN: Summer - daily 1000-1800; Winter Tues-Sun 1000-1600; closed 25/26 Dec. Ring to confirm.
ADMISSION: Charge for Museum.   *TEL:* 01604 862229.

JUSTIN CAPP

FACILITIES: A variety of tooled leather masks, showing native anilmals and artefacts
LOCATION: 4 Luddington-in-the-Brook, near Oundle.
OPEN: Ring for details.
ADMISSION: Ring.   *TEL:* 01832 293330.

CASTLE ASHBY CRAFT CENTRE AND RURAL SHOPPING YARD

FACILITIES: Ceramics, working potter, country furniture, tiles, knitwear, art gallery, farm shop and delicatessan. Coffee and tea room.
LOCATION: In the village of Castle Ashby, off the A428, east of Northampton.
OPEN: Tues-Sat 0930-1730; Sun 11.00-1700.
ADMISSION: Free.   *TEL:* 01604 636250.

CASTLE ASHBY POTTERY

FACILITIES: A wide range of practical stoneware, terracota and porcelain made on the premises. International ethnic crafts, including bags, hangings, jewellery, clothing and throwovers.

LOCATION: The Old Farm Yard, Castle Ashby, off the A428, east of Northampton.
OPEN: Tues-Sat 1000-1700; Sun 1100-1700; Bank Hol Mon.
ADMISSION: No charge. *TEL:* 01604 696076.

CHARLOTTE GARDEN

FACILITIES: Pot pourri.
LOCATION: Church End House, Church Street, Byfield.
OPEN: Ring.
ADMISSION: Ring. *TEL:* 01327 261969.

CLOTH AND CLAY

FACILITIES: Traditional and sculptural metalwork, ceramics and textiles.
LOCATION: 10 High Street, Irchester.
OPEN: Ring.
ADMISSION: No charge. *TEL:* 01933 413494.

CLOVER CRAFTS

FACILITIES: Specialises in the making of stained glass items using the Tiffany Technique. Items include clocks, vases, mirrors, jewellery boxes, photo frames and sun catchers (frogs, owls, butterflies, etc).
LOCATION: 120 Main Road, Duston.
OPEN: Ring John Beckwith before visiting.
ADMISSION: No charge. *TEL:* 01604 582378.

COLLECTIONS

FACILITIES: Glassware, leather, ceramics, toiletries, jewellery, knitwear, greetings cards and gifts.
LOCATION: Heart of The Shires Shopping Village, The Woodyard on the A5, 2 miles north of Weedon crossroads.
OPEN: Tues-Sat 1000-1700; Sun 1100-1700.
ADMISSION: Free. *TEL:* 01327 349552.

COPPER GALLERY

FACILITIES: Housed in a delightful tastefully restored Northamptonshire barn. A wide range of the best of British crafts including paintings, prints, porcelain, ceramics, hand blown glass, hand woven wall coverings and rugs. Copper repousse pictures and etchings are also produced and for sale, or you can commission your own design. The flower arranger corner include an array of materials to enhance floral decorations, and includes dried flowers, candles, containers and figurings.
LOCATION: Lower Street, Desborough, off the A6, and next to St Giles Church.

OPEN: Tues-Sat 1000-1730; Sun 1400-1700.
ADMISSION: No charge.   *TEL:* 01536 762333.

COTTAGE FLOWERS
FACILITIES: Dolls - kits or made to specification.
LOCATION: 144 Sywell Road, Overstone.
OPEN: Ring.
ADMISSION: No charge.   *TEL:* 01604 643420.

THE COUNTRY PINE SHOP
FACILITIES: Has quality stripped pine furniture from the Victorian and Edwardian era for sale; also offers a quality stripping service. Hand made kitchen units and wardrobes using old and reclaimed timber. Designs to individual specifications.
LOCATION: The Romney Buildings, Nurseries, Northampton Road, West Haddon.
OPEN: Ring for times.
ADMISSION: Free.   *TEL:* 01788 510430.

COUNTRY REFLECTIONS
FACILITIES: Farriers.
LOCATION: 8 East End, Scaldwell, Northampton.
OPEN: Ring for times.
ADMISSION: Free.   *TEL:* 01604 881856.

CRAFT CENTRE
FACILITIES: Specialises in American crafts, together wirth fabrics and patterns.
LOCATION: 23 Crabb Street, Rushden.
OPEN: Ring.
ADMISSION: N/A.   *TEL:* 01933 418876

CRAFT CENTRE, THE
FACILITIES: Large range of locally made crafts, including pottery, woodturned items, glass models, stained glass, local artists, etc. Children's and adults craft and pottery workshops.
LOCATION: Market Square, Raunds.
OPEN: Free - but charges for workshops.
ADMISSION: Mon/Tues/Thurs/Fri/Sat 0930-1200 & 1300-1700.
TEL: 01933 625004.

ENID CROUCH
FACILITIES: Knits pure wool jumpers.
LOCATION: Please ring for details.

OPEN: Ring for details.
ADMISSION: No charge.   *TEL:* 01604 621675

CULWORTH FORGE

FACILITIES: Provides a range of ornamental ironwork, stoves, fire and chimney systems, as well as gates, railings, hearth accessories and fire surrounds.
LOCATION: The Green, Culworth, reached off the A5 or A361, south of Daventry.
OPEN: Mon-Fri 0900-1300 and 1400-1730; Sat 0900-1500.
TEL: 01295 760439.

DAVENTRY TOURIST INFORMATION CENTRE

FACILITIES: Some local crafts.
LOCATION: Moot Hall, Daventry.
OPEN: Nov-Mar - Tues-Sat 1000-1530; Apr-Oct - 1000-1700; Sat 1000-1600.
ADMISSION: Free.   *TEL:* 01327 300277.

RON A DAVEY

FACILITIES: Produces gem trees.
LOCATION: Ring.
OPEN: Ring.
ADMISSION: N/A.   *TEL:* 01604 409058.

CLAIRE DENNY

FACILITIES: A painter working in oils and watercolours to explore landscapes, colour and light.
LOCATION: Ring.
OPEN: Ring.
ADMISSION: No charge.   *TEL:* 01327 340882.

DUET FURNITURE

FACILITIES: Handmade designer upholstery in a range of classical styles and fabrics.
LOCATION: Heart of the Shires Village, on A5 2 miles north of Weedon
OPEN: Ring.
ADMISSION: No charge.   *TEL:* 01327 342426.

JENNY DUNBAR

FACILITIES: Potter producing stoneware and one-off pieces in earthenware.
LOCATION: Pots and Prints, 12 High Street, Brigstock.
OPEN: Ring.

ADMISSION: No charge. *TEL:* 01536 373353.

ROGER EAMES
FACILITIES: Produces 'Quaint Little Places', model replicas of homes.
LOCATION: The Barn House, Glapthorn Road, Oundle.
OPEN: Ring.
ADMISSION: No charge. *TEL:* 01832 274112.

EARTHWALK
FACILITIES: Anything for the home and for the individual which is unconventional and hand crafted.
LOCATION: 28 Guildhall Road, Northampton.
OPEN: Mon-Sat 1000-1730.
ADMISSION: No charge. *TEL:* 01604 602101.

EAST CARLTON COUNTRYSIDE PARK
FACILITIES: A number of craft workshops specialising in glass craft, dried flowers, portraits, pottery, etc.
LOCATION: On the A427 between Corby and Market Harborough.
OPEN: Mon-Fri 0800-1700; Sat/Sun 12000-1700.
TEL: 01536 760165.

KEN EAST
FACILITIES: A painter whose works depicts constancy and change in a lifetime's teaching, examining and marking.
LOCATION: The Garden Studio, 99 Queens Park Parade, Kingsthorpe.
OPEN: Normal times but by arrangement only.
ADMISSION: No charge. *TEL:* 01604 716201.

EMPORIUM
FACILITIES: Arts and crafts from around the world, including fabrics from India and Africa, household and table decorations, knitwear from the Andes and Himalayas, international jewellery. Housed on three floors. Wholefood cafe.
LOCATION: 20/22 Abington Square, Northampton.
OPEN: Ring.
ADMISSION: Free. *TEL:* 01604 230642.

EQUINOX
FACILITIES: Third World (mostly) hand crafted items, from large wooden bananas to fridge magnets. Most are from overseas.
LOCATION: Sheaf Street, Daventry.
OPEN: Mon-Sat - 0930-1700.
ADMISSION: No charge. *TEL:* 01327 312150.

THE FLOWER DRUM
FACILITIES: Bouquets, basket arrangements for all occasions.
LOCATION: Rear of White Horse Inn, Welton.
OPEN: Ring.
ADMISSION: N/A.　　*TEL:* 01327 702820.

FORGET-ME-NOT FLOWERCRAFTS
FACILITIES: Wide range of artificial plants and trees; interior landscaping for office and home. Everything for the flower arranger; fabric flowers and plants.
LOCATION: Bishops Court, Daventry.
OPEN: Ring.
ADMISSION: N/A. *TEL:* 01327 706066.

FOTHERINGHAY FORGE AND WOODTURNERS
FACILITIES: Bespoke items in iron, forged on the fire. Also undertakes repair and restoration work and woodturning.
LOCATION: The Forge.
OPEN: Ring.
ADMISSION: No charge.　　*TEL:* 01832 226323.

FOXGLOVE FANTASIES POTTERY
FACILITIES: Is a small workshop producing completely black stoneware, which looks like iron. Fruit dishes, candleholders, stoneware (that looks like stone), old designs including hanging water bottles, Egyptian-like bottles, etc.
LOCATION: High Street, Eydon. At the corner of Moreton Pinkney road on an unclassified road, reached either from an unclassified road, formerly the B4525 at Canons Ashby or A361 from Byfield.
OPEN: Ring before visiting.
ADMISSION: No charge.　　*TEL:* 01327 261829.

FURNITURE WAREHOUSE
FACILITIES: Regency and Italian Repro furniture, with hundreds of items to choose from, occasional tables, bookcases, corner cabinets, etc.
LOCATION: Oakley Road (off Washbrook Road), Rushden.
OPEN: Mon 0900-1700; Wed-Sat 0900-1700.
ADMISSION: Free.　　*TEL:* 01933 53226.

THE GALLERY SHOWCASE
FACILITIES: Quality crafts on sale at very reasonable prices.
LOCATION: Within the shop at The Manor House Museum, Sheep Street, Kettering.

OPEN: Mon-Sat 0900-1700 (not Bank Hols).
ADMISSION: Free.
TEL: 01536 410333 (Mon-Fri) and 534219 (Sat).

THE GALLERY STABLE

FACILITIES: Part of The Blakesley Gallery, The Stable offers a range of beautiful silk flowers, furniture, gifts, garden containers, all with a garden or conservatory theme.
LOCATION: Barton House, Blakesley, near Towcester, and reached off the A5 or A43, north west of Towcester.
OPEN: Wed-Sun 1000-1700 and Bank Hols.
ADMISSION: Free.   *TEL:* 01327 860282.

CAROL GALVIN

FACILITIES: Sculptor/woodcarver.
LOCATION: The Old Forge, Chapel Street, Charwelton.
OPEN: Ring.
ADMISSION: Ring.   *TEL:* 01327 260594.

THE GARDEN GATE

FACILITIES: Barn full of terracotta glazed pots, garden funiture, baskets, edging bricks, tubs, etc.
LOCATION: Sholebroke, Whittlebury, Towcester.
OPEN: Ring for appointment.
ADMISSION: No charge.   *TEL:* 01327 857414/33293/50512.

GLASS WORKSHOP

FACILITIES: Produces glass ornaments over an oxygen/gas flame from clear and coloured glass rods. Lace makers accessories also available.
LOCATION: East Carlton Countryside Park, on the A427 Corby to Market Harborough road.
OPEN: Mon-Fri 0900-1730; Sun 1330-1730. Ring to confirm. Closed Christmas and New Year.
ADMISSION: Free.   *TEL:* 01536 7601265.

GLASS WORKSHOP

FACILITIES: Produces glass ornaments over an oxygen/gas flame from clear and coloured glass rods.
LOCATION: Wicksteed Park on the edge of Kettering on the A6.
OPEN: Ring for times.
ADMISSION: Free, although there may be a charge to get into Wicksteed.   *TEL:* 01536 512475.

GLAZED EXPRESSIONS
FACILITIES: Glazed ware.
LOCATION: 43 Main Street, Woodnewton.
OPEN: Ring.
ADMISSION: No charge.   **TEL:** 01780 470866.

HOBBYCRAFT
FACILITIES: Art and craft superstore selling a wide range of items for virtually every craft. Also runs regular courses.
LOCATION: Weedon Road, Northampton.
OPEN: Free to store. Charge for workshops.
ADMISSION: Mon-Fri 1000-2000; Sat 0900-1800; Sun 1100-1700.
TEL: 01604 591800.

KERSTIN GOULDING
FACILITIES: Produces hand-woven textiles, and especially rugs for floors and walls.
LOCATION: 2 Kiln Lane, Litchborough, near Towcester.
OPEN: Ring for details.
ADMISSION: Ring.   **TEL:** 01604 859161.

JOAN GRANT (RARE BREED) KNITWEAR
FACILITIES: Traditional designs, hard wearing garments, hand framed and hand finished from natural coloured wools. Unisex fun jumpers with animal motifs in Shetland and other wools. Also hand knitted quality fashion mohairs. Made to measure service. Quality yarns for sale.
LOCATION: The Old Shippon, Home Farm, Castle Ashby.
OPEN: Ring for times.
ADMISSION: No charge.   **TEL:** 01604 696369.

GRAPHITTI STAINED GLASS
FACILITIES: Restores and replicates existing internal and external stained glass panels in traditional or applied lead. Has a bespoke design service for both traditional, modern and own personal concepts. Produces a range of hand-crafted gifts and household items on commission.
LOCATION: Ring.
OPEN: Ring.
ADMISSION: No charge.   **TEL:** 01604 583620.

GRASSLANDS FARM SHOP
FACILITIES: Dried flowers, crafts, collectables, kitchenalia, watercolours, etc.
LOCATION: Grasslands Farm, Kelmarsh Road, Clipston.
OPEN: Most weekends and many weekdays.

ADMISSION: No charge.   *TEL:* 01858 525385.

MARGARET AND GERRY GREY

FACILITIES: The specialist shop for the specialist discerning collector for dolls, teddies and soft toys, including antiques, reproduction, new collectors, etc.
LOCATION: The Old Bakery Gallery, 7 and 38 Cambridge St, Wellingborough.
OPEN: Tues/Wed/Fri/Sat 1000-1700.
ADMISSION: No charge. *TEL:* 01933 272123 (shop) & 229191 (office).

GREEN MAN

FACILITIES: John Clare locally made oil-painted terra cotta plaques.
LOCATION: Plantsman, West Haddon, on A428 Northampton Road, Northampton side of the village.
OPEN: Ring.
ADMISSION: No charge.   *TEL:* 01788 510206.

SUSAN GROOM

FACILITIES: Makes authentic large scale replicas of butterflies in enamel.
LOCATION: 21 South Road, Oundle.
OPEN: Ring.
ADMISSION: No charge.   *TEL:* 01280 272059.

BARRY GUNNETT

FACILITIES: Artist specialising in figurative paintings and drawings, including animals, birds and still life.
LOCATION: Gunnett Antiques, 128 Northampton Road, Brixworth.
OPEN: Mon-Sat 0930-1730; Sun 1400-1700.
ADMISSION: No charge.   *TEL:* 01604 880057.

YVONNE HALTON

FACILITIES: Handthrown decorative and functional earthenware.
LOCATION: Hardingstone Pottery, 3 Back Lane, Hardingstone.
OPEN: Mon-Fri 1000-1500; Sat/Sun 1000-1700.
ADMISSION: No charge.   *TEL:* 01604 762124.

HANSLOPE HANDSPINNERS

FACILITIES: Craft fairs, demonstrations; sells Ashford spinning wheels.
LOCATION: 27 Hartwell Road.
OPEN: Ring.
ADMISSION: No charge.   *TEL:* 01908 510421.

HAPPICRAFT
FACILITIES: Supplies a wide range of craft materials, including pillow-lace, chess moulds, candle making materials, picture frames, marquetry, etc.
LOCATION: 5 Cannon Street, Wellingborough.
OPEN: Ring.
ADMISSION: No charge.   *TEL:* 01933 279542.

DEREK HAWKINS
FACILITIES: Wrought iron work, anything made to order, from chandeliers to flower pots.
LOCATION: The Old Dairy Farm Centre, Upper Stowe, off the A5 2 miles south of Weedon.
OPEN: Ring for details.
ADMISSION: No charge.   *TEL:* 01327 349034.

HEART OF ENGLAND TEAK COMPANY
FACILITIES: Specialises in teak garden and conservatory furniture from traditional to contemporary.
LOCATION: 23 High Street, Weedon.
OPEN: Ring.
ADMISSION: Free.   *TEL:* 01327 341928.

HEART OF THE SHIRES SHOPPING CENTRE
(formerly Architectural Heritage of Northamptonshire)
FACILITIES: A number of units within the complex, including Cavern Stove Shop, KY Gifts, Cabinet Maker, Posy Bowl (dried and silk displays), Memories (all periods of furniture and collectibles), Architectural Heritage (see separate entry), and Emily's Tea Room serving hot food, sandwiches, cakes, scones, clotted cream teas.
LOCATION: The Woodyard, on the A5, 2 miles north of Weedon crossroads.
OPEN: Ring.
ADMISSION: Free.   *TEL:* 01327 349242.

GINA HENMAN
FACILITIES: Decorative ceramic potter, producing brightly painted ceramic bowls, plates, clocks and jewellery.
LOCATION: Cloth and Clay, 10 High Street, Irchester, near Wellingborough.
OPEN: Thur 1000-1800; Fri/Sat 1000-1600.
ADMISSION: No charge.   *TEL:* 01933 413494.

MALCOLM HILL
(A member of the West Northants Wood Turners)
FACILITIES: A wide range of wood-turned items, including bowls, pens, teapot stands, etc.
LOCATION: Ring.
OPEN: By appointment - ring.
ADMISSION: No charge.   *TEL:* 01327 872982.

WENDY HOARE
FACILITIES: Produces a range of ceramics - for home and garden, mainly large scale.
LOCATION: 135 Billing Road Northampton.
OPEN: Ring for details.
ADMISSION: No charge.   *TEL:* 01604 622880.

ALICE HONEYBALL
FACILITIES: A painter specialising in 3-D pictures and copies of well known masters.
LOCATION: 45 Flintcomb Rise, Woodfield.
OPEN: Ring.
ADMISSION: No charge.   *TEL:* 01604 406661.

DEBORAH HOPSON WOLFE
FACILITIES: A potter producing functional ceramics, both commemorative and individual pieces.
LOCATION: Ring.
OPEN: Ring.
ADMISSION: No charge.   *TEL:* 01234 712306.

CHRISTOPHER M HORNE
FACILITIES: Balloons and flowers decorated and delivered for every occasion.
LOCATION: 195 Broadway East, Northampton.
OPEN: Ring.
ADMISSION: N/A.   *TEL:* 01604 401321.

PETER ILSEY
(Whilton Pottery)
FACILITIES: Stoneware, porcelain, crystalline glazes, ceramics, wood. Paintings - some by local artists.
LOCATION: Lower Lake Gate House, Whilton Locks, off the A5, and then off to the right just beyond the humpback bridge, and along canal towpath.
OPEN: 7 days - ring before going.
ADMISSION: No charge.   *TEL:* 01327 842886.

IRCHESTER COUNTRY PARK WOODLANDS

FACILITIES: Suppliers of rustic poles, round timber, fencing stakes, split rails.
LOCATION: In Gypsy Lane, on the B570 Little Irchester to Irchester road, and off the A509 south-east of Wellingborough.
OPEN: Ring for times.
ADMISSION: N/A.　　*TEL:* 01933 441143 (Woodland Officer)/276866 (Country Park).

IRCHESTER COUNTRY PARK WORKSHOPS

FACILITIES: Produces a range of outdoor furniture, etc., including picnic benches, ranging from very simple to more complex styles.
LOCATION: Irchester Country Park, Gypsy Lane, Irchester.
OPEN: Ring for information.
ADMISSION: N/A.　　*TEL:* 01933 279243.

MICHAEL IVENS

FACILITIES: Sculptor with 3-D items including bronze and stone. Also a painter, working in acrylics and watercolours.
LOCATION: Mill Pool Studios, Willow Mill, Long Buckby.
OPEN: Limited - ring for details.
ADMISSION: No charge.　　*TEL:* 01327 843885.

GEORGE JAMES AND SONS BLACKSMITHS

FACILITIES: New forged ironware and restoration work undertaken. Small hard forged items. Display and photographs show the work undertaken.
LOCATION: 22 Cransley Hill, Broughton.
OPEN: Ring.
ADMISSION: No charge.　　*TEL:* 01536 790295.

ALAN JENNINGS

FACILITIES: Hand made furniture with individual items to own design, both free standing and fitted. Repairs also undertaken.
LOCATION: 55 High Street, Braunston.
OPEN: Ring.
ADMISSION: No charge.　　*TEL:* 01788 890421.

FELICITY JONES

FACILITIES: Works with watercolours, producing landscape, conversation pieces and figures.
LOCATION: Overslade, 8 Teeton Rd, Ravensthorpe, Northampton.
OPEN: Ring for details.
ADMISSION: No charge.　　*TEL:* 01604 770653.

SUZANNE KATHKHUDA

FACILITIES: Produces a range of beautiful hand-painted ceramics. The workshop is open for the sale of these items including seconds.
LOCATION: Holdenby Designs, Holcot Road, Brixworth, off the A508.
OPEN: Ring for details.
ADMISSION: Free.   *TEL:* 01604 880800.

EDNA KENNEDY

FACILITIES: Painter on silk, producing painted and embroidered scarves and wall hangings.
LOCATION: Ring.
OPEN: Not available.
ADMISSION: No charge.   *TEL:* 01234 708305.

KETTERING HERITAGE QUARTER

FACILITIES: Museum shop selling toys and treats from a bygone age, including Victorian toys, Roman replica, jewellery, medieval brass rubbing kits and picture postcards. The Gallery Shop sells a range of posters and postcards.
LOCATION: Manor House Museum, Sheep Street.
OPEN: Mon-Sat 0930-1700 (closed Bank Hols).
ADMISSION: No charge.   *TEL:* 01536 534219/534381.

JONATHAN KNIGHT

FACILITIES: Furniture maker whose designs are informed by sculptural considerations, which are nevertheless practical.
LOCATION: Ring.
OPEN: Ring.
ADMISSION: No charge.   *TEL:* 01933 680807.

GUNTA ANITA KRUMINS

FACILITIES: Smoke-fired ceramics and porcelain.
LOCATION: Florence Villa, 22 Glapthorn Road, Oundle.
OPEN: Ring for details.
ADMISSION: Ring.   *TEL:* 01832 273083.

KY GIFTS

FACILITIES: Gifts for all tastes and occasions.
LOCATION: Heart of the Shires Shopping Village, on A5 2 miles north of Weedon.
OPEN: Ring.
ADMISSION: N/A.   *TEL:* 01589 039427.

JAN LANGAN

FACILITIES: Designer jeweller, with an exhibition and worshop where designer jewellery is made, and silversmithing takes place. Also runs evening classes.

LOCATION: The Castle, Castle Way, Wellingborough.

OPEN: Daily 1000-1900.

ADMISSION: Ring.   *RING:* 01933 229022 (The Castle).

CATHERINE LANGLEY

FACILITIES: Cast glass artist, specialising in lost wax method of primitive casting.

LOCATION: Ring.

OPEN: Ring.

ADMISSION: No charge.   *TEL:* 01933 272340.

GRAHAM LINNELL

FACILITIES: Cabinet maker, but also makes anything to order.

LOCATION: The Old Dairy Farm Centre, Upper Stowe, signposted off the A5 to the south of Weedon.

OPEN: Ring for details.

ADMISSION: No charge.   *TEL:* 01327 340525.

MANOR WOODWORKING

FACILITIES: Made to measure furniture in pine or hardwood. restorations undertaken - and anything in wood tackled. Designs and quotes are free, and all work is guarenteed.

LOCATION: Manor Farm, Guilsborough Road, West Haddon.

OPEN: Ring.

ADMISSION: No charge   *TEL:* 01788 510423.

BADEN R MAHONEY

FACILITIES: Produces water colours of local scenes.

LOCATION: Ring for information.

OPEN: Ring.

ADMISSION: Charge for work.   *TEL:* 01604 811018.

ALISON MARSH

FACILITIES: Pets, landscapes and families drawn and painted from pictures.

LOCATION: 22 Spring Gardens, Wellingborough.

OPEN: Ring.

ADMISSION: Charge for work.   *TEL:* 01933 222528.

ANN MARTIN PLANT DISPLAYS

FACILITIES: Living plants for home, office, etc. Hanging baskets, partition planters, etc.
LOCATION: Laudshill, 12 Boat House Lane, Crick.
OPEN: Ring.
ADMISSION: No charge.   **TEL:** 01788 822320.

JOHN MATHIESON

FACILITIES: Ceramics produced on the potters wheel - both raku and stoneware.
LOCATION: Old Dairy Farm, Upper Stowe. The Old Dairy Farm Centre is signposted off the A5.
OPEN: Mon-Fri 1000-1600; Sat 1000-1400.
ADMISSION: No charge.   **TEL:** 01327 340525.

MEADOWCRAFT CERAMICS

FACILITIES: Ceramic products for sale, also has shop and studio classes at most times.
LOCATION: 42 Oxford St, Kettering.
OPEN: Ring.
ADMISSION: Charge for courses.   **TEL:** 01536 410379.

GILL MEADOWS

FACILITIES: Potter producing hand thrown domestic stoneware.
LOCATION: 4 Park Street, Kings Cliffe, near Oundle.
OPEN: Ring.
ADMISSION: No charge.   **TEL:** 01780 470239.

MILLS STONEWARE

FACILITIES: Produces a range of garden ornaments, from small animals, birds, bats, seals, etc - to larger pieces, including bird baths. All are realistic and hand painted.
LOCATION: 53 High Street, Long Buckby.
OPEN: Ring,
ADMISSION: No charge.   **TEL:** 01327 843423.

MJS FURNISHINGS

FACILITIES: Family run business specialising in traditional elegant, timeless furniture made to perfection in mahogany, yew, oak and cherry.
LOCATION: 76 Artizan Road, Northampton.
OPEN: Mon-Wed & Fri-Sat 1000-1700; Sun 1000-1600.
ADMISSION: Free.   **TEL:** 01604 620499.

KA MEASURES

FACILITIES: Hand crafted furniture designed and manufactured on the premises, specialises in solid wood dining tables. Accepts commissions.
LOCATION: Heart of The Shires Shopping Village, The Woodyard, on the A5 2 miles north of Weedon crossroads.
OPEN: Tues-Sat 1000-1700: Sun 1100-1700.
ADMISSION: No charge.   *TEL:* 01327 341300.

GLYN MOULD

FACILITIES: A woodcarver working with timber like oak, ash and lime, using traditional tools. He is able to accommodate groups to see his work, usually in the evenings. Other crafts also housed in the same building (The Old Methodist Chapel). Demonstration and talk available.
LOCATION: 43 Main Street, Woodnewton, between Kings Cliffe and Oundle.
OPEN: Most weekdays and some weekend. Ring for details.
ADMISSION: No charge for visiting the workshops.   Charge for group visits.   *TEL:* 01780 470866.

NIGHTINGALE JEWELLERS

FACILITIES: Traditional and modern handcrafted jewellery. Nightingale specialises in 'one-off' designs to individual specifications. Jewellery repair service available.
LOCATION: Old Farmyard, Castle Ashby, off the A428, east of Northampton.
OPEN: Tues-Sat 1000-1700; Sun 1100-1700; Bank Hol Mon.
ADMISSION: Free.   *TEL:* 01604 696090.

R W NIGHTINGALE

FACILITIES: Blacksmith producing wrought ironwork and 'artistic' items.
LOCATION: Unit 5, JBJ Business Park, Northampton Road, Blisworth.
OPEN: Ring.
ADMISSION: Ring.   *TEL:* 01604 859252.

NORTHAMPTON LEADED LIGHTS

FACILITIES: Stockists of glass and craft materials.
LOCATION: 1 Marlborough Road, St James, Northampton.
OPEN: Ring.
ADMISSION: No charge.   *TEL:* 01604 755206.

NORTHAMPTON TOURIST INFORMATION CENTRE

FACILITIES: Crystal, tablemats, ceramics, doorstops, - some locally made.
LOCATION: Mr Grant's House, 10 St Giles Square, Northampton.

OPEN: 0930-1700 - Mon-Fri; 0930-1600 - Sat.
ADMISSION: No charge.   *TEL:* 01604 22677.

THE NORTHANTS GATE CENTRE

FACILITIES: Wrought iron gates of many designs; also strong plain or decorative security grilles. On display in the factory showroom.
LOCATION: 180-186 Regent Street, Kettering.
OPEN: Ring for details.
ADMISSION: Free.   *TEL:* 01536 85892.

MAGGIE AND RICHARD NORWELL

FACILITIES: Produce stained glass panels, lamps, boxes, terrariums. Commissions accepted.
LOCATION: Oundle Stained Glass Studio, 73 West Street, Oundle.
OPEN: Ring.
ADMISSION: No charge.
TEL: 01832 274113 (work) and 01733 235067 (home).

OAK FACTORY

FACILITIES: Manufacturer of a range of oak reproduction furniture.
LOCATION: Spencer Parade, Stanwick - near Potters the Butchers, and just off the A45 to the north east of Higham Ferrers.
OPEN: Mon-Sat 1000-1600; Sun 1200-1600.
ADMISSION: No charge.   *TEL:* 01933 623866.

OAKLEY MILL

FACILITIES: Gifts from around the world, including brass, coloured glass, jewellery ceramics, carved wood and clothes.
LOCATION: 10 Church Street, Woodford Halse - opposite the post office.
OPEN: Tues/Wed/Fri/Sat 0900-1730; Thurs 0930-1900.

OLD BAKERY GALLERY

FACILITIES: The specialist shop for the specialist discerning collector for dolls, teddies and soft toys, including antiques, reproduction, new collectors, etc.
LOCATION: The Old Bakery Gallery, 7 and 38 Cambridge Street, Wellingborough.
OPEN: Tues/Wed/Fri/Sat 1000-1700.
ADMISSION: No charge.   *TEL:* 01933 272123 (shop)/229191 (office).

THE OLD BAKEHOUSE STUDIOS

FACILITIES: Batiks on silk. Batik is a less well known craft, with an ancient tradition, and comes from the Japanese word meaning 'point of light' - and is due to the effects obtained by using wax. Courses also run.
LOCATION: The Old Bakehouse Studios, 7 Rushton Road, Wilbarston which is off the A427, which bypasses the village.
OPEN: Ring for details.
ADMISSION: Charge for courses.   *TEL:* 01536 771484.

OLD BREWERY STUDIOS

FACILITIES: Painting, prints and pottery. Also runs residential summer art courses. These are held in former forest 'bailiwick' villages.
LOCATION: The Manor House, King's Cliffe, off A43 south of Stamford.
OPEN: Ring for details.
ADMISSION: Free.   *TEL:* 01780 470247.

OLD CHAPEL CRAFTS

FACILITIES: Craft workshops and artists, exhibiting a variety of pictures in the craft workshops and adjoining Old Chapel Tea Room. The latter serves a wide range of meals and snacks, as well as coffee and afternoon teas. There is a delightful garden where meals can be taken during the summer.
LOCATION: Chapel Lane, Stoke Bruerne.
OPEN: Summer; April-Sept - everyday 1000-1800; Winter Oct-Mar 1100-dusk Tues-Sun.
ADMISSION: Exhibitions free.   *TEL:* 01604 863284.

OLD DAIRY FARM CENTRE

FACILITIES: Housed in a series of prize-winning converted 19 century farm buildings. There is a number of craft workshops (see separate listings), where crafts people can be seen working. Shops include antiques, Liberty of London, woollens loft, as well as a picnic area and free parking. There are also birds and animals on view. Restaurant/tea room serves home made food. Free parking. Groups by arrangement (including school visits - but see also Educational Visits). The barn conversion can be hired for demonstrations/meetings.
LOCATION: In Upper Stowe, reached off the A5 south of Weedon crossroads.
OPEN: 1 Mar-24 Dec 1000-1730; 1st Mon of New Year to end of Feb 1000-1630.
ADMISSION: Free, although charge made for certain events.
TEL: 01327 340525.

ORCHARD BLOSSOM FAVOURS

FACILITIES: Favours for all occasions. Traditional five sugar almonds representing health, wealth, happiness, good luck and fertility. Pot pourri, chocolates or a small gift can be added.

LOCATION: 6 Orchard Close, Hollowell.

OPEN: Ring for details.

ADMISSION: N/A.   *TEL:* 01604 740488.

OLD DUSTON FRAMING

FACILITIES: Wood turning and wood crafts.

LOCATION: 46a Main Road, Old Duston.

OPEN: Ring.

ADMISSION: No charge.   *TEL:* 01604 584934.

ELIZABETH PALMER

FACILITIES: Spins and weaves fabrics, also dyes. Also runs some residential and non-residential courses during the week and at weekends. Specialises in individual workshops. Equipment and material for spinning are stocked.

LOCATION: Crown Cottage, 46 High Street, Gretton, 2 miles off the A6003.

OPEN: By prior appointment all year.

ADMISSION: Free, charge for courses.   *TEL:* 01536 770303.

PARAPHERNALIA

FACILITIES: Has a wide range of local crafts, pictures, copper and brassware, painted pine furniture, baskets, dried flowers, china and collectables.

LOCATION: 2 Horsemarket, Kettering, (opposite taxi rank).

OPEN: Ring for details.

ADMISSION: Free.   *TEL:* 01536 414343.

PARKSIDE GALLERY

FACILITIES: Collectable craft gifts, including Lilliput Lane, Robert Harrop Silver Scenes, musical toys, scented candles, and many unusual gifts.

LOCATION: 17 Draymans Walk, Brackley.

OPEN: Mon, Wed, Thurs, Fri, Sat 0900-1700.

ADMISSION: Free.   *TEL:* 01280 706366.

JEREMY PEAKE CERAMICS

FACILITIES: Produces a basic line in kitchenware, including jugs, bowls, mugs, and special commissions for weddings, including personalised ware.

LOCATION: The Brick, 40 Addington Rd, Irthlingborough, near Wellingborough.
OPEN: Ring first.
ADMISSION: No charge.   TEL: 01933 653771.

PEARCE TANDY LEATHERCRAFT LTD
FACILITIES: Combines American and traditional Northamptonshire skills and techniques to produce leather work. Hides, tools, books, patterns and DIY kits and supplies. Indian lore and jewellery supplies. Free tuition available.
LOCATION: Billing Park, Wellingborough Road, Northampton.
OPEN: Ring.
ADMISSION: No charge.   TEL: 01604 407177.

PEEP HOLE CRAFTS AND GALLERY
FACILITIES: A craft boutique in a 17th century barn. A variety of crafts from around the country. The boutique also specialises in a nostalgic range of nightwear, lingerie, blouses, christening gowns, made in a variety of fabrics, including cotton, silk, satin and lace. Various exhibitions of artists work.
LOCATION: 5a High Street, Long Buckby, in the Coop precinct.
OPEN: Ring for details.
ADMISSION: Free.   TEL: 01327 843638.

ALISON PHILLIPS
FACILITIES: A painter with a wide range of techniques, including watercolours, pastels and oils.
LOCATION: Hinton Barn, Hinton-in-the-Hedges, near Brackley.
OPEN: Ring.
ADMISSION: Ring.   TEL: 01280 40577.

PHOENIX POTTERY
FACILITIES: A range of ware - ring for details.
LOCATION: High Street, Irchester.
OPEN: Ring for times.
ADMISSION: No charge.   TEL: 01933 57688.

PINEWOOD
FACILITIES: Quality pine furniture, with made to measure service, together with a variety of clocks, mirrors, pictures, etc.
LOCATION: 8 Bedford Road, Yardley Hastings.
OPEN: Wed/Thurs 1000-1700; Fri/Sat 1000-1730; Sun 1000-1600.
ADMISSION: No charge.   TEL: 01604 696466.

PINOCCHIO
FACILITIES: Wide selection of craft items, including Java lamps, Janson figures, pot pourri, prints, pine furniture, etc.
LOCATION: Ground Floor, Peacock Place, Market Sq., Northampton.
OPEN: 0900-1750.
ADMISSION: No charge.   *TEL:* 01604 601565.

PLENTI-FULL-POTS
FACILITIES: Stocks a large selection of containers and pots, including terracotta, baskets, wooden barrels, hanging baskets, stoneware, etc. Dried flowers and a wide range of 'mix and match' plants.
LOCATION: Falcutt Farm, Helmdon near Brackley, off the B4525 near Helmdon village.
OPEN: All year 1000-15730, but limited opening Jan. Closed 25/26 Dec/1 Jan.
ADMISSION: No charge. *TEL:* 01280 850479.

MALCOLM POLLARD
FACILITIES: Sculptor/woodcarver.
LOCATION: 42 East Park Parade, Northampton.
OPEN: Ring.
ADMISSION: Ring.   *TEL:* 01604 37932.

POLLY LONGFROCK
FACILITIES: Sells dolls houses and miniatures, all half scale.
LOCATION: 133 Simpson Avenue, Northampton.
OPEN: Tue/Wed/Fri 1030-1630: Sat 1000-1700; Sun 1200-1700.
ADMISSION: Free.*TEL:* 01604 26906.

POSY BOWL
FACILITIES: Specialist in dried silk flowers. Special arrangements undertaken.
LOCATION: Heart of the Shires Shopping Village on the A5 2 miles north of Weedon.
OPEN: Ring for times.
ADMISSION: No charge.   *TEL:* 01788 536879 (evenings).

THE POT SHOP
FACILITIES: A 'shop in a cottage' in the delightful stone built village of Geddington, there is a range of pots from different places, together with British made gifts, glass, china and greetings cards. Stockists of porcelain models of local buildings by Stanion Pottery.
LOCATION: 41 Queen Street, Geddington.
OPEN: Tues-Sun 0930-1700.
ADMISSION: Free.   *TEL:* 01536 742557.

PUNCHINELLO

FACILITIES: Quality picture framing, including tapestries and embroidery which can be stretched and framed. Large selection of prints and posters.
LOCATION: 49 Oxford Street, Wellingborough.
OPEN: Ring for information.
ADMISSION: Free.   *TEL:* 01933 410898.

DUDLEY RAVEN

FACILITIES: Full picture framing service - no job too small. 36 hour emergency service.
LOCATION: 34 Bliss Lane, Flore.
OPEN: Mon/Tues/Wed/Fri 1000-1700.
ADMISSION: N/A.   *TEL:* 01327 349012 (working hours).

GUY RAVINE

FACILITIES: Fine woodturning and treen. High quality products.
LOCATION: The Old Dairy Farm Centre, Upper Stowe, and reached of the A5, South of Weedon crossroads.
OPEN: Ring for details.
ADMISSION: Free.   *TEL:* 01327 340410.

DAVID READ

FACILITIES: Charcoal maker, woodland products and craft worker.
LOCATION: 1 Yorke Close, Finedon.
OPEN: Ring.
ADMISSION: N/A.   *TEL:* 01933 680522.

KATHLEEN RICHMOND

FACILITIES: Hand painted porcelain plates.
LOCATION: 34 Ilex Close, Hardingstone.
OPEN: Ring for details.
ADMISSION: No charge.   *TEL:* 01604 760021.

RIVERSIDE CERAMICS

FACILITIES: Kilns, potters wheels, slip, clay glazes, greenware and bisque. Tuition available, including wheel turning.
LOCATION: 6 Burwood Road, Northampton.
OPEN: Ring.
ADMISSION: Charge for tuition.   *TEL:* 01604 410480

RIVERVIEW CRAFTS

FACILITIES: Everything you need to make crafts - paints, beads, parchment, embroidery threads, glass paints - vast range. Free

demonstrations of specific crafts on Sundays. Details in free programme (send sae). Also runs workshops and knitters club.
LOCATION: Riverview, Station Road, Cogenhoe.
OPEN: Tues-Sun 1000-1700.
ADMISSION: Free - but charge for workshops.   *TEL:* 01604 891900

ROCK FOUNDRY
FACILITIES: House names, numbers and posy boxes.
LOCATION: Lakeside, Litchborough Road, Duncote, Towcester, and reached off the A5.
OPEN: Ring for details.
ADMISSION: Free.   *TEL:* 01327 351561.

PETER ROSE CERAMICS
FACILITIES: A range of hand painted ceramics, including wild life - foxes. rabbits, eagles, woodpeckers, owls and kingfishers, as well as wizards, dragons and castles. Also specialist pieces. Fine English bone china decorated to individual designs. White china always in stock.
LOCATION: The Old Farm Yard, Castle Ashby, off the A428, east of Northampton.
OPEN: Tues-Sat 1000-1700; Sun 1100-1700; Bank Hol Mon.
ADMISSION: No charge.   *TEL:* 01604 679949.

HUGH ROSS
FACILITIES: Traditional charcoal burner, also hazel woodland products.
LOCATION: The charcoal is available from various outlets, including the Northamptonshire Countryside Centre, 9 Guildhall Road, Northampton. The latter will also provide information.
OPEN: N/A.
ADMISSION: N/A.   *TEL:* 0385 536613 (mobile) or 01604 237220 (Countryside Centre).

SERENDIPITY
FACILITIES: Unusual gifts in wood, glass, together with a range of fancy gifts and ladies clothes.
LOCATION: 15 Sheaf Street, Daventry.
OPEN: Mon/Tues/Thurs/Fri/Sat 0930-1700; Wed 0930-1330.
ADMISSION: No charge.   *TEL:* 01327 702109.

PHILLIPA SMITH
FACILITIES: Painter, printmaker and muralist, specialising in animals, birds and flowers on paper canvas, using mixed media.
LOCATION: The Barn and Studio, Yew tree Cottage, Hinton-in-the-Hedges, near Brackley.

OPEN: Ring.
ADMISSION: Ring.   *TEL:* 01280 704577.

STANION POTTERY

FACILITIES: Produces an extensive range of handthrown kitchen ware and tableware. These include bread crocks, casseroles, jugs, mugs, vases, jars, bowls, etc. Commissioned work can be undertaken, and can include company logos, crests, etc. Also produces a range of porcelain models of local cottages, churches, pubs, etc. Demonstrations available.
LOCATION: 24 Willow Lane, Stanion.
OPEN: Mon-Fri 0900-1700; Sat/Sun by appointment.
ADMISSION: No charge - except demonstrations. *TEL:* 01536 400334.

ANN STEADMAN

FACILITIES: Painter and illustrator specialising in acrylic designs, dancers and a range of paintings.
LOCATION: Ring for details.
OPEN: Ring.
ADMISSION; Ring.   *TEL:* 01295 60398.

ANNA STEINER

FACILITIES: Produces printed textiles, including silk painting and textiles.
LOCATION: 2 Kiln Lane, Litchborough.
OPEN: Weekdays by appointment.
ADMISSION: No charge.   *TEL:* 01327 830095.

IAN STEVENS RE

FACILITIES: Wood engraver and printmaker, specialising in illustrations and printmaking.
LOCATION: Northampton - ring.
OPEN: By appoinment only.
ADMISSION: Ring.   *TEL:* 01604 842399.

MRS P STRATFORD

FACILITIES: Hand-crafted wooden toys, which include puzzles, ride on toys and climbing frames. Accepts commissions from playgroups and private individuals.
LOCATION: N/A.
OPEN: Ring.
ADMISSION: Charge for items.   *TEL:* 01832 272198.

SUSANNA THOMSON

FACILITIES: Storymask Craft. Performances for schools, youth groups, etc, where the emphasis is on mask making.

LOCATION: Ring.
OPEN: Ring.
ADMISSION: Charge for workshops.　　**TEL:** 01832 272048.

SUE'S FANCIES
FACILITIES: Specialises in needlework, including cross stitch. Large range of patterns, threads, kits, materials, accessories and craft sundries.
LOCATION: 37a Coffee Tavern Court, High Street, Rushden.
OPEN: Mon/Tues/Wed/Fri/ 0930-1630; Thurs 0930-1330.
ADMISSION: No charge.　　**TEL:** 01933 418882.

THREE SHIRES CRAFTS
FACILITIES: A true working craft shop demonstrating traditional methods. Variety of techniques and items for sale.
LOCATION: The Workshop, Spring Lane, Little Bourton, Banbury, Oxon
OPEN: Every day from 0900 to 1700.
ADMISSION: Free.　　**TEL:** 01295 750936.

JOHN THRUSSELL-JONES
FACILITIES: Studio pottery.
LOCATION: Castle Ashby Pottery, Old Farmyard, Castle Ashby.
OPEN: Tues-Sat 1100-1700.
ADMISSION: No charge.　　**TEL:** 01604 696076.

BOB TIMS
FACILITIES: Wood tuner - bowls, lamps, treen, stools, etc. Also teaches woodturning.
OPEN: Ring for information.
LOCATION: Ring.
ADMISSION: Does not have a shop.　　**TEL:** 01788 823266.

JOHN TIPLER
FACILITIES: Blacksmith.
LOCATION: Craft Workshops, East Carlton Countryside Park on the A427 Corby-Market Harborough road.
OPEN: Ring for times.
ADMISSION: No charge.　　**TEL:** 01536 770977 (Countryside Park).

THE TITHE BARN
FACILITIES: Crafts and antiques, as well as a farm shop with organically grown produce. There is a play area and pets corner. Free parking. Food available.

LOCATION: Home Farm, Thurning, off the A605, near Barnwell and South of Oundle.
OPEN: Ring for details.
ADMISSION: Free.   *TEL:* 01832 293511.

TRADELINE FENDERS
FACILITIES: Any splice, mooring lines, fenders, specials. All craft fancy ropework.
LOCATION: Bullfinch, The Wharf, Braunston, off the A45 to the north of Daventry.
OPEN: Ring.
ADMISSION: N/A.   *TEL:* 01788 891761.

HEATHER TROTTER
FACILITIES: Batik.
LOCATION: Old Dairy Farm Centre, Upper Stowe, off A5 south of Weedon crossroads.
OPEN: Ring for details.
ADMISSION: Free.
TEL: 01327 704694 (home); 01327 340525 (Office, Old Dairy Farm Centre).

VISCOUNT WOODCRAFTS
FACILITIES: Hand turned woodcraft items together with a large selection of woodturning and woodworking equipment and accessories.
LOCATION: 3 & 5 Brackley way, Towcester.
OPEN: Ring.
ADMISSION: No charge.   *TEL:* 01327 358510.

VR DESIGNS AND FORGE
FACILITIES: Situated on the same site as the Copper Gallery, and produces a wide range of ornamental ironwork, balustrades, fire baskets, fire screens, rise arches, etc, together with unusual weather vanes, sun dials, flower stands and garden lanterns. Commissions taken and restoration work carried out.
LOCATION: Lower Street, Desborough, off the A6, and next to St Giles Church.
OPEN: Tues-Sat 1000-1730; Sun 1400-1700.
ADMISSION: No charge.   *TEL:* 01536 762333.

WAKEFIELD FARM SHOP AND CRAFT CENTRE
FACILITIES: Range of craft gifts and dried flowers.

112

LOCATION: Assarts Farm, Wakefield Lodge Estate, Potterspury, reached off the A5.
OPEN: Tues-Fri 0930-1800; Sat 0900-1730; Sun 1000-1600.
ADMISSION: No charge.   *TEL:* 01327 811493.

R J WALDER
FACILITIES: Cabinet maker specialising in fine solid hardwood furniture, which is made to the requirements of individual clients.
LOCATION: 28 High Street, Milton Malsor.
OPEN: By appointment only.
ADMISSION: Ring.   *TEL:* 01604 858470.

HELEN WEST
FACILITIES: A jeweller working in gold and silver to produce handmade pieces.
LOCATION: Ring.
OPEN: Ring.
ADMISSION: No charge.   *TEL:* 01604 740043.

WEST COUNTRY PINE WORKSHOPS
FACILITIES: Reclaimed pine furniture and kitchens at Victorian prices. Bedroom and dining furniture, fitted kitchens. Made to measure service.
LOCATION: 117 Abington Avenue. Northampton.
OPEN: Ring.
ADMISSION: Free.   *TEL:* 01604 711000.

WEST NORTHANTS WOODTURNERS
FACILITIES: Club providing tuition and help for those interested in woodturning.
LOCATION: Long Buckby RF Club, Station Road.
OPEN: 3rd Wed of the month.
ADMISSION: Ring.   *TEL:* 01327 872982 (Secretary).

WHEEL CERAMICS
FACILITIES: Ceramics.
LOCATION: Pury Hill Farm, Pury Hill, Paulerspury.
OPEN: Ring.
ADMISSION: Ring.   *TEL:* 01327 811663.

WICKSTEED POTTERY
FACILITIES: Range of pots, etc. thrown on the premises.
LOCATION: Wicksteed Park, Kettering.
OPEN: Varies - ring.
ADMISSION: Charge for parking.   *TEL:* 01536 512475.

WILDER DREAMS HOBBY SHOP
FACILITIES: An open house ceramics workshop for all ages. No talent needed! Help is on hand. Spend a couple of hours in relaxing atmosphere and produce something which can be taken home.
LOCATION: 7 Midland Road, Thrapston.
OPEN: Mon-Fri 0900-1500; Mon/Wed evenings 1900-2100.
ADMISSION: Fees ranging from £2.00 to £30.00.   *TEL:* 01832 735506

WOODNEWTON CRAFT STUDIOS
FACILITES: Housed in the former Methodist Chapel, crafts including woodcarving, pottery and marionette puppets take place.
LOCATION: The Old Chapel, 43 Main Street, Woodnewton near Oundle.
OPEN: Most weekdays and some weekends - ring to check.
ADMISSION: Free.   *TEL:* 01780 470866.

WORLDWIDE REFINISHING SYSTEMS
FACILITIES: Renovates and resurfacing of bathrooms, kitchen units, showers, etc. Sells ceramic tiles.
LOCATION: Heart of The Shires Shopping Village, The Woodyard on the A5 2 miles north of Weedon crossroads.
OPEN: Tues-Sat 1000-1700; Sun 1100-1700. *TEL:* 01327 349899.

WOODPECKER STUDIO
FACILITIES: Woodcarving specialist in solid timber, making anything from lace bobbins to totem poles.
LOCATION: Knuston Hall.
OPEN: Mon-Fri 1000-1900; Sat/Sun 1400-1900.
ADMISSION: No charge.   *TEL:* 01933 410393.

CRICKET

See also Sporting Activities, including Spectator Sports.

NORTHAMPTONSHIRE COUNTY CRICKET CLUB
FACILITIES: County cricket and other matches held at home.
LOCATION: Wantage Road, Northampton.
TEL: 01604 632917.

A5 RANGERS CYCLING CLUB

FACILITIES: From 11 years upwards for cycle touring, racing, trialling and road racing.
LOCATION: 101 Watling Street West, Towcester.
OPEN: Ring for times.
ADMISSION: Membership fee.   *TEL:* 01327 352389.

AMATEUR CYCLING CLUB

FACILITIES: Facilities for the amateur.
LOCATION: Ring for details.
OPEN: Ring.
ADMISSION: Membership fee.   *TEL:* 01933 517564/525237

BIKING ROUND THE BOROUGH

FACILITIES: Produced by Kettering Leisure Services it gives details of family cycle tours through towns and villages around Kettering, covering Rothwell, Desborough, Stoke Albany, Wilbarston, Pipewell and Rushton.
LOCATION: As described in the leaflet.
OPEN: Can be cycled at any time.
ADMISSION: No charge.   *TEL:* 01536 410226 (TIC).

THE BLUEBELL LINE

FACILITIES One of Northamptonshire's Cycletours. Takes in the villages of Daventry, Staverton, Hellidon, Everdon, Preston Capes and Newnham. A full day cycle tour covering up to 20 miles through some of the county's most impressive countryside and attractive villages.
LOCATION: See leaflet.
OPEN: Can be taken at most times.
ADMISSION: Charge for leaflet.
TEL: 01604 237220 (Countryside Centre)/236735 (Cycling Officer).

BRAMPTON VALLEY CENTRAL

FACILITIES: Cottages and coverts - No 4 in the Cycletours series, and includes a network of routes for both touring and off-road cyclists helping them to enjoy the countryside of the Brampton Valley.
LOCATION: See leaflet.
OPEN: Can be cycled at most times.
ADMISSION: Charge for leaflet.
TEL: 01604 237220 (Countryside Centre), 236735 (Cycling Officer).

115

BRAMPTON VALLEY NORTH-EAST

FACILITIES: Ridge, roads and rivers, including Arthingworth, Harrington, Lamport.
LOCATION: See leaflet.
OPEN: Can be cycled at most times.
ADMISSION: Charge for leaflet.   *TEL:* 01604 237220 (Countryside Centre) and 236735 (Cycling Officer).

BRAMPTON VALLEY NORTH WEST

FACILITIES: A network of five routes for both touring and off-road cycling, including Naseby Field, Kelmarsh, Clipston, etc.
LOCATION: See leaflet.
OPEN: Can be cycled at most times.
ADMISSION: Charge for leaflet.   *TEL:* 01604 237220 (Countryside Centre)/236735 (Cycling Officer).

BRAMPTON VALLEY SOUTH

FACILITIES: Houses and Heaths - No 5 in the Cycletours series, covers a network of five routes for both touring and off-road cyclists enabling them to enjoy the countryside of the Brampton Valley.
LOCATION: See leaflet.
OPEN: Can be cycled at most times.
ADMISSION: Charge for leaflet.
TEL: 01604 237220 (Countryside Centre)/236735 (Cycling Officer).

BRAMPTON VALLEY SOUTH-EAST

FACILITIES: Scenes and greens - five rides, covering such places as Boughton, Holcot, Brixworth, Walgrave, Old, etc.
LOCATION: See leaflet.
OPEN: Can be cycled at most times.
ADMISSION: Charge for leaflet.   *TEL:* 01604 237220 (Countryside Centre)/236735 (Cycling Officer).

CLIFFE BAILIWICK AND WILLOW BROOK

FACILITIES: No 3 in the Cycletours series, takes in Kings Cliffe, Bulwick, Southwick, Woodnewton and Apethorpe, with the 16 mile tour giving an ideal day out which allows the cyclist to discover one of the ancient administrative areas of Rockingham Forest.
LOCATION: See leaflet.
OPEN: Can be cycled at most times.
ADMISSION: Cost of leaflet.
TEL: 01604 237220 (Countryside Centre)/236735 (Cycling Officer).

CYCLE ROUTES IN NORTHAMPTON

FACILITIES: A leaflet with map showing the cycle routes.
LOCATION: In Northampton.
OPEN: Can be cycled at any time.
ADMISSION: No charge.   *TEL:* 01604 22677 (TIC).

CYCLISTS' TOURING CLUB - KETTERING

FACILITIES: Organises rides of various distances.
LOCATION: In and around Kettering.
OPEN: Ring.
ADMISSION: Membership fee.   *TEL:* 01536 712570.

CYCLISTS' TOURING CLUB

FACILITIES: All day rides every Sunday - varying distances.
LOCATION: Meets outside Guildhall, Northampton.
OPEN: Sunday - 0915.
ADMISSION: Ring.   *TEL:* 01604 870534.

45 ROAD CYCLING CLUB

FACILITIES: Road cycling.
LOCATION: Ring.
OPEN: Ring.
ADMISSION: Charge.   *TEL:* 01933 224122.

GRAND UNION CANAL

FACILITIES: The London to Birmingham Waterway. Some sections of the towpath which are suitable for cycling, but a cycle licence is needed.
LOCATION: Ring for details.
OPEN: During daylight hours.
ADMISSION: Charge for licence.   *TEL:* 01788 890666.

GUIDED BIKE RIDES

FACILITIES: Held regularly throughout the County.
LOCATION: Various locations.
OPEN: Varies.
ADMISSION: Sometimes.   *TEL:* Contact your local TIC and library.

INVICTA ROAD CLUB

FACILITIES: Road racing.
LOCATION: Corby.
OPEN: Ring.
ADMISSION: Charge.   *TEL:* 01536 742814 (R Summerlin, 10 Brunswick Gardens, Corby, NN18 9ER).

KETTERING FRIENDLY CYCLING CLUB

FACILITIES: Friendly Cycling Club - Cliff Smith Design.
LOCATION: Write for details.
OPEN: Write for details.
ADMISSION: Membership fee.
TEL: Miss D Bull, 25 Boddington Road, Kettering, NN15 6DZ.

MOORS, MOATS AND MANORS

FACILITIES: No 1 in the Cycletours series, through the villages of Harrington, Thorpe Underwood, Braybrooke and Arthingworth in a tour which covers about 9.5 miles taking the cyclist through winding country lanes, pretty villages and gently rolling countryside.
LOCATION: See leaflet.
OPEN: Can be cycled at most times.
ADMISSION: Cost of leaflet.
TEL: 01604 237220 (Countryside Centre)/236735 (Cycling Officer).

NENE VALLEY - WEEDON TO NORTHAMPTON

FACILITIES: Takes in Gayton, Rotherthorpe, Kislingbury, Little Brington, Nether Heyford, with a choice of three tours which explore the history, landscape and wildlife of the Nene Valley.
LOCATION: See leaflet.
OPEN: Can be cycled at most times.
ADMISSION: Cost of leaflet.
TEL: 01604 237220 (Countryside Centre/236735 (Cycling Officer).

NENE VALLEY - OUNDLE TO WANSFORD

FACILITIES: No 9 in the Cycletours series, takes in Oundle, Ashton, Fotheringhay, Wansford, Yarwell and Nassington, and includes a choice of three tours allowing the cyclist to explore the history, landscape and wildlife of this area of the Nene Valley.
LOCATION: See leaflet.
OPEN: Can be cycled at most times.
ADMISSION: Charge for leaflet.
TEL: 01604 237220 (Countryside Centre)/236735 (Cycling Officer).

NENE VALLEY - OUNDLE TO THRAPSTON

FACILITIES: No 2 in the Cycletours series, takes in Oundle, Aldwincle, Clopton and Barnwell, allowing a choice of three tours, giving time to explore the history, landscape and wildlife of this part of the Nene Valley.
LOCATION: See leaflet.
OPEN: Can be cycled at most times.
ADMISSION: Charge for leaflet.
TEL: 01604 237220 (Countryside Centre)/ 236735 (Cycling Officer).

NORTHAMPTON VELO CLUB

FACILITIES: Regular rides for individuals from the age of eleven.
LOCATION: Meets at Abington Park gates, Wellingborough Road.
OPEN: Every Sun morning at 0900.
ADMISSION: Membership fee.   *TEL:* 01604 622747.

ROCKINGHAM FOREST WHEELERS

FACILITIES: Road and mountain bike racing, plus touring.
LOCATION: Ring.
OPEN: Ring.
ADMISSION: Charge.   *TEL:* 01536 771349.

SULGRAVE, THE WASHINGTONS AND THE SHEEP THAT EAT MEN

FACILITIES: There are two routes. The first takes in Bucknell Woods, Greens Norton, Bradden, Slapton, Wappenham and Abthorpe. The second covers Wappenham, Weedon Lois, Weston, Sulgrave, Helmdon and back to Wappenham.
LOCATION: See leaflet.
ADMISSION: Charge for leaflet.
TEL: 01604 237220 (Countryside Centre)/236735 (Cycling Officer).

VALLEY BIKE HIRE

FACILITIES: Has bikes for hire by the hour - or longer.
LOCATION: 5a West Street, Oundle.
OPEN: 0900-1700 Mon-Sat.
ADMISSION: Hire charge.   *TEL:* 01832 275381/278127.

See also Residential Centres, Farms, etc.

THE CANAL MUSEUM

FACILITIES: Housed in a restored cornmill, the Museum covers the 200 year history of the canals using models, videos, pictorial and three-dimensional displays, which explore every aspect of the waterways. These include crafts, boats, people, etc. From time to time demonstrations of traditional painting are held, as well as art and craft exhibitions. There is a first rate bookshop, which also sells a range of souvenirs, painted canalware, waterways gifts, etc. Boat trips and food close by.

LOCATION: Off the A5 south of Northampton, 10 mins from J15 of M1.

OPEN: Summer - daily from 1000-1800, including Bank Hols; Winter Tues-Sun 1000-1600. Closed 25/26 Dec. Ring to confirm opening times. Free parking for Museum visitors in Museum car park.

ADMISSION: Charge.   *TEL:* 01604 862229.

CALVERT ENVIRONMENTAL EDUCATION CENTRE

FACILITIES: Based at the Shanks and McEwan site, the Centre is the converted pavilion of the former Sports ground, and has a teacher in residence. There is a small aquatic study area, wide open spaces, small wood, and an area which can be 'developed' by schools. Some resource material available. Classroom, meeting room and a smaller kitchen, together with toilets in an adjacent building. Wheelchair access provided to the centre and nature trail. There is no public access to the site, and booking must be made.

LOCATION: Shanks and McEwan, Brackley Lane, Calvert, Bucks, just over the County border, available for schools in the south of the County.

OPEN: All year.

ADMISSION: No charge.

TEL: 01296 738837 (Shanks and McEwan)/01865 775476 (BBONT).

DAVENTRY MUSEUM

FACILITIES: Various displays and teaching sessions available, including workshops (Invaders, Romans etc.)

LOCATION: Moot Hall, Daventry.

OPEN: Ring.

ADMISSION: No charge for educational visits, but charge for workshops. **TEL:** 01327 302463.

FERMYN FOREST

FACILITIES: A remnant of the former Rockingham Forest, and consists of oak and ash trees, with some hazel. Good display of bluebells in the spring, together with violets and primroses. Autumn is good for fungi. A teachers pack is available. A Forest Ranger is available for which there is a charge. On site leaflet.
LOCATION: South end of Brigstock village, just off the Brigstock bypass (A6116).
OPEN: Can be used at most times.
ADMISSION: Charge for Ranger. **TEL:** 01780 444395 (Forest Enterprise).

FOREST ENTERPRISE

FACILITIES: Pack of material and Forest Ranger is available to work with groups in some woods.
LOCATION: Ring for information.
OPEN: Ring to book.
ADMISSION: Charge for pack and Ranger. **TEL:** 01780 444395

HOLDENBY HOUSE EDUCATION PROGRAMME

FACILITIES: Covers a wide subject range, including Victorians, Tudors, Stuarts, Medieval nature, mammals, trails, colour and light, wool story - from pre-school. Comparisons - furniture, shapes, textiles.
LOCATION: Signposted, 6 miles north west of Northampton off A5199.
OPEN: Mar-end Oct.
ADMISSION: Charge. **TEL:** 01604 770074.

HOLDENBY HOUSE FALCONRY CENTRE

FACILITIES: Courses for children during the holidays - need to be pre-booked. The Falconry Centre is open during term time when the House is available for school groups.
LOCATION: In the grounds of Holdenby House, signposted 6 miles north west of Northampton, off the A5199.
OPEN: Mar-end of Oct; other times by appointment from 1300-1700.
ADMISSION: Charge. **TEL:** 01604 770994.

INVADERS

FACILITIES: National Curriculum links for KS2 CSU1 - 'Invaders and Settlers' and KS2 CSU1 - 'The Roman Empire'. Workshops can include talk by Roman soldier, Roman trader, Viking warrior, Viking trader, trying on Roman costume, etc.

LOCATION: Manor House Museum, Kettering, Daventry Museum, Moot Hall.

OPEN: Ring.

ADMISSION: Charge. *TEL:* 01536 5343815 (Kettering) /01327 302463 (Daventry).

THE KNIGHTS OF THE ROSE

FACILITIES: Lectures and talks on the medieval way of life. Members dress in various costumes of the period, and there are vivid descriptions of life in medieval times.

LOCATION: Your school, club, etc.

OPEN: Ring to discuss details.

ADMISSION: Ring for information.   *TEL:* 01604 880668.

'LEARNING ABOUT THE ROCKINGHAM FOREST' PACK
See Rockingham Forest Trust.

LINDA CRUISES

FACILITIES: Can offer 10 different educational trips on the canal in narrowboats, lasting from 25 mins to 3 hours. These can be linked in with a visit to the Canal Museum at Stoke Bruerne.

LOCATION: Stoke Bruerne, reached off the A508 or A5.

OPEN: Ring for details - booking essential.

ADMISSION: Various charges depending on length of visit.

TEL: 01604 862107.

NORTHAMPTONSHIRE HERITAGE EDUCATION

FACILITIES: Provides schools and teachers with courses, etc, based on Historical/archaeological aspects of the County. On-site visits, together with work in schools.

LOCATION: Various parts of the County.

OPEN: Ring for times of courses, etc.

ADMISSION: Annual fee/charges.   *TEL:* 01604 237248.

NORTHFIELD FARM AND COUNTRY CENTRE

FACILITIES: Housed in a converted barn on a working farm. Arrangement for various groups to visit. Programme takes account of requests from teachers. There is a study centre, toilets, room for seating 50 people and small kitchen. Apart from school groups the Centre is available for pre-booking only.

122

LOCATION: Cransley - leave A14 at junction 7, and follow signs towards Thorpe Malsor. At the bottom of the hill, fork left towards Cransley. Northfield Farm is the first building on the left.
OPEN: Ring for details and to book.
ADMISSION: Charge made.   *TEL:* 01536 512305/510622.

OLD DAIRY FARM CENTRE

FACILITIES: A mixed arable and sheep farm, there is also a large turkey raising unit, as well as calves, pigs, poultry and other animals. The Farm welcomes school groups who can gain first hand experience. Situated in a delightful part of Northamptonshire, with open aspects in rolling countryside. There is also the added attraction of craft workshops, etc. Educational programme available, linked to the National Curriculum (where required). There are also lambing days. School parties are escorted around the farm and the trail. During the summer there are opportunities for pond dipping. Topics offered include Living and Growth, Materials, Machinery, Maps and Mapping. A booklet giving details of the farm and the above topics is available. There is free parking, a picnic area and eating room. Toilets, including one for disabled visitors. School visits book and worksheets available. Teachers are welcome to visit the farm to see and/or organise a visit.
LOCATION: In the village of Upper Stowe, off the A5 south of Weedon.
OPEN: Ring for details. Farm, is open from 0930-1530.
ADMISSION: £1 half day/£1.50 full day.   *TEL:* 01327 340525.

STEVE PARISH
See Past Lives Project

PAST LIVES PROJECT

FACILITIES: Trade and communications, food and farming, housing and architecture, making and doing for KS1, KS2 and KS3. Visits to schools include artifacts, costumes - and a lot of enthusiasm and knowledge.
LOCATION: At Holdenby House or at school.
Free information on living history.
OPEN: Ring - to suit individual groups.
ADMISSION: Charge.   *TEL:* 01604 584307.

SULGRAVE MANOR

FACILITIES: Provides a range of experiences, including those for various ages. Tudor period lifesyle is especially interesting, but courses can cater for anything up to the 18 century. The Manor is presented as a lived-in house, rather than a museum. Children's Guidebook and schools pack available, together with a wealth of resource material relating to the history of the house. Special events organised each year.

LOCATION: On an unclassified road, 7 miles north east of Banbury; 6 miles west of Brackley.

OPEN: Daily (not Weds) - 1 April-31 Oct 1030-1300 & 1400-1730 (Oct 1600). Weekends only Mar & Nov 1030-1300 & 1400-1800; Dec various times - ring for details. Open by appointment only in Feb, March, November and December.

ADMISSION: Charges made.   *TEL:* 01295 760205.

ROCKINGHAM CASTLE

FACILITIES: The building is on the site of a Saxon fortress and was built by William the Conqueror. It has been in the Watson family since the 16th century. There are interesting exhibits from the Civil War, as well as furniture and paintings. There is a large amount of educational material which covers art, literary studies and history, as well as a nature trail. Teachers contemplating taking a school group are encouraged to make a preliminary visit.

LOCATION: Off the A6116 between Corby and Oakham.

OPEN: 31 Mar-1Oct, daily by prior agreement; 1 April-30 Sept daily by prior arrangement, except Thurs.

ADMISSION: Charge. *TEL:* 01536 770240.

ROCKINGHAM FOREST TRUST

FACILITIES: Rockingham Forest covers a large part of north-east Northamptonshire, and it was the Norman Kings who designated the area a Royal Forest. They frequently visited the County on their hunting forays. Although much of the woodland has now gone, there are still some areas. Areas designated as forest included more than the tree, and in the countryside 'Forest Law' was upheld so that the area could be hunted at the king's pleasure. The Trust has produced a folder 'Learning about The Rockingham Forest', which includes details about the many places to visit, including some of the finest historic 'houses' - Kirby Hall, Rockingham Castle and Lyveden New Bield. The Pack contains introductory information, and suggests how the area can be used.

LOCATION: See pack for details of individual places.

OPEN: See pack.

ADMISSION: Various charges.   *TEL:* 01832 274278 (Coordinator).

WEST LODGE RURAL CENTRE

FACILITIES: A wide range of facilities for schools, including a working farm with trailer rides, crops of the UK, operations during the year, woods at different ages, flora and fauna, fungi forays, pond dipping, sculpture trail (in progress), monastic ruins, iron ore mining, etc. Orienteering and team leadership courses also available.

LOCATION: West Lodge, Pipewell Road, Desborough. Teachers' pack (priced) available.

OPEN: Throughout the year, but booking essential.

ADMISSION: Charge.   *TEL:* 01536 760552.

EQUESTRIAN CENTRES AND RIDING SCHOOLS

S ALLWORK

FACILITIES: Ring for details.
LOCATION: Home Farm, Delapre Park, Northampton.
OPEN: Ring.
ADMISSION: Charge.   *TEL:* 01604 764429.

ASHTON VALE STABLES

FACILITIES: Ring for information.
LOCATION: Bung Vale Farmhouse, Stoke Road, Ashton, Northampton.
OPEN: Ring.
ADMISSION: Charge.   *TEL:* 01604 864551.

BOUGHTON MILL RIDING SCHOOL

FACILITIES: Tuition, trekking, etc. - ring.
LOCATION: Boughton Mill, Welford Road, Chapel Brampton.
OPEN: Ring.
ADMISSION: Charge.   *TEL:* 01604 843319.

BRAMPTON STABLES

FACILITIES: Tuition for beginner to advanced rider.
LOCATION: Holdenby Road, Church Brampton.
OPEN: Ring.
ADMISSION: Charge.   *TEL:* 01604 842051.

CHURCH BRAMPTON EQUESTRIAN CENTRE

FACILITIES: Tuition for all ages - ring for further information.
LOCATION: Church Farm, Holdenby Road.
OPEN: Ring.
ADMISSION: Charge.   *TEL:* 01604 820622.

BUTTERFIELD LIVERIES AND RIDING SCHOOL

FACILITIES: A small friendly yard, with qualified BHS instructors for private and group tuition. All abilities catered for. All weather floodlit menage. Pony days, horse and rider away days, etc.
LOCATION: Butterfields Farm, Weedon Lane, Nether Heyford.
OPEN: Ring.
ADMISSION: Charges.　　*TEL:* 01327 340687.

CROMWELL EQUESTRIAN CENTRE

FACILITIES: Tuition all ages. Indoor school, liveries and hunter liveries.
LOCATION: Thurning is on an unclassified road south east of Oundle, off the A605 or A605 and B662.
OPEN: Ring.
ADMISSION: Charge.　　*TEL:* 01832 293436.

EAST LODGE FARM RIDING ESTABLISHMENT

FACILITIES: Tuiton for various ages and standards.
LOCATION: East Lodge Farm, Ecton, near Northampton.
OPEN: Ring.
ADMISSION: Charge made.　　*TEL:* 01604 810244.

EVERGREEN RIDING STABLES

FACILITIES: Jumping, countryside hacking, special occasions catered for, small classes or private tuition, all standards.
LOCATION: 18 High Street, Gayton, near Northampton.
OPEN: Tues-Sun 0900-1800.
ADMISSION: Charge.　　*TEL:* 01604 858247.

FOXHILL FARM EQUESTRIAN CENTRE

FACILITIES: Riding facilities.
LOCATION: On the Holcot to Sywell road.
OPEN: Tues-Thurs. Ring for further details.
ADMISSION: Ring for details of prices.　　*TEL:* 01604 781191.

GLEBE FARM EQUESTRIAN CENTRE

FACILITIES: Ring or details.
LOCATION: Glebe Farm, Bozeat.
OPEN: Ring.
ADMISSION: Charge.　　*TEL:* 01933 665083.

GREEN ACRES RIDING CENTRE

FACILITIES: Range of activities.

LOCATION: Green Farm, Puxley, on an unclassified road off the A5 south east of Towcester.
OPEN: Ring.
ADMISSION: Charge.   *TEL:* 01908 566092.

HARGRAVE RIDING CENTRE
FACILITIES: Ring for details.
LOCATION: Hargrave Lodge, Hargrave, Wellingborough.
OPEN: Ring.
ADMISSION: Charge.   *TEL:* 01933 622059.

HARRINGWORTH MANOR STABLES
FACILITIES: Riding for all ages and abilities, including safe off road hacking. Beginners and nervous rides welcome. Floodlit schooling area. Escorted rides through pleasant countryside.
LOCATION: Wakerley Road, Harringworth, near Corby.
OPEN: Ring.
ADMISSION: Fee.   *TEL:* 01572 747400.

HOLDENBY RIDING SCHOOL
FACILITIES: Indoor and outdoor schools. Beginners (adults and children) welcome. Training courses available.
LOCATION: Holdenby, Northampton - off A50/A428.
OPEN: Ring.
ADMISSION: Charge. *TEL:* 01604 770003.

HOME FARM
(Mr and Mrs T Spencer)
FACILITIES: Ring.
LOCATION: Off Tilbury Road, East Haddon.
OPEN: Ring.
ADMISSION: Charge. *TEL:* 01604 770208.

LADY MEADOW STABLES
FACILITIES: All weather arena for hire.
LOCATION: Newnham, near Daventry - details when booking.
OPEN: Mon-Fri 1200-1500; Tues/Fri 1700-1900; Sat/Sun 1300-1600 (Booking essential).
ADMISSION: Charge. *TEL:* 01327 311634/0421 632983.

R J LEE
FACILITIES: Ring for details.
LOCATION: New Tunnel Hill Farm, Stoke Road, Blisworth.
OPEN: Ring.

ADMISSION: Charge.   **TEL:** 01604 858041.

LITTLECOURT YARD AND EQUITATION CENTRE

FACILITIES: Livery, instruction, training and competition.
LOCATION: Littlecourt Yard, Farthingstone.
OPEN: Ring.
ADMISSION: Charge.   **TEL:** 01327 361211.

MANOR FARM RIDING SCHOOL

FACILITIES: Hacking, private and semi-private tuition, schooling, driving and jumping. All ages and abilities catered for. Tiny Tots classes are held for children under seven; 2-3 day courses held regularly.
LOCATION: Easton Maudit, Wellingborough.
OPEN: All year - ring for times.
ADMISSION: Fee.   **TEL:** 01933 663750.

MANOR YARD RIDING STABLES

FACILITIES: All weather equitation. Forest rides, cross-country course and indoor school for adults and children.
LOCATION: Manor Yard, Sudborough, off A6116, north west of Thrapston.
OPEN: Ring.
ADMISSION: Charge.   **TEL:** 01832 733208.

MOULTON COLLEGE EQUESTRIAN CENTRE

FACILITIES: Indoor and outdoor all weather facilities, cross country and show jumping; 35 horses. Training for professional qualifications and preparation for competitions. No casual riders.
LOCATION: Pitsford Rd, Moulton, Northampton.
OPEN: Varies - ring for details.
ADMISSION: Course fee/charges.   **TEL:** 01604 492653.

ORLINGBURY HOLD RIDING SCHOOL

FACILITIES: Beginners are welcome, wide range of activities, including indoor school for evening lessons.
LOCATION: Kettering Road, Hannington - A43 between Northampton and Kettering.
OPEN: Ring.
ADMISSION: Charge.   **TEL:** 01604 781283.

MRS R PIMLETT

FACILITIES: Ring for details.
LOCATION: Station road, Welton, on the edge of the village

OPEN: Ring.
ADMISSION: Charge. *TEL:* 01327 702191.

RIDING FOR THE DISABLED ASSOCIATION
FACILITIES: Provides riding and driving on a regular basis, based on medical consent.
LOCATION: Various sites in the County.
OPEN: Varies - ring.
ADMISSION: Ring. *TEL:* 01327 872146.

RYHILL CROSS COUNTRY TRAINING COURSE
FACILITIES: Over 30 jumps, including water, set in 60 acres of well drained grassland.
LOCATION: A5, halfway between the Long Buckby Wharf turn and the Watford turn.
OPEN: Ring for details.
ADMISSION: Ring. *TEL:* 01327 842250/0976 903548 (Doug Sheppard)

SHORTWOOD LODGE EQUESTRIAN CENTRE
FACILITIES: Ring for details.
LOCATION: Apethorpe Road, Nassington.
OPEN: Ring.
ADMISSION: Charge. *TEL:* 01780 470016.

SOUTH VIEW FARM EQUESTRIAN CENTRE
FACILITIES: Off road riding, with facilities for beginners and those wishing to improve. Private lessons available.
LOCATION: South View Farm, Irthlingborough Road, Wellingborough.
OPEN: Tues/Wed/Thurs 0900-dusk; Weekends 0900-1800.
ADMISSION: Charge. *TEL:* 01933 653110.

STOWE RIDING EQUESTRIAN CENTRE
FACILITIES: Tuition, livery 'breaking' schooling, events, shows, riders shop.
LOCATION: Stowe, near Buckingham.
OPEN: Ring. *TEL:* 01280 812363.

THREE SHIRES RIDING CENTRE
FACILITIES: Range of courses, tuition, off road racing, etc.
LOCATION: Elpeace, Airfield Road, Poddington, Wellingborough.
OPEN: Ring.
ADMISSION: Fee. *TEL:* 01234 782808.

TOP FARM RIDING SCHOOL
FACILITIES: Ring for details.
LOCATION: Top Farm, Great Doddington, near Wellingborough.
OPEN: Ring.
ADMISSION: Charge. *TEL:* 01933 227263.

UPLANDS EQUESTRIAN CENTRE
FACILITIES: Purpose built centre - variety of courses, etc.
LOCATION: Uplands Farm, off A6/A43 in Loddington village.
OPEN: All year.
ADMISSION: Charge. *TEL:* 01536 713210/710935.

WOODLANDS EQUESTRIAN CENTRE
FACILITIES: Riding and exam tuition for adults and children; stable management, livery and tack shop. Horse and pony sales. Horse feeds shop. Conference room for lectures.
LOCATION: Warren Lodge Farm, Dingley.
OPEN: Ring.
ADMISSION: Charge. *TEL:* 01858 535398.

WOODFORD RIDING SCHOOL
FACILITIES: Range of instruction offered.
LOCATION: The Manor House Farm, Addington Road, Woodford.
OPEN: Ring.
ADMISSION: Charge.   *TEL:* 01832 735500.

FACTORY SHOPS

BARKERS SHOES
FACILITIES: Makes high quality ladies and men's shoes - wide narrow and extreme sizes. Sells discontinued and imperfect lines.
LOCATION: Station Road, Earls Barton.
OPEN: Mon-Sat 1000-1700; Sun 1000-1600.
ADMISSION: No charge.   *TEL:* 01604 810387.

BARRATTS
FACILITIES: A wide range of footwear, including discontinued lines, rejects, sale stock and new lines, covering children's to adults, and from trainers to slippers, as well as boots, summer and winter wear.
LOCATION: Kingsthorpe Road, Northampton.

OPEN: Mon-Sat 0900-1730.
ADMISSION: No charge. *TEL:* 01604 718632.

CROCKET AND JONES

FACILITIES: High quality welted men's shoes and also walking shoes for ladies.
LOCATION: Perry Street, Northampton.
OPEN: Fri 1500-1800; Sat 0930-1400.
ADMISSION: No charge. *TEL:* 01604 31515.

DB SHOES

FACILITIES: Many types and styles of shoe including large sizes for men, the DB range and golf shoes.
LOCATION: Bunting Road, Kingsthorpe Hollow, Northampton.
OPEN: Mon 1000-1400; Fri 1000-1630; Sat 1000-1600.
ADMISSION: No charge. *TEL:* 01604 791088.

EDWARD GREEN AND CO LTD

FACILITIES: Men's welted shoes, riding boots and cavalry boots.
LOCATION: Oliver Street, Northampton.
OPEN: Mon-Fri 0900-1230.
ADMISSION: No charge. *TEL:* 01604 713199.

THE FABRIC WAREHOUSE

FACILITIES: Always has more than a quarter of a million metres of top quality curtain and upholsery fabrics in stock. Also nets, tracks, poles, cushions, tapes, floor cushions, etc.
LOCATION: Unit 2, Harvey Reeves Road, St James Mill Road Industrial Estate, Northampton.
OPEN: Seven days a week, including 1000-1600 on Suns.
ADMISSION: Free. *TEL:* 01604 759312.

T GROCOCK AND CO ROTHWELL LTD

FACILITIES: Sells mens and ladies direct moulded shoes. Extra wide fittings available.
LOCATION: Gordon Sreet, Rothwell.
OPEN: Mon-Fri 1000-1700; Sat 0900-1300.
ADMISSION: Free. *TEL:* 01536 418416.

HOLDENBY DESIGNS

FACILITIES: A range of hand-painted ceramics. Sale items including seconds.
LOCATION: Holdenby Designs, Holcot Road, Brixworth, off the A508.
OPEN: Ring.

ADMISSION: No charge. *TEL:* 01604 405285.

LEVIS - BIG L FACTORY OUTLETS

FACILITIES: Sells a range of Levi leisurewear, including jeans and sweatshirts. Generally items are not first quality, and have the 'Levi' tag removed, but are up to one-third cheaper than perfect price.
LOCATION: Commercial Street, Northampton, reached off the St Peter's Way roundabout - and then left. Car parking close by.
OPEN: Mon/Wed 1000-1730; Tues/Thurs/Fri 0930-1730; Sat/Bank Hols 0900-1800.
ADMISSION: No charge. *TEL:* 01604 603022.

NIMBUS

FACILITIES: This a commercial operation for blind and partially sighted people. Produces a range of toileteries, including soap, toothpaste, etc.
LOCATION: Lower Farm Road, Moulton Park, Northampton.
OPEN: Mon-Thurs 0800-1630; Fri 0800-1415.
ADMISSION: No charge. *TEL:* 01604 646411.

THE OAK FACTORY

FACILITIES: The only stockist and manufacturer of oak furniture in the County. Traditional furniture, including corner cabinets, dressers, wall units, bookcases, etc. Also stocks a range of occasional furniture, footstools, magazine racks, etc.
LOCATION: Spencer Parade. Stanwick, near Potters the Butcher, and just off the A45 to the north east of Higham Ferrers.
OPEN: Mon-Sat 1000-1600; Sun 1200-1600.
ADMISSION: Free. *TEL:* 01933 623866.

PIGGLY WRIGGLY

FACILITIES: Walking footwear and Dr Martens.
LOCATION: 178 Kettering Road, Northampton.
OPEN: Mon/Tues 1000-1700; Wed/Thurs 0930-1330 & 1400-1730; Fri/Sat 0900-1730.
ADMSSION: No charge. *TEL:* 01604 32798.

TECHNIC SHOE CO LTD

FACILITIES: Classical English shoes.
LOCATION: Bedford Road, Rothwell.
OPEN: Mon-Fri 1100-1600; Sat 0930-1230.
ADMISSION: No charge. *TEL:* 01933 53073.

TYRELLS FOOTWEAR LTD

FACILITIES: Ladies, mens and children's sports shoes.

LOCATION: Albert Road, Rushden.
OPEN: Mon/Wed 1000-1200; Tues/Fri 1000-1730; Sat 1000-1600.
ADMISSION: No charge.   *TEL:* 01933 319274.

WHITE AND CO (EARLS BARTON) LTD
FACILITIES: Mainly boots, including the world famous Dr Martens.
LOCATION: New Street, Daventry.
OPEN: Tues/Fri/Sat 1000-1600.
ADMISSION: Free.   *TEL:* 01327 702291.

FARM SHOPS AND PICK YOUR OWN

ARK FARM SHEEP DAIRY
FACILITIES: Shop with sheep's milk ice cream, yoghurt and other produce.
LOCATION: Ark Farm, High Street South, Tiffield, near Towcester. Tiffield signposted off the A5 South of Weedon or North of Towcester.
OPEN: All year (not 25 Dec) - 1430-1700.
ADMISSION: Free.   *TEL:* 01327 350202.

BERRYDALE GOATS
FACILITIES: Pasturised goats milk and fresh eggs.
LOCATION: Clint Hill Farm, Hanging Houghton.
OPEN: Ring.
ADMISSION: N/A.   *TEL:* 01604 880366.

IAN BRODIE
FACILITIES: Sells a selection of fresh farm turkeys, including portions, boned and rolled, and oven ready, together with turkey burgers, turkey sausages, breast rolls, cockerels, pheasants and geese.
LOCATION: Upper Stowe, reached off the A5, south of Weedon take the signs for Old Dairy Farm Centre.
OPEN: Ring for details.
ADMISSION: Free.   *TEL:* 01327 340545/341425.

CASTLE ASHBY FINE FOODS
FACILITIES: Farm shop and delicatessan. There is also a craft centre (see under Craft Workshops/Centres). Tea and coffee available.
LOCATION: Castle Ashby Craft Centre, The Old Farm Yard, Castle Ashby off A428.
OPEN: Tues-Sat 0930-1730; Sun 1100-1700.
ADMISSION: Free.   *TEL:* 01604 696742.

CHAWTON FORGE HERBS AND FRAGRANCES

FACILITIES: Herbs and fragrances.
LOCATION: High Street, Scaldwell.
OPEN: Ring.
ADMISSION: No charge.   *TEL:* 01604 880135.

CHURCH FARM SHOP

FACILITIES: Organic meats, organic vegetables and farm house cooking.
LOCATION: Church Street, Strixton, on the A509 between Bozeat and Wollaston.
OPEN: Tues-Fri 0900-1730.
ADMISSION: No charge.   *TEL:* 01933 664378.

COURT FARM SHOP

FACILITIES: Wide range of produce. Pick your own in season.
LOCATION: Court Farm, Overstone - entrance opposite Post Office.
OPEN: Wed-Sun 1000-1700.
ADMISSION: No charge.   *TEL:* 01604 491447/643610.

DAILY BREAD WHOLE FOODS

FACILITIES: Has a wide range of organic products, spices, herbs, grains, dried fruits, nuts, seeds, etc.
LOCATION: The Old Laundry, Bedford Road, Northampton.
OPEN: Mon-Fri 0830-1730; Sat 0830-1600.
ADMISSION: Free.   *TEL:* 01604 621531.

DOVECOTE FARM SHOP AND PICK YOUR OWN

FACILITIES: Has a range of soft fruits in season, including raspberries, strawberries, blackberries, blackcurrants, gooseberries, together with other farm produce. Teas, DIY barbecue and children's play area.
LOCATION: At Newton, off the A43 west of Kettering or A6003.
OPEN: Ring for details.
ADMISSION: Free.   *TEL:* 01536 742343.

CLARKES PICK YOUR OWN

FACILITIES: Blackcurrants, strawberries, raspberries, gooseberries - in season.
LOCATION: Turn off A43 at Redhouse Pub for Hannington.
OPEN: Daily 1000-late.
ADMISSION: Charge for fruit.   *TEL:* 01604 781256.

134

ESSENTIAL ENGLISH
FACILITIES: Delicatessen selling a wide range of cheese.
LOCATION: 10b West Street, Oundle.
OPEN: Ring.
ADMISSION: N/A. **TEL:** 01832 274396.

GRASSLANDS
FACILITIES: Freedom food. Organic produce - beef, pork, lamb, chicken, bacon, gammon pieces, eggs, 14 flavours of sausage, 3 flavours of beefburgers, range of pies, 18 varieties of nut roast and other vegetarian foods. All items are home-made.
LOCATION: Scotch Lodge Farm, Mears Ashby Road, Earls Barton.
OPEN: Tues/Wed 1400-1700; Thurs/Fri 0900-1200 & 1400-1700; Sat/Sun 0900-1200.
ADMISSION: No charge. **TEL:** 01604 810910.

GRASSLANDS FARM SHOP
FACILITIES: Farm produce, Christmas trees, mistletoe, decorations in season. Dried flowers, crafts etc.
LOCATION: Kelmarsh Road, Clipston.
OPEN: Most weekends, many weekdays.
ADMISSION: No charge. **TEL:** 01858 525385.

HILL FARM HERBS
FACILITIES: Situated in a pleasant area behind a traditional farmhouse, the plants being displayed in the old farmyard, and with a delightful garden. A large stone barn houses the shops. Herb plants, barn shop with a wide selection of gifts, dried flowers and herbs, pot pourri, essential oils, pots, baskets, and traditional preserves and kitchenware. Visitors are welcome to browse in the attractive garden and enjoy some time in the tea shop in summer.
LOCATION: Park Walk, Brigstock.
OPEN: Daily 1030-1730 (Mar-Oct); 1030-1630 (Nov-Feb).
ADMISSION: No charge. **TEL:** 01536 373694.

HOME FARM
FACILITIES: Strawberries, raspberries, gooseberries, tayberries and new potatoes - in season.
LOCATION: Great Harrowden - follow signs on A509 and A510.
OPEN: Daily 1000-2000.
ADMISSION: Free. **TEL:** 01933 678255.

HOMELEIGH FARM NURSERIES

FACILITIES: Bedding plants, shrubs, vegetables, trees, hay and straw, and animal food.
LOCATION: A45 near Dodford/Everdon turn between Daventry and Weedon.
OPEN: 1000-1700 daily.
ADMISSION: No charge.   *TEL:* 01327 341846.

ISHAM FARM SHOP AND PICK YOUR OWN CENTRE

FACILITIES: An established 'Pick your own' centre on the edge of a delightful village. Asparagus available from mid-April, followed by soft fruit. Home grown vegetables, free range eggs, cut flowers, etc. Teas and barbecues at weekends (weather permitting). Children's' play area and animal corner.
LOCATION: Isham Farm, Church Street, Isham, off the A509 on edge of village.
OPEN: 1 Apr-31 Oct - Tues-Fri 100-1800; Sat/Sun 1000-1900.
TEL: 01536 722756.

MAIDFORD LODGE FARM

FACILITIES: Produces finest quality additive free meat and poultry. Gloucester Old Spot pork, Aberdeen Angus beef and Jacob lamb. All livestock is reared indoors and fed on natural food with no growth promotors or chemicals. Free range hens.
LOCATION: On the Litchborough to Maidford road.
OPEN: Wed 1000-1600; Thurs 0900-1700; Fri 0900-1800; Sat 0900-1300.
ADMISSION: No charge.   *TEL:* 01327 860303 (day), 860827 (even).

MORETON MUSHROOMS

FACILITIES: Mushrooms and spent compost.
LOCATION: Home Farm, The Green, in the centre of the village, opposite the pub.
OPEN: Mon-Fri 0730-1900; Sat/Sun mornings (am).
ADMISSION: No charge.   *TEL:* 01295 760382.

MOULTON COLLEGE FARM SHOP

FACILITIES: Sells their own produced beef, pork and lamb joints hand-made deserts and Moulton Dairy ice cream.
LOCATION: Home Farm, Pitsford Road, Moulton, Northampton.
OPEN: Wed-Fri 1000-1800; Sat 1000-1700; Sun 100-1700.
ADMISSION: No charge.   *TEL:* 01604 494204.

NORTHAMPTONSHIRE COUNTRYSIDE CENTRE

FACILITIES: Run for people with learning difficulties, the Centre sells a range of produce, including a variety of seasonal vegetables and fruit. Bedding plants usually available, together with honey and home-made jams.
LOCATION: Kent Road, off the Weedon road, between Princess Marina Hospital and the former St Crispins Hospital buildings.
OPEN: 0900-1530. When shop shut people on site until 1700.
ADMISSION: No charge.   *TEL:* 01604 582414.

THE OLD DAIRY FARM CENTRE PRODUCE SHOP

FACILITIES: A variety of mouth-watering produce, including free range eggs, old fashioned preserves and chutneys, farm fresh cooked meats, cheese and country wines.
LOCATION: Signposted off the A5 south of Weedon.
OPEN: 9 Jan-28 Feb 1000-1630; 1 Mar-24 Dec 1000-1730. (Evenings by arrangement).
ADMISSION: No charge.   *TEL:* 01327 340525.

PITWELL FARM LIMITED

FACILITIES: Pick your own in season, including Bramleys, Worcesters, as well as ready picked.
LOCATION: Byfield/Priors Marston Road, Byfield, south of Daventry off A361.
OPEN: Ring for details.
ADMISSION: Free.   *TEL:* 01327 260252.

DEREK SMITH'S FARM SHOP

FACILITIES: A wide range of fruit and vegetables, home made cakes, jams, free range eggs, ice cream, drinks.
LOCATION: West View Farm, Brampton Lane, Chapel Brampton, 220 metres from Brampton Valley Way car park.
OPEN: Mon-Sat 0900-1600; Sun 0900-1700.
ADMISSION: N/A.   *TEL:* 01604 843206.

THE TITHE BARN

FACILITIES: Farm shop with organically grown produce. Also sells antiques and crafts. Pets Corner and Play area.
LOCATION: Thurning, off the A605 near Barnwell and South of Oundle.
OPEN: Ring for details.
ADMISSION: Free.   *TEL:* 01832 293511.

SUNNY MEADOW FARM SHOP

FACILITIES: A wide range of products including turkeys, cockerels, homemade pies, cakes and Wilja potatoes. Free range eggs and home produced fowl. Morning coffee and afternoon teas also available.
LOCATION: Sunny Meadow, Buckby Wharf 0.5 miles from the A5 Long Buckby/Daventry crossroads.
OPEN: Wed/Sat 9-1700; Sun 9-1330.
ADMISSION: Free.   *TEL:* 01327 842574.

SUNNY VALE FARM NURSERY

FACILITIES: Pick your own soft fruit and vegetables in season.
LOCATION: Off Lamport Road, Harrington.
OPEN: Ring for details.
ADMISSION: Charges for produce.   *TEL:* 01604 686608.

WAKEFIELD FARM SHOP AND PICK YOUR OWN CENTRE

FACILITIES: The Farm Shop specialises in naturally home grown game and meat. A wide range of delicatessan food with a cheese counter. Home-cooked hams and cakes available. Pick your own fruit and vegetables in season. Tea room serves breakfasts, lunches and teas.
LOCATION: Assarts Farm, Potterspury, reached off the A5, south east of Towcester.
OPEN: Tues-Fri 0900-1730; Sat 09000-1700; Sun 1000-1230.
ADMISSION: No charge.   *TEL:* 01327 811493.

K G YORK

FACILITIES: Soft fruits in season, including rasberries, strawberries, blackberries, tayberries, gooseberries and white, red and black currents.
LOCATION: Roe Farm, Whiston Road, Cogenhoe.
OPEN: Seasonal - ring.
ADMISSION: No charge.
TEL: 01604 890516.

FARMS

ADSTONE HOUSE

FACILITIES: Countryside Stewardship area. A farm where chemicals have not been used. Interesting habitat for a variety of plants and animals. School groups can visit by prior arrangement. booklet (priced) containing background information and ideas for work/follow up activities from Everdon Field Studies Centre (01327 361384).
LOCATION: On the edge of Adstone on the former B4525.
OPEN: Ring to arrange appointment.
ADMISSION: No charge.   *TEL:* 01327 860302.

ARK FARM SHEEP DAIRY

FACILITIES: A traditional farm with sheep, cattle and free-range hens. Sheep are also milked, although this is limited between October and November. Farm shop - see under Farm Shops.
LOCATION: Ark Farm, High Street South, Tiffield, near Towcester. The village is signposted off the A5 south of Weedon.
OPEN: All year (not Christmas Day) from 1430-1700.
ADMISSION: Free.   *TEL:* 01327 350202.

COUNTRYSIDE STEWARDSHIP SCHEME

FACILITIES: Under the Scheme farmers are given grants with the proviso that they open their farms a number of times a year to school groups.
LOCATION: Various around the county.
OPEN: Ring.
ADMISSION: No charge - although there may be for materials.
TEL: 01604 491131 (Farming and Wildlife Group (FWAG) Adviser for more information/details of farms).

GRASSHOPPERS

FACILITIES: Set in 40 acres of open countryside, the Children's Farm has many baby animals to cuddle and feed. Chicks and ducklings can be seen hatching. There are friendly pigs, red deer, pygmy goats and rare breeds. School visits arranged. Other groups catered for.
LOCATION: Horwell Farm, Baynards Green, near Bicester.
OPEN: 1 April-end Oct - Tues-Suns 1000-1700.
ADMISSION: Charge.   *TEL:* 01869 346554.

THE LIVING LANDSCAPE TRUST

FACILITIES: Based at the Duke of Buccleuch's Boughton Estate it has a wide range of activities. Apart from an extensive open days during the summer, the Director of the Living Landscape Trust can arrange a variety of visits and courses, with opportunities to see a commercial farm covering 350 acres. There are dairy cattle, sheep, arable crops, etc - as well as a dairy. Worksheets, ideas for activities, etc. available from the Director.

LOCATION: Estate is off the A43 at Boughton, to the north of Kettering.

OPEN: Arrangements made for individual groups.

ADMISSION: Charge made.   **TEL:** 01536 515731 (The Director)

MANVELL FARM PARK

FACILITIES: Designed for children, activities can be arranged for school groups to see and touch a wide variety of animals.

LOCATION: White Lodge Farm, Northampton Road, Walgrave.

OPEN: Ring for details.

ADMISSION: Various.   **TEL:** 01604 781969.

MOULTON COLLEGE

FACILITIES: An education officer can arrange a series of activities for school groups at the farm. There are also open days during lambing, which are advertised widely in the press and on local radio.

LOCATION: Moulton College is in the village of Moulton, just to the north of Northampton and off the A43.

OPEN: Ring for details - courses arranged to suit.

TEL: 01604 491131 (Schools Liaison Officer).

NFU

FACILITIES: Scheme for arranging visits to farms for school groups.

LOCATION: On various farms around the County.

OPEN: Varies.

ADMISSION: Varies.   **TEL:** 01604 634277.

OLD DAIRY FARM CENTRE

FACILITIES: Has a range of farm animals, including some 'rare' breeds. Apart from the general public, groups can also be catered for. School groups are welcome. Arrangements can be made to provide 'lessons' based on NC attainment targets. There is the possibility of seeing crafts, and demonstrations at certain times of the year. There is a 'pocket money' shop, as well as catering facilities, craft and gift shops. See also Educational Visits.

140

LOCATION: Upper Stowe, signposted off the A5 south of Weedon crossroads.
OPEN: Ring for details, special arrangements can be made for groups.
ADMISSION: No charge for individuals to look around animal enclosures, but charges for groups, etc. vary depending on requirements.
TEL: 01327 340525.

ROOKERY OPEN FARM

FACILITIES: Working farm with different demonstrations. Cows, baby calves, pet lambs, sheep, ducks, rabbits, ponies, tractor and trailer rides.
LOCATION: Rookery Lane, 300m from Stoke Bruerne Lock.
OPEN: 1st March-Mid Nov - Tues-Sun 1100-1730 - ring to confirm.
ADMISSION: Charge.   *TEL:* 01604 864477.

WEST LODGE RURAL CENTRE

FACILITIES: The Centre is in a totally modernised barn, which still retains its rustic charm. It is ideal for lectures, meetings, demonstrations and exhibitions. The Centre gives the visitor the opportunity to visit a working farm and discover the many aspects of the rural environment. The Centre is also available for school groups - see under Educational Visits.
LOCATION: West Lodge, Pipewell Road, Desborough.
OPEN: Sun - March to Nov and Bank Hols from May.
ADMISSION: Charge made. *TEL:* 01536 760552.

FISHING

BARNWELL COUNTRY PARK

FACILITIES: Day tickets, including facilities for the disabled. Free parking. Other facilities - see Country Parks.
LOCATION: Off A605, half a mile south of Oundle.
OPEN: Ring for details - Park open all year.
ADMISSION: Ring for details.   *TEL:* 01832 273435.

BILLING AQUADROME

FACILITIES: Coarse fishing.
LOCATION: Signposted off the A45.
OPEN: Ring for details.
ADMISSION: Charge.   *TEL:* 01604 408181.

BROOK MEADOW

FACILITIES: Five acre lake stocked with carp up to 18lbs and tench to 4lb.

LOCATION: The Wrongs, Sibbertoft on an unclassified road between the A508 and A5199/A427.

OPEN: Ring for details - fishing for those staying at Brook Meadow Lakeside Holidays or in the Farmhouse, but day tickets available.

ADMISSION: Charge.　　*TEL:* 01858 880886.

CASTLE ASHBY FISHERIES

FACILITIES: Coarse fishing.

LOCATION: Grendon Road.

OPEN: Ring.　　*ADMISSION:* Charge.　　*TEL:* 01604 696024.

DAVENTRY COUNTRY PARK

FACILITIES: Day tickets. Facilities for the disabled. Free parking. Other facilities - see Country Parks.

LOCATION: On B4036 about a mile from Daventry Town Centre.

OPEN: Ring for details - Park open all year.

ADMISSION: Charge.　　*TEL:* 01327 77193.

DELAPRE PARK LAKE

FACILITIES: Coarse fishing.

LOCATION: Ring.

OPEN: Ring for details.

ADMISSION: Ring.　　*TEL:* 01604 764847/636723.

EARLS BARTON ANGLING CLUB

FACILITIES: Has weekly meetings.

LOCATION: Silver Band Club (HQ).

OPEN: Second Tues of each month.

ADMISSION: Membership fee.　　*TEL:* 01604 812433.

ELINOR TROUT FISHERY

FACILITIES: Covers a 50 acre site, and is considered a 'bank anglers paradise', with fly fishing for browns, rainbows, some salmon and golden rainbows. Boats for hire. The fishery is re-stocked weekly.

LOCATION: Turn right in Aldwinkle. Immediately after the church turn left into Lowick Road.

OPEN: End Feb-end Dec from 0700 until one hour after sunset.

ADMISSION: Day, junior and evening tickets available.

TEL: 01832 720786 (Fishing Lodge) or 735071.

EYEBROOK RESERVOIR

FACILITIES: This is a natural water with rainbows and wild brownies.
LOCATION: Off the A6003 Corby to Uppingham road.
OPEN: 1 April - 31 October.
ADMISSION: Various charges - ring for details. *TEL:* 01536 770264.

FINESHADES ABBEY

FACILITIES: A mixed coarse fishery, mainly with carp.
LOCATION: Off the A43, half way between Corby and Stamford.
OPEN: Ring for details.
ADMISSION: Tickets £5 for two rods on the bank. *TEL:* 01780 83284.

FOXHOLES FISHERIES

FACILITIES: Has several lakes, with various arrangements for fishing.
Day ticket for carp and coarse fishing, season ticket for carp and coarse
fishing, match fishing and carp sales. Day ticket permits fishing on Day
Ticket Pool; Season Ticket permits fishing on four lakes.
LOCATION: Off A428 Northampton to Rugby road. If travelling in the
Crick direction turn right approximately one mile before the village, at
Mal Pratt Motors (Foxholes Garage), and the Fisheries are about 400
metres from the road down a track on the left.
OPEN: Dawn to dusk 1 May to 31 Dec. Closed Tues.
ADMISSION: Charge. *TEL:* 01788 823967.

GLEBE LAKES

FACILITIES: Coarse fishing.
LOCATION: Near Ecton.
OPEN: Ring for details.
ADMISSION: Charge. *TEL:* 01604 712591.

GRENDON LAKES FISHERY

FACILITIES: Four fully stocked lakes, with carp, bream, tench, perch,
roach, pike. Membership/day tickets, arrangements for match bookings.
LOCATION: Main Road, Grendon.
OPEN: Ring for information.
ADMISSION: Ring for details. *TEL:* 01933 665303/665335.

HEYFORD FISHERY

FACILITIES: Coarse fishing.
LOCATION: Off the A5 at the Narrow Boat, about 1mile south of
Weedon. The fishery is about 1.5 miles from the turn, just before the
village of Nether Heyford.
OPEN: Ring.
ADMISSION: Charge. *TEL:* 01604 714899.

HOLLOWELL RESERVOIR

FACILITIES: Has a reputation for big pike and tench.
LOCATION: Off the A5199 to the north west of Northampton.
OPEN: June 16-March 14.
ADMISSION: Charge. *TEL:* 01604 781350.

KINGFISHER LAKES

FACILITIES: Trout fishing. Restaurant and bar open to the public.
LOCATION: Buckingham Road, Deanshanger.
OPEN: 0900-dusk.
ADMISSION: Charge. *TEL:* 01908 562332.

OVERSTONE PARK COUNTRY CLUB

FACILITIES: Fishing for members/non-members.
LOCATION: Ecton Lane, Sywell.
OPEN: Ring.
ADMISSION: Charge. *TEL:* 01604 647709.

PERLO MILL TROUT FISHERY AND CLAY PIGEON SHOOTING

FACILITIES: Trout fishing.
LOCATION: Fotheringhay.
OPEN: Ring for details.
ADMISSION: Charge. *TEL:* 01832 226241.

PITSFORD RESERVOIR

FACILITIES: A natural water owned by Anglian Water. A large part of the area is also a nature reserve managed by the Wildlife Trust (see separate entry under Nature Reserves). Brown trout and rainbows. Boats are available, including some electric ones.
LOCATION: Pitsford Reservoir is off the A508 Northampton to Market Harborough road, and reached at the end of the bypass, signposted Holcot. The Fishing Lodge is just over the causeway on the left.
OPEN: Mar-Dec.
ADMISSION: Ring for prices. *TEL:* 01604 781350.

RAVENSTHORPE TROUT FISHERY

FACILITIES: Owned by Anglian Water, fishing for brown trout and rainbows. Rowing boats for hire.
LOCATION: Fishing Lodge, Teeton Road, off the A428 Northampton to Rugby road. Follow signs for Ravensthorpe. In village follow sign to Teeton. The Reservoir is on the left outside Ravensthorpe village, and the fishing lodge is at the western side of the dam.

OPEN: Mar-Dec.
ADMISSION: Ring for details.   *TEL:* 01604 781350.

RINGSTEAD GRANGE TROUT AND SALMON FISHERY

FACILITIES: Salmon and rainbow. Boats available. Fly fishing tuition by arrangement.
LOCATION: At Ringstead Grange, off the A605 between Ringstead and Great Addington.
OPEN: 0700 - one hour after sunset from 27 Feb-29 Oct.
ADMISSION: Ring for prices.   *TEL:* 01933 622960.

SOUTH VIEW FISHERY

FACILITIES: Coarse fishing.
LOCATION: Near Wellingborough.
OPEN: Ring for details.
ADMISSION: Charge.   *TEL:* 01933 650457.

SYWELL COUNTRY PARK

FACILITIES: Fishing available. Free car parking. See Country Parks.
LOCATION: Off A4500 Northampton-Wellingborough road at Earls Barton crossroads, and then signposted.
OPEN: Closed 15 Mar-15 June (inclusive). Main car park 0830-1600 (summer); 0830-1700 (winter). 'Out of hours' car park always open.
ADMISSION: Charge.   *TEL:* 01604 810970.

WADENHOE TROUT FISHERY

FACILITIES: Trout fishing.
LOCATION: Wadenhoe.
OPEN: Ring for times.
ADMISSION: Charge made.   *TEL:* 01832 272006/275222.

WILLOWBROOK

FACILITIES: Trout fishing.
LOCATION: Woodnewton near Oundle.
OPEN: Call at Manor House for permit.
ADMISSION: Charge. Permit needed.   *TEL:* N/A.

YARWELL MILL

FACILITIES: Coarse fishing in the River Nene and adjacent lake in season. All anglers need a rod licence.
LOCATION: Yarwell Mill Caravan Park, Yarwell near Oundle.
OPEN: Ring for times.
ADMISSION: Charge.   *TEL:* 01832 273701.

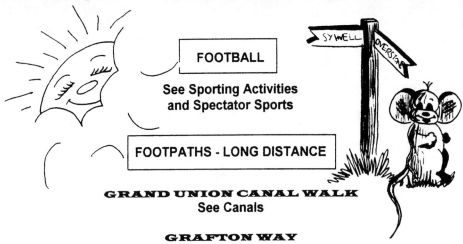

FOOTBALL

See Sporting Activities
and Spectator Sports

FOOTPATHS - LONG DISTANCE

GRAND UNION CANAL WALK
See Canals

GRAFTON WAY

FACILITIES: Links with the Knightley Way at Greens Norton, and carries on to Cosgrove, and then joins the North Buckinghamshire Way at Wolverton. The walk is named after the Dukes of Grafton who were large landowners in southern Northamptonshire during the 18th and 19th centuries. There is a leaflet describing the walk and places of interest.
LOCATION: See leaflet.
OPEN: Can be walked at all times.
ADMISSION: Free (charge leaflet).
TEL: 01604 237220 (Countryside Centre).

JURASSIC WAY

FACILITIES: Starts at Warkworth in the south west of the county and covers 83 miles before reaching Easton-on-the-Hill in the north. The Way links Banbury (Oxon) and Stamford (Lincs) and passes along the county's western and southern borders. Named the Jurassic Way it follows the upland spine of Jurassic limestone. It is thought to have been an earlier historic trade route linking the Humber and Severn estuaries.
FACILITIES: Pack produced which gives detailed information.
LOCATION: See publication.
OPEN: Can be walked at all times.
ADMISSION: Charge for pack.
TEL: 01604 237220 (Countryside Centre).

KNIGHTLEY WAY

FACILITIES: The footpath starts at Badby in the west of the County, and travels across undulating and unspoilt Northamptonshire countryside to Green Norton - distance of some 12 miles. Here it links

146

with the Grafton Way. The route takes in the historic Fawsley Park, and the delightful villages of Preston Capes, Farthingstone, Litchborough, etc. It is named because it travels over land which was formerly owned by the Knightley family.

FACILITIES: Walks leaflet with detailed map and more information is available.

LOCATION: Details in leaflet.

OPEN: Can be walked at any time.

ADMISSION: Charge for leaflet.

TEL: 01604 237223 (Recreational Routes Officer)/01604 237220 (Countryside Centre).

THE MACMILLAN WAY

FACILITIES: A 230 mile long distance footpath established to raise awareness of the Cancer Relief Macmillan Fund, and to assist with raising further help for the national charity. The Walk is only waymarked from North to South, and the special waymarker discs show the fund logo. A book is available.

LOCATION: The Walk starts at Oakham, and continues to Abbotsbury (Dorset coast). It enters the county near Weston by Welland, and passes south through Braybrooke, Maidwell, Creaton, Holdenby, the Bringtons, Flore, Farthingstone, Canons Ashby and Eydon (also many intermediate villages), and leaves Northamptonshire near Chipping Warden.

OPEN: Can be walked at any time.

ADMISSION: Charge for book.

TEL: Further information from Northamptonshire Countryside Centre - 01604 237220.

MIDSHIRES WAY

FACILITIES: A long distance footpath, the Midshires Way starts in Buckinghamshire and goes through Northamptonshire from Salcey Forest to the Welland Valley, a total distance of 46 miles. It passes through or close to a series of delightful villages, including Piddington, Bugbrooke, Upper Heyford, Upper Harlestone, the Bramptons, Brixworth, Arthingworth, Braybrooke and Sutton Bassett. It also has junctions with three other County long distance footpaths - the Nene Way (at Nether Heyford), the Jurassic Way (between Great Oxenden and Hermitage Wood) and the Grand Union Canal Walk (between Blisworth and Nether Heyford).

FACILITIES: It is suitable for walkers, horse-riders and off-road cyclists. A leaflet is available with details of the walk.

LOCATION: The Northamptonshire section starts at Salcey Forest on the Bucks border and ends on the Leicestershire border near Sutton Bassett.

OPEN: Can be used at all times.

ADMISSION: Charge for leaflet.   *TEL:* 01604 237220 (Countryside Centre).

NENE WAY

FACILITIES: A long distance footpath covering some 70 miles and like the Knightley Way it also starts in Badby and progresses through village and town, and open countryside to Wansford in Cambridgeshire. It has been established along present rights of way for most of its length - and along some 'permitted paths. It crosses the length and breadth of the Nene Valley.

LOCATION: See packs for details. Two packs available.

OPEN: Can be walked at all times.

ADMISSION: There is a cost for the packs.

TEL: 01604 237223 (Recreational Routes Officer) or 01604 237220 (Countryside Centre).

GARDEN CENTRES AND NURSERIES

BARN FARM PLANTS

FACILITIES: Bulbs, pansies, polyanthus, ornamental kale, winter/summer hanging baskets, conifers, heathers, garden sundries.

LOCATION: Upper Wardington on A361.

OPEN: Daily 0900-1800.

ADMISSION: No charge.   *TEL:* 01295 758080 (daytime).

BARBY NURSERIES

FACILITIES: Supplies plants to the general public as well as to wholesalers. Always good displays, including bedding plants, shrubs, hanging baskets and gifts.

LOCATION: Near the water tower on a unclassified road on the A361 side of Barby, and about 1.5 miles off the A361.

OPEN: Ring.

ADMISSION: Free.   *TEL:* 01788 890314.

JOHN BECKWITH - See CLOVER CRAFTS

148

THE BELL PLANTATION

FACILITIES: Tree and shrub nursery. Conifers, specimen trees, fruit trees, shrubs, roses, climbers, herbaceous, bulbs, bedding plants.
LOCATION: On A5, north of the Towcester roundabout.
OPEN: Ring.
ADMISSION: No charge.   *TEL:* 01327 354126.

BILLING GARDEN CENTRE

FACILITIES: Wide range of plants, together with trees and shrubs. Large range of houseplants, outdoor covered area with trees and shrubs, containers and equipment, ornamental garden furniture.
LOCATION: The Causeway Park, Great Billing, Northampton.
OPEN: Mon-Sat 0900-1800; Sun 1000-1600.
ADMISSION: No charge.   *TEL:* 01604 786666.

BLISS LANE NURSERY

FACILITIES: Range of shrubs, bedding plants, etc.
LOCATION: 34 Bliss Lane, Flore, off the A45 when entering Flore from the M1/Weedon directions.
OPEN: Ring for times.
ADMISSION: Free.   *TEL:* 01327 340918.

BOSWORTH NURSERIES AND GARDEN CENTRE

FACILITIES: Complete range of plants, shrubs, trees etc, with changing selection of herbaceous plants.
LOCATION: Finedon Road, Burton Latimer.
OPEN: Ring.
ADMISSION: Free.   *TEL:* 01536 722635.

BRESSINGHAM PLANT CENTRE

FACILITIES: Within the old walled garden at Elton Hall. Wide range of plants.
LOCATION: Elton Hall is just off the A605 to the north east of Oundle.
OPEN: Ring.
ADMISSION: Charge made to visit Hall.   *TEL:* 01832 280223.

BRITTONS NURSERY

FACILITIES: Trees and shrubs, houseplants, planted bowls, bedding plants a specialty.
LOCATION: Wellingborough Road, Mears Ashby.
OPEN: Ring for times.
ADMISSION: Free.   *TEL:* 01604 810287.

149

CEDAR NURSERIES

FACILITIES: A pleasant small village nursery with a garden, it sells a variety of bedding plants, etc.
LOCATION: Poplar Farm, Holcot.
OPEN: Ring for details.
ADMISSION: Free.   *TEL:* 01604 781267.

CEDAR VIEW NURSERY

FACILITIES: Wide range of bedding plants including antirrhinum, alyssum, aubretia, begonia, fuchsia, pansies, etc. Trailing plants for hanging baskets, heathers, roses, multi-purpose compost.
LOCATION: The Broadway, Norton, off the A5 road, north of Weedon or the Daventry to Whilton road.
OPEN: Ring.
ADMISSION: No Charge.   *TEL:* 01327 300799.

CLOVER CRAFTS

FACILITIES: A small nursery specialising in unusual alpines and dwarf perennials of some 100 varieties which are grown on site.
LOCATION: 120 Main Road, Duston.
OPEN: Ring John Beckwith before visiting.
ADMISSION: No charge.   *TEL:* 01604 582378.

COTON MANOR GARDENS

FACILITIES: Specialist nursery selling unusual plants and shrubs.
LOCATION: Near Ravensthorpe - tourist signs on A428 and A5199.
OPEN: All year normal working hours.
ADMISSION: No charge.   *TEL:* 01604 740219.

CRICK LODGE NURSERIES

FACILITIES: Range of bedding plants, garden shrubs, greenhouse.
LOCATION: Main Road, Crick.
OPEN: Mon-Sat 0900-1700; Sun 1030-1530.
ADMISSION: No charge.   *TEL:* 01788 822959.

DAVENTRY NURSERIES

FACILITIES: Shrubs, bulbs, bedding plants, herbaceous plants, perennials, conifers, heathers, hanging baskets filled, pot plants, composts, etc.
LOCATION: Reached from the Leamington Way roundabout, near the Civic Amenity Tip and Daventry Sports Park.
OPEN: Mon-Sat 0900-1800; Sun 1000-1600.
ADMISSION: No charge.   *TEL:* 01327 876855.

E DENNETT

FACILITIES: Wide range of bedding plants, shrubs, roses, heathers, trees, etc, together with compost. Landscaping service also available.
LOCATION: Ashby Road, Daventry.
OPEN: Ring for times.
ADMISSION: No charge.   *TEL:* 01327 702288.

DRYWOOD NURSERIES

FACILITIES: Wide range of specialised plants.
LOCATION: The Menagerie, Newport Road, Holcot
OPEN: Ring for times.
ADMISSION: Free.   *TEL:* 01604 870957.

DUSTON GARDEN CENTRE

FACILITIES: Large selection of plants, trees, shrubs, herbs, and a large pet department, accessories. Easy parking.
LOCATION: Millway, Duston, just off the large roundabout close to Sixfields Stadium on the edge of Northampton.
OPEN: Every day.
ADMISSION: Free.   *TEL:* 01604 752155.

E.L.F. PLANTS

FACILITIES: Small nursery growing conifers, specialises in other small growing plants.
LOCATION: Harborough Road North, along the track by Kingsthorpe Cemetery.
OPEN: Thurs-Sat 1000-1700.
ADMISSION: No charge.   *TEL:* 01604 846246.

EVERGREEN NURSERIES

FACILITIES: Specialist growers of heathers, alpines, shrubs and conifers.
LOCATION: Evergreen Lodge, Mawsley Road, Loddington, Kettering.
OPEN: Six days - closed Tues.
ADMISSION: No charge.   *TEL:* 01536 712177.

FIRCROFT GARDEN CENTRE

FACILITIES: Range of bedding plants, shrubs, etc.
LOCATION: Stamford Road, Corby.
OPEN: Ring.
ADMISSION: No charge.   *TEL:* 01536 268346.

GAGGINI'S PLANT CENTRE
FACILITIES: Specialist growers of container trees, shrubs, conifers, fruit, herbaceous plants.
LOCATION: Mears Ashby Nurseries, Glebe House, Glebe Road, Mears Ashby.
OPEN: 0930-1730 (Mon-Sat).
ADMISSION: No charge.   *TEL:* 01604 811811/812371.

THE GARDEN GATE
FACILITIES: Terracotta and glazed pots, garden furniture, edging bricks, tubs, Dutch pea sticks and more.
LOCATION: Sholebroke, Whittlebury, Towcester.
OPEN: Ring for details.
ADMISSION: No charge.   *TEL:* 01327 857414/33293/50512.

THE GARDENER'S CENTRE
(Salcey Forest Timber Products)
FACILITIES: Pot grown trees and shrubs, bedding plants, pots, ornaments, picnic benches, rose arches, trellis gates, fencing, etc. Made to measure service.
LOCATION: The Old Wood Yard, Hanslope Road, Salcey Forest, Hartwell.
OPEN: Ring.
ADMISSION: No charge.   *TEL:* 01604 406373.

GEDDINGTON GARDENS
FACILITIES: Hardy plant nursery.
LOCATION: Between Queen Eleanor Cross and Boughton House.
OPEN: Wed-Sun - Mar to Oct.
ADMISSION: No charge.   *TEL:* 01536 461020.

GREENFINGERS NURSERY AND GARDEN CENTRE
FACILITIES: Fuschias a specialty, but also a wide range of plants and shrubs. Pond liners stocked (and can be fitted), cold water fish.
LOCATION: Market House Courtyard, Brackley.
OPEN: Mon-Sun 0900-1700.
ADMISSION: No charge.   *TEL:* 01280 701677.

GREENLANE GARDEN CENTRE
FACILITIES: Shrubs, bedding plants, bulbs, perennials, herbs, alpine.
LOCATION: Brackley Road, Towcester, behind Little Chef A43 south.
OPEN: Mon-Sat 0900-1730; Sun 1000-1730.
ADMISSION: No charge.   *TEL:* 01327 350593.

THE GROWING GARDEN

FACILITIES: Large collection of plants with display beds, together with large pet and aquatic centre, tea room with homemade cakes and sandwiches. Children's farm and large adventure area.
LOCATION: Barnwell Road, Oundle - follow the signs for Barnwell Country Park.
OPEN: Nearly every day.
ADMISSION: No charge.   *TEL:* 01832 273478.

HALL PARK GARDEN CENTRE

FACILITIES: Range of plants, pet food and tool hire.
LOCATION: Hall Avenue, Rushden.
OPEN: Ring.
ADMISSION: No charge.   *TEL:* 01933 410562.

HARLESTONE HEATH GARDEN CENTRE

FACILITIES: Wide range of plants and shrubs, including house plants, seeds, gifts, etc.
LOCATION: Harlestone Road, Harlestone on the A428 Northampton-Rugby road.
OPEN: Ring for times.
ADMISSION: Free.   *TEL:* 01604 751346.

HILL FARM HERBS

FACILITIES: Attractive nursery selling herbs and cottage plants. Free mail order list Also sells dried flowers, pot pourri, seeds, etc.
LOCATION: Park Walk, Brigstock.
OPEN: Daily Mar-Dec from 1030.
ADMISSION: No charge.   *TEL:* 01536 373597.

HILLSIDE FARM NURSERY

FACILITIES: Set amidst a 150 acre farm it has a wide range of bedding plants, geraniums and fuschias. There are also rock plants, perennials, shrubs and conifers. During spring and summer hanging basket and container planting demonstrations held by arrangement. Picnic area.
LOCATION: Harrowden Lane, Finedon, off the A510 near Finedon.
OPEN: 0900-dusk daily (not Christmas and New Year).
TEL: 01933 681076.

HINWICK HALL HORTICULTURE

FACILITIES: Specialist bedding plants.
LOCATION: Hinwick, Wellingborough.
OPEN: 7 days a week.
ADMISSION: No charge for nursery.   *TEL:* 01933 50543.

HOWITTS HOME AND GARDEN VILLAGE

FACILITIES: Garden plants, building supplies, tropical fish, cold water and pond fish and plants.
LOCATION: 291 Rockingham Road, Corby.
OPEN: Mon-Sat 0900-1800; Sun 1000-1700.
ADMISSION: No charge.   *TEL:* 01536 203092/262078.

ISE GARDEN CENTRE

FACILITIES: Wide range of plants and shrubs, and accessories, including composts and seeds.
LOCATION: Warkton Lane, Kettering.
OPEN: Ring.
ADMISSION: No charge.   *TEL:* 01536 519792.

W J JONES

FACILITIES: Growers of a wide range of rock, alpine and hardy plants, including some unusual varieties. Bedding plants and hanging baskets also stocked - and seasonal plants. Provides a helpful service with advice.
LOCATION: Park View Nurseries, Towcester Road, Litchborough, off the A5.
OPEN: Ring for details.
ADMISSION: Free.   *TEL:* 01327 830222.

KENNEDYS GARDEN CENTRE

FACILITIES: Wide range of plants, shrubs and trees.
Also seasonal plants, and gift shop.
LOCATION: Millers Lane, Wellingborough.
OPEN: Ring for details.
ADMISSION: Free.   *TEL:* 01933 273728.

KINGS HEATH HOME AND GARDEN

FACILITIES: Wide range of plants.
LOCATION: 3 Park Square, Kings Heath, Northampton.
OPEN: Ring for times.
ADMISSION: Free.   *TEL:* 01604 750049.

MOULTON COLLEGE GARDEN CENTRE

FACILITIES: Sells a large selection of shrubs, evergreens, late bedding plants, hyacinths, poinsettias, etc.
LOCATION: Home Farm, Pitsford Road, Moulton, Northampton.
OPEN: Wed-Fri 100-1800; Sat 100-1700; Sun 1000-1600.
ADMISSION: No charge.   *TEL:* 01604 494206.

NORTHAMPTONSHIRE COUNTRYSIDE CENTRE
See under Farm Shops

THE NURSERY FURTHER AFIELD
FACILITIES: Hardy perennials, including geraniums and hemerocallis.
LOCATION: Evenley Road, Mixbury, near Brackley.
OPEN: Mid-March - mid Oct - Wed/Sat/Bank Hol Mons 1000-1700.
ADMISSION: No charge. *TEL:* 01280 848808 (day)/848539 (evening).

PAYNES NURSERIES (TOWCESTER) LTD
FACILITIES: More than 500 different species of shrubs, trees, perennials, roses, conifers, fruit trees, climbing plants, alpines, fruit trees, heathers, etc. Flowering and foliage plants, seeds, vegetable plants and peats, fertilisers, composts, tools, paving slabs, rockery stones, fencing, etc.
LOCATION: 192 Watling Street East, Towcester.
OPEN: Mon-Sat 0830-1800; Sun 1000-1300.
ADMISSION: No charge. *TEL:* 01327 50377.

THE PLANT WAREHOUSE (JACK HADDON)
FACILITIES: Indoor plants and planters.
LOCATION: The Riding, Northampton town centre - behind Woolworths
OPEN: Mon-Fri 0830-1730; Sat 0830-1630.
ADMISSION: N/A. *TEL:* 01604 633976.

PLANTSMAN
FACILITIES: This is the 'Gardener's Garden Centre' with a wide range of the finest quality plants, shrubs and trees. Advice freely given based on practical gardening experience. Always good displays.
LOCATION: On the A428 (Northampton Road) on the Northampton side of West Haddon.
OPEN: Ring for details.
ADMISSION: Free. *TEL:* 01788 510206.

PLENTI-FULL-POTS
FACILITIES: Grows and stocks a wide range of 'mix and match' plants, as well as containers, barrels, hanging baskets, baskets, stoneware, etc.
LOCATION: Falcutt Farm, Helmdon near Brackley, which is off an unclassified road formerly the B4525 near Helmdon village.
OPEN: All year 1000-1700, limited opening Jan. Closed 25/26 Dec/1 Jan.
ADMISSION: No charge. *TEL:* 01280 850479.

PODDINGTON GARDEN CENTRE
FACILITIES: A wide range of plants and accessories for the garden. Sections in this large centre include garden sundries, garden furniture, houseplants and floral department, aquatic and pet section, gnomes kitchen, books and giftware, peat and compost, decorative paving and stoneware. Free parking.
LOCATION: High Street, Poddington, reached from the A509, and signed in Bozeat.
OPEN: Seven days a week - 0900-1730 (winter); 0900-1830 (summer). Wednesday is Ladies Day.
ADMISSION: No charge.   *TEL:* 01933 53656.

RAVENSTHORPE NURSERY
FACILITIES: Over 3000 varieties of plants, including herbaceous, shrubs, trees, etc.
LOCATION: 6 East Haddon Road, Ravensthorpe.
OPEN: Tues-Sun, Bank Hols Mons - 1000-1800 (or dusk).
ADMISSION: No charge.   *TEL:* 01604 770548.

ROB'S NURSERY
FACILITIES: Trees, shrubs, bedding plants, hanging baskets.
LOCATION: Church Street, Moulton.
OPEN: Ring.
ADMISSION: No charge.   *TEL:* 01604 495073.

ROMAN WAY GARDEN CENTRE
FACILITIES: Wide range of plants and shrubs.
LOCATION: Five Elms Nursery, 8 Watling Street, Potterspury.
OPEN: Ring.
ADMISSION: No charge.   *TEL:* 01908 542427.

RYELANDS NURSERIES
FACILITIES: Large selection of cottage and garden plants.
LOCATION: Naseby Road, Clipston.
OPEN: Fri/Sat - Mar to Sept.
ADMISSION: No charge.   *TEL:* 01858 525564

SELBY SHOWJUMPS
FACILITIES: Hardwood and treated pine garden furniture, gates, sheds, kennels, chicken houses, pine kitchens, etc. Also showjumps and pine kitchen furniture. Cream teas also available - weather permitting.
LOCATION: The Bungalow, Littleworth, Duncote, off the A5 between Weedon and Towcester.
OPEN: Daily 0930-1900.

ADMISSION: No charge.   *TEL:* 01327 350345.

SPRING FARM NURSERIES

FACILITIES: Bedding plants, hanging baskets, pick your own fruit in season.
LOCATION: Spring Farm, Litchborough.
OPEN: Ring.
ADMISSION: No charge.   *TEL:* 01327 830799.

SUNNY VALE NURSERIES

FACILITIES: Small plant nursery.
LOCATION: Off Lamport Road, Harrington.
OPEN: Ring for details.
ADMISSION: No charge.   *TEL:* 01604 686608.

TAKEROOT NURSERIES LTD

FACILITIES: Range of bedding and other plants.
LOCATION: Yelvertoft Road, Crick.
OPEN: Ring for times.
ADMISSION: No charge.   *TEL:* 01788 824176.

J B & V A TEBBUTT
See Sunnyvale Nurseries

THISTLEHOLME NURSERIES

FACILITIES: General nurseries, with bedding plants, etc.
LOCATION: Taylors Green, Warmington.
OPEN: Ring.
ADMISSION: No charge.   *TEL:* 01832 380827.

C V WARWICK

FACILITIES: General nursery and garden centre.
LOCATION: The Nurseries, Yardley Hastings.
OPEN: Ring for times.
ADMISSION: Free.   *TEL:* 01604 696241.

WHILTON LOCKS GARDEN CENTRE

FACILITIES: Caters for all gardening requirements. There is also an Aquatic Centre and Pet Centre. Advice, easy car parking, coffee shop. Local free deliveries.
LOCATION: Off A5 3 miles north of Weedon, signposted to Whilton Locks.
OPEN: Every day - 0900 to 1800.
ADMISSION: Free.   *TEL:* 01327 842727.

WHITES NURSERIES

FACILITIES: Bedding plants, shrubs, etc.
LOCATION: 24 Broad Street, Earls Barton.
OPEN: Ring.
ADMISSION: No charge.   *TEL:* 01604 810350.

WOODMEADOW GARDEN AND AQUATICS CENTRE

FACILITIES: Has a range of trees, shrubs, slabs, sheds, summerhouse pavilions, leisure cabins.
LOCATION: Kettering Road, Hannington, at the Hardwick turn on the A43 Kettering to Northampton road.
OPEN: Daily.
ADMISSION: Free.   *TEL:* 01604 781260.

WYEVALE GARDEN CENTRE

FACILITIES: Wide range of garden plants, shrubs, compost, gifts, etc. Part of a large chain.
LOCATION: B526 Newport Pagnell Road, close to Turners Musical Merry-Go-Round.
OPEN: Daily.
ADMISSION: Free.   *TEL:* 01604 765725.

YOUNGS NURSERIES

FACILITIES: General nursery, peat/compost.
LOCATION: 33 Northampton Road, Blisworth.
OPEN: Ring for times.
ADMISSION: No charge.   *TEL:* 01604 858574.

GARDENS

**See also Historic
Houses and Buildings**

BOUGHTON HOUSE

FACILITIES: The Estate is run by the Living Landscape Trust. Gardens and ground only open. There is a garden shop, tearoom, gift shop and adventure playground.
LOCATION: On A43, 3 miles north of Kettering.
OPEN: Daily (except Fri) from 1300-1700.
ADMISSION: Ring for details.
TEL: 01536 515731 (The Living Landscape Trust).

CASTLE ASHBY GARDENS

FACILITIES: Consists of a combination of 18 and 19 century styles, with formal gardens and an arboretum. The 200 acre estate is unspoilt. The mile long avenue offers impressive views of Castle Ashby, the ancestral home of the Marquis of Northampton. There is also an arboretum and lakes. Plants for sale.
LOCATION: Signed off the A428.
OPEN: All year 1000-dusk.
ADMISSION: Charge.   **TEL:** 01604 696696 (Head Gardener).

COTON MANOR GARDENS

FACILITIES: An outstanding example of an Old English garden, which has been laid out on a variety of levels. There are lawns, a water garden, and excellent hedges, all of which are enhanced by the resident flamingoes, cranes and other waterfowl which roam around the 'estate'. Paths are well laid out. There is a gift shop and home made lunches and teas, together with a specialist plant nursery.
LOCATION: Off A428 or A5199 (follow tourist signs), near Guilsborough.
OPEN: Suns/Weds/Bank Hols Easter-end Sept; Thurs in July/Aug -1200-1800. Parties at other times by arrangement.
ADMISSION: Charge.   **TEL:** 01604 740219.

HOLDENBY HOUSE GARDENS

FACILITIES: The gardens and house date from Elizabethan times, and the House, although not open, provides a delightful backdrop. The building is one of the largest Elizabethan houses, and Charles I was imprisoned here. Built by Sir Christopher Hatton, the Chancellor to Elizabeth I, at the time it was the largest house in England. It was rebuilt in the Victorian era, using some materials from the original building. There are a number of facilities including teas, etc.
LOCATION: Signposted from the A5199 and A428, and 7 miles from Northampton.
OPEN: Apr-Sept - Sun 1200-1800; July-Aug - Thurs 1300-1700.
ADMISSION: Fee.   **TEL:** 01604 770074/777086.

GOLF COURSES AND CLUBS

CHERWELL EDGE

FACILITIES: 18 hole pay and play course, driving range, restaurant and bar facilities. Visitors welcome.

LOCATION: Chacombe - between Middleton Cheney and Sulgrave.
OPEN: Every day.
ADMISSION: Fees.   **TEL:** 01295 711591.

COLD ASHBY GOLF CLUB

FACILITIES: 27 hole golf course with clubhouse, including lounge bar and function room for 100, conference facilities.
LOCATION: Stanford Road, 1 mile from the A14.
OPEN: Daily - ring first.
ADMISSION: Club fee, also daily playing fee for non-members.
TEL: 01604 740548.

COLLINGTREE PARK GOLF COURSE

FACILITIES: 16 bay driving range, three testing practice holes, latest indoor teaching facilities.
LOCATION: Windingbrook Lane, Northampton, is less than 4 miles south of Northampton town centre.
OPEN: Ring for information.
ADMISSION: Charge.   **TEL:** 01604 700000.

CORBY GOLF RANGE AND LEISURE CLUB

FACILITIES: 9 hole golf course, 9 hole pitch and putt, 26 bay floodlit golf range, shop, private and group lessons.
LOCATION: Corby Road, Cottingham.
OPEN: 7 days a week.
ADMISSION: Charge.
TEL: 01536 403119.

CORBY PUBLIC GOLF COURSE

FACILITIES: 18 hole pay and play complex, with clubs for hire, a shop, bars, restaurant and snacks. Tuition available, practice greens, refreshments and car parking.
LOCATION: Stamford Road, Weldon, off the A43 and east of Corby.
OPEN: From 0800 daily.
ADMISSION: Charge made.   **TEL:** 01536 60756.

DAVENTRY AND DISTRICT GOLF CLUB

FACILITIES: A nine hole course on Borough Hill. Club room.
LOCATION: On the B4036 Daventry-Norton road, linking the town with the A5.
OPEN: Ring for details.
ADMISSION: Ring.   **TEL:** 01327 700829.

DELAPRE GOLF COMPLEX

FACILITIES: An 18 hole course, with additional activities including 25 covered floodlit practice bays, pitch and putt, putting greens, grass practice areas, with bunkers and sloping lies. Club House. Car Park.

LOCATION: Eagle Drive, Nene Valley Way, Northampton, signed half way between the Eleanor Cross roundabout and the Bedford Road flyover.

OPEN: Ring for times.

ADMISSION: Charge.   **TEL:** 01604 764036.

FARTHINGSTONE HOTEL, GOLF COURSE AND LEISURE CENTRE

FACILITIES: Set in picturesque surroundings on a mature 18 hole golf course. Fully licenced bar and carvery restaurant, full leisure facilities (squash, snooker aerobics), en suite rooms, etc.

LOCATION: On a minor road off the A5 south-west of Weedon or the A361 south-east of Daventry.

OPEN: 7 days a week.

ADMISSION: Charge.   **TEL:** 01327 361291.

HELLIDON LAKES

FACILITIES: The course is set in a delightful part of Northamptonshire, with a Hotel and Country Club. 18 hole Lakes course and 9 hole Holywell course set in 240 acres of beautiful countryside. 14 Lakes - covered driving range into water. Golf tuition available. There is also a sauna, Pro shop and much more.

LOCATION: Hellidon is off the A361 Daventry to Banbury road and south west of Daventry.

OPEN: Seven days.

ADMISSION; Various fees.   **TEL:** 01327 262575.

KETTERING GOLF CLUB

FACILITIES: Eighteen hole parkland course.

LOCATION: Headlands.

OPEN: Mon-Fri visitors

ADMISSION: Fees charged.   **TEL:** 01536 511104.

KINGFISHER LAKES

FACILITIES: Nine hole golf course. Restaurant and bar open to the public.

LOCATION: Buckingham Road, Deanshanger.

OPEN: 0900-dusk.

ADMISSION: Charge.   **TEL:** 01908 562332.

KINGSTHORPE GOLF CLUB

FACILITIES: An eighteen hole course, with a par of 69. Catering available except on Sundays. A handicap certificate is required.
LOCATION: Kingsley Road, Northampton.
OPEN: Daily but not at weekends for visitors.
TEL: 01604 710610 (Secretary).

NORTHAMPTON GOLF CLUB

FACILITIES: An 18 hole course, with a handicap of 72.
LOCATION: Harlestone, Northampton.
OPEN: Ring for details.
ADMISSION: Fees charged. *TEL:* 01604 845102/845155 (Secretary).

NORTHAMPTONSHIRE COUNTY GOLF CLUB

FACILITIES: An 18 hole course with a par of 71. Ring for details. Catering available, but limited on Mondays.
LOCATION: Sandy Lane, Church Brampton, Northampton.
ADMISSION: Membership fee/fees charged.
OPEN: Ring for details. *TEL:* 01604 843025 (Secretary).

OUNDLE GOLF CLUB

FACILITIES: 18 hole course; par 70, length 5600 yards. There are restrictions to visitors after 1030 at weekends. Catering available except Mondays.
LOCATION: Benefield Road.
OPEN: Daily - ring for details.
ADMISSION: Ring for details. *TEL:* 01832 273267 (Sec); 272273 (Pro).

RUSHDEN AND DISTRICT GOLF CLUB

FACILITIES: Ring.
LOCATION: Kimbolton Road, Chelveston.
OPEN: All week.
ADMISSION: Ring for details. *TEL:* 01933 314910. (Sec).

SILVERSTONE GOLF CLUB

FACILITIES: Unique 12 bay driving range, 18 hole par 72 course.
LOCATION: Silverstone Road, Stowe.
OPEN: 7 days.
ADMISSION: Charge. *TEL:* 01280 850005.

STAVERTON PARK

FACILITIES: 18 hole course, par 71, 6634 yards.
LOCATION: On A425, west of Daventry.
OPEN: Daily - but bookings needed 2 days ahead for weekend.

ADMISSION: Ring for details.
TEL: 01327 705911 (Sec); 01327 705506 (Pro).

STOKE ALBANY
FACILITIES: 18 holes. open to public. Membership available, corporate and society days.
LOCATION: Ashley Road, Stoke Albany.
OPEN: Ring.
ADMISSION: Charge.   *TEL:* 01858 535208.

WELLINGBOROUGH GOLF CLUB
FACILITIES: An 18 hole course.
LOCATION: Harrowden Hall, Great Harrowden, 2 miles north of Wellingborough on A509.
OPEN: To the public during the week.
ADMISSION: Fee charged.   *TEL:* 01933 677234 (Secretary).

WEST PARK GOLF AND COUNTRY CLUB
FACILITIES: A number of courses, including the 1905 Course, a reconstruction of the original golf course, Royal Whittlewood Course, The Grand Prix Course, The Wedgwood Course has par 3's and par 4's, and is designed with the testing short game, or novice player, in mind. There is also a Golf 'O' Drome and Practice Range.   Bar lounge and catering.
LOCATION: Whittlebury, off the A413 Towcester to Buckingham road, on the outskirts of the village.
OPEN: All year - seven days a week - booking advisable.
ADMISSION: Fees charged.
TEL: 01327 858092 (information)/858588 (reservations).

GROUPS AND ASSOCIATIONS

BAPS
FACILITIES: Based in Wellingborough a group for the blind and partially sighted. Meets regularly and arranges a variety of social activities, including visits and outings.
LOCATION: Ring for information.
OPEN: Ring.
ADMISSION: Charge,.   *TEL:* 01933 225266.

BODDINGTON VINTAGE ASSOCIATION

FACILITIES: A committee of people who organise agricultural based rallies.

LOCATION: The group meets in Upper Boddington, reached off the A361 Daventry to Banbury road.

OPEN: Ring for information.

ADMISSION: Ring.   *TEL:* 01295 760571.

COUNCIL FOR THE PROTECTION OF RURAL ENGLAND (CPRE)

FACILITIES: Groups in various parts of Northamptonshire campaigning for the 'protection of England' - campaign for the countryside.

LOCATION: Various.

OPEN: Ring.

ADMISSION: Membership fee.   *TEL:* 01280 703556.

DAVENTRY MODEL BOAT CLUB

FACILITIES: Builds and sails model boats.

LOCATION: Outdoor meetings at Daventry Country Park. Indoor meetings as arranged.

OPEN: Ring for details.

ADMISSION: Membership fee.   *TEL:* 01327 878705.

DAVENTRY PLAYERS

FACILITIES; Company which puts on regular productions. Always looking for new talent.

LOCATION: Daventry Community Centre, Ashby Road.

OPEN: Ring for details of rehearsels and performances.

ADMISSION: Charge for performances. *TEL:* 01327 706607 enquiries.

DAVENTRY RAMBLERS

FACILITIES: Arranges a range of walks and talks in the Daventry area.

LOCATION: Varies.

OPEN: See programme.

ADMISSION: Membership fee.   *TEL:* 01327 878695.

DAVENTRY VIP CLUB

FACILITIES: For visually impaired people, the Club meets monthly and arranges a variety of social activities. There is an annual produce and craft show with BAPS, Wellingborough. Produces a monthly tape.

LOCATION: Meets New Street Day Centre, opposite the shopping centre and next to the bus station.

OPEN: Ring for details.

ADMISSION: Subscription, plus charges for visits, etc.

TEL: 01788 890401.

FRIENDS OF NORTHAMPTON MUSEUM AND ART GALLERY

FACILITIES: For details contact Gill Lindsay, Secretary.
LOCATION: Central Museum, Guildhall Road, Northampton.
OPEN: Ring for details.
ADMISSION: Membership fee. *TEL:* 01604 713279.

HIGHAM FERRERS FOOTPATHS GROUP

FACILITIES: Arranges walks and practical activities.
LOCATION: Higham Ferrers.
OPEN: Ring for details.
ADMISSION: Membership fee. *TEL:* 01933 359237.

KETTERING AND DISTRICT RAMBLING CLUB

FACILITIES: Arranges rambles.
LOCATION: Varies.
OPEN: Sat/Sun and mid-week.
ADMISSION: Membership fee.
TEL: 01536 722407 (weekend walks); 01536 85185/514772 (mid-week)

KNIGHTS OF THE ROSE

FACILITIES: Arranges spectacular foot combat displays, medieval banquet entertainment, lectures, etc. on medieval way of life.
LOCATION: N/A
OPEN: N/A
ADMISSION: Membership fee/charge for activities. *TEL:* 01604 880668

LONG DISTANCE WALKERS ASSOCIATION
BEDS, BUCKS AND NORTHANTS GROUP

FACILITIES: Arranges long distance walks.
LOCATION: Various venues.
OPEN: Ring.
ADMISSION: Membership fee. *TEL:* 01933 314381.

MASQUE THEATRE

FACILITIES: Regular productions, the group welcomes new members interested in all aspects of theatre. Wide range of opportunities.
LOCATION: Productions take place at Northampton College Arts Centre, St Gregory's Road, Northampton. There is usually one open-air production each year.
OPEN: Ring for information.
ADMISSION: Ring. *TEL:* 01604 38201 (Secretary).

MOULTON PLAYERS
FACILITIES: Group which puts on regular performances.
LOCATION: Moulton School.
OPEN: Ring.
ADMISSION: Ring - charge for performances. *TEL:* 01604 792532.

NATIONAL COUNCIL FOR THE CONSERVATION OF PLANTS AND GARDENS
NORTHAMPTONSHIRE GROUP
FACILTIES: Indoor meetings: arranges visits to gardens.
LOCATION: Moulton School, Pound Lane, Moulton.
OPEN: First Monday of the month.
ADMISSION: Membership fee.   *TEL:* Jim Bond, 14 High St, Lamport.

NORTHAMPTONSHIRE FAMILY HISTORY SOCIETY
FACILITIES: Arranges regular meetings to enable members to research their ancestry.
LOCATION: Meets in Northampton and Kettering.
OPEN: Write.
ADMISSION: Membership fee.
TEL: Write to Mrs J Simmons, 187 Stamford Road, Kettering.

NORTHAMPTONSHIRE FAMILY HISTORY SOCIETY - KETTERING BRANCH
FACILTIES: A wide range of indoor meetings.
LOCATION: Cornmarket Hall, Kettering.
OPEN: Second Mon of the month at 1930.
ADMISSION: Membership fee.   *TEL:* N/A.

NORTHAMPTONSHIRE GARDENS TRUST
FACILITIES: Encourages awareness of gardens and landscapes of all periods. Surveys, researches and records large and small gardens, etc.
LOCATION: N/A.
OPEN: N/A.
ADMISSION: N/A.   *TEL:* 01604 843552.

NORTHAMPTONSHIRE INDUSTRIAL ARCHAEOLOGICAL GROUP
FACILITIES: An interesting series of talks.
LOCATION: University Centre, Barrack Road, Northampton.
OPEN: Second Fri of month - 1930.
ADMISSION: Membership fee.
TEL: Contact: Mr G Starmer, 34 The Crescent, Northampton, NN1 4SB.

NORTHAMPTONSHIRE POST CARD CLUB

FACILITIES: Talks and activities in connection with postcards.
LOCATION: NASO Rooms, St Michael's Road, Northampton.
OPEN: Second Tues of month - 1930.
ADMISSION: Membership fee.
TEL: Contact: Mr G Garner, 5 Cheriton Way, Northampton, NN1 5SB

NORTHAMPTONSHIRE PRESERVATION SOCIETY
CORBY BRANCH

FACILITIES: A variety of indoor meetings.
LOCATION: East Carlton Park Heritage Centre.
OPEN: Last Tues of month - 1930.
ADMISSION: Membership fee.   *TEL:* N/A.

NORTHAMPTONSHIRE PRESERVATION SOCIETY
WELLINGBOROUGH BRANCH

FACILITIES: A variety of indoor meetings.
LOCATION: Polish Club, 33 Winstanley Road.
OPEN: Second Tues of month - 1930.
ADMISSION: Membership fee.   *TEL:* N/A.

NORTHAMPTONSHIRE RECORD SOCIETY

FACILITIES: Includes copies of the Journal, free admission to lectures, etc.
LOCATION: Meets at the Record Office, Wootton Hall Park, off the A45.
OPEN: Meetings arranged at various times,
ADMISSION: Membership fee.   *TEL:* 01604 762297.

NORTHAMPTONSHIRE VICTORIA COUNTY HISTORY TRUST

FACILITIES: Set up to raise money to complete the Victoria County History for Northamptonshire, which covers 167 parishes. Topics to be covered include the boot and shoe industry, iron and steel, engineering, etc. If you want to get involved, please ring.
LOCATION: Secretary based at Northamptonshire Record Office, Wootton Hall Park.
OPEN: N/A.
ADMISSION: N/A.   *TEL:* 01604 762129.

NORTHAMPTONSHIRE WEAVERS, SPINNERS AND DYERS

FACILITIES: Runs groups, courses, etc.
LOCATION: Ring for details
OPEN: Ring.

ADMISSION: Membership fee.   *TEL:* 01604 890534/01908 542898.

OUNDLE AND DISTRICT PHAB-GATEWAY CLUB

FACILITIES: Wide range of activities including games, discos, outings, country dancing, etc. From age 9years upwards.
LOCATION: Ring for details.
OPEN: Wed 1930-2100.
ADMISSION: Small charge.   *TEL:* 01832 226246.

THE RAMBLERS ASSOCIATION
KETTERING AND DISTRICT RAMBLERS

FACILITIES: Varied programme including walks and indoor meetings.
LOCATION: Kettering area.
OPEN: As programme.
ADMISSION: Membership fee.   *TEL:* 01536 722407.

THE RAMBLERS ASSOCIATION
TOWCESTER AND DISTRICT RAMBLERS

FACILITIES: Arranges walks and meetings.
LOCATION: Towcester area.
OPEN: As programme.
ADMISSION: Membership fee.   *TEL:* 01908 674867.

THE RAMBLERS ASSOCIATION
WELLINGBOROUGH GROUP

FACILITIES: Arranges group walks and indoor activities.
LOCATION: In and around Wellingborough.
OPEN: Details in programme.
ADMISSION: Membership fee.   *TEL:* 01933 680032.

ROCKINGHAM FOREST WALKERS

FACILITIES: Arranges walks in the forest and other venues.
LOCATION: Varies.
OPEN: Membership fee.
ADMISSION: Ring.   *TEL:* 01536 722437.

ROTHWELL PRESERVATION TRUST

FACILITIES: A charity and limited company which works for the preservation of Rothwell's buildings. Offers advice.
LOCATION: Meets in the Market House.
OPEN: Not available to the 'general public' at the moment.
ADMISSION: N/A.   *TEL:* 01536 711086.

RUSHDEN HISTORICAL TRANSPORT SOCIETY

FACILITIES: Indoor meetigs - also possibility of practical work on their collection.
LOCATION: Conservative Club, High Street South, Rushden.
OPEN: Last Tues of month (not Dec) at 1945 for 2000.
ADMISSION: Fee.   *TEL:* N/A.

SEALED KNOT

FACILITIES: Re-enactments of battles, etc.
LOCATION: Ring.
OPEN: Ring for information.
ADMISSION: Membership fee.   *TEL:* 01327 877725

UNDER THE TOWER DRAMA

FACILITIES: Welcomes new members.
LOCATION: Parish Church Room, Earls Barton.
OPEN: Meets Fri/Sun evenings during productions.
ADMISSION: Check.   *TEL:* N/A.

UPPER NENE ARCHAEOLOGICAL SOCIETY

FACILITIES: Regular meetings: also preparing a museum at Piddington. Visits and archaeological digs.
LOCATION: Northampton.
OPEN: Write for details.
ADMISSION: Membership fee.
TEL: Mrs M Smedley, 57 Pinewood Road, Northampton, NN3 2RD.

WELLINGBOROUGH CIVIC SOCIETY

FACILITIES: Gives support on town matters and runs the heritage Centre.
LOCATION: Heritage Centre in Croyland Hall.
OPEN: Ring.
ADMISSION: Membership fee for Society.   *TEL:* 01933 276838.

WELLINGBOROUGH AND DISTRICT ARCHAEOLOGICAL SOCIETY

FACILITIES: An interesting selection of talks, which have included the history of the privy and historical gardens.
LOCATION: Friends Meeting House, St John's Street.
OPEN: Last Mon of the month at 1930.
ADMISSION: Charge.   *TEL:* N/A.

WILDLIFE TRUST FOR NORTHAMPTONSHIRE

Has groups in the following locations: Brackley and District, Desborough, Finedon and District, Geddington and District, Irchester, Kettering and District, Nassington and District, Northampton Wildlife Group, Oundle and District, Peterborough, Rushden and Wellingborough

TEL: 01604 405285 for details of addresses, contacts, etc.

GUIDED TOURS AND VISITS

BLUE BADGE GUIDES

FACILITIES: Qualified guides who arrange walks, excursions, themed coach tours etc. in various parts of the County. Routine tours and walks or 'made-to-measure'. Topics include Rockingham Forest, The Hunsbury Story, Crime and Punishment, Ghosts and Legends, Easton Neston and the Hesketh family, Hidden Treasures and Curiosities, The Life and Poetry of John Clare, Journey Along the Nene, The Civil War - the list is endless.

LOCATION: In and around the County - details from TIC's - or from the organiser.

OPEN: Various times.

ADMISSION: Charge made.   *TEL:* 01604 843175.

HERITAGE QUARTER, KETTERING

FACILITIES: A leaflet which enables the visitor to discover more about the Heritage Quarter, which includes The Manor House Museum, Heritage Quarter Gardens, Alfred East Gallery. Activities include events days, living history workshops, loans collection, identification service, gallery concerts, Saturday Art Club, young artists exhibitions, enquiry service, craft fairs, schools services.

LOCATION: Sheep Street area.

OPEN: 0930-1700 Mon-Sat (not Bank Hols) - Museum 0930-1630 Mon-Sat (not Bank Hols).

ADMISSION: Free.

TEL: 01536 410333 x 381 (Museum and Gallery); 01536 410266 (TIC).

NORTHAMPTON GUILDHALL

FACILITIES: Tours can be pre-booked through the local Visitor Centre.

LOCATION: 2 St Giles Square, Northampton.

OPEN: Ask for details.
ADMISSION: Charge.   *TEL:* 01604 22677 (Visitor Centre).

WINDMILL VINEYARD

FACILITIES: Tours of this Northamptonshire Vineyard, which produces medium dry white wine, and also country wines from fruit grown on the farm. Wine tasting in the windmill tower. Refreshments can be provided for groups if ordered.
LOCATION: Hellidon.
OPEN: Sat/Sun Bank Hols.
ADMISSION: Charge.   *TEL:* 01327 262023.

GYMNASIUM, HEALTH CLUBS AND FITNESS CENTRES

AEROBICS WAREHOUSE

FACILITIES: Aerobics and step centre.
LOCATION: 11a The Ridings, (near Woolworth), Northampton.
OPEN: Ring.
ADMISSION: Charge.   *TEL:* 01604 602712.

MIKE BAKER

FACILITIES: Health studio includes gymnasium for men, trimnasium for women, weight training, body building, short specialised exercises, etc.
LOCATION: Fetter Street, Northampton - between Angel Street and John Street, just around the corner from the Derngate's main entrance.
OPEN: Mon-Fri 1000-2130; Sat 1000-1630; Sun (men only) 1000-1300.
ADMISSION: Charge.   *TEL:* 01604 620468.

BETTER BODIES GYMNASIUM

FACILITIES: Spacious, well equipped gymnasium with fully trained instructors, large selection of machines. Facilities for men and women. Free car parking.
LOCATION: Unit 1, First Floor, Nene Enterprise Centre, Freehold Street, Northampton.
OPEN: Mon-Fri 0930-2130; Sat/Sun 1000-1600.
ADMISSION: Charge.   *TEL:* 01604 791294.

BODY SHAPERS

FACILITIES: Unisex gym, ladies gym and keep fit, sunbeds, saunas, massage machines, qualified instructors.
LOCATION: School Lane, Kettering.
OPEN: Mon-Thurs 0900-2100; Fri 0930-2000; Sat 0930-1700; Sun 1000-1300 & 1700-1900.

171

ADMISSION: Charge.   *TEL:* 01536 515766.

BODY AND SOUL GYMNASIUM
FACILITIES: Fully equipped gymnasium. Aerobics, badminton, table tennis, over 50's session, junior weight training, creche available.
LOCATION: YMCA, Cheyne Walk, Northampton.
OPEN: Ring.
ADMISSION: Charge.   *TEL:* 01604 638834.

BODYBITZ
FACILITIES: Qualified instructors and the latest equipment; step aerobics, sun beds and sauna.
LOCATION: 62 High Street. Weedon.
OPEN: Ring for times.
ADMISSION: Charge.   *TEL:* 01327 342306.

BODYTALK
FACILITIES: The complete health package, including fitness, sunbeds, Turkish rooms, sauna.
LOCATION: London Road, Kettering.
OPEN: Ring.
ADMISSION: Charge.   *TEL:* 01536 410253.

BUSTERS GYM AND HEALTH STUDIO
FACILITIES: Ring for details.
LOCATION: 1 Overstone Road, Northampton.
OPEN: Ring for information.
ADMISSION: Charge.   *TEL:* 01604 603052.

DALLINGTON COUNTRY CLUB
FACILITIES: Gym with apparatus.
LOCATION: Poyntz Lane, Off Mill Lane, Dallington, Northampton.
OPEN: Ring.
ADMISSION: Charge.   *TEL:* 01604 584923.

DERNGATE GYM AND FITNESS CLUB
FACILITIES: Gym apparatus.
LOCATION: 9 Derngate, Northampton.
OPEN: Ring.
ADMISSION: Charge.   *TEL:* 01604 639248.

FITNESS 2000
FACILITIES: Gym fitted with the latest equipment. Step classes, circuit training, etc. Coffee shop, reflexology.

LOCATION: 1 High Street, Long Buckby on the B5385.
OPEN: 7 days a week.
ADMISSION: Charge. *TEL:* 01604 843755.

HANOVER INTERNATIONAL HOTEL AND CLUB

FACILITIES: Swimming, whirlpool spa, exercise equipment, sauna, solarium and steam room.
LOCATION: Sedgemoor Way, off Ashby Road, Daventry.
OPEN: Ring.
ADMISSION: Membership fee.   *TEL:* 01327 301777, ext 422.

HARPERS FITNESS CLUB

FACILITIES: A fully equipped gym, plus sunbeds and relaxing sauna.
LOCATION: Pemberton Centre, H E Bates Way, Rushden.
OPEN: Ring for details.
ADMISSION: Charge.   *TEL:* 01933 50324.

HARPER'S FITNESS GYM

FACILITIES: Nutritional and dieting advice and guidance, together with a sports and fitness club. Up to date tecnically advanced equipment.
LOCATION: Daventry Leisure Centre, Lodge Road.
OPEN: Mon/Tue/Thurs 0900-2100; Wed 0900-2045; Fri 0900-1900; Sat 1000-1800; Sun 1000-1700.
ADMISSION: Charges.   *TEL:* 01327 871144.

HATTON PARK HEALTH AND FITNESS STUDIO

FACILITIES: Ladies and men's gym with full supervision, dance studio, sauna, sunbeds, body treatment, nutritional and diet advice.
LOCATION: Redwell Street, Wellingborough.
OPEN: Ring.
ADMISSION: Charge.   *TEL:* 01933 279974.

HEALTH AND FITNESS STUDIO

FACILITIES: Toning tables, sunbeds, ladies gymnasium with one to one instruction, sunbeds, etc.
LOCATION: 181A Watling St. West, Towcester (above D J Butchers).
OPEN: Ring.
ADMISSION: Charge.   *TEL:* 01327 359990.

HOPPITYS FITNESS FACTORY

FACILITIES: Gym and health equipment.
LOCATION: Grove Works, Grove Road, Northampton.

OPEN: Ring.
ADMISSION: Charge.   *TEL:* 01604 604674.

IMAGE GYM AND HEALTH STUDIO.

FACILITIES: Fully equipped gymnasium with qualified instructors, personalised training programmes, shaping, toning, large Finnish log sauna.
LOCATION: 12 Gregory Street, Northampton, opposite Carlsberg Brewery and St Peter's Way roundabout.
OPEN: Mon-Fri 1100-2100; Sat 1100-1400; Sun 1000-1300 & 1630-1900.
ADMISSION: Charge.   *TEL:* 01604 628793.

IMPULSE FITNESS SUITE

FACILITIES: Purpose-built studio, including facilities for individual computer-designed programmes.
LOCATION: Danes Camp Leisure Centre, Clannel Road, Northampton.
OPEN: Ring.
ADMISSION: Charge - no membership fee.   *TEL:* 01604 705469.

KINGFISHER HEALTH AND LEISURE CENTRE

FACILITIES: Gym, aerobics, toning tables, beauty treatments, etc.
LOCATION: Bective Road and Yelvertoft Road, Northampton.
OPEN: Ring for details.
ADMISSION: Ring for details.   *TEL:* 01604 710805.

THE LAKES GYMNASIUM

FACILITIES: All the latest in get fit technology.
LOCATION: In the Hellidon Lakes complex off the A361 south west of Daventry.
OPEN: Ring for details.
ADMISSION: Fee charged.   *TEL:* 01327 262550.

MIRAGE HEALTH AND FITNESS CENTRE

FACILITIES: Health and fitness programmes, with gym, etc.
LOCATION: 4 Park Road, Wellingborough.
OPEN: Ring.
ADMISSION: Charge.   *TEL:* 01933 228667.

OLYMPIA BODY GYM

FACILITIES: Complete fitness for men and women. Weight training, body building, qualified instructors, sunbeds, saunas, etc.
LOCATION: 30 High Street, High Ferrers.

OPEN: Ring.
ADMISSION: Charge.   *TEL:* 01933 412467.

ONE TO ONE
FACILITIES: Doesn't want fit people - but ordinary people who are unfit and overweight, people with back problems, people who don't want to go to a gym and feel intimidated by beautiful bodies, people who want to get fit safely by regular exercise with a personal qualified instructor.
LOCATION: 16 High March, Daventry.
OPEN: Ring.
ADMISSION: Fee charged.   *TEL:* 01327 871118.

OVERSTONE PARK COUNTRY CLUB
FACILITIES: Fully equipped gymnasium, circuit training, tennis courts, squash courts, snooker hall, outdoor swimming pool, etc. Refreshments and food.
LOCATION: Ecton Lane, Sywell, Northampton.
OPEN: Club 1000-2200; bar 1100-1500. Open all day Sunday.
ADMISSION: Charge.   *TEL:* 01604 647709.

PLANET PULSE
FACILITIES: A fully supervised 30 station fitness centre.
LOCATION: Lings Forum Leisure Centre, Weston Favell Centre, Welligborough Road, Northampton.
OPEN: Ring.
ADMISSION: Charges.   *TEL:* 01604 402833.

RUSHDEN HEALTH AND FITNESS CENTRE
FACILITIES: Qualified instructors on hand to offer regular fitness assessment, combined with body composition testing, used in the preparation of individual training programmes. Fully equipped gymnasium with pin select machines, olympic loose weights, cycles and stepping machines. Programes for fitness, body toning, weight gain, weight loss, body building or strength.
LOCATION: 38 Little Street.
OPEN: Ring.
ADMISSION: Charge.   *TEL:* 01933 56173.

THE SWEAT BOX
FACILITIES: Has a range of facilities, including a beauty therapist and sauna and steam room complex.
LOCATION: 5 Station Close Retail Park, Vicar Lane, Daventry, reached off Southway or from the town centre.
OPEN: Seven days a week - ring for times.

ADMISSION: Fees charged.   TEL: 01327 356173.

THE WATERMARK CLUB

FACILITIES: Pre-assessment and personal programmes, aerobic studio, 20m indoor swimming pool, gym with over 60 pieces of equipment.
LOCATION: Overstone Park, Billing Lane, Northampton.
OPEN: Daily 0700-2100.
ADMISSION: Charges.   TEL: 01604 647666.

THE WORKHOUSE FITNESS CENTRE

FACILITIES: Fast tanning solarium, cardiovascular equipment, ladies only sessions, exclusive range of health products. Free fitness session and personal assessment.
LOCATION: Unit 14, Middle March Industrial Estate, Daventry.
OPEN: Ring for times.
ADMISSION: Charge.   TEL: 01327 31010.

HISTORIC HOUSES AND BUILDINGS

ALTHORP HOUSE

FACILITIES: The seat of the Earl and Countess Spencer. The house was built in the 16th century. There are fine collections of paintings, French and English furniture and porcelain. Museum to Diana, Princess of Wales. She is buried on an island in the Park. There is also a display of carriages, a well laid out garden in 550 acres and an arboretum. Spencer Exhibition in the Courtyard. Shop and refreshments.
LOCATION: A428, 6 miles north west of Northampton.
OPEN: Ring for dates.
ADMISSION: Fee charged.   TEL: 01604 770209.

AYNHO PARK

FACILITIES: A 16th century Mansion rebuilt in the 17th century by Sir John Soane.
LOCATION: 6 miles south west of Brackley on the B4031.
OPEN: May-Sept Wed/Thurs 1400-1600.
ADMISSION: Charge.   TEL: 01869 810636.

BOUGHTON HOUSE

FACILITIES: The House is a vision of Louis XIV's Versailles - transported to the Northamptonshire countryside. The Dukes of Buccleuch and their ancestors have been resident since 1528. There is a world famous armoury and some priceless art treasures. A good collection of 17th/18th century English and French furniture, together with works of art and tapestries. In addition the park is open and there are lakes, nature trails, a picnic area and adventure playground. Teas and gift shop.

LOCATION: Off A43 north of Kettering near Geddington.

OPEN: Daily throughout August - ring for times.

ADMISSION: Charge

TEL: 01536 515731 (Director, Living Landscape Trust).

CANONS ASHBY HOUSE
(National Trust)

FACILITIES: Formerly the home of the Dryden Family it is now in the care of the National Trust. A small manor house with restored gardens, a small park, and church nearby. Some traces of Elizabethan wall panelling and also contemporary paintings in the Spencer Room. Formal garden with axial arrangement of paths and terraces and high stone walls dates mainly from 1708-1710. Free parking, gift shop and teas.

LOCATION: On an unclassified road off the A361 south of Daventry, or off A5 between Weedon and Towcester.

OPEN: 30 Mar-end Oct Wed/Sun/Bank Hol Mon 1300-1730.

ADMISSION: Charge.   *TEL:* 01327 860044.

CHICHELE COLLEGE
(English Heritage)

FACILITIES: Founded in 1422 by Henry Chichele, who was Archbishop of Canterbury. The College, which was built for secular canons, still contains parts of the quadrangle, which incorporates a chapel.

LOCATION: College Street, to the north of the Market Square, Higham Ferrers.

OPEN: Ring for details.

ADMISSION: Ring for details.   *TEL:* 01933 317182.

COSGROVE VIADUCT

FACILITIES: The aquaduct crosses a main road.

LOCATION: Cosgrove to the south of Towcester.

OPEN: Can be seen at any time.

ADMISSION: No charge.   *TEL:* N/A.

COTTESBROOKE HALL

FACILITIES: A Queen Anne House, which has an excellent collection of pictures, especially covering sporting and equestrian subjects. There are also good collections of porcelain and some fine furniture.

According to tradition, this was the house which was the 'model' for Jane Austin's 'Mansfield Park'. Excellent gardens with a wide variety of shrubs, plants, etc.
LOCATION: On an unclassified road off the A5199 to the north west of Northampton.
OPEN: Easter-end Sept, Thurs afternoons and Bank Holiday Mons - 1400-1730. (Parties on other days by prior arrangement).
ADMISSION: Charge.   *TEL:* 01604 505808.

DEENE PARK

FACILITIES: The historic family home of the Brudenell family since 1514, one of whom was the 7th Earl of Cardigan, who led the Charge of the Light Brigade, and some of his 'relics', together with other family heirlooms, are on display. Some additional building took place during the reign of George III. House open, and there are delightful lakeside gardens. Party bookings of 20 or more at any time by prior arrangement.
LOCATION: About half a mile off A43 half way between Kettering and Stamford
OPEN: Easter Sun/Mon, May Bank Hols, Suns - June, July and August, and August Bank Holiday Monday. Park 1300 onwards; House 1400-1700.
ADMISSION: Entrance fee.   *TEL:* 01780 450278/450223.

DELAPRE ABBEY

FACILITIES: Only one of two Cluniac nunneries in England, and was founded in 1145 by Simon de Saint Liz or Senlis - and got its name from the water meadows of the River Nene - de la pre. The present building dates from 1617-51. It became the home of the Northamptonshire Records Office (since moved) in 1958.
LOCATION: London Road.
OPEN: Outside only visible.
ADMISSION: N/A.   *TEL:* N/A.

EDGCOTE HOUSE

FACILITIES: Dating from the mid-18th century it was built by the Chauncey family.
LOCATION: One mile off the A361.
OPEN: By appointment only.
ADMISSION: Charge.   *TEL:* 01295 660257.

ELTON HALL

FACILITIES: Dates back to 1474, and has been the home of the Proby family since the early part of the 17th century, when it was completed by the grandson of the original builder, Sir Peter Proby, Lord Mayor of London, and the land was given to him by Queen Elizabeth I. Extensions were added in the 18th and 19th centuries. The house is an interesting mixtures of styles, which reflect the tastes of succeeding generations. There are many art treasures, including works by Gainsborough, Constable, Reynolds and Millais, as well as some interesting books, the most 'famous' of which is undoubtedly Henry VIII's Prayer Book The delightful gardens include herbaceous borders, a rose garden and extensive shrubberies. Teas available. There is a plant centre in the old walled garden and an oyster bar in the Old Dairy.

LOCATION: 5 miles west of Peterborough on A605.

OPEN: Easter, May, August Bank Hols, July Weds/Suns; August - Wed/Thurs/Sun.

ADMISSION: Charge made.   *TEL:* 01832 280468.

FINEDON WATER TOWER

FACILITIES: Victorian structure has some excellent decorative work and is built from polychromatic bricks. Outside only.

LOCATION: East end of Finedon on A6.

OPEN: Can be seen at all times.

ADMISSION: No charge.   *TEL:* N/A.

FOTHERINGHAY CASTLE

FACILITIES: Erected in the 12th and 13th centuries. Richard III was born here in 1452, and Mary Queen of Scots was beheaded in 1587. The only visible sign of the 'unhappy' place is a mound, which represents the remains of the Castle.

LOCATION: Off the A605 near Fotheringhay village.

OPEN: Farmer allows access to the site in daylight hours - Mid Jan-Dec.

ADMISSION: No charge.   *TEL:* 01832 274333 (Oundle TIC).

THE GUILDHALL

FACILITIES: Built in three phases - 1864, 1892 and 1992, the exquisitely carved outside depicts famous scenes and figures from Northampton's history, including The Trial of Thomas Becket at Northampton Castle, Henry II and the Town Charter of 1189, Henry VI bestowing the Town Charter, the Wedding of Walthheof and Judith, the niece of William the Conqueror. Below the ground floor windows fifty shields can be seen, which represent various villages and towns, trades, local families and crafts from the County. Statue sculptures include those of Thomas Becket, Dryden, Queen Eleanor, Queen Victoria, Richard I and Edward IV - all of whom had connections with the town. Richly decorated interior.

LOCATION: St Giles Square.
OPEN: Tours available.
ADMISSION: Charge for tour.
TEL: 01604 233500 (Northampton Borough Council).

HARRINGWORTH VIADUCT
FACILITIES: A three quarters of a mile long viaduct which spans the Welland Valley, with its 82 arches. It was opened in 1879. Can be viewed from various angles including roads and footpaths in the area.
LOCATION: Off A43 at Harringworth, north east of Corby. Best seen from the lane near Seaton, just to the north of the viaduct.
OPEN: Can be viewed at any time.
ADMISSION: No charge.
TEL: 01536 410266 (Kettering TIC - leaflet available).

HAWKING TOWER
FACILITIES: This folly was built by the second Earl of Stratford and Wentworth, who was responsible for a number of mock Gothic follies on his estate. This is a three stage tower dating from the mid 18th century, and Horace Walpole mentioned it in a letter of 1756.
LOCATION: Boughton.
OPEN: Can be seen at most times.
ADMISSION: No charge.   TEL: N/A.

HELMDON VIADUCT
FACILITIES: The nine-arched viaduct is across the River Tove and was constructed to carry the Geat Central Railway.
LOCATION: 5 miles north of Brackley on a minor road.
OPEN: Can be seen at any time.
ADMISSION: Free.   TEL: N/A.

HINWICK HOUSE
FACILITIES: Queen Anne style house with superb architecture. A distinctive feature is the collection of pictures by such famous masters as Kneller, Lely and Van Dyck. A display of garments - 'A century of clothes' - covers the period 1840-1940. Tapestries, lace, needlework, object d'art, furniture and china complete the displays.
LOCATION: 6 miles south east of Wellingborough and 3.5 miles Rushden off the A6.
OPEN: Mainly by appointment.
ADMISSION: Charge.   TEL: 01933 53624.

HOLDENBY HOUSE

FACILITIES: 16th-19th century furniture, historical and sporting pictures, King Charles I memorabilia and piano museum.

LOCATION: Signposted 6 miles north west of Northampton off A5199 or A428.

OPEN: Easter Mon, Mayday Bank Hol Mon, Aug Bank Hol Mon, and for groups of 25 by prior arrangement

ADMISSION: Charge. **TEL:** 01604 770241 (house visits).

KELMARSH HALL

FACILITIES: A red brick Palladian house which was built by James Gibbs in 1728, and later extended in 1870.

FACILITIES: Has a collection of porcelain jars, fine china, furniture, paintings, and gardens.

LOCATION: Kelmarsh is off the A508, 11 miles north of Northampton.

OPEN: Ring for details.

ADMISSION: Charge. **TEL:** 01604 686543.

KETTERING RAILWAY STATION

FACILITIES: Leaflet available giving details of the building.

LOCATION: Station Road, off the A43 Northampton-Stamford road.

OPEN: Can be seen at most times.

ADMISSION: No charge. **TEL:** 01536 410266.

KIRBY HALL
(English Heritage)

FACILITIES: Begun in 1570 alterations were made in the 17th century. Soon after completion it came into the hands of Sir Christopher Hatton. It is a fine example of a large, stone-built Elizabethan mansion. The House is open, and there are fine gardens currently being restored.

LOCATION: On a minor road off the A43 4 miles north of Corby.

OPEN: 1 April-31 Oct daily from 1000-1800; 1 Nov-31 Mar Wed-Sun 1000-1600. Closed 24-26 Dec, 1 Jan.

ADMISSION: Charge. **TEL:** 01536 203230.

LAMPORT HALL AND GARDEN

FACILITIES: The home of the Isham family for more than 400 years. The Hall contains a wealth of outstanding furniture, books and paintings collected by the Ishams when the third baronet did the Grand Tour of Europe in the 1670's. Events take place most months, and include craft, gift, doll and antique fairs, as well as opera, theatre and jazz evenings. The Hall is also available for Conferences, group visits and corporate entertainments, as well as private parties. Private group visits by arrangement.

LOCATION: On the A508 between Northampton and Market Harborough.
OPEN: Ring for details.
ADMISSION: Charges depending on event. *TEL:* 01604 686272.

LYVEDEN NEW BIELD
(National Trust)

FACILITIES: The original idea was that the building would symbolise the Passion of Christ, but it was never finished. Begun by Sir Thomas Tresham in 1595, he was later imprisoned, and was castigated because of his Catholic beliefs. When he died in 1605 work stopped on the building. Parking is available about half a mile from the New Bield.
LOCATION: On an unclassified road, off the A427 Corby-Oundle Road, or A6116, to the south east of Corby/south west of Oundle.
OPEN: All year 0900-dusk.
ADMISSION: Charge. *TEL:* 01832 205358 (Custodian).

THE MENAGERIE

FACILITIES: The folly was built in the 1750's and fell into disrepair, but has been restored. There is some outstanding Rococo plasterwork in the main room, and this includes the signs of the zodiac. Lord Halifax once kept animals in the gardens. New gardens have been created in recent years and include wetland, bog, shrubberies, etc. There is also a grotto and two thatched arbours.
LOCATION: Horton.
OPEN: Gardens - Thurs from April-end Sept - 1000-1600; house, grotto and gardens to parties of 20 or more.
ADMISSION: Charge. *TEL:* 01604 870957.

NEWNHAM MILL

FACILITIES: The mill was built in 1790 on the top of 600 foot Newnham Hill, but was not used after 1860. It has now been converted into an observation platform. Good views from the top. Maximum group of twelve people at any one time.
LOCATION: On the minor road from Newnham to Daventry. There is a car park just before the flyover across the A45. Footpath up the hill to the Mill.
OPEN: By arrangement. *TEL:* 01327 300277 (Daventry TIC to obtain key).

PREBENDAL MANOR HOUSE

FACILITIES: Considered to be the oldest building of its kind in the County. It stands on the site of what is thought to be one of King Canut's

Royal manors. The present house was constructed in the 13th century, although it is much reduced. It has been occupied since Saxon times. A substantial timber aisled hall was revealed as the result of archaeological work. There is a 15th century dovecote and medieval fishponds. A small museum is housed in the 18th century tithe barn.

LOCATION: Nassington, on an unclassified road reached from the A605, A47 or A1.

OPEN: By prior arrangement.

ADMISSION: Charge. **TEL:** 01780 782575.

PRIEST'S HOUSE
(National Trust)

FACILITIES: Pre-Reformation priest's lodge, built of local stone in 15th or 16th century and of architectural interest. There is a small museum showing bygones of the village of Easton-on-the-Hill.

LOCATION: South of Stamford and off the A43, at Easton-on-the-Hill.

OPEN: See noticeboard at site.

ADMISSION: Free. **TEL:** 01780 62506.

ROCKINGHAM CASTLE

FACILITIES: On the site of a former Saxon fortress, Rokingham Castle was built by William the Conqueror. Henry VIII gave it to Edward Watson in 1530, who carried out some restoration work on the Norman building. The Long Gallery contains a fine collection of paintings and furniture, and the Tudor Great Hall has many exhibits from the Civil War. Outside a street contains a bakery, laundry and brewhouse. There is also a church and chapel, together with Salvin's Flag Tower. Educational activities available with a supply of material, including topics covering literature, history and art, together with a trails leaflet. Gift shop and tea-room.

LOCATION: 2 miles north of Corby on A60003.

OPEN: Easter Sun-end Sept, Suns/Thurs/Bank Hol Mons and Tues. following/Tues during August. 1300-1730. Any other time by prior arrangement.

ADMISSION: Charge. **TEL:** 01536 770240.

ROUND HOUSE

FACILITIES: This is a circular house with a central chimney and was erected by General Arbuthnot of Woodford to commemorate the Duke of Wellington's visit and the Battle of Waterloo, after Wellington commented that the local landscape was like that when he

fought the Battle of Waterloo.
LOCATION: 2 miles north of Finedon on the A510.
OPEN: Exterior can be seen at any time.
ADMISSION: N/A.   *TEL:* N/A.

ROYAL THEATRE

FACILITIES: Opened on 5 May 1884, it was designed by Charles Phipps, who also designed the Savoy Theatre in London.   There was a serious fire in 1887, but the building was restored.   The Theatre has a typical Victorian interior, with a superbly embellished auditorium, and Corinthian pillars supporting the boxes.
LOCATION: Guildhall Road, Northampton.
OPEN: Open days arranged - tel for details.   *TEL:* 01604 38343.

RUSHTON TRIANGULAR LODGE
(National Trust)

FACILITIES: Built by Sir Thomas Tresham, the person responsible for Lyveden New Bield, it was a testimony to his devout Catholic beliefs. There are 3-storeys, each having three sided chimneys; three walls, 3 triangular gables and windows, all depicting the Trinity theme.
LOCATION: 3 miles from Desborough, 1 mile west of Rushton on minor road.
OPEN: April-September 0930-1830; Sun 1400-1830.
ADMISSION: Charge.   *TEL:* 01536 710761

SOUTHWICK HALL

FACILITIES: Dates from the early part of the 14th century, and has been owned successively by just three families. The House is interesting because it illustrates the development of the manor house, and at the same time remains the Capron family home.   Eleven rooms are open to the public, including an exhibition of Victorian clothes which were worn by members of the Capron family. There are several collections, including lace, children's toys and other artefacts dating from the Victorian era.   Victorian and Edwardian Exhibition, collection of carpentry and rural tools, home-made teas.   The Stable Block has an interesting exhibition; there is also a huge birch tree which is referred to as the 'Elephant Tree'.
LOCATION: On a minor road off the A427 Corby-Oundle road and to the north of Oundle.
OPEN: Bank Hol Suns/Mons from Easter to August. Wed from May-August. 1200-1700.
ADMISSION: Charge.   *TEL:* 01832 274064.

STOKE PARK PAVILIONS

FACILITIES: This was thought to have been the first Palladian country house to be built in Britain, and consists of two pavillions and a colomnade. Exterior only on view.
LOCATION: 7 miles from Northampton off the A508 and in the village of Stoke Bruerne.
OPEN: Jun/Jul/Aug Sat/Sun/Bank Hols 01400-1800.
ADMISSION: Charge.   *TEL:* 01604 862172.

SULGRAVE MANOR

FACILITIES: House of the ancestors of George Washington.   Good example of a small manor house, with various gardens one of which has a 16th century sundial. An intriguing kitchen and fine examples of furniture.   A wide range of activities arranged throughout the year.   The 18th century Brew House has been made into a Visitors' Centre.   This includes a shop, tea and coffee room and audio visual room, with a museum of the Manor and surrounding village.
LOCATION: Sulgrave village, on an unclassified road 8 miles north west of Brackley.
OPEN: Daily (not Wed) 1 April-31 Oct - 1030-1300 & 1400-1730 (1600 in Oct). Weekends Mar/Nov/Dec 1030-1300 & 1400-1600. Closed Jan, 25/26 Dec.
ADMISSION: Charge.   *TEL:* 01295 760205.

HISTORIC MONUMENTS, MEMORIALS AND SITES

AMERICAN MEMORIAL

FACILITIES: A memorial to the American airmen who used Spanhoe airfield.
LOCATION: On the road to Laxton, near the former Spanhoe airfield.
OPEN: Always.
ADMISSION: No charge.   *TEL:* 01832 274333.

APETHORPE STOCKS AND WHIPPING POST.

FACILITIES: Probably erected in the 18th century, and the only surviving example in the country of a stocks bench can also be seen.
LOCATION: In Bridge Street, opposite St Leonard's Church and the War Memorial. Please ensure you do not park near the bend. Cars can be parked in Main Street or further up Bridge Street.
OPEN: Can be seen at any time.
ADMISSION: No charge.

TEL: 01604 237272 (Northamptonshire Heritage) in case of difficulty.

AYNHO STOCKS
FACILITIES: Dating from the 18th century, they were in use until the middle of the last century.
LOCATION: 6 miles south west of Brackley, opposite 32 Roundtown - which is a busy point. Park in the centre of the village.
OPEN: Always.
ADMISSION: No charge.   **TEL:** 01280 700111 (Brackley TIC).

BOCASE STONE
FACILITIES: The Bocase tree is now marked by a stone, the significance of which has never been fully explained. It is believed that the tree was the one designated for the site of the Saxon Forest Courts, and the tree was immortalised by the stone. The stone was erected in the reign of Charles I.
LOCATION: Public bridleway near Brigstock.
OPEN: Can be viewed at most times.
ADMISSION: No charge.   **TEL:** N/A.

BOUGHTON - OBELISK
FACILITIES: Built in 1764 by Lord Stafford, who lived in what was then Boughton Park, it was erected to the memory of the 4th Duke of Devonshire to commemorate his associations with the village.
LOCATION: About 400 metres off the A508, 2.5 miles from Northampton.
OPEN: Can be seen at most times.
ADMISSION: No charge.   **TEL:** N/A.

CHARLES BRADLAUGH
FACILITIES: Statue erected in 1894 to this MP, a very radical and outspoken person on religious matters. He was the first aetheist to sit in the Houses of Parliament. First elected in 1880, he refused to take the oath, and was dismissed, again being elected in 1881, 1882, 1884 and 1885, but was dismissed each time until the Speaker eventually admitted him in 1886. He was Liberal MP for Northampton.
LOCATION: Abington Square.
OPEN: At all times.
ADMISSION: No charge.   **TEL:** N/A.

BRIGSTOCK MARKET CROSS
FACILITIES: Erected in 1586, the cross is engraved with the initials and coat of arms of Queen Elizabeth I. Other initials recorded include

James II, Queen Anne and Queen Victoria. It is 'used' each year in the May Queen crowning.

LOCATION: Brigstock is just off the A6116, 5 miles south east of Corby. The cross is on a traffic island on Hall Hill, and the junction of Mill Lane and Church Street, next to the war memorial. Take care when parking - Brigstock is a busy village.

OPEN: Can be viewed at any time.

ADMISSION: Free.

TEL: 01604 237272 (Northamptonshire Heritage) in case of difficulty.

ROBERT BROWNE

FACILITIES: A Monument erected to the founder of the Brownists, which later became the Congregational Church. He is buried in the churchyard. Thought to have been born about 1550, and after spending time preaching against the Church of England, he travelled around the country, eventually settling in Northampton. He died in Northampton Goal some people suggest for attacking a constable, others for not paying a parish rate.

LOCATION: South side of St Giles Churchyard in St Giles Terrace/Spencer Parade.

OPEN: Can be seen at most times.

ADMISSION: No charge. **TEL:** N/A

BULWICK

FACILITIES: Market cross with medieval base.

LOCATION: In the centre of the village.

OPEN: Can be seen at most times.

ADMISSION: No charge. **TEL:** N/A.

BULWICK DOVECOTE

FACILITIES: This circular building probably dates from the 18th century.

LOCATION: Ring for details.

OPEN: Ring.

ADMISSION: No charge. **TEL:** 01780 450249 (The Rectory, Church Lane).

CHARWELTON PACKHORSE BRIDGE

FACILITIES: Thought to date from the 15th century this miniature stone bridge, which is only about a metre wide, once spanned the infant River Cherwell.

LOCATION: On the A361 just as you enter Charwelton.

OPEN: Always.

ADMISSION: No charge. **TEL:** N/A.

COBBLERS LAST

FACILITIES: This sculpture 'dominates' the pedestrianised Abington Street, and is a continuing reminder of the importance of the shoe trade to the town.

LOCATION: Abington Street, near the entrance to the Grosvenor Centre.

OPEN: Can be seen at all times.

ADMISSION: No charge. **TEL:** N/A.

CORBY STEELWORKER

FACILITIES: A memorial to the men and women who built Corby into the bustling town which exists today.

LOCATION: In the centre of town.

OPEN: Can be seen at all times.

ADMISSION: No charge. **TEL:** N/A.

CRANFORD ST ANDREW DOVECOTE

FACILITIES: Dates from the late 17th century. It is circular with potence - revolving ladder.

LOCATION: Off St Andrews Lane - contact Dairy Farm, St Andrews Lane for access.

OPEN: Exterior only can be viewed at any time.

ADMISSION: No charge. **TEL:** 01536 330273.

DAVENTRY MONUMENT

FACILITIES: Known locally as the Burton Memorial, it was erected at the beginning of the 20th century in memory of a Mr Burton who had been a part-time town clerk. A well-known huntsman, he was also a point-to-point rider. The money for the memorial came from a public appeal. At the time of construction a drinking fountain and trough were incorporated.

LOCATION: Opposite the Market Square at the end of High Street.

OPEN: Always on view.

ADMISSION: No charge. **TEL:** N/A.

DENTON DOVECOTE

FACILITIES: This 17th century building is circular.

LOCATION: Access by calling at Holly Cottage, 3 Main Street.

OPEN: Ring

ADMISSION: No charge. **TEL:** 01604 890228 (Mr and Mrs Pendered).

DESBOROUGH - OLD TOWN CROSS

FACILITIES: Not unlike a gateway pillar, the town cross is in the form of a tall square column, on top of which is a stone sphere. It is believed to have come from Harrington Hall demolished in 1745.
LOCATION: High Street, Desborough, off the A6.
OPEN: Can be seen at all times.
ADMISSION: No charge. *TEL:* N/A.

DUDDINGTON DOVECOTE

FACILITIES: Dating from the 18th century this is a rectangular dovecote with two rooms.
LOCATION: Ring.
OPEN: Ring.
ADMISSION: No charge. *TEL:* 01780 52075 (Burghley Estate Office).

ALFRED EAST

FACILITIES: A bronze bust which was erected in front of the Art Gallery to this well known painter who was born in the town in 1849. He became an internationally recognised painter of landscapes, and left pictures to the town with the proviso that a gallery was built to house them.
LOCATION: In front of the Alfred East Art Gallery in Sheep Street in the centre of Kettering.
OPEN: Can be seen at all times.
ADMISSION: No charge. *TEL:* N/A.

ELEANOR CROSS, Geddington

FACILITIES: Considered to be the finest of the three remaining crosses. These were erected to mark the resting places of the cortege of Queen Eleanor of Castile, and put in place by her husband, Edward I. At Geddington there was also a royal hunting box, which has since gone, but the cross has survived. The slender, finely carved shaft has three statues of Queen Eleanor. Triangular in design, the cross has three storeys. Six small shields bear the arms of England, Castile and Leon-on-Ponthieu. The cross was built mainly from Weldon stone, although Stanion stone (slightly harder in texture) was used for the weatherings and string courses. The cross is in the open and can be viewed.
LOCATION: Situated in the village of Geddington and off the A43 Kettering to Stamford road.
OPEN: Always.
ADMISSION: Free. *TEL:* 01536 410266 (Kettering TIC).

ELEANOR CROSS, Hardingstone

FACILITIES: Was thought to be the first of (possibly) 12 which were built. Erected in 1291, it was on the old turnpike road leading to London. The cross is on the brow of a hill overlooking both the town of Northampton and the Nene Valley. There are four storeys to the cross, and each is smaller than the one below it. Sixteen different shields are displayed on a pointed pediment.
LOCATION: On the A508 south of Northampton.
OPEN: Viewing can be made at any time.
ADMISSION: Free.   *TEL:* 01604 22677 (Northampton Visitor Centre).

EYDON STOCKS AND WHIPPING POST
FACILITIES: Dating from the end of last century/beginning of this century.
LOCATION: The Green - but please park in the High Street.
OPEN: Can be viewed at any time.
ADMISSION: No charge.
TEL: 01604 237272 (Northamptonshire Heritage) in case of difficulty.

FINEDON - DIRECTION PILLAR
FACILITIES: This small pyramid shaped 'building' once had mileages recorded on it. It was erected by Sir English Dolben of Finedon Hall in thankfulness of a number of blessings for that year.
LOCATION: On the A510 by the crossroads and 3 miles north east of Wellingbrough.
OPEN: Can be seen at all times.
ADMISSION: No charge.   *TEL:* N/A.

FURTHO DOVECOTE
FACILITIES: This is a medieval building of circular design with additions being made in the 17th and 18th centuries.
LOCATION: Can only be reached on foot either from the Grafton Way or along a bridleway through Furtho Manor Farm.   Care must be taken as this is a working farm.
OPEN: Daylight hours.
ADMISSION: No charge.
TEL: 01604 237272 (Northamptonshire Heritage) in case of difficulty.

GRETTON STOCKS AND WHIPPING POST
FACILITIES: Thought to date from the 18th century, these were used until 1858.
LOCATION: The Green, High Street.
OPEN: Can be seen at all times.
ADMISSION: No charge.

TEL: 01604 237272 (Northamptonshire Heritage) in case of difficulty.

IRTHLINGBOROUGH CROSS

FACILITIES: Of late 13th century construction, this was a preaching cross. The shaft is 13 feet in height, and according to tradition it was used in medieval times as a standard for the pole to measure out shares in the open fields.
LOCATION: At the junction of Finedon Road, Station Road and High Street - on a roundabout. The cross should be viewed from the pavement as this is a very busy junction.
OPEN: Can be seen at any time.
ADMISSION: No charge.
TEL: 01604 237272 (Northamptonshire Heritage) in case of difficulty.

KINGS SUTTON STOCKS

FACILITIES: Thought to date from the 18th century.
LOCATION: The Square, near the Bell Inn.
OPEN: Can be seen at all times.
ADMISSION: No charge.
TEL: 01604 237272 (Northamptonshire Heritage) in case of difficulty.

KINGS SUTTON WELL HEAD

FACILITIES: This 19th century replica was built when the road passing the original well was diverted. The original St Rumbald's well was well known for its healing waters.
LOCATION: On the Charlton road, as you leave Kings Sutton. Please park in the village and walk.
OPEN: Can be seen at any time.
ADMISSION: No charge.
TEL: 01604 237272 (Northamptonshire Heritage) in case of difficulty.

LITTLE HOUGHTON STOCKS AND WHIPPING POST

FACILITIES: The original stocks date from the 18th century, but were replaced in 1835.
LOCATION: On Bedford Road, outside the Post office. The stocks are close to a junction, and care needs to be taken when parking.
OPEN: Any time.
ADMISSION: No charge.
TEL: 01604 237272 (Northamptonshire Heritage) in case of difficulty.

LONG BUCKBY CASTLE

FACILITIES: Constructed in the 12th century this Ringwork and Bailey now survives as an earthwork. There is an information board on site.

LOCATION: The castle is signposted from the Market Square and reached through The Poplars.
OPEN: Any reasonable time.
ADMISSION: No charge.   *TEL:* 01604 237272.

MARSTON TRUSSELL GATES

FACILITIES: These were originally erected at Brampton Ash Hall in the late 17th century, and moved to their present position when the Hall was demolished in 1750.
LOCATION: Marston Trussell Hall, Theddington Road. Very narrow road - take care when parking.
OPEN: Daylight hours.
ADMISSION: No charge.
TEL: 01604 237272 (Northamptonshire Heritage) in case of difficulty.

E R MOBBS

FACILITIES: A Monument to the Commanding Officer of the 7th Battalion the Northamptonshire Regiment who was killed in action at Ypres during the First World War. His bust is at the base of a pedstal depicting a battle scene together with a football scene, because he was also a well-known sportsman. The memorial was moved from the Market Place in 1931.
LOCATION: Abington Square, Northampton.
OPEN: At all times.
ADMISSION: No charge.   *TEL:* N/A.

NASEBY OBELISK (BATTLE MONUMENT)

FACILITIES: To commemorate the Battle of Naseby (1645) the obelisk was erected in 1823, but was later found to be on the wrong site. There is an information board near the obelisk.
LOCATION: East side of Clipston road. Park in layby.
OPEN: Can be viewed at all times.
ADMISSION: No charge.   *TEL:* N/A.

NASEBY BATTLE MONUMENT - 1936

FACILITIES: This was erected on the 'exact' site of the battle, and marks the position where Oliver Cromwell led the cavalry charge. Information board on site. Parking in layby.
LOCATION: Along a field path 50 metres to the left of the Sibbertoft Road and 1.5 miles from Naseby.
OPEN: Can be viewed at all times.
ADMISSION: No charge.   *TEL:* N/A.

ORLINGBURY DOVECOTE

FACILITIES: This is a square 17th century dovecote with a very low door!

LOCATION: Reached from The Green, and then into Rectory Lane. Dovecote Yard is on the left just before the Village Hall. Contact the keyholders - see below.

OPEN: Most reasonable times.

ADMISSION: No charge.   *TEL:* 01933 678386 or 01933 678474.

OVERSTONE GATES

FACILITIES: These were erected at Pytchley Hall at the beginning of the 17th century, but were moved to their present site when the building was demolished in 1824.

LOCATION: Half a mile from Overstone, on the Sywell Road.

OPEN: Can be seen at any time.

ADMISSION: No charge.

TEL: 01604 237272 (Northamptonshire Heritage) in case of difficulty.

PITSFORD - MEMORIAL TO CHARLES COMPTON

FACILITIES: The memorial was erected to Charles Compton who died as the result of a riding accident when hunting with the Pytchley on 9 Nov 1907.

LOCATION: Pitford, 5.5 miles north of Northampton off A508.

OPEN: Can be seen at all times.

ADMISSION: No charge.   *TEL:* N/A.

SISTERS OF NOTRE DAME

FACILITIES: A plaque and a memorial to the Sisters of Notre Dame of Namur who established the Notre Dame High School in Abington Street. There is also a small garden of remembrance to the Sisters.

LOCATION: Notre Dame Mews, off Abington Street.

OPEN: Daylight hours - plaques can be viewed at any time.

ADMISSION: No charge.   *TEL:* N/A.

SULGRAVE STOCKS AND WHIPPING POST

FACILITIES: Reconstructed in 1933.

LOCATION: On the Green at the junction of Magpie Lane and Park Road.

OPEN: Can be seen at any time.

ADMISSION: No charge.

TEL: 01604 237272 (Northamptonshire Heritage) in case of diificulties.

384th BOMBARDMENT GROUP (HEAVY)

FACILITIES: A granite monument erected for the above group.

LOCATION: Geddington-Grafton Underwood Road on the site of the main runway.

OPEN: Can be viewed at any time.

ADMISSION: No charge. *TEL:* N/A.

US 351 BOMBER GROUP

FACILITIES: Triangular memorial in Welsh marble to the bomber group which flew from Polebrook airfield.

LOCATION: On the runway on the Hemington road.

OPEN: Can be seen at most times.

ADMISSION: Free. *TEL:* 01832 274333 (Oundle TIC).

WADENHOE DOVECOTE

FACILITIES: Thought to date from the 18th century, this circular building has a potence (a revolving ladder).

LOCATION: The gated paddock on the east side of Pilton Road, and virtually opposite to the Wadenhoe Trust Office.

OPEN: Most reasonable times.

ADMISSION: No charge.

TEL: 01604 237272 (Northamptonshire Heritage) in case of difficulty.

WALGRAVE MOAT

FACILITIES: All that remains of the earthen banks and ditches which were part of the medieval moated manor house and the surrounding fishponds.

LOCATION: Turn off Old Road into Newlands Road, then second right into the Village Hall car park. It is necessary to walk to the bottom of the recreation field.

OPEN: Can be seen at most times.

ADMISSION: No charge.

TEL: 01604 237272 (Northamptonshire Heritage) in case of difficulty.

WARMINGTON DOVECOTE

FACILITIES: This circular 17th century dovecote has lathe and plaster nestboxes and a potence (a revolving ladder).

LOCATION: Reached from Eaglethorpe Farm, which is off Eaglethorpe Green in the village.

OPEN: Ring before visiting.

ADMISSION: No charge. *TEL:* 01832 280223 (Elton Estate Office).

WILBARSTON DOVECOTE

FACILITIES: The original dovecote was of medieval origin, and there is now only one rectangular wall left. This has eight rows of nesting boxes.
LOCATION: In the grounds of Wilbarston Primary School, School Lane.
OPEN: Term time - ring first.
ADMISSION: No charge. *TEL:* 01536 771252.

HORSE DRAWN VEHICLES

T A & M HARDING

FACILITIES: Horse drawn vehicles for hire.
LOCATION: The Bungalow Farm, Watford Road, Crick.
OPEN: Ring.
ADMISSION: Charges. *TEL:* 01788 822338.

TRADITIONAL HORSE DRAWN CARRIAGE CO

FACILITIES: Tours through country lanes, along forest trails, etc.
LOCATION: Horton Stables, Little Horton Drive, Horton, Northampton.
OPEN: Ring.
ADMISSION: Charges. *TEL:* 01604 870039.

YOUR CARRIAGE AWAITS

FACILITIES: Horse drawn vehicle hire.
LOCATION: Firs Cottage, 74 Queen Street, Weedon.
OPEN: Ring.
ADMISSION: Charges. *TEL:* 01327 342121.

HORSE RIDING

See Equestrian Centres

INFORMATION AND ADVICE

THE ASSISTANT COUNTY LIBRARIAN (INFORMATION)

FACILITIES: A comprehensive sports information service is available through the above officer of Northamptonshire County Council.
LOCATION: N/A.
OPEN: N/A.

195

ADMISSION: N/A.　　　　**TEL:** 01604 20252 EX 412.

BRIDLEWAYS
FACILITIES: Has details of bridleways in the county.
LOCATION: N/A.
OPEN: 0900-1700 - for information.
ADMISSION: N/A.　　　　**TEL:** 01604 237583.

CANALS IN NORTHAMPTONSHIRE
FACILITIES: Gives information about the canals in the county.
LOCATION: In the county.
OPEN: N/A.
ADMISSION:　Charge for leaflet available from Libraries, TIC's, Countryside Centre, Country Parks.
TEL: 01604 237220 (Countryside Centre).

CHURCH ARCHITECTURE IN NORTHAMPTONSHIRE
FACILITIES: Leaflet with text and illustrations to explain the church architectural styles in the County.
LOCATION: Useful when visiting churches.
OPEN: N/A.
ADMISSION:　Charge for leaflet available from Northamptonshire Libraries, TIC's, Country Parks, the Countryside Centre.
TEL: 01604 237220 (Countryside Centre).

COMSPORT
FACILITIES: Arranges sporting activities where it is not possible to have regular events,
LOCATION: One operates in Daventry District; the other in Wellingborough.
OPEN: Ring for information.
ADMISSION: Charges made.
TEL: 01327 786332 (Daventry District); 01933 440044(Wellingborough)

CONTACT - THE NORTHAMPTONSHIRE GUIDE TO SPORTING OPPORTUNITY
FACILITIES:　A comprehensive listing of national sporting organisations, local groups and organisations, as well as facilities, e.g. ice rinks/stadium.
LOCATION: N/A.
OPEN: N/A.
ADMISSION: N/A.
TEL: 01604 236454 (Leisure Services, Northamptonshire CC).

COUNTY HERITAGE SITES

FACILITIES: The leaflet lists the historic buildings and monuments in the care of Northamptonshire County Council.

LOCATION: The 25 buildings and monuments are in various parts of the County.

OPEN: See leaflet for details.

ADMISSION: No charge for visiting the sites. Leaflet available from Northamptonshire Heritage. *TEL:* 01604 237272.

COUNTRYSIDE PUBLICATIONS 'HERITAGE SERIES' AND 'OUT AND ABOUT HERITAGE' SERIES.

FACILITIES: A range of leaflets about various aspects of the Northamptonshire countryside - from folklore to village walks.

LOCATION: N/A.

OPEN: N/A.

ADMISSION: Charges for leaflets - for full list contact The Countryside Centre.

TEL: 01604 237220.

DAVENTRY DISTRICT - MINI GUIDE

FACILITIES: The leaflet gives background information to the area, together with places to visit and things to do, including a town trail, places of interest, sports and leisure.

LOCATION: Around the Daventry area.

OPEN: N/A.

ADMISSION: N/A.   *TEL:* 01327 300277 (TIC).

DAVENTRY DISTRICT SPORTS FEDERATION

FACILITIES: Aims to bring together sports organisations, clubs and key individuals to promote and develop participation in sport within Daventry District. Organises various events, including an annual sports forum and administers a sports fund. Produces a quarterly newsletter.

LOCATION: N/A.

OPEN: N/A.

ADMISSION: N/A.

TEL: 01327 302413 (Daventry DC Sports Development Unit).

DISCOVER NORTHAMPTONSHIRE'S COUNTRYSIDE

FACILITIES: Published regularly it gives up-to-date information about the county's country parks, footpaths, etc, with telephone numbers, etc.

Free, copies are available from The Countryside Centre, Guildhall Road, TIC's, Country Parks, Libraries, etc.
TEL: 01604 237220. (Countryside Centre).

EAST MIDLANDS REGIONAL SPORTS COUNCIL DIRECTORY
FACILITIES: A Directory gives details of various sporting activities in the County.
LOCATION: N/A.
OPEN: N/A.
ADMISSION: Charge for Directory.
TEL: 01602 821887/822586.

ENVIRONMENT BRANCH, NORTHAMPTONSHIRE COUNTY COUNCIL'S PLANNING AND TRANSPORTATION DEPARTMENT
FACILITIES: Able to offer advice and information on a number of aspects of the environment. These include landscape, recreation, nature conservation, cycling, tourism, environmental grants and environmental improvements. The Branch is also responsible for the Nene Valley Project, and has involvement with Rockingham Forest Trust.
LOCATION: N/A.
ADMISSION: N/A.
OPEN: 0900-1700 Mon-Thurs; 0900-1630 Fri. *TEL:* 01604 236737.

ENVIRONMENTAL PROJECTS AND TOURISM OFFICER, NORTHAMPTONSHIRE COUNTY COUNCIL
FACILITIES: Involved with envirornnental projects (such as picnic sites) and deals with tourism.
LOCATION: Countywide.
OPEN: Office hours.
ADMISSION: N/A.   *TEL:* 01604 236736.

EXPLORING THE NENE VALLEY
FACILITIES: A leaflet which gives details of the facilities along the Nene Valley, including trout fishing, nature reserves, picnic sites, horse riding centres, cycletours, countryside walks, etc.
LOCATION: In the Nene Valley.
OPEN: See leaflet.
ADMISSION: Charge for leaflet.
TEL: 01604 236633 (Nene Valley Project).

FUSION - THE YOUTH ZONE DROP IN AND INFORMATION SHOP

FACILITIES: For young people: there is information on anything and everything - education, employment training, environment, Europe, health, sport, leisure, travel, etc. Free and confidential service. Also pool, SkyTV, video games, refreshments.
LOCATION: 4 Cheyne Walk.
OPEN: Mon-Thurs 1300-1900; Fri 1300-1600; Sat 1000-1200 and 1300 1600.
ADMISSION: No charge.   *TEL:* 01604 38834.

GROUP TRAVEL GUIDE

FACILITIES: This guide gives information for groups visiting the county, and includes details of itineries, hotels, places to vsit, etc. There are clear maps and touring information.
LOCATION: In and around Northamptonshire.
OPEN: See brochure.
ADMISSION: Guide is free to restricted clientelle. *TEL:* 01604 671400.

HERITAGE EDUCATION AND INTERPRETATION

FACILITIES: Provides services for schools on heritage education and interpretation; sometimes has displays.
LOCATION: N/A.
OPEN: 0900-1700.
ADMISSION: Charges for services.   *TEL:* 01604 237248.

HISTORIC SITES AND LANDSCAPES - NORTHAMPTONSHIRE COUNTY COUNCIL.

FACILITIES: Has a list of the historic sites and historic landscapes in the County.
LOCATION: N/A.
OPEN: 0900-1700   *TEL:* 01604 237242.

MONUMENTS IN NORTHAMPTONSHIRE

FACILITIES: Gives details of many of the interesting monuments in the County.
LOCATION: Around Northamptonshire.
OPEN: Monuments can be 'visited' at most times.
ADMISSION: Charge for leaflet - available from Countryside Centre, Northamptonshire Libraries, TIC's, Country Parks, etc.
TEL: 01604 237220 (Countryside Centre).

NENN - NORTHAMPTONSHIRE ENVIRONMENTAL NETWORK NEWSLETTER

FACILITIES: Carries details of local groups, activities, calendar of activities, etc.

LOCATION: Across the County.

ADMISSION: Subscription fee to newsletter.

OPEN: N/A.   *TEL:* 01604 630719.

NORTHAMPTON CENTRAL LIBRARY

FACILITIES: Sports Information Point. Points exist at other places in the County.

LOCATION: Abington Street

OPEN: Usual library hours - ring for times.

ADMISSION: No charge.   *TEL:* 01604 626774.

NORTHAMPTONSHIRE CHAMBER OF COMMERCE, TRAINING AND ENTERPRISE TOURISM AND CONFERENCE BUREAU

FACILITIES: Produces a series of leaflets and provides other information about the county. Publications include Touring Map, Where to Stay brochure, Waterways Guide, Tales of the Unexpected and Calendar of Events.

LOCATION: N/A.

OPEN: N/A.

ADMISSION: Charges for some events/activities. *TEL:* 01604 671400.

NORTHAMPTONSHIRE COUNTRYSIDE CENTRE

FACILITIES: Has an up-to-date list of countryside activities, together with information on groups, including addresses and telephone numbers. If they don't have it, they are usually able to find out through their links with many other organisations.

FACILITIES: Apart from a visit to the Centre help is available by telephoning. Also has a wide range of leaflets, booklets, books, information, gifts, etc.

LOCATION: 9 Guildhall Road, Northampton.

OPEN: Tues-Fri 1000-1700, Sat 1000-1600.

ADMISSION: Free.   *TEL:* 01604 237220.

NORTHAMPTONSHIRE COUNTRYSIDE SERVICES

FACILITIES: Part of the County Council's Planning and Transportation Department. Offers advice and information on a wide variety of topics. including the six country parks - as well as involvement and links with numerous other groups around the county.

200

LOCATION: Telephone calls only.
OPEN: Office Hours.
ADMISSION: N/A.
TEL: 01604 236236 (ask for Countryside Services) or 237220 (Countryside Centre).

NORTHAMPTONSHIRE FARM HOLIDAYS
FACILITIES: This group of independent working families provides accommodation and is registered with the English Tourist Board. A range of farmhouse bed and breakfast and self catering accommodation in the county. Covers areas as far apart as Sibbertoft (with fishing and 4WD off road track) to Fotheringhay in the Nene Valley.
LOCATION: Various places around the County.
OPEN: Most open all year.
ADMISSION: Charges. TEL: 01604 770990 (Secretary).

NORTHAMPTONSHIRE HERITAGE
FACILITIES: Able to offer advice about archaeological sites in the County.
LOCATION: Telephone calls only.
OPEN: Office hours.
ADMISSION: N/A. TEL: 01604 237246.

NORTHAMPTONSHIRE LIBRARIES
Can help with natural history, history, geology, etc. Please see under main heading LIBRARIES.

NORTHAMPTONSHIRE ON HORSEBACK
FACILITIES: This guide gives details of 23 interesting trails throughout Northamptonshire.
LOCATION: Different parts of the county.
OPEN: Usually accessible.
ADMISSION: Publication priced £5.95. TEL: 01604 237220.

NORTHAMPTONSHIRE RECORD OFFICE
FACILITIES: Has a wealth of material relating to villages and towns around the county, including charters, court rolls, deeds, parish and nonconformist registers, maps, letters, photographs and films. It also publishes a number of booklets, etc. Documents can be photocopied, provided there is no infringement of copyright, which will be discussed by the Record Office.
LOCATION: Wootton Hall Park on the A45.

OPEN: Mon/Tues/Wed 0900-1645; Thurs 0900-2045; Fri 0900-1615. Two Sats in each month 0900-1215. Ring before visiting.
ADMISSION: No charge for viewing - but cost for any photocopying.
TEL: 01604 767562.

RAILWAYS IN NORTHAMPTONSHIRE
FACILITIES: A leaflet which gives background information to the railways in the County.
LOCATION: N/A.
OPEN: N/A.
ADMISSION: Charge for leaflet.   *TEL:* 01604 237220 (Countryside Centre).

RIGHTS OF WAY
FACILITIES: Details of rights of way in the County, and takes reports of problems with access along these routes.
LOCATION: N/A.
OPEN: 0900-1700.
ADMISSION: N/A.   *TEL:* 01604 237582/3.

THE RIVER NENE IN NORTHAMPTONSHIRE
FACILITIES: A leaflet which gives further information about the river.
LOCATION: N/A.
OPEN: N/A.
ADMISSION: Charge for leaflet available from libraries, TIC's, country parks, Countryside Centre.
TEL: 01604 237220 (Countryside Centre).

THE ROAD SAFETY CENTRE
FACILITIES: The Northamptonshire Cycle Training Scheme is administered by the Road Safety Centre, and can be taken advantage of by any child aged 10 and over. The scheme is offered free through schools in the county.
LOCATION: Delapre Middle School Annexe, Main Road, Far Cotton, Northampton.
OPEN: As advertised.
ADMISSION: Free.   *TEL:* 01604 763438.

SITES AND MONUMENTS RECORD
FACILITIES: Details of the sites and monuments in Northamptonshire.
LOCATION: N/A.
OPEN: 0900-1700.
ADMISSION: N/A.   *TEL:* 01604 237246.

THE SUNDAY ROVER
FACILITIES: A new leisure travel ticket, available under the Travelwise initiative. Offering excellent value and superb travel opportunities, linking bus services, and some train operators, within nine Midland counties, including Northamptonshire.
LOCATION: See literature available from TIC's, for details.
OPEN: Sundays and Bank Hol Mons.
ADMISSION: Charge.
TEL: 01536 407507 (Corby TIC), 01327 300277 Daventry TIC), 01536 410266 (Kettering TIC), 01604 22677 (Northampton Visitor Centre), 01843 27433 (Oundle TIC), 01933 228101 (Wellingborough TIC).

VILLAGE INITIATIVES FUND
FACILITIES: It is basically a 'fund for new ideas', aimed at providing cash (to a limited extent) for self-help objects which will benefit villages.
LOCATION: N/A.
OPEN: Office hours.
ADMISSION: N/A.   *TEL:* 01604 765888.

WHAT'S ON MAGAZINE
FACILITIES: A regular publication which llists events in Northants, Bucks and Beds.
LOCATION: Around the County.
OPEN: N/A.
ADMISSION: Complimentary copies available from tourist outlets/also by subscription.
TEL: 01327 843778.

LASER

CORBY LASERDROME
FACILITIES: Theme nights, special members nights.
LOCATION: 24 Market Walk, Queens Square.
OPEN: Ring for details.
ADMISSION: Charges, with special family tickets on certain days.
TEL: 01536 408282.

PLANET QUASAR LASER GUN
FACILITIES: Laser games centre.
LOCATION: 222A Kettering Road, Northampton.
OPEN: Ring for times.
ADMISSION: Charge.   *TEL:* 01604 638498.

QUASER

FACILITIES: Laser games centre.
LOCATION: Unit E, Whittle Cl, Park Fm Industrial Est, Wellingborough.
OPEN: Ring for times.
ADMISSION: Charge made.   *TEL:* 01933 679702.

ZAP ATAX 2000

FACILITIES: The ultimate laser combat arena. Special midweek madness.
LOCATION: 20 Kingswell Street, Northampton.
OPEN: Ring for times.
ADMISSION: Charge.   *TEL:* 01604 621112.

LEISURE AND SPORTS CENTRES

See also Swimming Pools

BARBY SPORTING

FACILITIEs: Covered 10 bay floodlit driving range, 2 colour coated tennis courts, clay pigeon shooting ground. Families welcome.
LOCATION: Barby Lane, between the village and Hillmorton (Rugby).
OPEN: All week -1000-2100.
ADMISSION: Charge.   *TEL:* 01788 891873.

BENHAM SPORTS ARENA

FACILITIES: Wide range, including archery, athletics, badminton, fencing, gymnastics, netball, volleyball, table tennis, snooker/pool.
LOCATION: Kings Park, Kings Park Road, Moulton Park, Northampton.
OPEN: Ring for times.
ADMISSION: Charges.   *TEL:* 01604 494100.

BRACKLEY RECREATION CENTRE

FACILITIES: Wide range, including athletics, badminton, basketball, gymnastics, netball, table tennis, etc. Gallery Restaurant and fitness suite.
LOCATION: Springfield Lane.
OPEN: Ring for times.
ADMISSION: Charge.   *TEL:* 01280 701787.

BURTON LATIMER RECREATION CENTRE

FACILITIES: Various facilities.
LOCATION: Pioneer Road.
OPEN: Ring.

204

ADMISSION: Charge.   TEL: 01536 723390.

CLUB DIANA
WELLINGBOROUGH SQUASH CLUB AND
HEALTH CENTRE
FACILITIES: Fully equipped gymnasium, sauna, 2 full size snooker tables, 5 squash courts, organised fitness classes, jacuzzi and solarium.
LOCATION: Finedon Road.
OPEN: 7 days a week.
ADMISSION: Charge.   TEL: 01933 73332/77344.

CORBY LEISURE POOL COMPLEX
FACILITIES: Competition swimming pool, leisure pool, water slide, squash courts, sauna, steam room, sunbeds, fitness room, spectator and bar facilities. Swimming lessons for all age groups.
LOCATION: George Street.
OPEN: Ring for information.
ADMISSION: Charge.   TEL: 01536 400085.

CRESCENTS COMMUNITY CENTRE
FACILITIES: Wide range including basketball, bowls, six-a-side football, netball and table tennis.
LOCATION: Laburnum Crescent, Kettering.
OPEN: Ring for times.
ADMISSION: Charges.   TEL: 01536 415648.

DANES CAMP LEISURE CENTRE
FACILITIES: Various, including badminton, climbing walls, 5-a-side football, netball, karate, kung fu, rollerskating, snooker/pool, etc. Horseshoe shaped leisure pool with water cannons, flume and fountains. Beach area for paddling.
LOCATION: Clannel Road, south of the town, off the A45 ring road, near Tesco Supermarket.
OPEN: Ring for times.
ADMISSION: Charges.   TEL: 01604 763536 (Recorded information).

DAVENTRY LEISURE CENTRE
FACILITIES: Main sports hall with 1 Badminton court, five a side, cricket, tennis and squash courts. Gymnasium, dance studio with sprung floor. 25m six lane pool with wave machine, beach area and rapids. Teaching pool, spectator seating, solarium, viewing gallery, creche, restaurants/bars, adventure play for children. Saxon Hall for arts, theatre, etc.

LOCATION: Lodge Road, opposite Daventry District Council offices and next to the Methodist Church..
OPEN: Mon-Fri 0630-2100;Sat 0800-1800;Sun 0800-2200.
ADMISSION: Charges. *TEL:* 01327 871144.

DESBOROUGH LEISURE CENTRE
FACILITIES: Children's play areas, cricket pitch, hockey pitch, rounders pitch, squash courts, family area, licenced bar, snack bar. Multi-purpose main hall, multi-purpose floodlit play area.
LOCATION: The Hawthorns.
OPEN: Ring for times.
ADMISSION: Charge. *TEL:* 01536 761239.

FINEDON COMMUNITY SPORTS AND LEISURE CENTRE
FACILITIES: Indoor bowls, badminton and children's activities. Also available for bookings.
LOCATION: Wellingborough Road.
OPEN: Ring.
ADMISSION: Charge. *TEL:* 01933 681061.

HIGHFIELD LEISURE CENTRE
FACILITIES: Badminton, basketball, indoor football, indoor cricket, volleyball, karate.
LOCATION: Highfield Road, Wellingborough.
OPEN: Ring.
ADMISSION: Charge. *TEL:* 01933 274330.

INDOOR CRICKET STADIUM AND QUASER
FACILITIES: 8-a-side indoor cricket (male/ladies/mixed), 5-a-side football, showers, changing facilities.
LOCATION: Unit E, Whittle Cl, Park Fm Industrial Est, Wellingborough.
OPEN: 1200-2100.
ADMISSION: Charges. *TEL:* 01933 679702.

INTERLEISURE SQUASH AND SPORTS CLUB
FACILITIES: Squash courts, sauna, sunbeds, gym, step and aerobics, snooker, pool, darts, skittles.
LOCATION: Central Avenue, Whitehills, Northampton.
OPEN: Ring.
ADMISSION: Charges. *TEL:* 01604 843512.

KETTERING LEISURE VILLAGE.

FACILITIES: Squash courts, main arena for badminton, five-a-side, leisure pool, quasers, bowling. Full health suite and gymnasium.
LOCATION: On the edge of Kettering in Thurston Drive, off Northampton Road.
OPEN: Ring.   **ADMISSION:** Charges.   **TEL:** 01536 414414.

KETTERING RECREATION CENTRE

FACILITIES: Main hall with badminton courts, basketball, indoor soccer, netball, volleyball, roller skating, short tennis. Annexe - martial arts, keep fit, table tennis and aerobics. Indoor nets - cricket and archery. Wide range of activities in addition to those mentioned - gymnastics, keep fit, karate, discos. pool.
LOCATION: Northampton Road.
ADMISSION: Charges.   **TEL:** 01536 410254.

LINGS FORUM LEISURE CENTRE

FACILITIES: Various including badminton, basketball, bowls, dance/aerobics, fitness/dance studio, 5-a-side football, gymnastics, judo, karate, keep fit, table tennis, tae kwando, trampoline, weight training, etc. 25m swimming pool.
LOCATION: Lings Forum, just off the A4500 Northampton-Wellingborough Road and opposite Weston Favell Shopping Centre.
OPEN: Ring for times.
ADMISSION: Charge.   **TEL:** 01604 763616.

LODGE PARK SPORTS CENTRE

FACILITIES: Two multi-sports halls, fitness area, sauna and bar and lounge. Badminton, volley-ball, 5-a-side, weight training, short tennis, archery, martial arts, sun beds.
LOCATION: Lodge Park.
OPEN: Ring for times.
ADMISSION: Charges made.   **TEL:** 01536 400033.

MCDIARMID SPORTS HALL

FACILITIES: Multi-purpose sports hall.
LOCATION: The Connaughty Centre, Cottingham Road, Corby.
OPEN: Ring.
ADMISSION: Ring.   **TEL:** 01536 204258

MOULTON LEISURE AND COMMUNITY CENTRE

FACILITIES: Has a wide range of facilities including fitness, aerobics, step aerobics, cricket, fencing, table tennis, weight training, etc.

LOCATION: Pound Lane.
OPEN: Ring for information.
ADMISSION: Charges for various activities/events.
TEL: 01604 670506.

MOUNTS HEALTH SUITE
FACILITIES: A range of exercise programmes incuding work out with weights, circuit training, ladies training, step aerobics, etc.
LOCATION: Mounts Baths, Upper Mounts, Northampton.
OPEN: Ring for times.
ADMISSION: Charge.   **TEL:** 01604 636003.

NORTHAMPTON ROAD RECREATION GROUND
FACILITIES: Bowling greens, hard tennis courts, putting green.
LOCATION: Northampton Road, Kettering.
OPEN: Ring.
ADMISSION: Charges.   **TEL:** 01536 414141.

OUNDLE SCHOOL SPORTS FACILITIES
FACILITIES: Multi-purpose sports hall.
LOCATION: Milton Road, Oundle
OPEN: Ring.
ADMISSION: Ring.   **TEL:** 01832 272407.

OVERSTONE PARK COUNTRY CLUB
FACILITIES: Fully equippped gymnasium, squash and tennis courts, snooker and pool, circuit training, aerobics, sunbeds and beauty salon, massage. Refreshments and food.
LOCATION: Ecton Lane, Sywell, Northampton.
ADMISSION: Charge for membership.   **TEL:** 01604 647709.

PEMBERTON CENTRE
FACILITIES: Two squash courts, multi-purpose sports hall, which caters for badminton, volley-ball, netball, skating, table tennis, short tennis, five-a-side football and special events. Harpers Fitness Club has a fully equipped gym, two sunbeds and a relaxing sauna.
LOCATION: H E Bates Way, Rushden.
OPEN: Ring for details.
ADMISSION: Charge.   **TEL:** 01933 350324.

REDWELL LEISURE CENTRE
FACILITIES: A multi-purpose sports hall with outdoor bowling, fitness suite and squash courts. Licenced bar and Mrs Waendels Pantry.

Outside bowls, football pitches, tennis courts, netball courts, hockey pitch. A range of activities is organised. Ladies Recreation morning (creche available) and Tiny Tumblers. Special events organised, including exhibitions, tournaments, seminars, dances, birthday parties, etc.
LOCATION: Barnwell Road, off Gleneagles Drive, Wellingborough.
OPEN: Ring for details.
ADMISSION: Charge.   *TEL:* 01933 402045.

ROCKINGHAM TRIANGLE SPORTS STADIUM
FACILITIES: All weather 8-lane x 400 metre track, 12 lane x 100m track, 10 outdoor grass tracks, polygan-fitness suite, 3 netball courts, indoor multi use hall.
LOCATION: Rockingham Road, Corby.
OPEN: Ring.
ADMISSION: Charge.   *TEL:* 01536 401007.

RUSHDEN SPORTS CENTRE
FACILITIES: 4 badminton courts, 5-a-side football, 4 squash courts, 12 station multi-gym, sauna. Aerobic and step classes through the day and evening. Meeting rooms and function rooms with licenced bars.
LOCATION: Birchall Road, Rushden.
OPEN: Ring for details.
ADMISSION: Charge.   *TEL:* 01933 50324.

STANION VILLAGE HALL ASSOCIATION
FACILITIES: Badminton court, gym room, changing room, lounge bar. Main hall and meeting room for hire with kitchen facilities.
LOCATION: Brigstock Road.
OPEN: Ring.
ADMISSION: Charge.   *TEL:* 01536 407026.

THRAPSTON POOL
FACILITIES: Open for public use throughout the week. Early risers (0730-0900), aquarobics, crazytime for kids, ladies only, relax 'n' swim, swimming lesson, family swim, private hire. Lesson programmes include those for non-swimmers, novice swimmers, early swimmers, splashers and improvers.
LOCATION: Market Road, off the A604.
OPEN: Ring for information.
ADMISSION: Charge.   *TEL:* 01832 733116.

TOWCESTER CENTRE FOR LEISURE

FACILITIES: Five-lane swimming pool, leisure pool with wave machine and eighty-foot flume. Bar, bistro, creche, gynmasium, floodlit tennis court and sports hall with wide range of activities including badminton, trampoline, gynmastics, etc. Computerised fitness testing.
LOCATION: Springfields - off A43 roundabout.
OPEN: Every day except 25/26 Dec.
ADMISSION: Charge.   **TEL:** 01327 358188.

WEAVERS LEISURE CENTRE

FACILITIES: Multi-purpose sports hall, gymnasium, sauna, solarium and floodlit outdoor all weather training areas.
LOCATION: Weavers Road.
OPEN: Ring for details.
ADMISSION: Charge.   **TEL:** 01933 276883.

THE WILLISON CENTRE

FACILITIES: Multi-purpose sports hall.
LOCATION: Roade School, Stratford Road, Roade.
OPEN: Ring.
ADMISSION: Ring.   **TEL:** 01604 862125

LEISURE DRIVES

DAVENTRY LEISURE DRIVE

FACILITIES: Covers this interesting and unspoilt part of the county. The tour, which can be either a half or full day, takes in Daventry, Daventry Country Park, Sulgrave Manor, Canons Ashby House, Old Dairy Farm Centre, etc.
LOCATION: As detailed in the drive leaflet.
OPEN: Can be used at most times - but some features may not always be open.
ADMISSION: Charges for certain visits.   **TEL:** 0604 237220.

OUTINGS FROM OUNDLE - 1

FACILITIES: Takes in Brigstock, Ringstead and Wadenhoe.
LOCATION: See leaflet.
OPEN: Can be taken during daylight hours.
ADMISSION: No charge.   **TEL:** 01832 274333 (TIC).

210

OUTINGS FROM OUNDLE - 2

FACILITIES: Covers Lilford and Barnwell.
LOCATION: See leaflet.
OPEN: Daylight hours.
ADMISSION: No charge.   *TEL:* 01832 274333 (TIC).

OUTINGS FROM OUNDLE - 3

FACILITIES: Ashton and Fotheringhay.
LOCATION: See leaflet.
OPEN: Daylight hours.
ADMISSION: No charge.   *TEL:* 01832 274333 (TIC).

OUTINGS FROM OUNDLE - 4

FACILITIES: Kings Cliffe-Easton-on-the-Hill-Harringworth-Deene.
LOCATION: See leaflet.
OPEN: Daylight hours.
ADMISSION: No charge.   *TEL:* 01832 274333 (TIC).

ROCKINGHAM FOREST LEISURE DRIVE

FACILITIES: In the Welland Valley a half day or full day self-guided car tour through this delightful part of Northamptonshire. The drive covers a wide range of interesting places, including Brigstock Country Park, East Carlton Countryside Park, Hill Farm Herbs, Triangular Lodge, Rockingham Castle, The Living Landscape Trust, Kirby Hall, Barnwell Country Park, etc.
LOCATION: In the Welland Valley - see leaflet.
OPEN: Can be taken at most times - although some facilities might not always be open.
ADMISSION: Charge for certain 'activities'.
TEL: 01604 237220 (Countryside Centre) and local TIC's.

WORLD WAR II AMERICAN AIRFIELD NOSTALGIA

FACILITIES: A drive which takes the visitor on 'A journey down memory lane', looking at World War II United States Army Air Force Bases in Northamptonshire It covers airfields at Harrington, Grafton Underwood, Poddington, Chelveston, Deenethorpe, Spanhoe, Kings Cliffe and Polebrook.
LOCATION: See leaflet.
OPEN: Daylight hours.
ADMISSION: Free.   *TEL:* From local TIC's.

LIBRARIES

Libraries are a useful source of information, especially when looking for local 'connections' and information. The libraries in the County are listed below. Opening times have been omitted. Please contact individual libraries.

BRACKLEY
LOCATION: Manor Road.   *TEL:* 01280 70345

BRAUNSTON
LOCATION: The Village Hall.   *TEL:* 01788 891423.

BRIXWORTH
LOCATION: Spratton Road.   *TEL:* 01604 880764.

BURTON LATIMER
LOCATION: High Street.   *TEL:* 01536 723357.

CORBY
LOCATION: 9 The Links, Queens Square.   *TEL:* 01536 203304.

DANESHOLME
LOCATION: 14 Neighbourhood Centre, Corby.   *TEL:* 01536 742862.

DAVENTRY
LOCATION: North Street.   *TEL:* 01327 703130.

DEANSHANGER
LOCATION: Little London.   *TEL:* 01908 562889.

DESBOROUGH
LOCATION: High Street.   *TEL:* 01536 761085.

EARLS BARTON
LOCATION: Broad Street.   *TEL:* 01604 810726.

FINEDON
LOCATION: Town Hall, Berry Green Road.   *TEL:* 01933 680208.

HIGHAM FERRERS
LOCATION: Midland Road.   *TEL:* 01933 314842.

IRCHESTER
LOCATION: High Street.   *TEL:* 01933 312539.

IRTHLINGBOROUGH
LOCATION: High Street. *TEL:* 01933 650641.

KETTERING
LOCATION: Sheep Street. *TEL:* 01563 512315.

KINGSTHORPE
LOCATION: 2 Welford Road. *TEL:* 01604 714021.

LONG BUCKBY
LOCATION: Station Road. *TEL:* 01327 842796.

MIDDLETON CHENEY
LOCATION: Main Road. *TEL:* 01295 710796.

MOULTON
LOCATION: Doves Lane. *TEL:* 01604 646796.

NORTHAMPTON - ABINGTON
LOCATION: Lindsay Avenue. *TEL:* 01604 401402.

NORTHAMPTON CENTRAL LIBRARY
FACILITIES: The local loans collection is invaluable.
LOCATION: Abington Street. *TEL:* 01604 26771.

NORTHAMPTON - DUSTON
LOCATION: Pendle Road. *TEL:* 01604 585882.

NORTHAMPTON - FAR COTTON
LOCATION: Towcester Road. *TEL:* 01604 762192.

NORTHAMPTON - HUNSBURY
LOCATION: Overslade Close, East Hunsbury. *TEL:* 01604 702830.

NORTHAMPTON - ST JAMES
LOCATION: St James Road. *TEL:* 01604 751037.

NORTHAMPTON - WESTON FAVELL
LOCATION: Weston Favell Centre. *TEL:* 01604 413327.

WOLLASTON
LOCATION: Newton Road. *TEL:* 01933 664805.

WOODFORD HALSE
LOCATION: Village Hall. *TEL:* 01327 260101.

OUNDLE
LOCATION: Glapthorn Road.　　*TEL:* 01832 272584.

RAUNDS
LOCATION: High Street.　　*TEL:* 01933 623671.

ROTHWELL
LOCATION: Market Hill.　　*TEL:* 019536 711880.

RUSHDEN
LOCATION: Newton Road.　　*TEL:* 01933 312754.

THRAPSTON
LOCATION: High Street.　　*TEL:* Thrapston 733251.

TOWCESTER
LOCATION: Richmond Road.　　*TEL:* 01327 50794.

WELLINGBOROUGH
LOCATION: Pebble Lane.　　*TEL:* 01933 225365.

LOCAL HISTORY SOCIETIES

Local history societies are situated in the towns and villages listed below.

BODDINGTON HISTORY SOCIETY
FACILITIES: Indoor meetings covering a variety of topics.
LOCATION: Peel Cottage.
OPEN: Ring.
ADMISSION: Charge.　　*TEL:* 01327 61081.

BOZEAT HISTORICAL AND ARCHAEOLOGICAL SOCIETY
FACILITIES: Indoor meetings on various topics.
LOCATION: Meets at Bozeat Working Men's Club, 65 High Street.
OPEN: Second Tuesday of month at 2000.
ADMISSION: Membership fee　　*TEL:* N/A.

BRACKLEY AND DISTRICT HISTORY SOCIETY
FACILITIES: Meets regularly.
LOCATION: Methodist Hall.
OPEN: 1945.

ADMISSION: Membership fee.
TEL: N/A. Details in local library. Contact Brackley Library.

BRIGSTOCK LOCAL HISTORY SOCIETY
FACILITIES: Arranges indoor meetings.
LOCATION: British Legion Club Room.
OPEN: Second Wednesday in month at 1930.
ADMISSION: Membership fee.   *TEL:* N/A.

BRINGTON AND NOBOTTLE LOCAL HISTORY ASSOCIATION
FACILITIES: Regular indoor meetings.
LOCATION: Reading Room, Great Brington.
OPEN: Third Mon of month at 2000.
ADMISSION: Membership fee.   *TEL:* N/A.

BRIXWORTH HISTORY SOCIETY
FACILITIES: Regular meetings covering a variety of topics of local and national interest.
LOCATION: Sports Pavilion, St David's Close.
OPEM: Third Tues of month at 1945.
ADMISSION: Membership fee.   *TEL:* 01604 880604.

COTTINGHAM AND MIDDLETON LOCAL HISTORY SOCIETY
FACILITIES: Indoor talks.
LOCATION: Methodist Chapel, Corby Road, Cottingham.
OPEN: Mons 1930.
ADMISSION: Membership fee.   *TEL:* N/A.

EARLS BARTON AND DISTRICT HISTORICAL SOCIETY
FACILITIES: Non-members are welcome at all meetings, which cover a variety of topics.
LOCATION: Barkers Canteen, Station Road, Earls Barton.
OPEN: Third Fri of month 1930.
ADMISSION: Fee.   *TEL:* N/A.

FLORE HERITAGE SOCIETY
FACILITIES: Indoor meetings and visits.
LOCATION: Ring.
OPEN: First Wed of month except Jul/Aug - 1945
ADMISSION: Membership fee.   *TEL:* 01604 340387.

GREAT EASTON AND DISTRICT LOCAL HISTORY SOCIETY

FACILITIES: Indoor speakers.
LOCATION: Village Hall, High Street.
OPEN: 1930.
ADMISSION: Membership fee.   *TEL:* N/A.

GRETTON LOCAL HISTORY SOCIETY

FACILITIES: A wide range of subjects covered - of local and County interest.
LOCATION: Village Hall.
OPEN: Thurs 1930.
ADMISSION: Membership fee.   *TEL:* N/A.

HARLESTONE HISTORICAL SOCIETY

FACILITIES: Meetings, talks, etc.
LOCATION: Ring.
OPEN: Ring.
ADMISSION: Membership fee.   *TEL:* 01604 842238.

HISTORICAL ASSOCIATION (NORTHAMPTON BRANCH)

FACILITIES: Wide range of meetings.
LOCATION: St Giles Church Centre, St Giles Terrace.
OPEN: Thurs at 1930.
ADMISSION: Membership fee.
TEL: Contact: C A Linfield, Platt's House. The School, Wellingborough, Northants, NN8 2BX.

HOUGHTONS (THE) AND BRAFIELD LOCAL HISTORY SOCIETY

FACILITIES: Indoor meetings.
LOCATION: Parish Hall, Little Houghton.
OPEN: 2000.
ADMISSION: Fee.   *TEL:* N/A.

LONG BUCKBY LOCAL HISTORY SOCIETY

FACILITIES: A range of indoor meetings.
LOCATION: St Lawrence Church Schoolrooms.
OPEN: Information in local library.
ADMISSION: Membership fee.   *TEL:* N/A.

ORLINGBURY HISTORY SOCIETY

FACILITIES: Indoor meetings.
LOCATION: Village Hall.

OPEN: 1st Wed of month.
ADMISSION: Ring. *TEL:* 01933 878250.

RUSHDEN AND DISTRICT HISTORY SOCIETY
FACILITIES: Range of speakers.
LOCATION: Rushden Hall.
OPEN: Third Fri of month at 1930.
ADMISSION: Charge. *TEL:* N/A.

THRAPSTON DISTRICT HISTORICAL SOCIETY
FACILITIES: Indoor meetings covering a range of topics.
LOCATION: St James Sunday School Hall.
OPEN: Third Thurs in month at 1930.
ADMISSION: Membership fee. *TEL:* N/A.

TOWCESTER LOCAL HISTORY SOCIETY
FACILITIES: Variety of meetings about local county and national topics.
LOCATION: Riverside Centre, Islington Road.
OPEN: Second Wed of month at 1945.
ADMISSION: Charge. *TEL:* N/A.

WEEDON BEC HISTORY SOCIETY
FACILITIES: Meetings cover a range of topics.
LOCATION: Riverside Court, Riverside Drive.
OPEN: Ring.
ADMISSION: Charge. *TEL:* 01327 341350.

WELDON LOCAL HISTORY SOCIETY
FACILITIES: Meetings vary - some cover local area (Rockingham Forest) to more general topics.
LOCATION: See parish notice board.
OPEN: Third Tues of Month.
ADMISSION: Charge *TEL:* N/A.

WELLINGBOROUGH CIVIC SOCIETY
FACILITIES: Indoor talks/meetings.
LOCATION: Leighton Coach House, off High Street.
OPEN: Ring.
ADMISSION: Ring. *TEL:* 01933 228310.

WOODFORD HALSE HISTORY SOCIETY
FACILITIES: Talks vary from wall paintings to pottery.
LOCATION: Memorial Centre, Station Road.
OPEN: Third Tues of month at 1930.

ADMISSION: Charge.   TEL: N/A.

MARKETS

BRACKLEY MARKET
FACILITIES: A general market.
LOCATION: Centre of town.
OPEN: Fridays.
ADMISSION: No charge.   TEL: 01280 700111(TIC).

CORBY MARKET
FACILITIES: A wide spectrum of goods, including fruit and vegetables, clothing, shoes, etc.
LOCATION: The Square in the centre of Corby.
OPEN: Mon (bric-a-brac); Tues, Sat - and a smaller market on Thurs, Sun (out of town).
ADMISSION: No charge.   TEL: 01536 407507 (Corby TIC).

DAVENTRY MARKET
FACILITIES: Was successfully moved from the Market Place to the High Street. The market has long traditions, and was probably in existence before it was mentioned in 1255. A wide range of stalls on either side of the High Street, with a good selection from fish to meat, pet foods, etc.
LOCATION: High Street, Daventry. Free parking nearby.
OPEN: Tues and Fri. Extra markets at holiday times.
ADMISSION: Free.
TEL: 01327 871100 (Daventry District Council).

KETTERING MARKET
FACILITIES: A charter was granted in 1227 by King Henry II to the Abbot of Peterborough and his monks. Various stalls, with smaller markets on Tues.
LOCATION: Market Street.
OPEN: Tues (small), Wed (bric-a-brac/antiques), Fri, Sat.
ADMISSION: No charge.   TEL: 01536 410266.

NORTHAMPTON CATTLE MARKET
FACILITIES: In addition to the normal activities at the previous cattle market, there will be antique and modern house furniture sales, and other sales, including pedigree sales.
LOCATION: Brackmills, A428 Bedford Road.
OPEN: Ring.   TEL: As now.

218

NORTHAMPTON MARKET

FACILITIES: Dates from 1235, when Henry III made merchants move from All Saints Churchyard to what is now the Market Square. Fruit and veg, with general market and some bric a brac.

LOCATION: Market Square.

OPEN: Mon (fruit/veg), Tues/Wed/Thurs/Fri/Sat - general markets with bric-a-brac on Thurs.

ADMISSION: No charge.

TEL: 01604 233500 (Northampton Borough Council).

NORTHAMPTON MARKET HALL

FACILITIES: Fresh meat, fish, vegetables, fruit, bread and cakes. Cheese and Caribbean food. Clothes, footwear, etc.

LOCATION: Sheep Street.

OPEN: Tues/Wed/Fri/Sat - early a.m. to 1500.

ADMISSION: Free.   *TEL:* 01604 233500.

OUNDLE MARKET

FACILITIES: General market.

LOCATION: Centre of town.

OPEN: Thurs.

ADMISSION: No charge.

TEL: 01832. 742000 (East Northamptonshire District Council)/274333 (Oundle TIC).

RAUNDS MARKET

FACILITIES: General market.

LOCATION: Centre of town.

OPEN: Fri.

ADMISSION: Free.   *TEL:* 01933 228101 (Welingborough TIC).

ROTHWELL MARKET

FACILITIES: General market.

LOCATION: Centre of town.

OPEN: Mon.

ADMISSION: Free.   *TEL:* 01536 410266 (Kettering TIC).

RUSHDEN MARKET

FACILITIES: General market.

LOCATION: High Street.

OPEN: Saturdays.

ADMISSION: Free.   *TEL:* N/A.

THRAPSTON CATTLE MARKET

FACILITIES: A typical cattle market, and one of only two left in Northamptonshire. It deals with a variety of livestock, and at one time the Bedford and Kettering Cattle Markets were moved here when they closed.
LOCATION: In the centre of Thrapston.
OPEN: Tues/Fri.
ADMISSION: Free. *TEL:* 01832 274333 (Oundle TIC).

THRAPSTON MARKET

FACILITIES: A market has been held weekly since 1205 when the rights to the town were secured by one Baldwin de Vere. A street market selling a variety of wares.
LOCATION: Along the High Street.
OPEN: Tues.
ADMISSION: Free. *TEL:* 01832 274333 (Oundle TIC).

TOWCESTER FRIDAY MARKET

FACILITIES: Antiques, bric-a-brac, furniture, linen, lace, china - cafe with home-made cakes.
LOCATION: Town Hall.
OPEN: Fri - 0900-1500.
ADMISSION: No charge. *TEL:* 01908 225579.

TOWCESTER MARKET

FACILITIES: General market.
LOCATION: On A5 by Racecorse.
OPEN: Fri.
ADMISSION: Free. *TEL:* 01280 700111 (Brackley TIC).

WELLINGBOROUGH MARKET

FACILITIES: A bric-a-brac/antiques market is held on Tues, and general markets on Wed/Fri/Sat.
LOCATION: Market Square.
OPEN: Tues/Wed/Fri/Sat.
ADMISION: Free.
TEL: 01933 229777 (Wellingborough Borough Council).

THE ABBEY COMMUNITY RESOURCE CENTRE

FACILITIES: Advice, information, photocopying, meeting rooms, training, conferences, support networks, creche facilities, exhibition hall, office accommodation, function facilities, information on local groups. Organisations using the Centre include Abbey Parent and Toddler Group, Adult Basic Education, Daventry District Scouting - Association Resource Shop, Dial, PPA Bulk Buy, etc.

LOCATION: Abbey Street, Daventry and reached from the Market Square.

OPEN: Varies for different groups, etc. Ring for details.

ADMISSION: Ring for information.   *TEL:* 01327 872466.

ANGLIAN WATER

FACILITIES: Arranges open days at various sites.

LOCATION: In and around the County.

OPEN: Ring for details.

ADMISSION: Ring for details.   *TEL:* 0345 145145.

CARLSBERG BREWERY

FACILITIES: Produces Danish lager by a special process. Brewing, bottling/canning and packaging processes can be seen during a tour of the works.

LOCATION: Bridge Street, Northampton.

OPEN: All year - by arrangement.

ADMISSION: Ring.   *TEL:* 01604 234333.

CHRONICLE AND ECHO

FACILITIES: The Chronicle and Echo is Northampton's evening paper. Guided tours of the newspaper available.

LOCATION: Upper Mounts, Northampton.

OPEN: Ring for information.

ADMISSION: Ring.   *TEL:* 01604 231122 (Visitors Department).

CORN MARKET HALL

FACILITIES: Drama, music, etc.

LOCATION: London Road, Kettering.

OPEN: Various times.

ADMISSION: Charge.   *TEL:* 01536 410266 (TIC).

THE DIAMOND CENTRE
FACILITIES: Arranges a wide range of activities from music to snooker and pool, including events open to the public.
LOCATION: Nene Park, Irthlingborough.
OPEN: Various times.
ADMISSION: Charge.   *TEL:* 01933 650354.

DUKE OF EDINBURGH AWARD SCHEME
FACILITIES: Details of the Scheme which operates around the county.
LOCATION: Various venues used.
OPEN: Ring for information.
ADMISSION: Ring for information.
TEL: 01933 663318 (Development Worker)/01327 877022 (Daventry area Office).

EXPLORER TICKET
FACILITIES: Unlimited travel on day of purchase. The easiest way to see Northamptonshire from the top of a bus.
LOCATION: Details of routes, etc. from Greyfriars Bus Station.
OPEN: Daily.
ADMISSION: Charge.   *TEL:* 01604 620077.

GLAPTHORN COW PASTURE NATURE TRAIL
FOR PEOPLE WITH A VISUAL HANDICAP
FACILITIES: Cassette tape which takes visually impaired people around a marked trail. There are six stops on the tape.
LOCATION: Glapthorn Cow Pasture.
OPEN: Can be used at most times.
ADMISSION: No charge.   *TEL:* 01832 272741.

HILL FARM HERBS
FACILITIES: Organises a series of walks around the gardens.
LOCATION: Park Walk, Brigstock.
OPEN: Ring for details.
ADMISSION: Charge.   *TEL:* 01536 373694.

HOLDENBY FALCONRY CENTRE
FACILITIES: There are 19 different species of birds managed by the Falconry Centre and displays are arranged in the grounds of Holdenby House. The birds which are not being flown can be seen in the aviaries. A trained falconer is always on hand to answer questions about the birds, their habits and habitats. Courses held for children.
LOCATION: Holdenby House.
OPEN: 1200-1800 daily (April-Oct) - weather permitting. Ring for details.

ADMISSION: Charge.   TEL: 01604 770074.

MISTER GRANT'S HOUSE
FACILITIES: Includes the tourist information centre for Northampton. Also has exhibitions, sales. etc.
LOCATION: 10 St Giles Square, Northampton.
OPEN: Ring for details.
ADMISSION: Free.   TEL: 01604 22677.

MOOT HALL
FACILITIES: A varied programme of exhibitions and events.
LOCATION: Near the Market Square, Daventry.
OPEN: Oct-Mar 1000-1530 - Tues-Sat; Apr-Sept 1000-1700 Mon-Sat.
ADMISSION: Exhibitions usually free; may be charge for some events.
TEL: 01327 300277.

NEWBOTTLE WOODS NATURE TRAIL
FACILITIES: Waymarked nature trail.
LOCATION: Kings Sutton to Charlton Road near Banbury
OPEN: Can be walked at most times.
ADMISSION: No charge.   TEL: 01280 700111 (TIC).

NORTHAMPTON MERCURY COMPANY
FACILITIES: Tours of the making of the Chronicle and Echo, Northampton's evening newspaper.
LOCATION: Upper Mounts, Northampton.
OPEN: Ring for times.
ADMISSION: Charge.   TEL: 01604 231122.

NORTHAMPTONSHIRE WEAVERS, SPINNERS AND DYERS
FACILITIES: Group involved with spinning, weaving and dyeing.
LOCATION: Ring.
OPEN: Ring.
ADMISSION: Ring.   TEL: 01604 890534/01908 542898

ROTHWELL HERITAGE INFORMATION PANEL
FACILITIES: The panel gives information about Rothwell's many historic buildings.
LOCATION: Market Hill.
OPEN: Can be seen at any time.
ADMISSION: No charge.   TEL: N/A

ST JAMES'S LAKE

FACILITIES: The lake was excavated as part of the flood control system for water draining from the new areas of the town.

LOCATION: Brackley-Hinton-in-the-Hedges road, which joins the A43 on the southern edge of Brackley.

OPEN: All times.

ADMISSION: No charge.   *TEL:* 01280 700311.

SWAN'S WAY

FACILITIES: This long distance bridle route starts in Salcey Forest and goes into Buckinghamshire, finishing near Aylesbury.

LOCATION: See map.

OPEN: Can be ridden at most times.

ADMISSION: No charge.   *TEL:* 01296 382796.

TOURS OF THE UNEXPECTED

FACILITIES: An insight into the working lives of the people of Northamptonshire, these tours are organised by the Tourism and Conference Bureau, Northamptonshire Chamber of Commerce, Training and Enterprise. They cover a wide range of guided tours, which include gardens, museums, skin care companies, breweries, commercial organisations, etc.

LOCATION: Details in a leaflet with the same title.

OPEN: Varies.

ADMISSION: Charge for some.

TEL: 01604 671200 (Tourism unit) or obtain leaflets from TIC's.

SAUNTERBUS

FACILITIES: A special service run by Northamptonshire County Council in conjunction with Stage Coach United Counties.   Various routes are planned, enabling passengers to stop off at various places of interest, including the County's principal attractions.

LOCATION: Around the county.

OPEN: The service operates from Easter to September on Sunday, Bank Holiday Mondays and other weekends.

ADMISSION: Bus fare plus any admission charges (sometimes reduced for Saunterbus users).

TEL: 01604 236712 (County Council Public Transport Section) during office hours.

TURNER'S
FACILITIES: Seasonal activities, Christmas parties, Back to the 60's' nights, etc.
LOCATION: On the Newport Pagnell road about 800m from the Wootton Hall roundabout.
OPEN: Most evenings/afternoons
ADMISSION: Charges.   *TEL:* 01604 763314.

MOTOR SPORTS

ARNCO QUADS AND KARTS
FACILITIES: Mini quad bikes (ages 4-11), junior quad bikes (age 10-16), rally karts (12-adult). Helmets and tuition provided. Football area and picnic tables.
LOCATION: Half way between Buckingham and Brackley, on the south Northamptonshire border.
OPEN: Varies - ring for details.
ADMISSION: Charges.   *TEL:* 01280 703625/812327.

GP KARTING
FACILITIES: Indoor Karting Centre, which offers racing and enduring sessions.
LOCATION: St James Mill Road, Northampton.
OPEN: Ring.
ADMISSION: Charges.   *TEL:* 01604 591591.

GRASSHOPPERS
FACILITIES: Quads for a wide range including adults.
LOCATION: Horwell Farm, Banyards Green, 5 miles south of Brackley on B4100 towards Aynho from the B4100/A43.
OPEN: Sat/Sun 0900-dark (1800 summer), school hols, half term, Bank Hols.
ADMISSION: Charges.   *TEL:* 01869 345902.

HUNTS KART RACING CLUB LTD
FACILITIES: Kart racing aged 8 upwards; 60cc, 100cc and 250cc - twin-engined machines. Professional circuit, inside race control, catering, toilets.
LOCATION: Kimbolton on B660.
OPEN: Second Sat/Sun of month.
ADMISSION: Charge for racing and for spectators.
TEL: 01327 876444.

NORTHAMPTON STADIUM
FACILITIES: Stock car, hot rod and banger racing.
LOCATION: Horton Road, between Horton and Brafield-on-the-Green, off the A428.
OPEN: Ring for details.
ADMISSION: Charge made.   *TEL:* 01604 870206.

ROUGH RIDER OFF ROAD KARTS
FACILITIES: Off road karting in Phillips 570cc Super Fours. Own private parties, or open race meeting. Practice sessions on Sundays.
LOCATION: Kart Track, Boughton Fair Lane, off Holcot Road, off the A43 on the edge of village.
OPEN: Sat/Sun/Bank Hol Mon 1100-1900. Mid-week by arrangement - Mid-March to Mid-Nov.
ADMISSION: Charge.   *TEL:* 01933 276525.

SANTA POD RACEWAY
FACILITIES: Range of activities.
LOCATION: Poddington Airfield, Sharnbrook 6 miles south east of Wellingborough between Wymington and Poddington.
OPEN: Ring for details.
ADMISSION: Charge made.
TEL: 01234 782828.

SELF DRIVE MOTOR SPORT
FACILITIES: Car and kart racing. Equipment supplied free. Refreshments available. Spectators free.
LOCATION: Northampton Stadium, Horton Road, between Horton and Brafield-on-the-Green off the A428.
OPEN: Daily 1000-2100 - times may vary on Stock Car nights.
ADMISSION: Charge.   *TEL:* 0891 474983 (Race line).

SILVERSTONE CIRCUIT
FACILITIES: A range of motoring events take place at Silverstone, including the British Grand Prix. There are also facilities for testing cars, as well as a motor racing school.
LOCATION: Silverstone on A43.
OPEN: Ring for programme.
ADMISSION: Charge made.   *TEL:* 01327 857271.

226

SILVERSTONE CIRCUIT - KARTING

FACILITIES: Karting tuition is considered the training ground for Formula One drivers - and most begin their lessons at an early age. Tuition for 8-16 year olds. Includes an informative classroom briefing, with video presentation, and this is followed by a circuit familiarisation, a trackside driving demonstration - and then the real driving starts! There are further courses after the introductory sessions. Suitable for drivers without previous karting experience. Everything provided - including overalls and helmets.
LOCATION: Silverstone on the A43.
OPEN: Ring.
ADMISSION: Charge.   *TEL:* 01327 857788.

SILVERSTONE DRIVING CENTRE TRACK OPEN DAY

FACILITIES: The day includes a selection of activities from Circuit Driving - race prepared saloons; single seaters - Formula Ford Racing cars; Kart Racing, Skid cars, Autotest in the Caterham Seven.
LOCATION: Silverstone, on the A43.
OPEN: Various days - ring for brochure/details.
ADMISSION: Fee.
TEL: 01327 857788 (bookings)/858560 (direct line)/857177 (Customer Care).

SILVERSTONE RALLY SCHOOL

FACILITIES: Rally tuition and gift days.
LOCATION: Silverstone Circuit, on the A43.
OPEN: Ring.
ADMISSION: Charge.   *TEL:* 01327 857413.

TOUGH TERRAIN TRACK

FACILITIES: For 4wd experiences on a specially constructed off-road track to test driving skills, improve driving control, and the true capabilities of 4wd vehicles. Steep inclines, side slopes, deep water, every kind of terrain you're likely to come across. - only 'street-legal' vehicles are allowed. Dealers can use it to give customers the chance to drive a 4wd vehicle before purchase.
LOCATION: The Wrongs, Welford Road, Sibbertoft off A5100.
OPEN: Third weekend each month from 0900-1800. Other times by arrangement.
ADMISSION: £15 per driver per day.   *TEL:* 01858 880886.

JOHN WATTS PERFORMANCE DRIVING CENTRE

FACILITIES: Learn to drive a racing or rally car. Specialist tuition in every sphere of driving, even on simulated ice!

LOCATION: Silverstone Circuit, off the A43 near Silverstone village.

OPEN: Ring for details.

ADMISSION: Charge.   *TEL:* 01327 857177.

WHILTON MILL RALLY CARTING CENTRE

FACILITIES: A range of options available, including open rally kart sessions, party sessions and private race meetings. A variety of off-road vehicles available. Also other outdoor activities, including clay pigeon shooting.

LOCATION; Whilton Locks, about 1 mile from A5, signposted Whilton Locks (and just over canal and M1 bridge), 3 miles north of Weedon.

OPEN: Sat/Sun 1300-1700 subject to availability; corporate/groups by prior arrangement at other times.

ADMISSION: Charge.   *TEL:* 01327 843822.

MUSEUMS

ABINGTON MUSEUM

FACILITIES: Housed in a 15th century manor house, which was once the home of Elizabeth Bernard, Shakespeare's daughter, who is buried in the nearby church. It is set in the delightful grounds of Abington Park. The house includes an oak panelled room and Great Hall. Displays include the social history of the house. There is a room with 16th century oak panelling, a Victorian Cabinet of Curiosities, Northampton life - from birth to death, the County's military history - at home and abroad - and a 19th century fashion gallery.

LOCATION: 1 mile from the town centre, in Abington Park reached off the A4500 Kettering road.

OPEN: Tues-Sun 1300-1700; Bank Hol Mons 1300-1700. Closed 25/26 Dec.

ADMISSION: Free.   *TEL:* 01604 31454.

ASHTON MILL AND FISH MUSEUM

FACILITIES: Housed in the former mill it still has late 19th century mill machinery for water and electricity supply. There is also a fish museum, as well as antique farm machinery, basket making and thatching exhibitions, and forge and tools. Tea room on site.

LOCATION: Ashton Wold Estate, off the A605 in the village of Ashton, N of Oundle.

OPEN: Sat/Sun 1400-1800. Other days by prior arrangement.

ADMISSION: Charge. Car and coach parking free.

TEL: 01832 272264.

THE CANAL MUSEUM

FACILITIES: Is housed in former canalside warehouses. There are two floors of displays, which gives an intriguing insight into the canals as they were at the dawn of the Industrial Revolution. The Museum exhibits bring to life more than 200 years of a rich and varied history on the canals and waterways of the country - not just the county. Free parking for museum visitors.

LOCATION: Signposted off the A5/A508/A43 and south of Northampton 10 mins from J15 of the M1.

OPEN: Tues-Sun 1000-1600.

ADMISSION: Charge.   *TEL:* 01604 862229.

CARPET BAGGERS AVIATION MUSEUM

FACILITIES: Is on an old admin site of airfield No 179. This was used during the Second World War by the US 8th Airforce 801st, 492. Carpet Baggers was the group's code name when dropping people and material into Europe. Exhibits feature the work of this period of the airfield's history, and includes memorabilia and photographs. Free car park/coach parking. Refreshments, souvenirs, pick your own soft fruits and vegetables in season, small plant nursery, toilets, picnic site, information.

LOCATION: Off Lamport Road, Harrington.

OPEN: Weekend/Bank Holidays 1000-1800. Other times for groups by arrangement.

ADMISSION: Charge - combined with Northants Aviation Museum.

TEL: 01604 686608.

CENTRAL MUSEUM AND ART GALLERY, NORTHAMPTON

FACILITIES: Northamptonshire's main museum has a wide range of exhibits, including the internationally famous shoe collection. These include a variety of decorative items like buckles, as well as the machines which were introduced to 'mechanise' the industry. The small room which has been reconstructed to show a shoemaker' shop is a must. Northamptonshire's history includes objects, sound and film combined to tell the history of the town from earliest Stone Age times to the 20th century. There is an outstanding collection of decorative arts, which include Oriental and British ceramics. Temporary exhibitions are also put on, and there is an art gallery (see Art Galleries). Limited street parking. Car and coach parking close by.

LOCATION: Guildhall Road, near town centre.

OPEN: All year - Mon-Sats 1000-1700; Sun 1500-1700. Closed 25/26 Dec.

ADMISSION: Free.   *TEL:* 01604 639415.

DAVENTRY MUSEUM

FACILITIES: Is located in the historic 18th century Moot Hall. Local interest collections and exhibitions on permanent display, with a variety of temporary exhibitions throughout the year. These include the Story of Borough Hill, the social history of the town and district, local trades (including whip making), rural life and the development of Daventry. Educational facilities available if booked in advance.

LOCATION: In the Moot Hall opposite the Market Square.

OPEN: Oct-March 1000-1300 Tues-Sat; April-September 1000-1700 Mon-Fri; April-Sept 1000-1600 Sats.

ADMISSION: Free.   **TEL:** 01327 300277.

EARLS BARTON MUSEUM OF LOCAL LIFE

FACILITIES: Contains collections to show aspects of working life and leisure in the 19th and 20th centuries. Reconstructions include the ground floor of the home of a shoe-worker's family at the beginning of the 20th century. There is a reconstruction of a 'shop' of a shoe-worker, including equipment like sewing machines. There is also a parlour and yard with 'traditional' washing kit - dolly tub and mangle. In addition there are other exhibits and changed displays. Sales counter with books and souvenirs.

LOCATION: West Street.

OPEN: Sat/Sun/Bank Hol Mon 1430-1700 (Mar-Sept); 1430-1600 (Oct-mid-Dec). Groups by arrangement.

ADMISSION: Ring for details.   **TEL:** 01604 810349.

GRANDAD'S ATTICS MUSEUM

FACILITIES: Small museum on two floors above Drapers furniture shop. The eight rooms have different themes - music, domestic, barn, hobbies and workshops. There is a piano player and a scenic railway - and much more.

LOCATION: Drapers (Furniture), Barrack Road, Northampton and opposite the Royal Mail Sorting Office.

OPEN: Mon-Sat 1000-1600.

ADMISSION: Charge.   **TEL:** 01604 638935/639907.

GRENDON HALL DOVECOTE CENTRE

FACILITIES: Exhibits and artefacts from between the wars.

LOCATION: In the grounds of Grendon Hall,

OPEN: Ring for details.

ADMISSION: No charge.   **TEL:** 01933 663853.

HANNINGTON VINTAGE TRACTOR CLUB MUSEUM

FACILITIES: A superb collection of agricultural and other bygones. These include vintage tractors. The Museum is administered by the Tractor Club. There is a collection of hedging instruments, dairy ware, etc. Picnic area.

LOCATION: Behind Lamport Hall, which is on the A508 Northampton-Market Harborough road.

OPEN: Suns/Bank Holidays 01415-1715 - at other times during events. Other groups by prior arrangement.

ADMISSION: Free if visiting Lamport Hall.   **TEL:** 01933 314320.

HUNSBURY HILL IRONSTONE RAILWAY MUSEUM
See Northamptonshire Ironstone Railway Trust Museum

IRCHESTER NARROW GAUGE RAILWAY MUSEUM

FACILITIES: A range of material linked to the railway which used to be part of the excavations in the area. Includes narrow gauge locomotives and rolling stock - not only from the area.
LOCATION: Irchester Country Park.
OPEN: Ring.
ADMISSION: No charge.   *TEL:* 01234 750469.

MANOR HOUSE MUSEUM

FACILITIES: Housed in an 18th century Manor House. There is a series of collections of social, industrial history and archaeology, together with geology, which gives a fascinating insight into the past history of Kettering.
LOCATION: Sheep Street, Kettering in town centre.
OPEN: Ring.
ADMISSION: Free. Parking (charge) nearby.   *TEL:* 01536 410263.

MUSEUM OF NORTHAMPTONSHIRE REGIMENT

FACILITIES: Situated in Abington Park Museum. A pictorial exhibition of the history of the Northamptonshire Regiment from 1741 to 1960. The collection of medals is of especial interest.
LOCATION: Abington Park, 1 mile from town centre off A4500.
OPEN: Tues-Sun 1300-1700; Bank Hol Mon 1300-1700. Closed 25/26 Dec.
ADMISSION: Free.   *TEL:* 01604 631454.

NASEBY BATTLE AND FARM MUSEUM

FACILITIES: The Museum has a miniature layout of the Battle of Naseby (1645), when Oliver Cromwell's Parliamentarians defeated King Charles I. There is a commentary on the battle, together with relics from the fields, village history and farm hand tools and machinery, and some vintage tractors. Two monuments can be seen close to the site.
LOCATION: Purlieu Farm, Naseby off the B4036 between Daventry and Market Harborough. Or off the A5199 Northampton-Leicester road.
OPEN: Bank Holiday Suns and Mons 1400-1700; some other times from Easter-Sept, and other times by arrangements for groups.

ADMISSION: Charge.   **TEL:** 01604 740241.

THE NATIONAL DRAGONFLY MUSEUM AT ASHTON MILL

FACILITIES: The only museum of its kind in Europe. Indoor sections feature displays and exhibitions, together with live dragonfly larvae in tanks. Outdoors there are dragonfly observation platforms where it is possible to watch dragonflies above the mill pond and specially created lake.

LOCATION: Ashton Wold, Ashton, near Oundle.

OPEN: Ring.

ADMISSION: Charge. **TEL:** 01832 272427.

NATIONAL FAIRGROUND MUSEUM

FACILITIES: The Museum will house the Fairground Heritage Trust's collection of vintage fairground rides, etc. It is planned to have the rides open, including the oldest known 'switchback'. There will be stalls, and special forms of transport for taking fairs around the country. There will also be historical exhibitions which show the development of the fairground.

LOCATION: Riverside, Northampton.

OPEN: Possibly 1998.

ADMISSION: Not known.

TEL: 0181 9830844 - further information from Northampton TIC 01604 622677.

THE NORTHANTS AVIATION MUSEUM

FACILITIES: Displays the remains of recovered World War II aircraft, including parts of a Junkers Bomber, a Dornier Do 217K Night Bomber and a USAF Liberator, together with a collection of instruments and other items of equipment. Free car/coach parking. Refreshments, souvenirs, pick your own soft fruits and vegetables in season, small plant nursery. toilets, picnic site, information.

LOCATION: Off Lamport Road, Harrington.

OPEN: Weekend before Easter-31 Nov - Weekends/Bank Hols from 1000-1800.

ADMISSION: Charge - combined with Carpetbaggers Museum.

TEL: 01604 686608.

NORTHAMPTONSHIRE IRONSTONE RAILWAY MUSEUM

FACILITIES: On the site of former ironstone workings, the Museum contains a variety of railway engines and wagons rescued from the local iron workings. There is also an Alichin steam roller. Diesel-hauled rides

233

along a piece of track. The exhibits show how ironstone was carried to the blast furnaces to be made into iron.

LOCATION: In Hunsbury Hill Country Park and on Hunsbury Hill Road, Camp Hill Northampton, close to the A45.

OPEN: Sun and Bank Hol Mons 0900-1700.

ADMISSION: Free, but charges for special events. Charge for rail trips.

TEL: 01604 890229.

OUNDLE MUSEUM

FACILITIES: Living heritage displays, with changing exhibitions, offering a unique view of the development of the area from Roman times. Temporary exhibition gallery.

LOCATION: Drill Hall Centre.

OPEN: Ring for times.

ADMISSION: Free.   *TEL:* 01832 274333 (TIC).

RUSHDEN HISTORICAL TRANSPORT MUSEUM

FACILITIES: Housed in the Old Railway Station, there is an interesting and colourful display of many forms of transport, representing different transport themes. A wide range of artefacts, including lamps, signs, ticket machines, signal equipment, and other railway relics. There is a gift shop. Regular programme of special events. The Society linked to the Museum arranges a variety of activities.

LOCATION: Station Approach.

OPEN: All year Suns 1030-1630. Other times by arrangement.

ADMISSION: Ring.

TEL: 01933 318988 (Sat/Sun 12000-1400/evenings 1930-2230).

SIR HENRY ROYCE MEMORIAL FOUNDATION

FACILITIES: Comprehensive collection of documents, memorabilia and photographs illustrating the history of the Rolls Royce, and Sir Henry Royce, the car's creator. Housed in the Hunt House.

LOCATION: Paulerspury, is 3 miles south of Towcester and off to the west of the A5.

OPEN: Ring.

ADMISSION: Charge.   *TEL:* 01327 797811

STEEL-MAKING HERITAGE CENTRE

FACILITIES: Within East Carlton Countryside Park. The steel-making Centre traces the history of the excavation of iron and steel making from early times. There is some equipment, plus displays, videos, etc.

LOCATION: East Carlton Countryside Park is 4.5 miles west of Corby on A427.
OPEN: Daily April-Oct 0930-1745; Nov-Mar 10.00-1600. School groups at other times by prior arrangement. Closed 25/26 Dec and 1 Jan.
ADMISSION: Free. Car/coach parking free. **TEL:** 01536 770977.

TURNER MUSICAL MERRY-GO-ROUND
FACILITIES: Pre-booked parties to see a range of shows. There is a variety of interesting items, including old cars and mechanical musical instruments (organs) and a merry-go-round.
LOCATION: On B526 Northampton-Newport Pagnell road, south of Northampton.
OPEN: Ring for details of events.
ADMISSION: Charge made. **TEL:** 01604 763314.

WELLINGBOROUGH HERITAGE CENTRE
FACILITIES: Housed in Croyland Hall, which derives its name from a medieval grange, it was built by the monks of Croyland (Lincolnshire) more than 1000 years ago. It is administered by the Wellingborough Civic Society. The displays are in four rooms, and cover all aspects of the history of Wellingborough, with the oldest exhibits going back 2000 years. Souvenirs, etc. for sale. Leaflets about local events available. Rooms are available for hire in this building and Leighton Coach House.
LOCATION: Behind the Hind Hotel and close to the Tithe Barn and Sharman Road car park. Demonstrations held from time to time.
OPEN: Mon/Tues/Wed/Fri/Sat 1000-1630; Sun 1400-1630. Open most Bank Hols. Closed Mons in Jan.
ADMISSION: Free, but donations for the upkeep welcomed.
TEL: 01933 276838.

WOLLASTON VILLAGE MUSEUM
FACILITIES: A range of exhibits which include archaeological finds, photographs, old prints, documents - all relating to the daily life of the village. There are also lace-making and footwear exhibits, as well as domestic, agricultural and industrial equipment. Some paintings by local artists.
LOCATION: 104 High Street, Wollaston, on A509 4 miles south of Wellingborough.
OPEN: Sun (from Easter-end of Sept) 1430-1630 - other times by prior arrangement.
ADMISSION: Charge. **TEL:** 01933 664468.

MUSIC

ACCOUSTIC MUSIC AND SONG SESSION
FACILITIES: Anyone welcome.
LOCATION: King William IV, Kingsthorpe.
OPEN: Second Sun each month.
ADMISSION: Ring.   *TEL:* 01604 587974.

ALL SAINTS CHOIR
FACILITIES: A choir made up of boy choristers, male altos, tenors and basses. Always looking for new members.
LOCATION: All Saints Church, town centre.
OPEN: Ring.
ADMISSION: Ring.   *TEL:* 01604 32914.

THE BLACK BOTTOM CLUB
FACILITIES: Jazz and other music.
LOCATION: George Row, Northampton.
OPEN: Ring for times.
ADMISSION: Charge.
TEL: 01604 233401 (information)/30666 (Box Office).

BRACKLEY MUSIC CENTRE
FACILITIES: Part of Northamptonshire Music Service. Regular tuition.
LOCATION: Southfield School, Banbury Road.
OPEN: Ring.
ADMISSION: Charge.   *TEL:* 01280 704622.

BUGBROOKE CHORAL SOCIETY
FACILITIES: Ring.   *TEL:* 01327 340956.

CABARET CAFE
FACILITIES: Jazz-cafe restaurant. Live music.
LOCATION: Derngate Theatre, 19-21 Guildhall Road, Northampton.
OPEN: Music - Thurs/Fri/Sat evenings.
ADMISSSION: Ring.   *TEL:* 01604 626222.

CAVENDISH SINGERS
BURTON LATIMER
FACILITIES: Ring.
LOCATION: Ring.
OPEN: Ring
ADMISSION: Membership fee.   *TEL:* 01536 726400.

COCK INN

FACILITIES: Regular sessions - ring for details.
LOCATION: Harborough Road, Kingsthorpe, Northampton.
OPEN: Ring for details.
ADMISSION: Ring for information.   *TEL:* 01604 715221.

COLLEGE STREET MINSTRELS

TEL: 01604 403225.

CORBY MUSIC CENTRE

FACILITIES: Part of Northamptonshire Music Service. Arranges regular activities.
LOCATION: Kingswood School, Gainsborough Road.
OPEN: Ring.
ADMISSION: Charge.   *TEL:* 01933 681594.

CORBY CHORAL SOCIETY

FACILITIES: New members welcome for this society.
LOCATION: Church of the Epiphany Hall, Elizabeth Street.
OPEN: Mon 1930-2130.
ADMISSION: Charge.   *TEL:* 01536 745010.

CORBY CO-OP SINGERS

FACILITIES: Female unaccompanied choir, always welcomes new singers by informal auditions.
LOCATION: Ring.
OPEN: Weds during term time.
ADMISSION: Ring.   *TEL:* 01536 263156 (answerphone).

CORBY MALE VOICE CHOIR

FACILITIES: New members always welcome.
LOCATION: Willow Room, Civic Centre.
OPEN: Ring.
ADMISSION: Ring.   *TEL:* 01536 744727.

DANETRE BRASS
Formerly Daventry Silver Band

FACILITIES: Rehearsals for Junior and Senior members.
LOCATION: Ring.
OPEN: Mon/Fri - Juniors 1830-1930; Seniors 2000-2200.
TEL: 01327 341388.

DAVENTRY AND DISTRICT CHORAL SOCIETY

FACILITIES: Meets each week and is involved with a range of performances in and around Daventry. Has a Junior Section.

LOCATION: Meetings held at Daventry Methodist Church.
OPEN: Tues 1930.
ADMISSION: Ring for details.   *TEL:* 01327 878529.

DAVENTRY LEISURE CENTRE

FACILITIES: The venue for a variety of concerts held throughout the year and organised by Daventry District Council in association with a variety of other bodies.
LOCATION: Daventry Leisure Centre, Lodge Road, Daventry.
OPEN: The concerts are held at various times.
ADMISSION: Charge.   *TEL:* 01327 302407.

DAVENTRY MUSIC CENTRE

FACILITIES: Wide range of tuition, the Centre is administered by Northamptonshire Music Service.
LOCATION: Daventry Tertiary College, Badby Road West.
OPEN: Ring for information.
ADMISSION: Charges.   *TEL:* 01604 37117.

THE DIAMOND CENTRE

FACILITIES: Organises a wide range of popular music events, including soul, rock 'n' roll, discos, etc. Part of Rushden and Diamonds.
LOCATION: Nene Park, Irthlingborough.
OPEN: Various times.
ADMISSION: Charge.   *TEL:* 01933 650345.

DINGLEY HALL AND CHURCH

FACILITIES: Music throughout the year.
LOCATION: Dingley.
OPEN: Ring for information.
ADMISSION: Charge.   *TEL:* 01536 410266 .

DUN COW FOLK CLUB

FACILITIES: Regular meetings/sessions.
LOCATION: Dun Cow, Brook Street, Daventry.
OPEN: Ring.
ADMISSION: Ring.   *TEL:* 01327 871545.

EARLS BARTON MUSIC

FACILITIES: Sings a variety of musical pieces and welcomes new members.
LOCATION: Details from Secretary.
OPEN: As per programme.
ADMISSION: Membership fee/charge for evenings.*TEL:* 01604 810106.

EARLS BARTON SILVER BAND

FACILITIES: Opportunities for new members.
LOCATION; Silver Band Club, Queen Street.
OPEN: Thurs from 1945-2145.
ADMISSION: Ring.   *TEL:* 01604 810697.

FAVELL MUSIC CENTRE

FACILITIES: Provides musical training for all abilities from the age of eighteen months. Activities with a wide range of instruments.
LOCATION: Lings Upper School.
OPEN: Saturday mornings during term time.
ADMISSION: Termly charge.   *TEL:* 01604 712717/37117.

FERRERS MUSIC CENTRE

FACILITIES: Part of the Northamptonshire Music Centre a variety of tuition is available.
LOCATION: Ferrers School, Queensway, Higham Ferrers.
OPEN: Ring for information.
ADMISSION: Charge.   *TEL:* 01604 637117.

FIORI MUSICALI

FACILITIES: 18th century music performed in period settings. The music includes familiar work and forgotten masterpieces. This professional ensemble consists of between 5-50 musicians depending on the venue/pieces.
LOCATION: Performed at various venues in Northamptonshire (and outside the County).
OPEN: Ring for details of performances.
ADMISSION: Charges for performances.
TEL: 01327 361380 for bookings and programmes.

THE GUILDHALL

FACILITIES: Has a wide range of musical events, from big bands to smaller groups.
LOCATION: St Giles Square, Northampton.
OPEN: Ring for information.
ADMISSION: Charge.   *TEL:* 01604 792948 (Box Office).

GUILSBOROUGH MUSIC CENTRE

FACILITIES: Northamptonshire Music Service provides tuition on a regular basis.
LOCATION: Guilsborough Primary School, High Street.
OPEN: Ring for details.

ADMISSION: Charge. **TEL:** 01604 648207.

GUILSBOROUGH AND DISTRICT CHORAL SOCIETY

FACILITIES: Members welcome.
LOCATION: Ring for details of venue.
OPEN: Ring.
ADMISSION: Membership fee. **TEL:** 01604 740573.

HANDBELL RINGERS OF GREAT BRITAIN

FACILITIES: Details of handbell ringing groups in Northamptonshire.
LOCATION: Ring for information.
OPEN: N/A.
ADMISSION: N/A. **TEL:** 01832 205340.

JUBILEE CHOIR

FACILITIES: Ring.
LOCATION: Meets in Brackley.
OPEN: Ring.
ADMISSION: Ring. **TEL:** 01280 702880

KETTERING AND DISTRICT CHORAL SOCIETY

FACILITIES: Members welcome - ring for details.
LOCATION: Ring.
OPEN: Ring.
ADMISSION: Ring. **TEL:** 01536 514714.

KINGS CLIFFE MUSIC CENTRE

FACILITIES: Operated by Northamptonshire Music Service.
LOCATION: Kings Cliffe Middle School.
OPEN: Ring.
ADMISSION: Charge. **TEL:** 01604 637117.

KETTERING MUSIC CENTRE

FACILITIES: Tuition provided by Northamptonshire Music Service.
LOCATION: William Knibb Centre, Montagu Street.
OPEN: Ring for information.
ADMISSION: Charge. **TEL:** 01933 317222.

LAMPORT HALL

FACILITIES: A variety of musical evenings arranged, from opera to jazz.
LOCATION: On A508 Northampton to Market Harborough road.
OPEN: Ring for programme.
ADMISSION: Varies. **TEL:** 01604 686272.

MEREWAY MUSIC CENTRE

FACILITIES: Provided by Northamptonshire Music Service with a wide range of tuition available.
LOCATION: Mereway Upper School, Mereway, Northampton.
OPEN: Ring.
ADMISSION: Charge.   *TEL:* 01604 231788.

MOULTON BRASS BAND

TEL: 01604 405375.

MUSIC FACTORY

FACILITIES: Activity to enable young people to make music.
LOCATION: Bective Youth Centre, Whiston Road, Northampton.
OPEN: Mon 2000-2200; Wed 2100-2300; Fri 1700-2200; Sun 1300-1700.
ADMISSION: Ring for details.   *TEL:* 01604 712924.

NENE VALLEY MUSIC CENTRE

FACILITIES: Regular tuition and group meetings for young people.
LOCATION: Prince William School, Herne Road, Oundle.
OPEN: Ring for information.
ADMISSION: Charge.   *TEL:* 01280 272881.

NORTHAMPTON BACH CHOIR

FACILITIES: The choir performs a variety of concerts.
LOCATION: Ring for details.
OPEN: Ring for meetings.
ADMISSION: Membership fee, concert charges. *TEL:* 01604 583754.

NORTHAMPTON COLLEGE ARTS CENTRE

FACILITIES: A range of musical evenings, including folk.
LOCATION: Booth Lane.
OPEN: Ring.
ADMISSION: Charge.
TEL: 01604 734218 (Information, tickets, bookings).

NORTHAMPTON CONTEMPORARY JAZZ

FACILITIES: Ring for details.
LOCATION: County Tavern, Abington Avenue.
OPEN: Ring for times.
ADMISSION: Charge.   *TEL:* 01604 28935.

NORTHAMPTON GILBERT AND SULLIVAN GROUP

FACILITIES: Puts on regular performances of Gilbert and Sullivan works.
LOCATION: Ring.
OPEN: Ring
ADMISSION: Charge for performances. *TEL:* 01604 402996.

NORTHAMPTON RECORDED MUSIC SOCIETY

FACILITIES: Aims to let music-lovers hear their interest and love of music with other people who have similar musical interests. The annual programme covers a wide spectrum of classical and not so serious music. Members and guests are able to listen to music without interruption and in conditions which are similar to those in a concert.
LOCATION: N.A.S.O. Centre, St Michael's Road, Northampton.
OPEN: Alternate Mondays from 1930-2200.
ADMISSION: Annual membership fee plus attendance fee; non-members pay by the session.
TEL: 01604 405327.

NORTHAMPTON SYMPHONY ORCHESTRA

FACILITIES: Series of concerts.
LOCATION: Various venues, including Derngate, Northampton and The Castle, Wellingborough.
OPEN: See programme.
ADMISSION: Charge. *TEL:* 01604 20103 (bookings).

NORTHAMPTONSHIRE MUSIC SCHOOL

FACILITIES: Organises a range of music tuition, youth bands, etc.
LOCATION: 125 Kettering Road, Northampton.
OPEN: Ring.
ADMISSION: Fees. *TEL:* 01604 637117.

OUNDLE CONCERTS

FACILITIES: Concerts have been organised for more than a decade, and the variety of musical evenings ranges from 'classical buskers' to jazz.
LOCATION: Great Hall, Oundle School.
OPEN: Usually held Saturdays or Sundays each month from Oct to March.
ADMISSION: Charge or subscribers fee.
TEL: 01832 272227, or individual tickets from Oundle Music 273669 or TIC 274333.

OUNDLE AND DISTRICT CHORAL SOCIETY
FACILITIES: Welcomes new members - ring.
ADMISSION: Membership fee.   *TEL:* 01832 273302.

PETERBOROUGH DIOCESAN GUILD OF CHURCH BELLRINGERS
FACILITIES: The Guild is divided into ten branches - Culworth, Daventry, Guilsborough, Kettering, Northampton, Peterborough, Rutland, Thrapston, Towcester and Wellingborough.   Many of the Anglican churches in the Diocese of Peterborough have ringing bands.
LOCATION: In Annual Report (see above).
OPEN: Each Branch has a regular monthly meeting, usually on a Saturday evening.   The programme for the year can be obtained from Derek Jones (0153626907I).   A list of practice evenings and times can be found in the Guild's Annual Report, obtainable from Jim Hedgcock (01933 312355).
ADMISSION: Annual subscription.   *TEL:* 01536 517699.

RACEHORSE
FACILITIES: The place to go to see good live original music 2-3 times a week. Bar menu, including vegetarian meals.
LOCATION: Abington Square, Northampton.
OPEN: Normal pub hours.
ADMISSION: No charge.   *TEL:* 01604 631997.

THE ROADMENDER
FACILITIES: Billed as Northamptonshire's premier art and music venue.   A wide range of musical events, including artists like, The Damned, King Kurt, etc.   Also a centre for dancers, writers and arts workshops.
LOCATION: 1 Lady's Lane, Northampton, near the bus station.
OPEN: Ring for programme.
ADMISSION: Various prices.   *TEL:* 01604 604222 (information).

ROTHWELL UNITED CHOIR
FACILITIES: Opportunities for male and female voices.
LOCATION: Ring.
OPEN: Ring.
ADMISSION: Ring.   *TEL:* 01536 516835.

ST CECILIA SINGERS
LOCATION: Rushden.
ADMISSION: Membership fee.   *TEL:* 01933 314198.

ST EDWARDS CHOIR
LOCATION: Meets in Kettering.
TEL: 01536 513711.

THE SKYLARKS OVER 60'S CHOIR AND TAMBOURINE GROUP
FACILITIES: Available to entertain at special events and welcomes new members.
LOCATION: Ring.
OPEN: Ring.
ADMISSION: Ring. *TEL:* 01869 810294.

THE STUDIO
Daventry Tertiary College, Daventry
FACILITIES: Concerts are held from time to time, sponsored by Daventry Leisure (Daventry District Council), etc.
LOCATION: Daventry Tertiary College is in Badby Road West.
OPEN: Ring for further information.
ADMISSION: Various prices. *TEL:* 01327 302407.

TOWCESTER CHORAL SOCIETY
FACILITIES: Members always welcome.
TEL: 01327 350088.

TOWCESTER MUSIC CENTRE
FACILITIES: Provides opportunities for children of all ages with a wide range of instrument tuition available. Run by Northamptonshire Music Service.
LOCATION: Nicholas Hawksmoor School, Towcester.
OPEN: Ring for times.
ADMISSION: Charge. *TEL:* 01604 637117.

JOHN TOWNLEY
FACILITIES: A converted barn houses organs dating back to the 1800's, and musical evenings are put on for groups, etc.
LOCATION: Home Farm, Whilton.
OPEN: By arrangement only.
ADMISSION: Charge. *TEL:* 01327 842297.

TRINITY MUSIC CENTRE
FACILITIES: Provides tuition for youngsters in a wide variety of instruments. Run by Northamptonshire Music Service.
LOCATION: Trinity School, Trinity Avenue, Northampton.
OPEN: Ring.

244

ADMISSION: Termly charge.   *TEL:* 01604 37117.

VARIATIONS

FACILITIES: Music and dramatic entertainment - mixed and for all ages.
LOCATION: Varies.
OPEN: Ring for information.
ADMISSION: Ring.   *TEL:* 01536 732522.

THE VOGUE SINGERS

FACILITIES: Details by ringing.
LOCATION: Ring.
OPEN: Ring.
ADMISSION: Ring.   *TEL:* 01604 891307.

THE WELLINGBOROUGH ART BARN
GILBERT AND SULLIVAN SOCIETY

FACILITIES: Produces regular performances, also needs singers, etc.
LOCATION: Ring.
OPEN: Ring.
ADMISSION: Charge for performances.   *TEL:* 01604 410028.

WELLINGBOROUGH MUSIC CENTRE

FACILITIES: A range of tuition for children provided by Northamptonshire Music Service.
LOCATION: John Lea School, Doddington Road.
OPEN: Ring.
ADMISSION: Charge.   *TEL:* 01933 625255.

WELLINGBOROUGH ORPHEUS CHOIR

FACILITIES: Ring.
LOCATION: Meets in Wellingborough.
OPEN: Ring.
ADMISSION: Ring.   *TEL:* 01933 678417.

NATURE RESERVES

The reserves marked with an * are owned or managed by the Wildlife Trust for Northamptonshire. Further information can be obtained by ringing the Reserves Ranger on 01604 405285. There is no charge for admission, but the Trust would welcome your membership which will be used for wildlife conservation in the County. It is not possible to give details of all the Wildlife Trust Reserves. Those listed here are the ones which have leaflets available (at the time of writing).

ASHTON WATER DRAGONFLY SANCTUARY

FACILITIES: This is one of only three such places in the world. Dragonflies are 'ancient' insects, fossils having been discovered which date back approximately 350 million years. Covering a five acre site it aims to protect and breed these interesting insects. There are now 16 resident species of dragonflies in the Sanctuary, which is up from 5 when it was established in 1969. Visitors are encouraged to discover more about these creatures, and there is a Visitor Centre. Free tours are available on open days.
LOCATION: Ashton Wold, Ashton, near Oundle. Entrance is along a bridletrack from Polebrook village.
OPEN: Every Sat/Sun throughout August - 1000-1600, with three guided tours each day.
ADMISSION: Ring for details. *TEL:* 01832 272427.

BARNACK HILLS AND HOLES*

FACILITIES: Covers 555 acres of limestone grassland, which was quarried for stone from Roman to medieval times. Considered one of the finest pieces of relict limestone grassland in England, and plants include pasque flower, horseshoe vetch, cowslip, purple milk vetch, squinancywort and man orchid.
LOCATION: Two miles east of A1, south west of Barnack Village. Although strictly in Cambridgeshire it is still administered by the Wildlife Trust for Northamptonshire.
OPEN: Access usually available.

BARNES MEADOW LOCAL NATURE RESERVE*

FACILITIES: Jointly owned by Northamptonshire County Council and Northampton Borough Council, it was declared a statutory local nature reserve in 1990 and covers 2.5 acres, with a great deal of wildlife interest. It consists of an arm of the River Nene, and most of the site is open water, with plenty of plants associated with such an area. It is also important for dragonflies, and waterfowl also find a refuge here. A boom has been put across the backwater so that boats are unable to gain access. The site can be walked, and there is car parking at the nearby Midsummer Meadow picnic site. Managed by the Wildlife Trust.

LOCATION: 2 miles (approx) south east of Northampton town centre, and isolated when the Barnes Meadow roundabout/flyover was constructed.

OPEN: Access usually available.

BEDFORD PURLIEUS

FACILITIES: 53 acres where 460 species of plants recorded, including columbine, wild liquorice, wood spurge, etc. Small leaved lime and oak, and beech also present.

LOCATION: On the southern side of the A47 and 1.5 miles west of Wansford.

OPEN: Usually available.

BODDINGTON MEADOW NATURE RESERVE*

FACILITIES: On the north-west bank of Boddington reservoir, which belongs to British Waterways. Traditionally managed as a hay meadow, the site covers 5.57 acres (2.4 ha), and was purchased by the Wildlife Trust in 1986 to prevent it from being ploughed up. The area has never been ploughed and so retains much of its old meadow fauna and flora. The plants are allowed to grow and the meadow is cut in July/August and is then grazed by cattle in the autumn. A pond was dug in 1992 to increase the wildlife value.

FACILITIES; The reserve can be walked, and a small car park is on the Byfield to Upper Boddington road, at the north west corner of the reservoir.

LOCATION: Off the A361,1 mile west of Byfield.

OPEN: Access available at most times.

COLLYWESTON QUARRIES*

FACILITIES: Known locally as 'The Deeps', it is as an area of limestone grassland with a rich insect fauna and flora. The largest area (19 acres) of semi-natural limestone grassland in the County, and is a Site of

Special Scientific Interest (SSSI). The reserve is leased by the Wildlife Trust from the Burghley Estate and Easton-on-the-Hill Parish Council, and has been managed by the Trust since 1983. Like others areas, this was originally mined for its mellow building stone and quarry slates. There is a good network of paths through the reserve.

LOCATION: Entry is at two points through kissing gates.The reserve is between Collyweston and Easton-on-the-Hill just off the A43. There is no car park, and cars should park in the lay by close to the reserve.

OPEN: Access usually available.

FARTHINGHOE NATURE RESERVE*

FACILITIES: The area is part of a cutting used by the former Banbury to Buckingham railway, a section of which was filled in as a landfill site. The reserve is leased from the County Council, and has a number of habitats including water (which attracts many dragonflies), meadow (which attract butterflies and has many wild flowers), scrub, etc.

LOCATION: Off the A422, 1 mile west of Farthinghoe, turn by bungalow.

OPEN: Access usually available.

GLAPTHORN COW PASTURE*

FACILITIES: Covering 69 acres (28ha) the reserve was purchased by the Trust in 1968 with help from WWF and RSNC. Visitors might expect to find a pasture, but they will discover a wood. Originally grazed for cattle around the turn of the century it was left, and blackthorn colonised the site, providing a dense scrub cover valuable to nesting birds and for the black hairstreak butterfly. The northern area of the reserve is high woodland which is dominated by ash, and the undulating nature of this part of the reserve reveals its former farming pattern as ridge and furrow. There are open grassy rides, and ponds and damp areas. A Site of Special Scientific Interest (SSSI) the site is frequented by nightingales in the spring. The site can be walked, although there are marshy areas and it can be very wet at certain times of the year. Dogs should be kept on leads. There is no car park, but a wide verge by the crossroads can be used.

LOCATION: Reached from the A604 Oundle to Peterborough road just to the south of Oundle.

OPEN: Access usually available.

GREAT OAKLEY MEADOW LOCAL NATURE RESERVE*

FACILITIES: The reserve covers an area which was saved from urban development through the generosity of the Commission for New Towns and with co-operation from Corby District Council. The Wildlife Trust now manages the site for the District Council. The meadow is an old established area and was mentioned in the Domesday Survey of 1085, and although the upper part of the area has been in arable cultivation for several hundred years, the lower section is thought to be 'natural meadow'. The area is grazed and cut in order to maintain the grassland plants, and the top part is grazed from April to October, the number of cattle allowed varies to prevent over-grazing. The area is open for visits, and there are opportunities for educational activities. Harper's Brook runs alongside the site. There are stiles from the A6014 and Lewin Road, and an entrance gate and stile from The Headway.

LOCATION: From the roundabout where the A6003 and A6014 converge, the signs for Great Oakley should be followed.

OPEN: Although access is usually available, it is important that dogs are not taken onto the site because of the grazing animals. Open days are arranged when experts are available to show visitors around.

HIGH WOOD AND MEADOW NATURE RESERVE*

FACILITIES: Approximately 40 acres of old woodland and meadowland, the reserve forms a Site of Special Scientific Interest. The wood is traditionally managed by 'coppicing', which involves cutting the shrubs close to ground level. This encourages the growth of new stems, and these can be used for fencing and thatching. Coppicing also allows light to reach the woodland floor, encouraging plants like primroses, bluebells and some orchids to grow. Coppiced woodland is also good for other forms of wildlife. The meadow is mainly acidic, and there are a number of plants which grow in these conditions, including sheep's sorrel, cat's ear and heath bedstraw. Cattle graze the grassland to keep it in good condition. Paths go through the woodland, and there is an information panel. The area is good for birdwatching, and more than eighty species have been recorded, including many which have bred in the reserve. Birds include grasshopper warbler, redstart, and woodwarbler. There are also many mammals, including badger, fox, stoat, rabbit, hedgehog and mice.

LOCATION: The Reserve is off the gated road between Stowe and Preston Capes. The entrance is along the Knightley Way until you come to the first hedge (on right), follow the line of this to the entrance to the Reserve.

OPEN: Access available at most times - ring for details.

KINEWELL LAKES LOCAL NATURE RESERVE

FACILITIES: Consists of 50 acres of mature gravel pits, with a hide and good birdwatching. There is also another 80 acres. Picnic tables and car parking.

LOCATION: Off the A605, immediately west of Ringstead.
OPEN: Can be visited at most times.
ADMISSION: No charge.   *TEL:* 01933 623039.

KINGS WOOD LOCAL NATURE RESERVE*

FACILITIES: An area of woodland which is thought to be at least 1600 years old, and contains a wide range of tree and shrub species, together with associated wildlife. By managing the wood by coppicing, the diversity of wildlife is retained, and the work being carried out will hopefully return the wood to its former state. It takes several years to produce a coppice cycle which, when complete, may lead to the return of the nightingale. Birds are a speciality at Kings Wood and include sparrowhawk, treecreeper, nuthatch, all three species of woodpecker (great spotted, lesser spotted and green), tawny owl, and jay - as well as members of the tit family and a variety of finches.
LOCATION: Kings Wood is about 1 mile south of Corby Civic Centre. Car parking is limited and at the eastern and of the wood - and adjacent to the south and east sides of the wood.
OPEN: Access is usually available.

KINGSTHORPE LOCAL NATURE RESERVE

FACILITIES: This is part of an area which is known as Kingsthorpe Mill Meadows, and was declared a statutory local nature reserve in 1990, one of a number in the Borough of Northampton. Owned by Northampton Borough Council and managed jointly by the Council and the Wildlife Trust, it is beside the Brampton arm of the River Nene, and covers some 12 acres (5ha), formerly being part of the flood meadows, and also has the site of he former Kingsthorpe Mill. There are large numbers of insects - including butterflies and dragonflies - as well as birds and mammals. The Borough Council works in close co-operation with the Wildlife Trust for Northamptonshire and together the two bodies have carried out important management work. Parts of the reserve are on either side of the 'new' road.

250

FACILITIES: There are good paths and bridges, with gates around the reserve, and seats are also on site. There are no parking facilities at the reserve.

LOCATION: The Reserve is in Kingsthorpe, 3 miles north of the town centre and off the Mill Way road about 400m metres from the traffic lights at the Cock Hotel.

OPEN: The reserve is accessible at all times.

TEL: 01604 405285 Local Reserves Manager, Wildlife Trust for Northamptonshire.

LINGS WOOD LOCAL NATURE RESERVE*

FACILITIES: Covering an area of 56 acres it is predominantly woodland, with some areas of scrub, grassland and wetland. In the Eastern District of Northampton, the area belongs to Northampton Borough Council and is managed by the Wildlife Trust, who have their headquarters on the site in Lings House. The name 'ling' suggests that the original area was heathland, and during the 16th century it was common land, which eventually became deciduous woodland by the turn of the century. Some of this was felled to be replaced by conifers. There are plans to try to recreate the heather habitat. The wood is a popular place for local people for dog walking. There are a large number of footpaths which criss-cross the area. There is a spring pond, with opportunities for educational groups to pond dip. A dew pond also exists. There is a car park just off Lings Way - and access to the Reserve is easy from this point.

LOCATION: 4 miles east of Northampton, and the entrance is signposted (Northamptonshire Wildlife Trust) off Lings Way reached from the mini roundabout signposted Lings/Goldings, off the A4500.

OPEN: Access available at all times.

MILL CROOK HAY MEADOW NATURE RESERVE*

FACILITIES: 14 acres in extent, Mill Crook is a traditionally managed hay meadow, in the valley of the River Tove near Towcester. The Trust bought the reserve to prevent 'development' and to protect the plants and animals. There are more than 20 different grass species, together with an interesting collection of other plants. The area is managed as a hay meadow. Reaching down to the banks of the River Tove, flooding occurs from time to time. Kingfishers nest along the Tove, and the calls of curlew are not unfamiliar. The Reserve is a 30-40 minute walk from the nearest parking, which is the grass verge on the Grafton Regis road. It is important that vehicles do not obstruct farm gates, etc.

LOCATION: The Reserve is near Grafton Regis and reached over a bridge from Grafton Regis or the A508. It is advisable to contact the Wildlife Trust before visiting the Reserve, to obtain a leaflet with a map. It is important to keep to the paths marked on the map.

OPEN: Can be visited at most times, although the Meadow floods periodically.

NEWBOTTLE SPINNEY NATURE RESERVE*

FACILITIES: A former stone quarry, deciduous trees were planted in the 18th and 19th centuries including ash, oak, lime sweet chestnut and sycamore.There is a good selection of woodland flowers including violets, primrose, spotted orchids and twayblade. Good bird population, including little and tawny owls.

LOCATION: 5 miles west of Brackley on both sides of an unclassified road from Kings Sutton to Newbottle. Several parking places.

OPEN: Can be visited at most times.

PITSFORD NATURE RESERVE*

FACILITIES: The reserve has been established by an agreement with Anglian Water and the Wildlife Trust for Northamptonshire. The Reserve area covers 194ha north of the causeway. In 1971 the whole reservoir was designated an SSSI (Site of Special Scientific Interest), mainly because of the large numbers of wintering wildfowl. The reserve has four streams, each of their valleys forming large shallow bays. It is during the winter that the visiting wildfowl find food and shelter. When the water level drops unusual plants grow up. The plants and their seeds provide valuable food for migrating waders. With the appointment of a Reserve Warden recording and management have become priorities. There are several hides dotted around the reserve, and access is by way of a number of paths. Parking is well provided for at the western end of the causeway, which allows excellent views over the reserve. Limited provision at the end of a sunken road which overlooks the Walgrave Arm - but security can be a problem here.

LOCATION: The Reserve is reached from Holcot or from the A508 at the roundabout north of Brixworth Country Park. Follow signs for Holcot.

OPEN: Access is restricted and permits are needed to visit the Reserve.

THE PLENS NATURE RESERVE*

FACILITIES: On the site of a former ironstone quarry on the north edge of Desborough and covers 14 acres. British Steel agreed a 21 year lease with the Wildlife Trust in 1986. There is a range of habitats, including open grassland, hawthorn scrub, and developing woodland. The site has a range of wildlife, but butterflies and wild flowers are the most noticeable. There is a footpath which goes across the Reserve to the Stoke Albany road. Some steep areas become slippery in wet weather; suitable footwear is essential. The site is suitable for educational activities - consult the Trust.

LOCATION: The Reserve is reached by foot from the north end of the railway bridge leading to Pipewell. Cars can park on the roadside not far from the start of the path.

OPEN: Normally accessible, but some areas may be dangerous in wet weather.

RAMSDEN CORNER PLANTATION*

FACILITIES: A remnant of the ancient and once extensive Stowe Wood, the reserve boasts a number of habitats, including several wet flushes. Rare plants in the County include wood vetch, bitter vetch, opposite-leaved golden saxifrage and wood horsetail. Good bird population including grasshopper warbler, treecreeper, redpoll, brambling and green and great spotted woodpeckers.

LOCATION: 6 miles south east of Daventry on an unclassified road between Preston Capes and Upper Stowe.

OPEN: Reasonable times.

SALCEY FOREST*

FACILITIES: 34 acres of ancient woodland are managed jointly by the Wildlife Trust for Northamptonshire and BBONT. An area of native oak, with ash, maple and sycamore, sweet chestnut, turkey oak, and a good mixture of shrubs, including guelder rose, dogwood and midland hawthorn. Many unusual plants and butterflies, including the wood white. Nightingales can be heard in the spring.

LOCATION: 6 miles south of Northampton and west of the B526 Northampton-Newport Pagnell Road, following the turning for Hartwell and car park is about half a mile on left. The entrance is via a track on the opposite side of the road.

OPEN: Can be visited at most times.

SHORT WOOD*

FACILITIES: The 62 acres woodland was purchased by the Trust in 1974, to prevent clearance for agriculture. There are many uncommon plant species, as well as different woodland types. A remnant of the old Rockingham Forest, it is mainly made up of a mixed coppice of hazel, field maple and ash, with some oaks as standards. Shrubs of interest include spindle, dogwood, wild service tree, guelder rose and spindle. A number of paths cross the area. The rides become very muddy; stout footwear advisable. Stay on the footpaths.

LOCATION: The reserve is off the Southwick-Glapthorn road north of Oundle. A bridlepath leads from this road into the Reserve. Park close by, but do not obstruct the gate.

OPEN: Access usually available.

SOUTHORPE PADDOCK*

FACILITIES: A small area of (basically) grassland covering some 4 acres, it is a Site of Special Scientific Interest. Although small, it is important because few areas of this kind remain in the County (and in the country). The site is grazed annually to provide the necessary conditions for the survival of limestone plants, and in the spring there are many wild flowers, including a good display of cowslips. The succession of wild flowers continues throughout the summer, and these flowers attract a variety of butterflies. Part of the old Ermine Street Roman Road runs across the site, marked by the raised ground. Parking is on the grass verge just before the humpback bridge. Dogs are not permitted when sheep are being grazed. Access is via a stile near the gate on the east side of the Wansford-Southorpe road.

LOCATION: On the Wansford-Southorpe road, off the A47.

OPEN: Access usually available.

SOUTHWICK WOOD*

FACILITIES: Fifty-six acres in extent and managed by the Wildlife Trust in conjunction with the owner's agents, the area has a variety of habitats, including scrub, woodland and grassland. An ancient woodland, such areas are fast disappearing, and the site has been continuously wooded since the beginning of the 17th century. The elms were affected by Dutch elm disease, which in turn affected the habitat structure. Management has also improved the area for wildlife. Paths and glades are mown to add to the variety of habitat, and coppicing allows light to get to the woodland floor, increasing the range of plant life. There are footpaths and some rides through the wood. Parking is on the west of the road between Glapthorn and Southwick. There is then a short walk N up the road past the water tower to the reserve.

LOCATION: Southwick Wood on the Glapthorn-Southwick road.

OPEN: Access usually available.

STOKE BRUERNE NATURE RESERVE*

FACILITIES: The reserve has been leased by the Wildlife Trust since 1988. Adjacent to the Grand Union Canal, it is a low lying area due to the removal of clay in the past. There are several ponds, reed beds and marshy areas, with patches of rough grassland and scrub, all of which are surrounded by tall hedges. More than fifty species of birds have been recorded, and grass snakes use the site for basking and feeding. Butterflies are also found in good numbers, and include species like the common blue, small heath and small skipper. The areas of water - as well as the GU Canal - attract dragonflies which feed and rest around the ponds. The area is managed by grazing sheep during the autumn and winter. A track goes across part of the area and there is also a 'circular' footpath. Dogs must be kept on leads. There is no parking at the reserve, and Stoke Bruerne is very busy during the summer. Take care when parking to avoid blocking drives, etc.

LOCATION: The reserve is in Stoke Bruerne on the Stoke Bruerne to Alderton road, and the entrance is not far from he cottage at lock 15.

OPEN: Access usually available.

SUMMER LEYS LOCAL NATURE RESERVE

FACILITIES: A former gravel pit, there are a number of islands and from the hides excellent birdwatching. Car parking and picnic area. Tree planting scheme in progress. Hides available, including one for wheelchair users.

LOCATION: Hardwater Road, between Wollaston and Hardwater Crossing.

OPEN: Always.

ADMISSION: No charge.

TEL: 01604 236633 (Nene Valley Project).

TAILBY MEADOW LOCAL NATURE RESERVE*

FACILITIES: 12 acres in extent it has been traditionally managed as a hay meadow. Situated in the valley of the River Ise, it is owned by Kettering Borough Council and managed by the Wildlife Trust. One of the best examples of a hay meadow to be found in the Ise Valley, this habitat is now very rare nationally. The Reserve is named after the former owners who were keen to see it preserved. There are 15 species of grass and many other wild flowers, including meadowsweet, pignut, pepper saxifrage, cuckoo flower (lady's smock), great burnet and bird's-foot trefoil. Popular with local people, the best time to see the reserve is during May to July when the wild flowers are at their best and butterflies abound. Parking is in the Leisure Centre car park.

LOCATION: Behind Desborough Leisure Centre, which is in Broadlands, off the Rushton to Desborough road.

OPEN: Accessible at most times.

TITCHMARSH LOCAL NATURE RESERVE*

FACILITIES: The reserve covers 73 acres and it is an important refuge for wildlife along the Nene Valley. One of many wetlands which have resulted from gravel extraction in the Valley, it was the only site which was protected by local nature reserve status. There is a heronry, which is not open to the public. The best time to visit is during the winter when the scrapes and ponds attract wildfowl and waders. Accessible hides enable the visitor to get a better glimpse of these birds. There is also a range of plant life, which in turn attracts many different insects. It was here that Sir Peter Scott watched wildlife before the area was devastated by gravel workings. The Peter Scott Hide, North Hide, Heronry Hide and Kirby Hide are well placed for views over different areas of water. Car parking, and a picnic site. There are paths around the reserve.

LOCATION: Reached from either A605 at Thorpe Waterville (turn off main road by public house) or from A6116 before Islip, following signs to Aldwinkle. Park in car park.

OPEN: Access available at most times.

THORPE WOOD NATURE RESERVE*

FACILITIES: This ancient piece of woodland was managed in the past, and similar techniques are being applied to open up the canopy and allow light to reach the ground where woodland flowers can grow. This is an area of coppice-with-standards. Some trees were cut down to near ground level at regular intervals. This produced a number of trunks which could then be harvested and the cycle repeated. Some trees were allowed to grow tall, and were cut down for a supply of larger timber. A good path takes you around the Reserve, and the Thorpe Wood leaflet explains what can be seen. Parking is available at the entrance to the reserve. Although in Cambridgeshire the area is a Wildlife Trust for Northamptonshire reserve.

LOCATION: On the edge of Peterborough, and can be reached from Nene Parkway between Woodston and Bretton.

OPEN: Access available at all times.

TWYWELL HILLS AND DALES

FACILITIES: 135 acres, with waymarked trail. Limited parking at present. Trail showing how to walk from site to local villages and vice versa.

LOCATION: Cranford Road ,just beyond AI4/A510 junction.

OPEN: Most times.   *TEL:* 01832 274278.

ORIENTEERING

BARNWELL COUNTRY PARK
FACILITIES: Orienteering course to assist in learning the basic skills.
LOCATION: Barnwell Country Park is off the A605, half a mile south of Oundle.
OPEN.. All year round.
ADMISSION: Charge for maps.   **TEL:** 01832 273435.

BRIGSTOCK COUNTRY PARK
FACILITIES: Orienteering course to assist in learning the basic skills.
LOCATION: On the A6116 south east of Corby.
OPEN: All year round.
ADMISSION: Charge for maps.   **TEL:** 01536 373625.

BRIXWORTH COUNTRY PARK
FACILITIES: Orienteering course to assist in learning the basic skills.
LOCATION: Just off the A508 to the south of Brixworth.
OPEN: All year round.
ADMISSION: Charge for maps.   **TEL:** 01604 882322.

DAVENTRY COUNTRY PARK
FACILITIES: Orienteering course to assist in learning the basic skills.
LOCATION: On B4036 Daventry to Market Harborough road and about 1 mile from the town centre.
OPEN: All year round.
ADMISSION: Charge for maps.   **TEL:** 01327 877193.

EAST CARLTON COUNTRY PARK
FACILITIES: Orienteering course to assist in learning the basic skills.
LOCATION: Off the A427 5 miles west of Corby.
OPEN: All year round.
ADMISSION: Charge for maps.   **TEL:** 01536 770977.

IRCHESTER COUNTRY PARK
FACILITIES: Orienteering course.
LOCATION: Irchester Country Park is in Gypsy Lane on the B570, and off the A509.
OPEN: Course can be tackled at most times.
ADMISSION: Charge for materials.   **TEL:** 01933 276866.

SALCEY FOREST

FACILITIES: Permanent orienteering course. It is necessary to acquire a pack before starting the course. This includes maps and information.

LOCATION: Salcey Forest is on a minor road between the A509 and A43 and M1.

OPEN: The trail can be used at most times.

ADMISSION: The pack, containing map, etc costs £1.50, and must be obtained from Forest District Office, Top Lodge, Fineshades, Corby, Northants, NN17 3BB.

TEL: 01780 444394.

WAKERLEY GREAT WOOD

FACILITIES: There is a permanent orienteering course, the maps for which need to be purchased before attempting the activity.

LOCATION: Wakerley Great Wood in off the A43 between Corby and Stamford.

OPEN: Can be used at most times.

ADMISSION: Charge for materials, which must be ordered before attempting the course from Forest District Office, Top Lodge, Fineshades, Corby, Northants, NN17 3BB.

TEL: 01780 444394.

OUTDOOR ACTIVITIES

See also Birdwatching, Motor Sports, Fishing etc.

ASTRONOMY SECTION
NORTHAMPTONSHIRE NATURAL HISTORY SOCIETY

FACILITIES: Has its own observatory.
LOCATION: On the southwest edge of Northampton.
OPEN: Write for details.
ADMISSION: Membership fee.
TEL: N/A. Write to the Secretary, Northamptonshire Natural History Society, Humphrey Rooms, Castilian Terrace, Northampton NN1 1LD.

BUTTERFLY CONSERVATION

FACILITIES: Organises regular meetings, activities, etc.
LOCATION: Ring.
OPEN: Ring.
ADMISSION: Charge.   *TEL:* 01933 663924/01604 758909.

JUNIOR OUTREACH GROUP

FACILITIES: This is the junior section of the Northamptonshire Natural History Society and Field Club and has been set up to provide younger members with practical projects. Activities arranged for studying natural history out of doors; indoor activities also arranged.
LOCATION: At various venues, some held in the Society's Humphrey Rooms, Castilian Terrace, Northampton, off St Giles Street or Derngate (close to town centre).
ADMISSION: Junior membership of the Society necessary.
TEL: Write to Colin Fuller, Northamptonshire Natural History Society, Humfrey Rooms, Castilian Terrace, Northampton, NN1 1LD.

KETTERING AND DISTRICT NATURAL HISTORY SOCIETY

FACILITIES: A range of natural history activities is organised.
LOCATION: Ring.
OPEN: Ring.
ADMISSION: Membership fee.   *TEL:* 01536 512315.

KETTERING AND DISTRICT NATURAL HISTORY SOCIETY - BOTANICAL SECTION

FACILITIES: Botanical activities - including field meetings and indoor lectures, etc.
LOCATION: Ring for details.

OPEN: Ring.
ADMISSION: Membership fee.   *TEL:* 01536 267606.

NORTHAMPTONSHIRE NATURAL HISTORY SOCIETY

FACILITIES: Founded in 1876 through the efforts of eminent naturalists of the day, including Lord Lilford and George Druce. There are a number of sections covering archaeology, astronomy, botany, conchology, geology, microscopy, natural history walks, ornithology, photography and zoology. Many sections have outdoor meetings.
LOCATION: The Humphrey Rooms, Castilian Terrace, close to the centre of Northampton.
OPEN: Meeting times are published in the quarterly programme.
ADMISSION: Annual membership fee.
TEL: N/A. Please write to the Secretary, The Humphrey Rooms, Castilian Terrace, Northampton, NN1 1LD for further information.

WILDLIFE WATCH

FACILITIES: The Junior branch of the Wildlife Trusts. A variety of indoor and outdoor activities organised.
LOCATION: At various venues around the County.
OPEN: Activities arranged at weekends during term-times and the holidays.
ADMISSION: Membership of a Wildlife Watch group necessary.
TEL: 01604 405285 (Wildlife Trust for Northamptonshire).

WILDLIFE TRUST FOR NORTHAMPTONSHIRE

FACILITIES: A number of groups throughout the county, arranging courses, social events, fund-raising, etc.
FACILITIES: Slide evenings, walks round nature reserves, etc.
LOCATION: At various places around the County.
OPEN: N/A.
ADMISSION: Membership of the Trust, but friends usually welcome.
TEL: For details of local groups ring 01604 405285.

PARKS AND PARKLAND

ABINGTON PARK

FACILITIES: This is the largest Park in Northampton. Available all through the year, with facilities at different times. These include playgrounds, ornamental gardens, lake with wildfowl, boating lake and boat hire, bandstand (during summer) and aviary. The Blind Garden is a delight in summer, and this has braille notices. Toilets. Parking on the road.

LOCATION: Can be reached from various directions, including Abington Avenue South, Wellingborough Road, etc.

OPEN: Always open.

ADMISSION: Park free, but charges for activities like boating.

TEL: 01604 233500 (Northampton Borough Council).

BECKETS PARK

FACILITIES: Named after Thomas a Becket who escaped from his trial being held in Northampton Castle in 1164. A large grassed area it is beside the River Nene and along canal banks. Boating at certain times of the year. There are play areas and walks, together with picnic benches and seats. Tennis, bowls and putting available during summer.

LOCATION: Five mins from town centre - Bedford Road..

OPEN: Always.

ADMISSION: Free.   **TEL:** 01604 637982.

BRACKLEY PARK

FACILITIES: Children's play area set in 3 acres.

LOCATION: High Street.

OPEN: Daylight hours.

ADMISSION: No charge.   **TEL:** 01280 702941.

BRADLAUGH FIELDS

FACILITIES: Approximately 100 acres, the area is part of the now defunct Northampton Golf Course, and is open to the public. Seating, park furnitiure and play equipment, together with a boardwalk for the pond have been installed. It is looked after by Northampton Borough Council, with an input from the Wildlife Trust and BTCV.

LOCATION: Several entrances including those from the end of Spinney Hill Road, from Greenview Drive and Holtons Lane.

OPEN: Can be visited at any time.

ADMISSION: No charge.

TEL: 01604 233500 (Northanpton Borough Council).

CROYLAND PARK, WELLINGBOROUGH

FACILITIES: Parkland, with stream.   There are also games pitches.

LOCATION: Off the A4500 in Croyland Road.

OPEN: Daylight hours.

ADMISSION: Free to park; some charges for other facilities.

TEL: N/A.

DELAPRE ABBEY GARDENS

FACILITIES: There is a walled garden, which includes herbs and bushes which have been shaped by topiary into elephants. There is a wilderness garden, lily pond, and plenty of grass to let off steam.

LOCATION: On the A508, London Road, about a mile south of Northampton town centre.

OPEN: Walled garden day light hours - May to September. The grassed area can be walked most times.

ADMISSION: Free.

TEL: 01604 233500 (Northampton Borough Council)/22677 (TIC).

DELAPRE PARK

FACILITIES: An open space with grassed areas, and the historic Delapre Abbey (not open). Elizabethan gardens, ornamental flower beds, fountains, ponds, statues.

LOCATION: About a mile south of Northampton town centre on the A508 London Road.

OPEN: Daylight hours.

ADMISSION: No charge.

TEL: 01604 233500 (Northampton Borough Council)/22677 (TIC).

DELAPRE RECREATION GROUND

FACILITIES: Children's playground with swings, roundabouts, etc.

LOCATION: Towcester Road, Northampton.

OPEN: Daylight hours.

ADMISSION: Free.

TEL: 01604 233500 (Northampton Borough Council).

DUNKIRK AVENUE

FACILITIES: Open space with a play area.

LOCATION: Dunkirk Avenue, Desborough.

OPEN: Daylight hours.

ADMISSION: Free.

TEL: 01536 410266 (TIC) or 410333 (Promotions and Tourism Association).

EASTFIELD PARK

FACILITIES: Consists of 52 acres of lakes and woodland.

LOCATION: Booth Lane North/Grange Road, Northampton.

OPEN: Daylight hours.

ADMISSION: No charge.   *TEL:* 01604 22677 (TIC).

EMBANKMENT, WELLINGBOROUGH

FACILITIES: An area of green space beside the River Nene.

LOCATION: On the edge of Wellingborough, away from the hustle and bustle of the town.
OPEN: Can be visited at most times.
ADMISSION: No charge.
TEL: 01933 228101 (Wellingborough TIC).

GEORGE V RECREATION CENTRE
FACILITIES: Play equipment, seats, skateboard ramp.
LOCATION: Pioneer Avenue, Burton Latimer.
OPEN: Daylight hours.
ADMISSION: Free.   TEL: 01536 410266 (Kettering TIC).

HALL PARK
FACILITIES: Woods, bandstand, flower gardens.
LOCATION: Hall Avenue, Rushden.
OPEN: Daylight hours.
ADMISSION: Free.   TEL: N/A.

HUNSBURY HILL COUNTRY PARK
FACILITIES: Covers 73 acres of semi-rural parkland. It includes the site of a former Iron Age camp. Part of the area includes some of the former Banbury Green Lane, a drovers route. There is plenty of walking, an adventure playground and picnic and barbecue areas.
LOCATION: Hunsbury Hill Road, Camp Hill, Northampton, close to the A45.
ADMISSION: No charge.
TEL: 01604 233500 (Northampton Borough Council).

ISE VALLEY PARK AND RIVERSIDE WALK
FACILITIES: Follows the course of the River Ise and the Riverside Walk takes in the different habitats at Cook's Spinney Nature Reserve There is also a skateboard ramp.
LOCATION: Barton Seagrave, south east of Kettering and off Deeble Road.
OPEN: Daylight hours.
ADMISSION: No charge.   TEL: 01536 521204.

KINGS GEORGE V RECREATION GROUND
FACILITIES: 10 acres which include football, tennis, children's play areas, The Paddocks Bowling Green, bowls, putting, car park, pavilion.
LOCATION: Desborough.
OPEN: Daylight hours.
ADMISSION: May be charge for some activities.   TEL: N/A.

MANOR HOUSE GARDENS
FACILITIES: Open space with seats in a quiet area in centre of Kettering.
LOCATION: Sheep Street, Kettering.
OPEN: Daylight hours.
ADMISSION: No charge.   *TEL:* 01536 410266 (TIC).

MANOR PARK
FACILITIES: Park with benches.
LOCATION: Squires Hill, Rothwell.
OPEN: Daylight hours.
ADMISSION: No charge.   *TEL:* N/A.

MIDSUMMER MEADOW
FACILITIES: The River Nene flows through the recreational area.
LOCATION: Adjacent to the Bedford Road.
OPEN: Daylight hours.
ADMISSION: Charge for car parking.
TEL: 01604 233500 (Northampton Borough Council).

THE PADDOCKS
FACILITIES: An area of park with seats and a play area.
LOCATION: Churchill Way, Burton Latimer.
OPEN: Daylight hours.
ADMISSION: Free.   *TEL:* N/A.

THE RACECOURSE, NORTHAMPTON
FACILITIES: An area of 114 acres, used for horse racing until 1904. Available for sporting activities, including tennis, bowls, rugby, hockey and cricket.
LOCATION: On the Kettering Road, north of the town centre.
OPEN: Always.
ADMISSION: Charge for some events - but generally free.
TEL: 01604 22677 (TIC).

ROCKINGHAM PARK
FACILITIES: Mature trees, bandstand, seats, play area with trains and a station, bowling and putting greens.
LOCATION: Rockingham Road, Kettering.
OPEN: Daylight hours.
ADMISSION: No charge.
TEL: 01536 410333 (Kettering Borough Council).

ST ANDREWS ROAD PARK

FACILITIES: A grassed area beside the river. There is a children's playground.
LOCATION: Bounded by St Andrews Road and Spencer Bridge Road.
OPEN: Always open.
ADMISSION: Free. *TEL:* N/A.

ST JAMES LAKE

FACILITIES: Open space with footpaths and water.
LOCATION: Brackley - Hinton-in-the-Hedges road, which joins the A43 on the southern edge of the town.
OPEN: Can be visited at most times.
ADMISSION: No charge. *TEL:* N/A.

SPENCER PARK

FACILITIES: Putting, bowls, games pitches, tennis, paddling pool - some only available 'in season'.
LOCATION: Washbrook Road, Rushden.
OPEN: Daylight hours.
ADMISSION: Charges for certain activities. *TEL:* N/A.

SWANSPOOL GARDENS

FACILITIES; Ornamental gardens, with putting, bowls and tennis.
LOCATION: London Road, Wellingborough.
OPEN: Daylight hours.
ADMISSION: Free to Gardens, but charge for some facilities.
TEL: 01933 278043.

THORNTONS PARK

FACILITIES: A sloping area going from the Kingsthorpe Road, there are play facilities. One area is the traditional kind; the other is an adventure fort. There are ornamental gardens.
LOCATION: Kingsthorpe Road.
OPEN: Daylight hours.
ADMISSION: Free.
TEL: 01604 233500 (Northampton Borough Council).

WELL LANE

FACILITIES: Play area and open space with usual equipment.
LOCATION: Well Lane, Rothwell.
OPEN: Daylight hours.
ADMISSION: Free. *TEL:* N/A.

PICK YOUR OWN
See Farm Shops

PICNIC SITES

There are also picnic areas in all country parks.

BADBY
FACILITIES: Picnic benches and parking, with views across Badby village and wood - and across the Northamptonshire countryside. Tourist information.
LOCATION: On A361 about 2 miles south of Daventry, and between Daventry and Badby village.
OPEN: Always.
ADMISSION: No charge. **TEL:** 01327 300277 (TIC).

EARLS BARTON RIVERSIDE PICNIC SITE
FACILITIES: Picnic tables, information boards, wildlife pond, canoe launch site.
LOCATION: On the unclssified road to Grendon, near Dunkleys Restaurant and opposite traffic lights at the bridge over the river.
OPEN: Most times.
ADMISSION: Free.
TEL: 01604 237220 (Countryside Centre)/236633 (Nene Valley Projects).

GREAT OXENDEN
FACILITIES: Picnic benches/ interpretation.
LOCATION: A508 near Great Oxenden.
OPEN: Always.
ADMISSION: Free. **TEL:** 01604 236644.

HARRINGWORTH VIADUCT
FACILITIES: Picnic benches/interpretation.
LOCATION: Road between Gretton and Harringworth
OPEN: Always.
ADMISSION: No charge. **TEL:** 01604 236644.

266

KINGSTHORPE LOCAL NATURE RESERVE
FACILITIES: Picnic area in this delightful local natures reserve, with the river and walks. No parking in the reserve.
LOCATION: On Mill Lane, Kingsthorpe, Northampton.
OPEN: Can be used at any time.
ADMISSION: No charge.   *TEL:* 01604 405285 (Wildlife Trust).

MIDSUMMER MEADOW
FACILITIES: Picnic area in a delightful park.
LOCATION: Adjacent to the Bedford Road.
OPEN: Daylight hours.
ADMISSION: No charge - but charge for parking.
TEL: 01604 233500 (Northampton Borough Council).

RIVER TOVE BENDS
FACILITIES: Picnic benches/interpretation.
LOCATION: A508 south of Stoke Brueme and between here and Grafton Regis.
OPEN: Always.
ADMISSION: Free.   *TEL:* 01604 236644.

RIVERSIDE PARK
FACILITIES: Picnic benches.
LOCATION: Weston Mill, near Northampton Boat Club.
OPEN: Always.
ADMISSION: Free.   *TEL:* 01604 236644.

SUMMER LEYS LOCAL NATURE RESERVE
FACILITIES: Picnic benches.
LOCATION: Hardwater Road, between Wollaston and Hardwater Crossing.
OPEN: Can be visited at most times.
ADMISSION: Free.   *TEL:* 01604 236633.

TITCHMARSH LOCAL NATURE RESERVE
FACILITIES: Car park, picnic benches.
LOCATION: Reached from either A605 at Thorpe Waterville (turn off main road by public house) or from A6116 before Islip, following signs for Aldwinkle. Park in car park.
OPEN: Always.
ADMISSION: No charge.   *TEL:* 01604 405285 (Wildlife Trust).

WHISTON
FACILITIES: Picnic benches/interpretation.

LOCATION: Cogenhoe to Grendon road.
OPEN: Always
ADMISSION: Free.   *TEL:* 01604 236633 (Nene Valley Project)

WICKEN

FACILITIES: Picnic benches/interpretation.
LOCATION: Area of land between the old A422 and the new A422 near Cranley Oak, approximately half way between Buckingham and Old Stratford.
OPEN: Always.
ADMISSION: Free.   *TEL:* 01604 236644.

WOOLPACK PIGGERIES/MOORINGS

FACILITIES: Picnic benches/interpretation.
LOCATION: From Thrapston towards Islip, turn right immediately over the bridge, opposite Woolpack Hotel. No parking.
OPEN: Always.
ADMISSION: Always.   *TEL:* 01604 236644.

YARWELL MILL

FACILITIES: Lakeside picnic site.
LOCATION: Yarwell Mill Caravan Park, Yarwell near Oundle.
OPEN: Ring for times.
ADMISSION: Ring for details.   *TEL:* 01780 782344.

POCKET PARKS

A pocket park has three elements. It is owned and managed by local people for their peaceful enjoyment and for wildlife. There is full public access, and it has nature conservation - or potential nature conservation - value. There are more than sixty pocket parks in Northamptonshire, ranging from small areas to much larger ones, covering a wide variety of 'habitat' from water to meadowland - and every alternative in between. If you want further information about any pocket park, please contact Sue Paice (01604 237222) in the first instance, and she will put you in touch with the correct person who 'looks after' a particular pocket park.

Pocket parks can be found at:

Aldwincle	Aston-le-Walls
Barton Seagrave	Blackthorn, (Northampton)
Boughton	Broughton Lane, Northampton
Brackley	Braunston
Brigstock	Brooke Weston College, Corby
Broughton	Burton Latimer
Byfield	Cogenhoe
Cottingham	Croughton
Desborough	Dog Kennel Spinney, Kettering
Easton-on-the-Hill	Evenley
Finedon	Great Billing
Greens Norton	Gretton
Hannington	Higham Ferrers
Hollowell	Kettering General Hospital
Kings Cliffe (1)	Kings Cliffe (2)
Levis Strauss, Northampton	Long Buckby
Lowick	Moulton
Nassington	Old
Old Stratford	Oundle
Ringstead	Rothwell
Rushden-Higham Ferrers	Rushton
Silverstone (1) Olney Meadow	Silverstone (2) Brickle
Spring Borough (Northampton)	Stanion
St Brendan's, Corby	Stoke Albany
Sulgrave	Thurning
Towcester	Walgrave
Warmington	Wellingborough - Brookfield
Weldon	Welton
West Haddon	Woodford Halse
Wootton	Yardley Hastings

POOL, SNOOKER AND BILLIARDS

BARRATTS CLUB

FACILITIES: 25 snooker tables, 6 pool tables, skittles, darts, 3 private rooms, restaurant - all day menu; Victorian bars, family room, children's play equipment. Good parking.
LOCATION: Kingsthorpe Road, Northampton.
OPEN: 0900-2300.
ADMISSION: Charge.　　**TEL:** 01604 721777.

CHALKIES SNOOKER CLUB

FACILITIES: Two pool tables, 5 full-size snooker tables. Function room, fully licenced bar with menu, and catering service for up to 150.
LOCATION: 64-70 Gold Street, Kettering.
OPEN: Every day from 1000-0200.
ADMISSION: Membership fee.　　**TEL:** 01536 415761.

CUE CLUB

FACILITIES: Twelve snooker tables/one pool table. Licenced bar with hot and cold food.
LOCATION: 32 Bridge Street, Northampton.
OPEN: Ring for times.
ADMISSION: Membership fee.　　**TEL:** 01604 639247.

DERNGATE SNOOKER CENTRE

FACILITIES: Fourteen tables, includes 2 snooker tables in private room. Licenced bar with hot and cold food.
LOCATION: 9 Derngate, Northampton.
OPEN: Every day from 0900-2400; closed Christmas Eve/New Year.
ADMISSION: Membership fee.　　**TEL:** 01604 635749.

EXCLUSIVE SNOOKER CLUB

FACILITIES: 15 tables, including 4 in private rooms. Bar, bar snacks/food, weekly entertainment in social areas.
LOCATION: Horsemarket, Northampton.
OPEN: 0930-1130.
ADMISSION: Membership fee.　　**TEL:** 01604 634355.

EXECUTIVE CLUB

FACILITIES: Ring.
LOCATION: 40 Market Street, Wellingborough.
OPEN: Ring.

270

ADMISSION: Charge.   TEL: 01933 226017.

MILL ROAD SOCIAL CLUB
FACILITIES: Six snooker, 3 pool tables and bar.
LOCATION: Mill Road, Kettering.
OPEN: Mon-Thurs 1830-2100.
ADMISSION: Charge.   TEL: 01536 511116.

KINGSTHORPE SNOOKER CENTRE
FACILITIES: Nine snooker tables and private room with darts. Large satellite TV, hot and cold food, lounge bar.
LOCATION: 3 High Street, Kingsthorpe.
OPEN: Seven days 0900-1200; evenings 1900-2030; Fri/Sat 1200-2300.
ADMISSION: Free membership.   TEL: 01604 634143.

OVERSTONE ROAD SNOOKER CLUB
FACILITIES: 12 snooker and 2 pool tables; food available.
LOCATION: Overstone Road, Northampton.
OPEN: Mon-Sat 0900-2300; Sun 0900-2130.
ADMISSION: Membership fee and guest fee.   TEL: 01604 647709.

PALACE SNOOKER CENTRE
FACILITIES: 18 tables with social area, bar and food.
LOCATION: Cinema Buildings, Gloucester Place, Park Road, Wellingborough.
OPEN: Every day 0930-2300.
ADMISSION: Membership fee. Temporary membership also available.
TEL: 01933 227855.

RUSHDEN EMBASSY SNOOKER AND BILLIARDS CLUB
FACILITIES: 6 snooker/billiards tables. Snacks available.
LOCATION: 85-87 High Street.
OPEN: 0900-2300.
ADMISSION: Membership fee; also daily membership.
TEL: 01933 314528.

RUSHDEN SNOOKER CENTRE
FACILITIES: 12 snooker/billiard tables. Bar and sandwiches, also tea, coffee, etc.
LOCATION: Windmill Club, Glassbrook Road.
OPEN: Every day from 1000-2400.
ADMISSION: Membership fee.   TEL: 01933 319191.

ST JAMES SNOOKER CLUB

FACILITIES: 3 snooker tables, one of which is in a private room; 5 pool tables. Food available.
LOCATION: 6 Harlestone Road, Northampton.
OPEN: 0900-2130.
ADMISSION: Membership fee.   *TEL:* 01604 583591.

THE SNOOKER CLUB

FACILITIES: 5 snooker tables, together with billiards, pool, darts and skittles.   Bar, hot and cold meals.   Social Club with entertainment fortnightly.
LOCATION: Station Road, Long Buckby.
OPEN: 1200-2300.
ADMISSION: Membership fee.   *TEL:* 01327 842239.

WINDMILL SNOOKER CLUB

FACILITIES: 11 snooker/billiard full-size tables, bar area, gaming machines, tea, coffee, sandwiches, sunbeds.
LOCATION: 72 Edmund Street, Kettering.
OPEN: Mon-Sat 0900-2300; Sun 0900-2130.
ADMISSION: Membership fee.   *TEL:* 01536 523917.

RACECOURSES

TOWCESTER RACES

FACILITIES: Held several times during the year, with areas for picnics, and special events are arranged to entertain children.
LOCATION: A5 south of Towcester - well signposted.
OPEN: Meetings held throughout the year - ring for details.
ADMISSION: Varies depending on the part of the course - ring for details.
TEL: 01327 353414.

RAILWAYS

IRCHESTER NARROW GAUGE RAILWAY

FACILITIES: Railway of locomotives and rolling stock from the former ironstone workings.

LOCATION: Irchester Country Park in Gypsy Lane on the B570, off the A509.

OPEN: Ring.

ADMISSION: Ring.

TEL: 01234 750469.

NORTHAMPTON IRONSTONE RAILWAY TRUST

FACILITIES: Rolling stock, etc.

LOCATION: Hunsbury Hill Country Park, on Hunsbury Hill Road, Camp Hill, Northampton, close to A45.

OPEN: Sun and Bank Hol Mons 0900-1700.

ADMISSION: Charge for rides.   **TEL:** 01604 890229.

NORTHAMPTON AND LAMPORT RAILWAY PRESERVATION SOCIETY
(NLR for short)

FACILITIES: Formed in 1981 with the intention of re-opening the branch line from Market Harborough to Northampton. Phase 1 is almost complete, and consists of the Pitsford and Brampton Station, two signal boxes, 1240 metres of running line together with additional sidings. Phase 2 is about to start shortly. Eventually the line will be just over 6 miles when complete. The railway recaptures the bygone days of steam and diesel, with signalling of the period. Various locomotives including three steam and many diesel, and a large collection of rolling stock. There is a souvenir shop, light refreshments, free car park and toilet facilities. *Colwyn* starred in the Royal Train scene in an episode of Dad's Army on BBC TV. *Yvonne* spent all its working life in a Brussels Gas Works. Fare paying service.

LOCATION: Pitsford and Brampton Station, Pitsford Road, Chapel Brampton, and reached off either the A50 or A508.

OPEN: 1030-1500 every Sun.

ADMISSION: Charge. Membership also available which includes regular newsletters, etc.

TEL: 01604 820327 (operating days), 01536 723522 (evenings).

BADBY YOUTH HOSTEL

FACILITIES: Recently renovated the Youth Hostel provides simple accommodation in the delightful village of Badby close to Badby Woods, the Nene Way, Knightley Way, Fawsley Park and not far from Everdon Stubbs.

LOCATION: Church Green, Badby; the village is reached off the A361.

OPEN: All year round.

ADMISSION: For prices ring Warden.   *TEL:* 01327 703883(Warden).

BRIXWORTH COUNTRY PARK

FACILITIES: Facilities for up to 24 people (2x12), including those with mobility problems. Wheelchair access. Self catering.

LOCATION: Off the A508, south of Brixworth.

OPEN: All year.

ADMISSION: Ring.   *TEL:* 01604 882322.

EVERDON FIELD STUDIES CENTRE

FACILITIES: Established in 1974 the Centre is housed in the former Victorian Village School. It caters for pupils from 5-13 from the County, and also runs adults courses from time to time. Two dormitories sleeping 30 students, together with staff accommodation. Groups are catered for, and programmes arranged with schools before they visit. Maximum age 13.

LOCATION: Everdon, off the A45 betwen Weedon and Daventry, in the centre of the village behind the village green.

OPEN: Courses run throughout the school term, and the centre is open at weekends for schools groups, and during the summer (and some other holiday periods) for Brownie and other youth groups.

ADMISSION: Fees charged depending on the use of the Centre - e.g. school group, weekend group, holiday group, etc.

TEL: 01327 361384.

FLETTON HOUSE

FACILITIES: The Centre is self-catering, and a wide range of activities is available in the vicinity. These include Fotheringhay Castle and Barnwell Country Park. Oundle is worth a visit. Fishing, boating and bird-watching are possible on the nearby River Nene.

LOCATION: Take the first left in Glapthorn Road into Fletton Way and follow the road round behind The Surgery.

OPEN: All year round.

ADMISSION: Ring for details of charges.   *TEL:* 01832 272179.

FRONTIER CAMP

FACILITIES: Owned by NAYC and set in 11 acres of its own ground, it has a river frontage, and offers a range of activities for school and youth groups. The Centre has accommodation in the Frontier Lodge, Splinters (cabins) and camping sites. It is able to provide qualified staff for activities. Catering is included in cost. Wide range of activities on and off site for which there is an extra charge. All-weather pitch and assault course.
LOCATION: Irchester, near Wellingborough.
OPEN: Ring for details of availability.
ADMISSION: Residential fees, plus fees for activities.
TEL: 01933 651718.

GRENDON HALL

FACILITIES: A youth residential centre available on a self-programming basis. The Hall is a Queen Anne house set in 17 acres of grounds, including a spinney, orchard and garden, as well as a pond. Dovecote Centre - heritage environmental centre - is situated in the grounds. The 60-bed centre includes full catering service, together with a wide range of ancillary 'services'. Outdoor activities available include swimming pool in the grounds, water polo, raft building, horse riding, river crossing, archery, canoeing, orienteering and initiative games.
LOCATION: On the edge of Grendon.
OPEN: Seven days a week, fifty weeks of the year.
ADMISSION: Charges for courses.   *TEL:* 01933 663853.

KINGS PARK

FACILITIES: Owned and operated by the NAYC, it backs onto Nene College, and is set in extensive grounds which includes a spinney. Wide range of activities in the Benham Sports Centre, including badminton, netball, volleyball, table tennis, roller skating, etc. There are various places of interest nearby.
LOCATION: In Boughton Green Road, Moulton Park, Kingsthorpe, Northampton, about a mile from Kingsthorpe, and close to Nene College.
OPEN: Ring for availability.
ADMISSION: Various prices - details on request. *TEL:* 01604 493111.

LONGTOWN ADVENTURE CENTRE

FACILITIES: Run by the Youth and Residential Service of Northamptonshire County Council and is an 'out-county' facility for schools from Northamptonshire. Set in 15 acres of grounds on the edge of the Black Mountains, and within easy reach of the Wye Valley, Forest of Dean and Brecon Beacons. Fully qualified and experienced staff organise and run courses for visiting groups. Within the grounds there is an absail tower, climbing wall, canoe training pool, a zig-wire, navigation courses and problem solving exercises. The Centre is able to offer a range of courses including caving, rock-climbing, kayaking, gorge-walking, camping, orienteering, canoeing, photography, painting, nature study, hill walking, industrial archaeology - the list is almost endless.

LOCATION: The Court House, Longtown, Hereford.

OPEN: Ring for details.

ADMISSION: Fees charged for courses.   *TEL:* 01873 860225.

MOULTON COLLEGE

FACILITIES: A residential block which is suitable for school groups. There are extensive grounds, but children must be supervised. It is possible to look at many farm-related topics, including butter and cheese making - by special arrangement. There are plenty of environmental activities which can be planned in the area. Lecturers/tutors are available for which there is a charge. Visits can be made to farms. Schools packs available.

LOCATION: Home Farm, Pitsford Road.

OPEN: Ring for details of availability.

ADMISSION: Charges for accommodation and for any tutoring.

TEL: 01604 491131.

NEWTON FIELD CENTRE

FACILITIES: In a former church which has been converted for use as a field studies centre. Dormitories available for 7 boys/7girls plus staff accommodation. Self catering; some equipment available. The surrounding area is available, but groups must be accompanied by a member of the centre staff. Courses during term time centre-taught: weekends and holidays self taught.

LOCATION: Newton Field Centre is near Geddington.

ADMISSION: Charges for day/residential visits vary.

OPEN: Most of the year.   *TEL:* 01536 741643.

YARDLEY HASTINGS UNITED REFORMED CHURCH NATIONAL YOUTH RESOURCE CENTRE

FACILITIES: Housed in an old chapel, it has accommodation for up to 40 people, including those with special needs. Various activities including a Soccer School, Christian Youth weekends, etc. The Centre is also available to school groups and all those involved with youth activities. Sports equipment available, together with the use of a minibus. There are schools' village study packs. Rooms include a chapel, refreshment bar, small library, outdoor chapel, attractive gardens, open air theatre and campfire circle.

LOCATION: Yardley Hastings off the A428 Northampton to Bedford road.

OPEN: Ring for details.

ADMISSION: Charges vary - ring for information.   *TEL:* 01604 696307.

SAILING
See Water Sports

SHOOTING

BARBY SPORTING

FACILITIES: Clay pigeon shooting grounds.

LOCATION: Barby Lane between the village and Hillmorton (Rugby).

OPEN: All week - 1000-2100.

ADMISSION: Charge.   *TEL:* 01788 891873.

CHERWELL VALLEY SHOOTING SCHOOL

FACILITIES: Practice, tuition, corporate days, etc.

LOCATION: Nellbridge Farm, Aynho.

OPEN: Ring.

ADMISSION: Charge.   *TEL:* 01280 702519 (Brackley Gunsmiths).

COURTENHALL SHOOTING SCHOOL

FACILITIES: Offers a range of facilities for all the family.

LOCATION: Courtenhall.

ADMISSION: Charge made.

OPEN: Ring. *TEL:* 0880 754418 or 01604 862993 (evenings/weekends).

HIS MASTERS SHOOT

FACILITIES: Clay pigeon shoot set in beautiful open countryside. Professional tuition, refreshments and guns provided.

LOCATION: Manor Farm, Adstone, off A43 at Towcester and north of Blakesley.

OPEN: All year round.
ADMISSION: Charge.   *TEL:* 01327 860284.

NENE VALLEY GUN CLUB
FACILITIES: Mobile clay pigeon shoots for corporate hospitality, but also suitable for groups. Plus a range of other activities, including archery, air rifle shooting, paint ball, full bore rifle, stalking, game shooting, etc.
LOCATION: Ring for details.
OPEN: Ring.
ADMISSION: Charge.   *TEL:* 01933 650129.

NORTHAMPTONSHIRE SHOOTING GROUNDS (SYWELL RANGE)
FACILITIES: Range of activities.
LOCATION: Hannington Lane, Walgrave.
OPEN: Ring.
ADMISSION: Charge.   *TEL:* 01604 781741.

PERLO MILL TROUT FISHERY AND CLAY PIGEON SHOOTING
FACILITIES: Set in a delightful part of Northamptonshire with tuition and guns available.
LOCATION: Fotheringhay, reached off the A650 beyond Oundle.
OPEN: Ring for times.
ADMISSION: Charge.   *TEL:* 0183 226241.

WEST PARK GOLF AND COUNTRY CLUB
FACILITIES: Clay pigeon shooting.
LOCATION: Whittlebury, near Towcester.
OPEN: Ring for information.
ADMISSION: Charge.   *TEL:* 01327 858092 (enquiries).

WHILTON MILL
FACILITIES: Clay pigeon shooting.
LOCATION: Whilton Locks, about a mile from A5, signposted Whilton Locks (and just over canal and M1 bridge), 3 miles north of Weedon.
OPEN: Ring.
ADMISSION: Charge.   *TEL:* 01327 843822.

SPORTS ACTIVITIES
including Spectator Sports

ARCHERS OF RAUNDS
FACILITIES: Regular practice and competitions.
LOCATION: Pemberton Centre indoors - Oct-Apr. Raunds Manor School outdoors - May-Sept.
OPEN: Ring.
ADMISSION: Charge.   *TEL:* 01933 350324.

BRACKLEY AND DISTRICT BOWLING CLUB
FACILITIES: Three and Two rink centre.
LOCATION: Westminster Road.
OPEN: Ring.
ADMISSION: Ring.   *TEL:* 01280 702525.

BROAD GREEN ARCHERS
FACILITIES: Ring for details of membership.
LOCATION: Meets in Wellingborough.
OPEN: Ring.
ADMISSION: Charge.   *TEL:* 01933 224814.

CORBY ATHLETICS CLUB
FACILITIES: Athletics coaching and training.
LOCATION: Rockingham Triangle.
OPEN: Ring.
ADMISSION: Membership fee.   *TEL:* 01536 263759.

CORBY INDOOR TENNIS CENTRE
FACILITIES: Indoor courts.
LOCATION: Rockingham Road.
OPEN: Ring.
ADMISSION: Ring.   *TEL:* 01536 407851.

CORBY RUGBY AND CRICKET CLUB
FACILITIES: Ring.
LOCATION: Rockingham Road.
OPEN: Ring.
ADMISSION: Ring.   *TEL:* 01536 204466.

CORBY TOWN FOOTBALL CLUB
FACILITIES: Regular home matches held.
LOCATION: Rockingham Triangle, George Street.
OPEN: See fixture list.
ADMISSION: Charge.   *TEL:* 01536 406640.

DALLINGTON ROAD RUNNERS
FACILITIES: Coaching and training.
LOCATION: Ring.
OPEN: Ring.
ADMISSION: Membership fee.   *TEL:* 01327 352090.

DANES CAMP LEISURE CENTRE
FACILITIES: Gym minis for under 5's and also mini-sports for 4-7 year olds.
LOCATION: Clannel Road, south of town centre off A45 ring road near Tesco Supermarket.
OPEN: Ring for times.
ADMISSION: Charge.   *TEL:* 01604 763595 (enrolments).

DAVENTRY AMATEUR ATHLETICS CLUB
FACILITIES: Coaching and training.
LOCATION: Ring.
OPEN: Ring.
ADMISSION: Membership fee.   *TEL:* 01327 879651.

DAVENTRY ARCHERY CLUB
FACILITIES: Ring for information.
LOCATION: Ring for details.
OPEN: Ring.
ADMISSION: Charge.   *TEL:* 01327 704064.

DAVENTRY BADMINTON CLUB
FACILITIES: Arrangements for members to play.
LOCATION: Stefan Hill Sports Centre, Western Avenue.
OPEN: Ring.
ADMISSION: Membership fee/charge.   *TEL:* 01327 878736.

DAVENTRY DISTRICT COUNCIL
FACILITIES: The Sports Development Officer is able to offer advice and help to groups wanting to set up their own sports activities.
LOCATION: Villages in the Daventry District Council area.
OPEN: N/A.
ADMISSION: Charges may be made.   *TEL:* 01327 302413.

DAVENTRY AND DISTRICT SPORTS CLUB
STEFEN HILL SPORTS GROUND

FACILITIES: A wide range of facilities for all the family, including squash club (four courts, with a fifth glass backed), Rugby Club with three full-size pitches, and for participants at all levels, Athletics Club, with comprehensive championship facilities. Bowls Club, which is on a self-constructed green suitable for representative matches. Tennis Club with three all weather floodlit courts. Cricket Club - an old established club with a grass cricket wicket.

LOCATION: Western Avenue, just off London Road and close to the Esso petrol station.

OPEN: Ring for details of activities.

ADMISSION: Charges.   *TEL:* 01327 703802.

DAVENTRY NEW STREET RECREATION
GROUND

FACILITIES: Tennis and bowls - also grassed area suitable for games. 'Redundant' steam locomotive.

LOCATION: New Street Recreation Ground is opposite the Bowen Square Shopping Precinct.

OPEN: Seasonal, usually from the beginning of May.   Grassed area always open.

ADMISSION: Charge made.   *TEL:* 01327 879381.

DAVENTRY PITCH AND PUTT COURSE

FACILITIES: An 18 hole pitch and putt course.

LOCATION: On the A361 behind the Community Centre, Ashby Road, Daventry, about 1 mile from town centre.

OPEN: Late March to early autumn.

ADMISSION: Charge made.   *TEL:* 01327 705781.

DAVENTRY ROAD RUNNING

FACILITIES: Organises road running.

LOCATION: Ring.

ADMISSION: Ring.

OPEN: Ring.   *TEL:* 01327 876749.

DAVENTRY RUGBY FOOTBALL CLUB

FACILITIES: Spectators welcome.

LOCATION: Stefan Hill Sports Centre, Western Avenue.

OPEN: See fixture list.

ADMISSION: Ring.   *TEL:* 01327 706286.

DAVENTRY SPORTS PARK
FACILITIES: Full size artificial pitch suitable for hockey, football, coaching courses, tournaments and training sessions. Five grass sports pitches for hire. Club house has bar and social area, and can be used for other activities, including receptions, parties, etc. Changing rooms; foyer can be used as a lecture room
LOCATION: Off the Leamington Way roundabout at the junction of the A45/A425.
OPEN: Ring for details.
ADMISSION: Charges made.   *TEL:* 01327 312223.

DAVENTRY SQUASH CLUB
FACILITIES: Meets regularly and provides facilities for a wide range of abilities. There are five courts, including one glass backed; five competitive teams; adult and junior coaching.
LOCATION: Daventry and District Sports Club, Western Avenue.
OPEN: Ring for details.
ADMISSION: Various charges, including off-peak rates.
TEL: 01327 871307.

DAVENTRY TOWN BOWLING CLUB
FACILITIES: Ring.
LOCATION: Stefan Hill Sports Centre - see previous entry.
OPEN: Ring for details.
ADMISSION: Charge. *TEL:* 01327 310300.

DAVENTRY TOWN FOOTBALL CLUB
FACILITIES: Spectators welcome for home matches.
LOCATION: Elderstubbs, Leamington Way.
OPEN: See fixture list.
ADMISSION: Charge.   *TEL:* 01327 706286.

DERNGATE GYM
FACILITIES: Apart from the usual activities, others include tae kwon-do for all ages. Activities for youngsters including Jumping Joe's Toddlers Fun and Fit Kids.
LOCATION: Derngate, Northampton.
OPEN: Ring for details.
ADMISSION: Fee charged.   *TEL:* 01604 39248.

DESBOROUGH INDOOR BOWLING CLUB
FACILITIES: Six rink centre.
LOCATION: Victoria Street, Desborough.
OPEN: Ring.

ADMISSION: Ring.　　　　*TEL:* 01536 762921.

EARLS BARTON CRICKET CLUB
FACILITIES: Fields two teams in the Northants County League and plays friendly games.
LOCATION: The Grange, Northampton Road.
OPEN: As advertised. Friendlies played on Sundays.
ADMISSION: Club membership fee.　　*TEL:* 01604 810632.

EARLS BARTON LADIES HOCKEY CLUB
FACILITIES: Ring for information.
LOCATION: Ring.
OPEN: Ring.
ADMISSION: Ring.　　*TEL:* 01604 880574.

THE ELLIOTT STARMER TENNIS ACADEMY
FACILITIES: Tennis coaching by LTA qualified coaches.
LOCATION: Varies - ring.
OPEN: Ring.
ADMISSION: Charge for coaching.
TEL: 01850 442022 or 01536 790876.

ENGLISH CONTACT KARATE ASSOCIATION
FACILITIES: Freestyle sparring classes
LOCATION: Martial Arts Sch, Grove Works, Grove Road, Northampton.
OPEN: Suns - Juniors 1300-1400; Adults 1400-1500.
ADMISSION: Ring for details.　　*TEL:* 01604 604914.

FENCING AT THE YMCA
FACILITIES: Teaches the art to 9-15 year olds. Booking in advance to ensure a place. Open fencing competitions are held regularly around the county.
LOCATION: 4-5 Cheyne Walk, Northampton.
OPEN: Wed - 1800-1900.
ADMISSION: Charge.　　*TEL:* 01604 638834.

KIDS FOOTBALL
FACILITIES: Football for youngsters.
LOCATION: Derngate Gym, Derngate, Northampton.
OPEN: Sats - starts 1000.
ADMISSION: Fee charged.　　*TEL:* 01604 639248.

INDOOR CRICKET STADIUM
FACILITIES: Indoor nets and pitches.

LOCATION: Unit 6, Whittle Close, Park Farm Industrial Estate.
OPEN: Ring.
ADMISSION: Ring. *TEL:* 01933 679702.

INTERLEISURE SQUASH AND SPORTS CLUB
FACILITIES: Squash, badminton, etc.
LOCATION: Central Avenue, White Hill, Northampton.
OPEN: Ring.
ADMISSION: Charge. *TEL:* 01604 843512.

KETTERING ARCHERS
FACILITIES: Caters for all levels.
LOCATION: Ring.
OPEN: Ring for meeting times.
ADMISSION: Charge. *TEL:* 01536 790668.

KETTERING LODGE BOWLING CLUB
FACILITIES: Four rink centre.
LOCATION: 15 Northampton Road.
OPEN: Ring.
ADMISSION: Ring. *TEL:* 01536 512763.

KETTERING RUGBY FOOTBALL CLUB
FACILITIES: See fixture list.
LOCATION: Waverley Road, Kettering.
OPEN: See fixture list.
ADMISSION: Charge. *TEL:* 01536 85588.

KETTERING TOWN CRICKET CLUB
FACILITIES: Senior sides, U17, U15, U13 Youth Teams.
LOCATION: Ring.
OPEN: Ring.
ADMISSION: Ring. *TEL:* 01536 510392.

KETTERING TOWN FOOTBALL CLUB
FACILITIES: Known locally as the 'Poppies', home matches held at the Club's ground.
LOCATION: Rockingham Road, Kettering.
OPEN: Home matches and other special matches.
ADMISSION: Charge made. *TEL:* 01536 483028/410815.

KETTERING TOWN HARRIERS
FACILITIES: Caters for 10 years upward for cross country, track and field events.
LOCATION: Ring.
OPEN: Ring.
ADMISSION: Membership fee. *TEL:* 01536 514542.

KETTERING TOWN SQUASH CLUB
FACILITIES: Ring.
LOCATION: Riley Road, Telford Way Industrial Estate.
OPEN: Ring.
ADMISSION: Membership fee. *TEL:* 01536 520099.

LODGE PARK ARCHERS
FACILITIES: Both able and disabled archers welcome.
LOCATION: Lodge Park Leisure Centre, Corby.
OPEN: Ring.
ADMISSION: Charge. *TEL:* 01536 744802.

LONG BUCKBY ASSOCIATION FOOTBALL CLUB
FACILITIES: Ring.
LOCATION: Station Road, Long Buckby.
OPEN: See fixture list.
ADMISSION: Charge. *TEL:* 01327 842682

MARTIAL ARTS SCHOOL
FACILITIES: Provides activities for a wide age range.
LOCATION: Martial Arts Sch, Grove Works, Grove Road, Northampton.
OPEN: Sun - 1300-1400 (children); 1400-1500 (adults).
ADMISSION: Charge. *TEL:* 01604 604914.

NORTHAMPTON ARCHERY CLUB
FACILITIES: Welcomes new members.
LOCATION: Meets in Northampton - details available.
OPEN: Ring.
ADMISSION: Charge. *TEL:* 01604 706787.

NORTHAMPTON BOYS GYMNASTICS CLUB
FACILITIES: Run by BAGA coaches, classes held for boys and girls.
LOCATION: Benham Sports Arena, Moulton Park, Northampton.
OPEN: Ring for details.
ADMISSION: Ring for details. *TEL:* 01604 645612.

NORTHAMPTON AND DISTRICT BOWLS ASSOCIATION

FACILITIES: Ring.
LOCATION: The Recreation Ground, Harborough Road, Kingsthorpe, Northampton.
OPEN: Ring for information.
ADMISSION: Charge.   **TEL:** 01604 721200.

NORTHAMPTON AND DISTRICT INDOOR BOWLS ASSOCIATION

FACILITIES: Ring.
LOCATION: Kingsthorpe Recreation Ground, Harborough Road, Kingsthorpe, Northampton.
OPEN: Ring.
ADMISSION: Ring.   **TEL:** 01604 721200.

NORTHAMPTON COUNTY GROUND BOWLING CLUB

FACILITIES: A number of first class bowling greens.
LOCATION: Wantage Road.
OPEN: Ring.
ADMISSION: Charge.   **TEL:** 01604 632518.

NORTHAMPTON JUDO CLUB

FACILITIES: Mixed juniors.
LOCATION: Unitarian Rooms, Abington Square, Northampton.
OPEN: Sats - 0930-1045 and 1045-1200.
ADMISSION: Ring for details.   **TEL:** 01604 791579.

NORTHAMPTON PHOENIX ATHLETICS CLUB

FACILITIES: Ring for full details.
LOCATION: In Northampton.
OPEN: Ring.
ADMISSION: Membership fee.   **TEL:** 01604 763714.

NORTHAMPTON RUGBY FOOTBALL CLUB

FACILITIES: Home matches are held at Franklin Gardens.
LOCATION: Off the Weedon Road.
OPEN: Details in annual programme.
ADMISSION: Charge.   **TEL:** 01604 751543.

NORTHAMPTON SWIMMING CLUB

FACILITIES: Training, matches, etc.
LOCATION: Various venues.
OPEN: Varies.

ADMISSION: Charge.   TEL: 01604 22849.

NORTHAMPTON TAE KWON-DO
FACILITIES: Adult classes held weekly.
LOCATION: Kingsley Park Middle Sch, St George's Av, Northampton.
OPEN: Sun 1830-1930.
ADMISSION: Fee charged.   TEL: 01604 414142.

NORTHAMPTON TOWN FOOTBALL CLUB
FACILITIES: A second division side, which plays at home at the new Sixfields Stadium, the A45 ring road. Catering facilities.
LOCATION: Upton Way off A45 ring road.
OPEN: Matches as advertised in the League fixture list.
ADMISSION: Various prices.   TEL: 01604 757773.

NORTHAMPTON TOWN FOOTBALL CLUB IN THE COMMUNITY SCHEME
FACILITIES: Early bird coaching for boys and girls aged 10 and under.
LOCATION: Held at the Racecourse Pavilion, Kettering Road.
OPEN: Each Saturday (during football season) from 1000-1300.
ADMISSION: Charge.   TEL: 01604 858134.

NORTHAMPTON WATER SKI CLUB
FACILITIES: Training, etc. Also for disabled.
LOCATION: Ring.
OPEN: Varies.
ADMISSION: Charge.   TEL: 01604 412303.

NORTHAMPTON YMCA
FACILITIES: Keep fit, weight training and aerobics.
LOCATION: 4-5 Cheyne Walk, Northampton.
OPEN: Details on request.
ADMISSION: Charge.   TEL: 01604 638834.

NORTHAMPTONSHIRE ATHLETICS ASSOCIATION
FACILITIES: Training, events, etc.
LOCATION: Various venues.
OPEN: Ring for information.
ADMISSION: Charges.   TEL: 01536 514542.

NORTHAMPTONSHIRE BASKETBALL ASSOCIATION
FACILITIES: Coaching, matches, etc.
LOCATION: Various venues.

OPEN: Various times.
ADMISSION: Charge.   TEL: 01604 712331.

NORTHAMPTONSHIRE BOWLS ASSOCIATION
FACILITIES: Training, matches, etc.
LOCATION: Various venues.
OPEN: Various times.
ADMISSION: Charge.   TEL: 01604 493193.

NORTHAMPTONSHIRE COUNTY COUNCIL
FACILITIES: Advises disabled people about sports facilities/activities.
LOCATION: N/A
OPEN: Office hours.
ADMISSION: No charge for advice.
TEL: 01604 236454 (Special Needs Training Officer).

NORTHAMPTONSHIRE COUNTY CRICKET CLUB
FACILITIES: Variety of matches in season, including County Cricket, various shields and other matches. Kiosks, gift shops, etc.
LOCATION: County Ground, Wantage Road, off Wellingborough Road, Northampton.
OPEN: As advertised.
ADMISSION: Charge made.   TEL: 01604 632917.

NORTHAMPTONSHIRE GYMNASTICS ASSOCIATION
FACILITIES: Provides, training, meetings, etc.
LOCATION: Ring.
OPEN: Ring.
ADMISSION: Details on request.   TEL: 01604 810549.

NORTHAMPTONSHIRE IVC CLUB
FACILITIES: Multi-activity sports, social and leisure club. Organises various events including skiing and ten pin bowling.
LOCATION: Meets at White Hart, Great Houghton.
OPEN: Club - Mon 2100 onwards.
ADMISSION: Charge.
TEL: 01604 411403/491389; 01536 83164; 01327 860606.

NORTHAMPTONSHIRE JUNIOR CRICKET TRAINING
FACILITIES: Ring for details of training schemes.
LOCATION: County Cricket Ground, Wantage Road, Northampton.
OPEN: Ring.

ADMISSION: Ring. **TEL:** 01604 632917.

NORTHAMPTONSHIRE SPORTS DEVELOPMENT FORUM COACH EDUCATION PROGRAMME

FACILITIES: The programme of courses, which covers a wide range of activities, is coordinated by the Forum. The programme (including the Coach Education Programme) can access individuals and groups into a wide range of sports, including archery, athletics, badminton, bowls, canoeing, cycling, fencing, football, gymnastics, skating, shooting, table tennis, water skiing and yachting.
LOCATION: Courses in Corby, Daventry, East Northants, Kettering, Northampton, South Northants and Wellingborough.
OPEN: At various times.
ADMISSION: Various charges.
TEL: 01604 236454 (Coaches Hotline - 24 hours a day).

NORTHAMPTONSHIRE TABLE TENNIS ASSOCIATION

FACILITIES: Arranges training, matches, etc.
LOCATION: At various venues - ring for information.
OPEN: Various times.
ADMISSION: Charge for membership.   **TEL:** 01604 633835.

NORTHANTS STORM

FACILITIES: American Football Team for over 18's.
LOCATION: Ring.
OPEN: Ring.
ADMISSION: Ring.   **TEL:** 01604 491210.

NORTHANTS TRIATHLON CLUB

FACILITIES: Coaching and training.
LOCATION: Ring.
OPEN: Ring.
ADMISSION: Club fee.   **TEL:** 01604 415225.

NORTHANTS VIKINGS AMERICAN FOOTBALL

FACILITIES: Youth kitted team 15-19 years.
LOCATION: Lings Upper School.
OPEN: Suns 1100.
ADMISSION: Ring.   **TEL:** 01933 356835.

OBELISK ATHLETICS CLUB

FACILITIES: Caters for disabled athletes, includes those who have competed in the Disabled Olympics.
LOCATION: Ring.
OPEN: Ring.
ADMISSION: Membership fee. **TEL:** 01604 843032.

RAUNDS TOWN FOOTBALL CLUB

FACILITIES: Ring.
LOCATION: Kiln Park, London Road.
OPEN: See fixture list.
ADMISSION: Charge. **TEL:** 01933 623351.

ROCKINGHAM REBELS AMERICAN FOOTBALL TEAM

FACILITIES: 18 and overs welcome.
LOCATION: Ring.
OPEN: Ring.
ADMISSION: Ring. **TEL:** 01536 723684.

ROTHWELL TOWN CRICKET CLUB

FACILITIES: Regular matches - welcomes new members.
LOCATION: Ring for details.
OPEN: During season.
ADMISSION: Charge. **TEL:** Mrs W Swingler, 24 Leys Avenue.

RUSHDEN TOWN INDOOR BOWLING CLUB.

FACILITIES: Six rink centre.
LOCATION: 144 Northampton Road.
OPEN: Ring.
ADMISSION: Ring. **TEL:** 01933 312680.

SIXFIELDS LEISURE

FACILITIES: Includes an eight lane athletics track. Other activities as advertised.
LOCATION: Off the A45 Upton Way between the A45 roundabout and the A508 roundabout.
OPEN: Ring for details.
ADMISSION: Charge. **TEL:** 01604 588338

SKEW BRIDGE SKI SCHOOL

FACILITIES: Dry ski slope for beginners, improvers, group fun, birthdays, school groups, tuition, private lessons, snow boarding, rental of equipment for holidays. ski shop, ski servicing, etc. Can also arrange activities for the disabled.

LOCATION: Northampton Road, Rushden.
OPEN: Ring for details.
ADMISSION: Charge made.   *TEL:* 01933 359939.

SOUTH NORTHAMPTONSHIRE COUNCIL LEISURE SERVICES

FACILITIES: Organises a series of sports programmes around the District, held at playing fields, sports, pitches, etc.
LOCATION: Around the District.
OPEN: Ring for information.
ADMISSION: Variable.   *TEL:* 01327 350211 x 445.

TARGETCRAFT ARCHERY CLUB

FACILITIES: Club for anyone interested in archery.
LOCATION: Meets in Burton Latimer.
OPEN: Ring for times.
ADMISSION: Charge.   *TEL:* 01536 726677.

TENNIS BUBBLE

FACILITIES: Tennis courts in an enclosed 'bubble'.
LOCATION: The Racecourse, Kettering Road, Northampton.
OPEN: Ring for details.
ADMISSION: Details on request.   *TEL:* 01604 639250.

TOWCESTER KARATE CLUB

FACILITIES: Classes for all ages.
LOCATION: Islington Road Community Centre, Towcester.
OPEN: Sun 1030-1300.   *TEL:* 01327 353455.

TRAIL RUNNING

FACILITIES: Running purely for the pleasure of running.
LOCATION: Any suitable area.
ADMISSION: Free.
OPEN: To suit you!   *TEL:* 01604 237273.

UNITED TRADERS ROAD RUNNERS

FACILITIES: Meets regularly - there are facilities for changing and shower rooms for men/women.
LOCATION: Balmoral Road, Northampton.
ADMISSION: Ring.
OPEN: Sun 0900; Wed & Fri 1900.   *TEL:* 01604 710199.

WACKIES SPORTS CLUB

FACILITIES: Offers a range of activities. Sports coaching, activity holidays, day trips, etc.
LOCATION: Little Houghton Cricket Club.
OPEN: Ring for details.
ADMISSION: Phone for details of membership.
TEL: 01604 762981.

WELLINGBOROUGH AND DISTRICT ATHLETICS CLUB

FACILITIES: Wide range of coaching and training.
LOCATION: Redwell Leisure Centre, Barnwell Road.
OPEN: Ring.
ADMISSION: Membership fee.   *TEL:* 01933 270025.

WELLINGBOROUGH BOWLING CENTRE

FACILITIES: Six rink centre.
LOCATION: Hatton Street.
OPEN: Ring.
ADMISSION: Ring.   *TEL:* 01933 222527.

WELLINGBOROUGH RUGBY CLUB

FACILITIES: Ring.
LOCATION: Cut Throat Lane, Great Doddington.
OPEN: See fixture list.
ADMISSION: Ring.   *TEL:* 01933 222260.

WELLINGBOROUGH TOWN FOOTBALL CLUB

FACILITIES: Indoor matches played at the Club's ground.
LOCATION: Dog and Duck ground, London Road.
OPEN: See fixture list.
ADMISSION: Charge.   *TEL:* 01933 223536.

WICKEN ARCHERY CLUB

FACILITIES: Mainly for recurve archers with outdoor and indoor shooting ranges.
LOCATION: Ring.
OPEN: Ring.
ADMISSION: Charge.   *TEL:* 01327 857640.

YARDLEY OUTDOOR PURSUITS (ABSAILING)

FACILITIES: Organises absailing.
LOCATION: 6 Highfield Way, Yardley Hastings.
OPEN: Ring for information.

ADMISSION: Charge.   **TEL:** 01604 696760.

YMCA
FACILITIES: Wide range of facilities including step aerobics, aerobics, badminton, table tennis, archery, etc.
LOCATION: 4-5 Cheyne Walk, Northampton.
OPEN; Ring for times.
ADMISSION: Charge.   **TEL:** 01604 638834.

YMCA ADVENTURERS
FACILITIES: Sports activities for 8-12 year olds.
LOCATION: 4-5 Cheyne Walk, Northampton.
OPEN: Sats 1830-2030.
ADMISSION: Charge.   **TEL:** 01604 638834.

SWIMMING

See also Leisure Centres, many of which have swimming facilities.

BRACKLEY SWIMMING POOL
FACILITIES: Aqua aerobics, swim and fitness, fitness suite, fun pool and basic pool.
LOCATION: Manor Road.
OPEN: Ring.
ADMISSION: Charge.   **TEL:** 01280 704906.

DAVENTRY OUTDOOR POOL
FACILITIES: The complex consists of a main pool, learner pool and paddling pool, lawns, cafe, play equipment. Free parking.
LOCATION: At the bottom of Ashby Road.
OPEN: From the beginning of May - ring for times.
ADMISSION: Charge.   **TEL:** 01327 702817.

MOUNTS BATHS
FACILITIES: Swimming pool with various activities, including aqua aerobics, ladies training, etc.
LOCATION: Upper Mounts, Northampton.
OPEN: Ring.
ADMISSION: Charge.   **TEL:** 01604 635221.

KETTERING SWIMMING POOL
FACILITIES: Range of courses as well as 'open' swimming.
LOCATION: London Road.

293

OPEN: Mon/Wed/Fri from 0900; Tues/Thurs 0730; Sat/Sun 0800.
ADMISSION: Charge.   *TEL:* 01536 410253.

OUNDLE PUBLIC SCHOOL POOL
FACILITIES: Indoor swimming pool.
LOCATION: Milton Road.
OPEN: Ring - limited public use.
ADMISSION: Ring.   *TEL:* 01832 272407.

ROTHWELL SWIMMING POOL
FACILITIES: A number of intensive courses for beginners or elementary improvers, but other courses run where there is a demand.
LOCATION: Greening Road.
OPEN: Weekday evenings, all day weekends; holidays 1300-1700.
ADMISSION: Charge.   *TEL:* 01536 710835/710151.

SPLASH LEISURE POOL, RUSHDEN
FACILITIES: Main pool, learner pool, beach pool, wet 'n' wacky flume, jucuzzi, water mushroom and finger spray. There are various swimming sessions, including those for parents and toddlers (0-5), children 5+ and adults. Lessons are normally in blocks of ten weeks. There is a creche, and a terraced servery, and arrangements can be made to hold parties at the centre. Free parking.
LOCATION: Station Road in the centre of the town, and well signposted from all directions.
OPEN: Ring for details.
ADMISSION: Charges.   *TEL:* 01933 410505.

THRAPSTON POOL
FACILITIES: Aquarobics, crazytime for kids, ladies only, relax 'n' swim. Lessons.
LOCATION: Market Road.
OPEN: Open for public use all week. Early risers 0700-0900.
ADMISSION: Charge.   *TEL:* 01832 733116.

WELLINGBOROUGH SWIMMING POOL
FACILITIES: 25m x 12.8 metres, with learners pool and diving. Various activities including lane swimming, fun time, mums and tots, swim school, 50+, ladies only, etc. Also sauna and sunbed.
LOCATION: Croyland Road.
OPEN: Ring for details.
ADMISSION: Charges.   *TEL:* 01933 225816.

THE WILLISON CENTRE

FACILITIES: Indoor Pool - limited public use.
LOCATION: Roade School, Stratford Road, Roade.
OPEN: Ring.
ADMISSION: Ring.   *TEL:* 01604 862125.

TENPIN BOWLING

GX SUPERBOWL

FACILITIES: 24 fully computerised lanes, bars, cafe, games area.
LOCATION: St James Retail Park, Towcester Road, on the A508 about 1 mile from town centre.
OPEN: Daily 1000-0100 - bookings usually need to be made in advance.
ADMISSION: Charge made.   *TEL:* 01604 234010.

HOLLYWOOD BOWL, WELLINGBOROUGH

FACILITIES: Arranges free 'Learn to Bowl' evenings.
LOCATION: Whitworth Way, Victoria Retail Park.
OPEN: Bookings must be made.
ADMISSION: Free admission, but fee charged for bowling.
TEL: 01933 441020.

ROCK 'N' BOWL

FACILITIES: Sixteen fully computerised lanes; private function suite, amusements, tuition, Senior Roller Club, Youth Bowling Club.
LOCATION: Rockingham Road, Kettering.
OPEN: Seven days a week.
ADMISSION: Charge.   *TEL:* 01536 414004.

THEATRES

ARTS CENTRE

FACILITIES: Variety of performances arranged.
LOCATION: Northampton College, Booth Lane, 2 miles from the town centre.
OPEN: Performances at various times - ring for details.
ADMISSION: Charge made.   *TEL:* 01604 403322.

THE CASTLE

FACILITIES: Wellingborough's Theatre and Centre for the Arts, it has a mixture of amateur and professional shows, and all events take place in the main theatre, unless indicated in the programme of activities. Includes live stage performances by bands and groups
LOCATION: In centre of town - signposted.
OPEN: Ring for details - times of performances vary.
ADMISSION: Charge.
TEL: 01933 270007 (Box Office)/229022 (Admin).

DERNGATE

FACILITIES: A registered charity providing a wide range of entertainment including plays, artists, shows, etc. These range from orchestra to pop stars, from pantomime to Solid Silver shows - and much more. Cabaret theatre cafe-bar.
LOCATION: 19/21 Guildhall Road, Northampton.
OPEN: Depends on programme.
ADMISSION: Varies.   **TEL:** 01604 24811.

FESTIVAL HALL

FACILITIES: This is the largest in the Theatre complex, with a seating capacity of 1328. Range of productions, including 'big name' concerts, wrestling, boxing, concerts and shows. - ring for programme.
LOCATION: George Street, Corby.
OPEN: Various times.
ADMISSION: Charge made.
TEL: 01536 402551 (information)/402233 (box office).

MCKINLEY THEATRE

FACILITIES: Range of amateur and professional productions.
LOCATION: Tresham College, St Mary's Road, Kettering.
OPEN: Various show times.
ADMISSION: Charge.   **TEL:** 01536 85765.

MOULTON LEISURE AND COMMUNITY CENTRE

FACILITIES: A range of productions, which include those by local groups and visiting theatres.
LOCATION: Pound Lane, Moulton.
OPEN: Most events start at 1930.
ADMISSION: Charges.   **TEL:** 01604 670506.

THE PLAYHOUSE

FACILITIES: A small intimate theatre with various productions - programme available.
LOCATION: 115 Clare Street, Northampton.
OPEN: Ring for details.
ADMISSION: Charge.   *TEL:* 01604 27791.

ROYAL THEATRE

FACILITIES: A highly rated theatre presenting a wide range of plays. It is possible to book a complete season at discount prices. Friends of the Royal also offers advantageous membership, etc. There is a bar, and a restaurant close by. The Royal and Derngate now share some facilities. A 'season' of plays is announced in good time. Has an annual pantomime.
LOCATION: Guildhall Road, Northampton.
OPEN: Performances usually start at 1930; there are also matinees on certain days and for certain performances.
ADMISSION: Ring for details.   *TEL:* 01604 632533/24811.

SAXON SUITE

FACILITIES: Theatre, arts and music centre.
LOCATION: In Daventry Leisure Centre.
OPEN: Ring.
ADMISSION: Ring.   *TEL:* 01327 871144.

SPINNEY HILL HALL

FACILITIES: Range of productions, including musical shows, etc. Ring for details.
LOCATION: Spinney Hill Road, off Kettering Road, Northampton, about 3 miles from town centre.
OPEN: Performances at various times.
ADMISSION: Charge.   *TEL:* 01604 499188.

STAHL THEATRE

FACILITIES: A converted church, plays are performed by local groups, including Oundle School, and there are also touring productions, from groups like the Theatre Sans Frontiere, The Magnificent Theatre Company, Stage One Theatre Company, etc. Pre-theatre supper can be arranged. There is a bar. A mailing list is held.
LOCATION: West Street, Oundle.
OPEN: Ring for details.
ADMISSION: Varies from production to production.
TEL: 01832 273930 (Information and Box Office).

```
┌─────────────────────────────────────────┐
│      TOURIST INFORMATION CENTRES          │
└─────────────────────────────────────────┘
```

The Tourist Information Centres have a wealth of information, and they keep up-to-date programmes of activities. In addition they are able to suggest accommodation, and they carry a wide variety of leaflets (priced and unpriced) of sites and activities in their area.

BRACKLEY TOURIST INFORMATION CENTRE

LOCATION: 2 Bridge Street.
OPEN: 0930-1630 Mon-Fri; 0930-1230 Sat. *TEL:* 01280 700111.

CORBY TOURIST INFORMATION CENTRE

LOCATION: Civic Centre, George Street.
OPEN: 0840-1700 Mon-Fri; 0930-1230 (Sat). *TEL:* 01536 407507.

DAVENTRY TOURIST INFORMATION CENTRE

FACILITIES: A wide range of local information including walks, places to visit, churches, town trail, etc. National leaflets, some souvenirs and guide books, etc. Publishes 'What's on Guide'.
LOCATION: Moot Hall, Market Square.
OPEN: Apr-Oct 1000-1700; Sat 1000-1600; Mar-Nov Tues-Sat 1000-1730.
TEL: 01327 300277.

KETTERING TOURIST INFORMATION CENTRE

FACILITIES: Local information, including places to visits, trails, Heritage Quarter, as well as bed booking service, and national information.
LOCATION: The Coach House, Sheep Street.
OPEN: 0930-1630 Mon-Sat (not Bank Hols). *TEL:* 01536 410266.

NORTHAMPTON VISITOR CENTRE

FACILITIES: Has a wide range of leaflets about local places of interest. Also stocks books, gifts, bus and train information, wide range of souvenirs, postcards, greeting cards, YHA membership, holiday information service, local accommodation booking service and book-a-bed ahead, local and national maps and publications, local guided walks, bookings for a range of concerts locally and at selected London and provincial theatres.
LOCATION: Mr Grant's House. 10 St Giles Square.
OPEN: 0930-1700 - Mon-Fri; 0930-1600 - Sat.
ADMISSION: Free. *TEL:* 01604 22677.

298

OUNDLE TOURIST INFORMATION CENTRE

FACILITIES: Holds a wide range of leaflets about walks, places to visit, etc. In addition, has national tourist information, bed booking service, theatre tickets, YHA membership, local craft and souvenirs, guidebooks, etc.
LOCATION: 14 West Street.
OPEN: Mon-Sat 09000-1700; Sun during summer 1300-1600.
TEL: 01832 274333.

WELLINGBOROUGH TOURIST INFORMATION CENTRE

FACILITIES: Wide range of local tourist information, places to visit, churches, walks, etc. Also publishes a monthly guide to what is on locally.
LOCATION: Wellingborough Library, Pebble Lane.
OPEN: 0930-1730 Mon-Thurs; 0930-1715 - Fri; 0930-1600 - Sat.
TEL: 01933 228101.

TOWN TRAILS

BRACKLEY CONSERVATION AREA

FACILITIES: The original conservation area, designated in 1971, was revised in 1977 and 1985, and includes the Market Place, High Street, Manor Road, Pebble Lane and Old Town.
LOCATION: Off the A43.
OPEN: Always.
ADMISSION: No charge.   *TEL:* 0327 350211.

BRACKLEY WALK

FACILITIES: The walk takes in the historic part of Brackley and covers St James Graveyard, Castle Hill, St James Lake, Town Hall, etc.
LOCATION: In Brackley as detailed in the leaflet.
OPEN: Can be walked a most times.
ADMISSION: No charge.   *TEL:* 01280 700111 (TIC).

BURTON LATIMER - A LOOK AT

FACILITIES: A walk leaflet detailing some of the interesting features in the town, including the church, Free School, memorial and Baptist Church.
LOCATION: In and around Burton Latimer.
OPEN: Can be walked at most times.
ADMISSION: No charge.   *TEL:* 01536 410266 (TIC) for leaflet.

DAVENTRY TOWN TRAIL
FACILITIES: Takes the visitor on a tour of the historical features of the town.
LOCATION: In and around Daventry town centre.
OPEN: Can be walked at most times.
ADMISSION: No charge.   *TEL:* 01327 300277 (TIC).

DESBOROUGH - DISCOVERING
FACILITIES: Describes the interesting places in Desborough including the Church, Church House and Desborough House, as well as the Old Town Cross and Manor House. There is an interesting resume of the history of the town.
LOCATION: Desborough is on the A6.
OPEN: Can be walked at most times.
ADMISSION: No charge.   *TEL:* 01536 410266.

GUIDED WALKS IN AND AROUND NORTHAMPTON
FACILITIES: A range of walks covering a variety of topics including 'Myths, Legends and other tales', 'Hidden treasures', 'Northampton's story', 'Share the memories', 'When the Normans came', etc. All in a leaflet.
LOCATION: As detailed in a leaflet of the same name.
OPEN: Takes place at various times.
ADMISSION: Charge.
TEL: 01604 22677 (Visitor Centre), 01604 843175 (Blue Badge).

KETTERING BAPTIST SITES
FACILITIES: Leaflet describing the Baptist sites around Kettering.
LOCATION: In and around Kettering Town centre - detailed in leaflet.
OPEN: Can be walked at most times.
ADMISSION: No charge.   *TEL:* 01536 410266 (TIC).

KETTERING - AN OFFBEAT LOOK AT
FACILITIES: Leaflet which enables the walker to gain an impression of twenty-seven interesting and offbeat things about Kettering. Available from TIC.
LOCATION: In and around the town centre.
OPEN: Can be walked at most times.
ADMISSION: No charge.   *TEL:* 01536 410266 (TIC).

KETTERING BAPTIST SITES - A WALKING TOUR
FACILITIES: The leaflet gives details of the sites of interest in Kettering.

LOCATION: Kettering.
OPEN: Can be walked at most times.
ADMISSION: No charge.   TEL: 01536 410266 (TIC).

KETTERING PARISH CHURCH

FACILITIES: A leaflet describing the parish church, and its interesting history and what to see.
LOCATION: Kettering.
OPEN: Can be viewed most days.
ADMISSION: No charge, but donations to upkeep welcome.
TEL: 01536 410266.

NORTHAMPTON - A GUIDED TOUR

FACILITIES: This book enables the visitor to discover innumerable areas of the town, and pinpoints historical features, places of interest etc. Available from bookshops.
LOCATION: See book for details.   Published by Meridian Books, distributed by Jema Publications.
OPEN: Can be walked at most times.
ADMISSION: Charge for book from bookshops and TIC.
TEL: 01604 644380 (Jema Publications).

NORTHAMPTON - HISTORIC TOWN TRAIL

FACILITIES: The trail takes in many of the historic sites in the town, with a tour of about 3 miles. The tour starts and finishes at the Visitor Centre in St Giles Square.
LOCATION: See leaflet for details.
OPEN: Can be walked at most times.
ADMISSION: No charge.   TEL: 01604 22677 (Visitor Centre).

NORTHAMPTON - THE MARKET SQUARE

FACILITIES: Looks at the historical aspects of the Square, and highlights some of the events which have taken place in the past. Buildings of interest are also highlighted.
LOCATION: Market Square in the centre of town.
OPEN: Can be seen at any time.
ADMISSION: No charge.   TEL: 01604 22677 (Visitor Centre).

OUNDLE TOWN TRAIL

FACILITIES: Takes the walker around the historic town of Oundle, with its many interesting buildings. Available from the TIC.
LOCATION: In Oundle.
OPEN: Can be walked at most times.

ADMISSION: Charge for leaflet.   *TEL:* 01832 274333.

ROTHWELL - A SHORT TOUR AND GUIDE
FACILITIES: Leaflet describing the interesting features of the town, including the parish church, United Reformed Church, Nunnery, and Manor House.
LOCATION: In and around Rothwell, which is on the A6.
OPEN: Can be walked at most times.
ADMISSION: No charge.   *TEL:* 01536 410266 (TIC) for leaflet.

ROTHWELL
FACILITIES: The town still retains its ancient fair, the charter for which was granted by King John in 1204. The locals call it 'Rowel', and the name comes from the Danish Rodwell, meaning 'the settlement by the red well' or 'the clearing by the stream where the roes feed'. Takes in part of Rothwell and nearby Desborough. Other features include the Triangular Lodge at Rushton, the memorial cross to the men of Rothwell, Jesus Hospital, Holy Trinity Church, Manor House, United Reformed Church, Rothwell House and Market House.
LOCATION: On the A6 to the north west of Kettering - see leaflet.
OPEN: Can be walked at any time.
ADMISION: Charge for leaflet.
TEL: 01604 237200 (Visitor Centre)/01536 410266 (TIC).

RUSHDEN TOWN WALKS
FACILITIES: Three walks - 'World War II', 'HE Bates' and 'Wymington Walk'.
LOCATION: In and around Rushden.
ADMISSION: No charge.
OPEN: Can be walked at most times. *TEL:* Available from TIC'S.

THRAPSTON
FACILITIES: An interesting circular walk, the trail takes in 22 houses of historical interest in a circular trail. The leaflet can be obtained from the Rockingham Forest Visitor Centre during summer or from Oundle TIC.
LOCATION: In Thrapston.
OPEN: Can be walked at any time.
ADMISSION: Charge for leaflet.
TEL: 01832 274333 (Oundle TIC).

TOWCESTER CONSERVATION AREA
FACILITIES: The original designation of 1970, was revised in 1977 and 1984, and now includes Moat Lane, much of Watling Street, the area around Towcester Mill and Sawpits Green.

LOCATION: On the A5.
OPEN: Can be visited at any reasonable time.
ADMISSION: Free.   *TEL:* 01327 350211 (South Northants Council).

THE WELLS OF WELLINGBOROUGH
FACILITIES: A leaflet which describes where the various wells were in the town. Leaflet available from TIC.
LOCATION: In Wellingborough.
OPEN: Most times.
ADMISSION: Charge for leaflet.   *TEL:* 01933 228101.

VILLAGE TRAILS

This section includes the village conservation leaflets produced by South Northamptonshire Council.

ABTHORPE CONSERVATION AREA
FACILITIES: The historic centre of the village including the Church of St John The Baptist and the area around the Green, where many of the older buildings are to be found including the 17th century (former) village school.
LOCATION: On an unclassified road 4 miles south west of Towcester.
OPEN: Can be seen at most reasonable times.
ADMISSION: No charge. *TEL:* 01327 350211 (Sth Northants Council).

ALDERTON CONSERVATION AREA
FACILITIES: Highlights the interesting aspects of this village and gives details of the history of the settlement.
LOCATION: 5 miles south east of Towcester between the A508 and A5.
OPEN: Can be seen at most reasonable times.
ADMISSION: No charge. *TEL:* 01327 350211 (Sth Northants Council).

AYNHO CONSERVATION AREA
FACILITIES: The area was originally designated in 1968, and has recently been looked at again, with the result that the modern development at the edge of the village has been eliminated.
LOCATION: 7 miles south west of Brackley on the A41.
OPEN: Can be seen at reasonable times.
ADMISSION: No charge. *TEL:* 01327 350211 (Sth Northants Council).

BLAKESLEY CONSERVATION AREA

FACILITIES: Originally designated in 1970, the boundary has since been extended. Gives a resume of the area.
LOCATION: 4 miles west of Towcester at the junction of a number of unclassified roads, all of which 'meet' near the village green.
OPEN: Most reasonable times.
ADMISSION: No charge. *TEL:* 0327 350211 (Sth Northants Council).

BLISWORTH CONSERVATION AREA

FACILITIES: Designated in 1991, the conservation area covers the important historical houses in the village, many of them 'clustered' around the church.
LOCATION: 4 miles north east of Towcester, off the A43 on A508.
OPEN: Most reasonable times.
ADMISSION: No charge. *TEL:* 01327 350211 (Sth Northants Council).

BRIGSTOCK

FACILITIES: This historical walkabout takes in the many features of the area, including Brigstock Country Park.
LOCATION: Brigstock is off the A6116 Thrapston to Corby road.
OPEN: Daylight hours.
ADMISSION: Cost of leaflet.
TEL: 01604 237220 (Countryside Centre).

BROUGHTON

FACILITIES: Leaflet showing the interesting places in the village.
LOCATION: Off the A43 to the south west of Kettering.
OPEN: Can be walked at most times.
ADMISSION: No charge. *TEL:* 01536 410266 (TIC) for leaflet.

CASTLE ASHBY CONSERVATION AREA

FACILITIES: The conservation area was designated in 1986, and includes Castle Ashby House, together with most of the village.
LOCATION: 8 miles south east of Northampton, off the A428 Bedford-Northampton road.
OPEN: Always.
ADMISSION: No charge. *TEL:* 01327 350211 (Sth Northants Council).

CHARLTON CONSERVATION AREA

FACILITIES: The Conservation area was designated in 1971, and includes much of the older parts of the village. The boundary of the area has recently been changed.
LOCATION: 6 miles south east of Banbury, 4 miles west of Brackley, just north of the B4031.

OPEN: Any time.
ADMISSION: No charge. *TEL:* 01327 350211 (Sth Northants Council).

CHACOMBE CONSERVATION AREA

FACILITIES: April 1986 saw the designation of this conservation area. It includes a ford, now an unusual feature in most villages, and a 17th century thatched house.
LOCATION: 4 miles NE of Banbury, and 1 mile W of the B4525.
OPEN: Always.
ADMISSION: No charge. *TEL:* 01327 350211 (Sth Northants Council).

CHIPPING WARDEN CONSERVATION AREA

FACILITIES: Originally designated in January 1970, the area has recently been revised, with the focal point being the 13th century church in Perpendicular and Decorated styles. The village has a number of interesting buildings, some of which are listed.
LOCATION: On the A361, 10 miles south of Daventry.
OPEN: Always.
ADMISSION: Free. *TEL:* 01327 350211 (Sth Northants Council).

COSGROVE CONSERVATION AREA

FACILITIES: Designated in 1991, this small linear village has medieval origins. There is a church with parts dating from the 13th, 14th and 15th centuries and, close to the Green and St Vincent's Well.
LOCATION: Just west of the A508.
OPEN: Always.
ADMISSION: Free. *TEL:* 01327 350211 (Sth Northants Council).

CRANFORD

FACILITIES: A leaflet describing the interesting features of the village.
LOCATION: To the east of Kettering.
OPEN: Can be walked at most times.
ADMISSION: No charge. *TEL:* 01536 410266 (TIC) for leaflet.

CULWORTH CONSERVATION AREA

FACILITIES: The first designation was in 1978, which was altered in 1987 to include an area at the eastern end of the village. Most of the village now comes within the conservation area. There are some interesting buildings, including the church and Old Rectory.
LOCATION: North of an unclassified road formerly the B4525 Banbury to Northampton road.
OPEN: Always.
ADMISSION: No charge. *TEL:* 01326 350211 (Sth Northants Council).

DENTON CONSERVATION AREA
FACILITIES: Amended in 1987 the conservation area was originally designated in 1971. The church forms the most impressive aspect to the village, but there are other buildings of interest.
LOCATION: On the A428 6 miles south east of Northampton.
OPEN: At any time.
ADMISSION: Free. *TEL:* 01327 350211 (Sth Northants Council).

EVENLEY CONSERVATION AREA
FACILITIES: The original conservation area, dating from 1968, was based around the village green, and revised in 1987 to take in Church Lane. It includes a number of listed buildings most of which are adjacent to the Green.
LOCATION: Off the A43, 2 miles from Brackley.
OPEN: Any time.
ADMISSION: No charge. *TEL:* 01327 350211 (Sth Northants Council).

EXPLORING AROUND WHISTON
FACILITIES: Village interpretation panel provides information on local footpaths and bridleways, illustrated with local landmarks.
LOCATION: Village Green.
OPEN: Can be seen at any time.
ADMISSION: No charge. *TEL:* 01604 236633 (Nene Valley Project).

EYDON CONSERVATION AREA
FACILITIES: Revision of the 1970 original conservation area took place in 1987. It includes a number of narrow lanes with delightful cottages generally hidden from view.
LOCATION: 2 miles west of the B4525 and 2 miles east of the A361, approximately half way between Daventry and Banbury.
OPEN: Any time.
ADMISSION: No charge. *TEL:* 01327 350211 (Sth Northants Council).

FARTHINGHOE CONSERVATION AREA
FACILITIES: The designation took place in 1978, but the boundary has recently been changed to include a large area of earthworks.
LOCATION: On the A422, 4 miles west of Brackley.
OPEN: Any time.
ADMISSION: Free. *TEL:* 01327 350211 (Sth Northants Council).

GEDDINGTON
FACILITIES: Leaflet giving information about the interesting aspects of the village.

LOCATION: Geddington, off the A43 north of Kettering.
OPEN: Can be viewed at most times.
ADMISSION: Free.   *TEL:* 01536 410266 (TIC) for leaflet.

GET OUT OF TOWN
Creaton, Cottesbrooke and Lamport landscapes. Take a bus ride to the countryside.

FACILITIES: The 'trail' leaflet gives details of places to visit, buses to catch and contains all the information anyone needs to take a bus trip, country walk and pub stop in the Brampton Valley. A number of facilities are given in the leaflet, including bus times, pubs, etc. Various walks, etc. are suggested with catchy titles like 'Slow Stroll': 'Swift Snack', 'Perfect Picnic Perambulation'. The leaflet folds out to form a useful map showing how to get around the 'course'! It is meant for people living in Northampton, Kingsthorpe and Market Harborough.
LOCATION: In the Brampton Valley.
OPEN: Visits need to be arranged linked to the bus services, times of which are given in the leaflet.
ADMISSION: Cost of bus fare; leaflets are free from The Countryside Centre in Northampton, TIC's etc.
TEL: 01604 686594 (Brampton Valley Project).

GET OUT OF TOWN
Pitsford Water - walks and wildlife.

FACILITIES: Aims to get people into the countryside by bus, and explores the delightful Pitsford Water and the surrounding countryside. It is meant for people living in Northampton, Moulton and Kettering. The leaflet lists bus times, where to eat, together with a number of suggested walks including 'Reservoir Romp', 'Wildlife Wander' and 'Rapid Reserve Race and Refreshment'. The leaflet opens to provide a clear map. Available from country parks, the Countryside Centre, etc.
LOCATION: Around Pitsford Water in the Brampton Valley.
OPEN: Your visits need to be timed to catch buses there and back - information in leaflet.
ADMISSION: Cost of bus fares - the leaflet is free from The Countryside Centre in Northampton, TIC's, country parks, etc.
TEL: 01604 686594 (Brampton Valley Project).

GRAFTON UNDERWOOD
FACILITIES: The leaflet gives a brief resume of the history of the village, and then looks at some of the interesting buildings, including The Church of St James, The Old School House, the former Manor House, the airfield and the church.

LOCATION: On a minor road between the A14 and the A6116, east of Kettering.
OPEN: Can be walked at most times.
ADMISSION: No charge. *TEL:* 01536 410266 (TIC) for leaflet.

GREATWORTH CONSERVATION AREA
FACILITIES: Designated in 1985, the village is unusual in having two manors. This is because there were originally two villages - Westhrop and Greatworth - which were joined in 1935.
LOCATION: At the junction of several unclassified roads 5 miles north of Brackley.
OPEN: Any time.
ADMISSION: Free. *TEL:* 01327 350211 (Sth Northants Council).

HARPOLE CONSERVATION AREA
FACILITIES: The conservation area includes the most historic parts of the village, which is along the High Street, and north and south of the church.
LOCATION: Off the A45, 4 miles west of Northampton.
OPEN: Always.
ADMISSION: Free.   *TEL:* 01327 350211 (Sth Northants Council).

HULCOTE CONSERVATION AREA
FACILITIES: All of the small 19th century estate village is within the conservation area. The village is quite unique in that virtually all the houses are listed because of their unusual character.
LOCATION: 1 mile north of Towcester off the A43.
OPEN: Always.
ADMISSION: No charge. *TEL:* 01327 350211 (Sth Northants Council).

KINGS SUTTON AND UPPER ASTROP
FACILITIES: First designated in 1970, the conservation area was revised in 1983. There are two areas. Kings Sutton includes the village centre; Astrop covers the House and parkland.
LOCATION: 6 miles west of Brackley, 4 miles south east of Banbury.
OPEN: Any time.
ADMISSION: Free.   *TEL:* 01327 350211 (Sth Northants Council).

LITCHBOROUGH CONSERVATION AREA
FACILITIES: Designated in 1978, the Conservation area was amended in 1987. Centred round the village green, Church of St Martin, and Litchborough house.

LOCATION: On an unclassified road 9 miles south west of Northampton.
OPEN: Always.
ADMISSION: No charge. TEL: 01327 350211 (Sth Northants Council).

LITTLE HOUGHTON CONSERVATION AREA
FACILITIES: The area takes in most of the village, with the older buildings mainly of sandstone construction, with the Church of St Mary at the centre of the settlement.
LOCATION: 2 miles south of Northampton just off the A428.
OPEN: Always.
ADMISSION: No charge. TEL: 01327 350211 (Sth Northants Council).

MIDDLETON CHENEY CONSERVATION AREA
FACILITIES: The Conservation Area includes an area to the north of the village centre, incorporating All Saints Church, and another area known as Lower Middleton Cheney.
LOCATION: 3 miles east of Banbury on the A422.
OPEN: Any time.
ADMISSION: No charge. TEL: 01327 350211 (Sth Northants Council).

MILTON MALSOR CONSERVATION AREA
FACILITIES: Includes most of the historic centre of the village, and Holy Cross Church, parts of which date from the12th century.
LOCATION: 5 miles north of Towcester to the east of the A43.
OPEN: Any time.
ADMISSION: Free.   TEL: 01327 350211 (Sth Northants Council).

MORETON PINKNEY CONSERVATION AREA
FACILITIES: The Conservation Area takes in most of the village, with many listed buildings.
LOCATION: 9 miles north of Brackley on the B4525.
OPEN: Any time.
ADMISSION: No charge. TEL: 01327 350211 (Sth Northants Council).

NETHER HEYFORD CONSERVATION AREA
FACILITIES: Nether Heyford has the distinction of having the largest village green in Northamptonshire and the conservation area includes the Green, and the Grade II listed Church of St Peter and St Paul.
LOCATION: Off the A45, 7 miles from Daventry.
OPEN: Always.
ADMISSION: No charge. TEL: 01327 350211 (Sth Northants Council).

NEWBOTTLE CONSERVATION AREA

FACILITIES: Designated in 1983, the main feature of the area is the Church of St James of 13th century origin. There is also a good example of a 16th century manor house, and areas of woodland and open spaces.

LOCATION: Midway between Brackley and Banbury, and forms a parish with the village of Charlton, half a mile to the south.

OPEN: Can be seen at most times.

ADMISSION: No charge. *TEL:* 01327 350211 (Sth Northants Council).

OVERTHORPE CONSERVATION AREA

FACILITIES: Last amended in 1987, the historic part of the village is included, and most of the older properties are listed buildings, with many dating from the 17th and 18th centuries.

LOCATION: 1 mile from Banbury on a minor road off the A422.

OPEN: At any time.

ADMISSION: No charge. *TEL:* 01327 350211 (Sth Northants Council).

PASSENHAM CONSERVATION AREA

FACILITIES: The conservation covers all the buildings in this small village, as well as some fields of Manor Farm and water meadows.

LOCATION: Half a mile south of the A422 Old Stratford-Deanshanger road.

OPEN: All times.

ADMISSION: No charge. *TEL:* 01327 352011 (Sth Northants Council).

STOKE BRUERNE CONSERVATION AREA

FACILITIES: The Conservation Area centres around the canal bridge and the canal centre.

LOCATION: 3 miles east of Towcester off the A508 Northampton to Stoney Stratford road.

OPEN: Always.

ADMISSION: No charge. *TEL:* 01327 350211 (Sth Northants Council).

SULGRAVE CONSERVATION AREA

FACILITIES: Most of the village is included within the designated area. Listed buildings include Sulgrave Manor.

LOCATION: 10 miles west of Towcester, 7 miles east of Banbury and 5 miles north of Brackley.

OPEN: Always.

ADMISSION: No charge. *TEL:* 01327 350211 (Sth Northants Council).

TREE TALES OF SOUTH NORTHAMPTONSHIRE

FACILITIES: A map which locates the sites of a number of interesting tree stories from the 'grisly' account of the Middleton Cheney Oak to Paulerspury's pear tree.
LOCATION: In South Northamptonshire Council's area.
OPEN: The trees can be seen during daylight hours.
ADMISSION: Free - but charge for map.
TEL: 01280 700111 (Brackley TIC).

THE TREES OF SULGRAVE

FACILITIES: A leaflet with map showing some of the trees of Sulgrave and where they are to be found.
LOCATION: Sulgrave.
OPEN: Can be used at most times.
ADMISSION: Charge for leaflet. **TEL:** 01327 700111 (Brackley TIC).

THENFORD CONSERVATION AREA

FACILITIES: The original conservation area boundary was revised in 1987, and includes the Church of St Mary and this, together with Thenford House and some farmhouses, are listed buildings.
LOCATION: 4 miles north of Banbury on an unclassified road.
OPEN: Can be seen at any time.
ADMISSION: Free. **TEL:** 01295 350211 (Sth Northants Council).

TIFFIELD CONSERVATION AREA

FACILITIES: Includes the central core of the village containing the older properties, including the 13th century Church of St John, Bridge House, Lower End Farm and Tiffield Grange.
LOCATION: 3 miles north of Towcester, just off the A43.
OPEN: Always.
ADMISSION: Free. **TEL:** 01327 350211 (Sth Northants Council).

TREE TRAIL, SYWELL COUNTRY PARK.

FACILITIES: A simple guide to the identification of trees below the dam.
LOCATION: Sywell Country Park is in Washbrook Lane, and reached off the A4500 at the Earls Barton crossroads.
OPEN: Daylight hours.
ADMISSION: Charge for leaflet.
TEL: 01604 810970 (Sywell Country Park)/237220 (Countryside Centre).

WALGRAVE
Landscapes from the past
FACILITIES: Produced by Northamptonshire Heritage, this circular trail around the village explores the still visible traces of the medieval village and its landscapes.
LOCATION: Walgrave.
OPEN: Can be walked at most times.
ADMISSION: No charge. **TEL:** 01604 237272 (Northants Heritage).

WICKEN CONSERVATION AREA
FACILITIES: The conservation area is mainly centred on the northern area of the village, and includes the Church, Home Farm and Manor House.
LOCATION: 5 miles west of Milton Keynes, on a quiet unclassified road, just S of Whittlewood Forest.
OPEN: Any time.
ADMISSION: Free. **TEL:** 01327 35221 (Sth Northants Council).

WILBARSTON - AROUND
FACILITIES: Takes visitors in and around this interesting village.
LOCATION: In and around the village.
OPEN: Can be walked at most times.
ADMISSION: Free. **TEL:** 01536 410266 (Kettering TIC).

YARDLEY HASTINGS CONSERVATION AREA
FACILITIES: The conservation area includes some former farm buildings which have been converted to residential use, as well as the Square, High Street and St Andrew's Church.
LOCATION: 8 miles south east of Northampton on the A428.
OPEN: Always.
ADMISSION: Free. **TEL:** 01327 350211 (Sth Northants Council).

VOLUNTEER BUREAUX

The five volunteer Bureaux in the County offer a wide range of opportunities for those wishing to volunteer, and those wanting volunteers. The 'jobs' are endless - from work in the countryside to helping with a variety of old people's groups, charities, etc. Ring for further information.

DAVENTRY VOLUNTEER CENTRE
LOCATION: The Bureau is situated in the Library in North Street.
OPEN: Tues/Fri 0930-1430.
TEL: 01327 300614.

KETTERING VOLUNTEER BUREAU
LOCATION: 15 London Road.
OPEN: Tues-Fri 0900-1500.
TEL: 01536 81116.

NORTHAMPTON VOLUNTEER BUREAU
LOCATION: 21 St Giles Street.
OPEN: Mon-Fri 1000-1600.
TEL: 01604 637522.

SOUTH NORTHANTS VOLUNTEER BUREAU
LOCATION: Town Hall, 86 Watling Street, Towcester.
OPEN: Ring for times.
TEL: 01327 358264.

WELLINGBOROUGH VOLUNTEER BUREAU
LOCATION: 6 Park Road.
OPEN: Mon-Wed & Fri 0900-1630; Thurs 0900-1130.
TEL: 01933 276933.

VOLUNTEERING IN THE COUNTRYSIDE

BARNWELL AND BRIGSTOCK CONSERVATION VOLUNTEERS

FACILITIES: A range of conservation tasks and activities in these two country parks.
LOCATION: Barnwell is just south of Oundle on the Thrapston road, the old A605; Brigstock on south side of village off A6116 Brigstock bypass.
OPEN: Ring.
ADMISSION: No charge.
TEL: 01832 273435 (Barnwell)/01536 373625 (Brigstock).

BRACKLEY AMENITY SOCIETY

FACILITIES: The Society aims to encourage a high standard of architecture and town planning in Brackley, to stimulate public interest in a care for beauty, history and the character of Brackley, to encourage the preservation, development, improvement and beautification of features of general public amenity or historic interest.
LOCATION: Meets in Brackley.
OPEN: Ring.
ADMISSION: Membership fee.   *TEL:* 01280 703253.

BRAMPTON VALLEY COUNTRYSIDE PROJECT

FACILITIES: Set up by Northamptonshire County Council and is grant-aided by the Countryside Commission. Different from a country park, the Project recognises that there are many needs within an area, and it aims 'to increase the potential for nature conservation, recreation and education by working with landowners and local communities; encouraging good practice and developing ideas for the benefit of both local people and visitors to the area'. There are opportunities for volunteers in the area to plant trees, clear ponds, etc.
LOCATION: Between Northampton and Market Harborough. The Project Officer is based at Lamport.
OPEN: N/A.
TEL: 01604 686327/0860 601593 (Project Officer).

BRAMPTON VALLEY WAY

FACILITIES: Volunteers always needed for a variety of jobs along this 14 mile linear park.
LOCATION: Between Northampton and Market Harborough.

314

OPEN: Ring for information.
ADMISSION: No charge.   *TEL:* 01604 686594.

BRIGSTOCK COUNTRY PARK
see Barnwell and Brigstock Conservation Volunteers

BRITISH TRUST FOR CONSERVATION VOLUNTEERS
FACILITIES: Always on the lookout for people who can spend some time in the countryside engaged in a wide range of practical conservation projects. A regular programme is drawn up, and this includes work with organisations like the Woodland Trust, the Wildlife Trust for Northamptonshire and British Waterways. There are some residential courses. Skills are taught, and include hedge-laying and coppicing. In addition to 'in-county' activities, the British Trust for Conservation Volunteers (BTCV) arranges a wide range of courses in different parts of the country.
LOCATION: At various places in the County - transport is provided.
OPEN: Projects usually take place on Tues and Thurs.
TEL: 01604 266456.

BRIXWORTH COUNTRY PARK
FACILITIES: Range of opportunities for volunteers to carry out conservation work in this 'new' country park overlooking Pitsford Water.
LOCATION: Just off the A508, signposted at the roundabout at the Northampton end of the Brixworth bypass.
OPEN: Ring for details.
ADMISSION: No charge.   *TEL:* 01604 882322.

BROCKWATCH AND NORTH NORTHANTS BADGERS
FACILITIES: Protection of setts, dealing with injured badgers, interference with setts, etc.
LOCATION: Covers the County.
OPEN: Anytime.
ADMISSION: Membership of one of the groups.
TEL: Emergency 0831 45124. Brockwatch: 01327 706349/01604 281761; North Northants: 01536 760141/510469/761088.

BUTTERFLY CONSERVATION
FACILITIES: Organises work parties from time to time on sites which are important for butterflies.
LOCATION: At sites to be announced.
OPEN: Details in newsletters, etc.

ADMISSION: Work parties usually consist of members of Butterfly Conservation.
TEL: 01582 663784.

DAVENTRY COUNTRY PARK CONSERVATION VOLUNTEERS

FACILITIES: Volunteers meet to help maintain various areas in the country park. Projects are arranged at various times of the year and announced in a leaflet which can be obtained from the country park, local library and TIC.
OPEN: Varies - see leaflets.
ADMISSION: No charge.
LOCATION: The Park is situated on the B4036 Daventry to Market Harborough road about 1 mile from the town centre.
TEL: 01327 877193 (Ranger).

FRIENDS OF THE DONKEY SANCTUARY

FACILITIES: Provides donkeys at home and abroad with new homes, and also has a welfare and educational service. Periodically looking for suitable homes for donkeys, as well as people able to fund-raise - provided your are over 18. The Sanctuary also provides indoor centres to bring together special needs children and donkeys.
LOCATION: N/A.
OPEN: N/A.
ADMISSION: N/A.   *TEL:* 01536 510622.

HIGHAM FERRERS NATURE CONSERVATION GROUP

FACILITIES: Manages various wildlife areas in the town.
LOCATION: In and around Higham Ferrers.
OPEN: Ring.
ADMISSION: Ring.   *TEL:* 01234 222304 (Dr N Lindner - work).

IRCHESTER COUNTRY PARK CONSERVATION VOLUNTEERS

FACILITIES: Meets to carry out management work in the country park. A programme of activities is drawn up regularly.
LOCATION: On B570 Little Irchester to Irchester road, and off A509 south east of Wellingborough.
OPEN: Varies.
ADMISSION: No charge.   *TEL:* 01933 276866.

NATIONAL TRUST

FACILITIES: Needs volunteers to help with management, professional and technical tasks.

LOCATION: Sites in the East Midlands (which includes Northamptonshire).

OPEN: Ring for information.

ADMISSION: No charge.   *TEL:* 01909 486411.

NENE VALLEY PROJECT

FACILITIES: Volunteers always needed for a range of activities, from re-stocking leaflet dispensers to conservation work.

LOCATION: Various points along the Nene Valley.

OPEN: Ring for details.

ADMISSION: No charge.   *TEL:* 01604 236633.

NENN - NORTHAMPTONSHIRE ENVIRONMENTAL NETWORK

FACILITIES: Always has 'jobs' - from conservation work out of doors to mailing and newsletter production.

LOCATION: Across the County.

ADMISSION: Fee for Newsletter.

OPEN: N/A.   *TEL:* 01604 630719.

NORTHAMPTON AND LAMPORT RAILWAY

FACILITIES: Is situated along part of the now disused Northampton to Market Harborough Railway line. Volunteers are needed every Sunday.

LOCATION: Brampton Station, Pitsford Road, Chapel Brampton.

OPEN: For volunteers - 1030-1700 Suns.

ADMISSION: Free for volunteers. *TEL:* 01604 820327 (Operating days)

NORTHAMPTONSHIRE DORMOUSE GROUP

FACILITIES: The Group arranges indoor and outdoor meetings. Most of the outdoor meetings are to check dormouse nesting boxes, and there are also training days for members, so that they can handle the mammals and record data, especially important if you wish to become a dormouse licence holder. The mammal is a protected species.

LOCATION: Indoor meetings are held at the Fox Inn, Wilbarston (North) and White Hart, Grafton Regis (South).

ADMISSION: Small charge for meetings/social gatherings.

OPEN: Indoor meetings are held bi-monthly - 1930 (North) 2000 (South). Outdoor meetings are per programme.

TEL: 01536 761712/01604 405285.

NORTHAMPTONSHIRE RECORD OFFICE

FACILITIES: Volunteers needed to do (almost) anything connected with records and who will help in a variety of ways. There is a need for people to transcribe records.
LOCATION: Wootton Hall Park, close to Police Headquarters at the Wootton Hall roundabout.
ADMISSION: N/A.
OPEN: Ring.   *TEL:* 01604 762129.

NORTHAMPTONSHIRE RURAL ACTION FOR THE ENVIRONMENT

FACILITIES: Offers grants, advice and training, to help you take action in your village. Set up to help with local projects which relate to the environment and encourages local residents of a community to get involved. The following can be carried out: recruit and train volunteers, environment evening classes, woodland management plan, village appraisal, photographic study, village appraisal, village trail, landscaping of a public area, energy saving study, pond restoration, wildlife survey, guided walks, parish map production, nature trail, etc.
LOCATION: In your village!
ADMISSION: The scheme is open to any local community group in a rural area. You don't have to be an expert.
OPEN: In your parish.
TEL: 01604 76588 (Northamptonshire ACRE who will give details of local advisers).

OTTER GROUP

FACILITIES: Needs help with survey work.
LOCATION: Various places in the County.
OPEN: Various times.
ADMISSION: No charge.
TEL: 01604 405285 (Wildlife Trust).

PARISH PATHS WARDEN SCHEME

FACILITIES: The Project has been set up to protect and manage the various paths in and around villages. Help is always needed via the local parish paths contact, and also to set up new projects. Each village involved has its own Parish Path Warden. Individuals needed to run groups. Volunteers also needed.
LOCATION: Various villages around the county.
OPEN: Programme arranged locally.
ADMISSION: N/A.   *TEL:* 01604 237224.

318

PARISH TREE WARDEN SCHEME

FACILITIES: The Scheme operates in many villages in Northamptonshire, and is part of a national initiative in which volunteers are appointed to collect information, offer advice, etc. Training days are held.
LOCATION: Various villages around the County - ask your Parish Council.
OPEN: Varies.
ADMISSION: No charge.
TEL: 01604 236763 (Northamptonshire County Council Trees and Landscape Officer).

POCKET PARKS

FACILITIES: Pocket Parks are sited in various places around the County. They are usually small areas of countryside and town which have been 'acquired' by local people, and are managed by them, and involve the local community. Those already established require regular work, and new ones are being set up all the time. There are now more than sixty of these areas in the County, each of which has a local management committee. Large range of activities take place, as well as valuable management work. A pack is available to those groups wishing to set up their own parks.
LOCATION: In various villages and towns around Northamptonshire. See also separate entry POCKET PARKS.
OPEN: Varies from park to park.
ADMISSION: No charge.   *TEL:* 01604 237222 (Pocket Parks Officer).

SYWELL LEMMING CATCHERS

FACILITIES: The group was set up to provide a conservation task force for Sywell Country Park. Various programmes of work are arranged. Further information can be obtained from the rangers.
LOCATION: Sywell Country Park is situated off the A4500 Northampton to Wellingborough road, and reached from the crossroads at Earls Barton on the A4500.
OPEN: Ring for information.   *TEL:* 01604 810970.

TUESDAY GROUP

FACILITIES: Meets each week at Irchester Country Park, and will suit students, the unemployed, retired, etc. A variety of conservation projects is organised by the Rangers.
LOCATION: Gypsy Lane on the B570, Little Irchester to Irchester road and off the A509, south east of Wellingborough.
OPEN: Every Tuesday - ring for details.

ADMISSION: Ring for details.   *TEL:* 01933 276866.

WILDLIFE TRUST FOR NORTHAMPTONSHIRE

FACILITIES: Has a regular conservation volunteer group which carries out work in the Trust's reserves around the County. The Conservation Volunteers are taught traditional countryside skills, such as coppicing and hedge-laying in return for their work on the reserves. A leaflet is produced at regular intervals giving details of the areas where work is being carried out. Also carries out surveys - help needed.

LOCATION: Work is carried out at any of the Trust's 45 reserves around the County.

OPEN: Volunteers usually work on Wed/Suns.

ADMISSION: No charge and a minibus takes volunteers to the site.

TEL: 01604 405285 (Wildlife Trust).

WILDLIFE TRUST

FACILITIES: Carries out a variety of surveys and is always looking for assistance. Those at present in progress include dormice and water voles.

LOCATION: At various places around the county.

OPEN: Ring for details of surveys in progress.

ADMISSION: N/A.   *TEL:* 01604 405285.

WOODPECKER VOLUNTEER GROUP

FACILITIES: Meets regularly at Irchester Country Park and is open to everyone, but many families get involved.

FACILITIES: A range of conservation activities aimed at a wide age range.

LOCATION: Gypsy Lane on the B570 Little Irchester to Irchester Road and of the A509 SE of Wellingborough.

OPEN: Once a month - ring for details.

ADMISSION: Ring for details.   *TEL:* 01933 276866.

WALKS
COUNTRYSIDE AND CANALS

See also village walks

BARNWELL'S NATURE TRAIL

FACILITIES: A half mile walk, with the aim of helping visitors to discover the wildlife in the country park. Audio tape available.

LOCATION: On the former A650 between the Oundle bypass and Oundle.
OPEN: Can be walked most times.
ADMISSION: Charge for leaflet. **TEL:** 01832 273435.

BLISWORTH

FACILITIES: Blisworth has evolved into a large village, much of it due in the recent past to the arrival of the canals. This leaflet takes the walker around the village, looking at places of interest, including the former brickworks house, the well-known Blisworth tunnel, boat yard, tunnel airshafts, etc.
LOCATION: Blisworth is reached off the A508.
OPEN: Can be walked at most times.
ADMISSION: Charge for leaflet.
TEL: 01604 237220 (Countryside Centre).

BLUE BADGE GUIDES

FACILITIES: Arranges a variety of walks in different parts of the County. They are also able to offer 'tailor-made' walks for specific occasions.
LOCATION: In various parts of the County.
OPEN: The walks take place at different times and in different venues.
ADMISSION: Charge made. **TEL:** 01604 843175 (Organiser).

BODDINGTON RESERVOIR

FACILITIES: The footpath between Byfield and Lower Boddington runs along part of the southern bank of the reservoir.
LOCATION: On the Byfield to Boddington Road, just off the A361 at Byfield, and about a mile on the left.
OPEN: Daylight hours.
ADMISSION: No charge. **TEL:** N/A.

BRAUNSTON

FACILITIES: The village came into its own with the arrival of the canals, and at one time it was the busiest trans-shipment port on the canal system. Features seen along the walk include the pump house, with the letters GJC on the side, Braunston tunnel, All Saints Church, the triangular junction of the Oxford and Grand Union Canals, as well as views of the village, the Warwickshire Plain, and ridge and furrow.
LOCATION: Braunston is just off the A45 Daventry to Dunchurch road.
OPEN: Can be walked all year.
ADMISSION: Charge for leaflet.
TEL: 01604 237220 (Countryside Centre).

COUNTRYSIDE WALKS IN ROCKINGHAM FOREST

FACILITIES: Six walks in the Rockingham Forest areas, produced by the Rockingham Forest Trust and Countryside Services, Northamptonshire County Council.
ADMISSION: Charge for leaflets.
OPEN: Can be walked at most times.
TEL: 01603 237220 (Countryside Centre)

DAVENTRY GROUP OF THE RAMBLERS

FACILITIES: A regular programme of walks arranged, together with talks, etc.
LOCATION: In and around Daventry.
OPEN: Ring for programme.
ADMISSION: Charge for membership. *TEL:* 01327 878695.

DITCHFORD LAKES

FACILITIES: Lakeside walks and birdwatching.
LOCATION: Ditchford Lane, Ditchford.
OPEN: Daylight hours.
ADMISION: No charge. *TEL:* N/A.

EVENLEY

FACILITIES: One of South Northamptonshire Heart of the Countryside Walks. Takes in some interesting features on the walk with information about buildings, a short history of Evenley, etc.
LOCATION: From Brackley TIC to Evenley and the around the village.
OPEN: Can be walked at most times.
ADMISSION: Free. *TEL:* 01280 700111.

EXPLORING THE OXFORD CANAL.

FACILITIES: The Walk runs between Oxford and Coventry, with a section in Northamptonshire.
LOCATION: See leaflet - available from TIC's and British Waterways offices.
ADMISSION: No charge.
TEL: 01788 890666 (BW - Oxford and Grand Union Canal office).

GRAND UNION CANAL

FACILITIES: The towpath starts in the county at Braunston and passes through a large part of Northamptonshire before reaching the Buckinghamshire border. BW organise guided walks and family expeditions in conjunction with Northamptonshire County Council Countryside Services. These include out on foot and back by boat.

Informative commentary is provided, and the walks are at a leisurely pace. Suitable for all ages.
LOCATION: At various points along the Grand Union Canal.
OPEN: Ring for details.
ADMISSION: Charge made. *TEL:* 01604 237220 (Countryside Centre).

GRAND UNION CANAL WALK

FACILITIES: It is possible to walk along the towing-path between London and Birmingham. Books and leaflets available, together with accommodation guides.
LOCATION: See publication.
OPEN: Can be walked during daylight hours.
ADMISSION: Charge for some publications/accommodation guides.
TEL: 01788 890666.

HIGHAM WHARF GRAVEL PITS

FACILITIES: Waterside walks around old gravel workings with natural history interest.
LOCATION: Footpath from Ditchford Lane, off the A45 halfway between Wellingborough and Rushden. Also reached by footpaths from Higham Ferrers.
OPEN: Always.
ADMISSION: No charge. *TEL:* N/A.

HOLLOWELL RESERVOIR

FACILITIES: Walks around the edge of this 140 acre Anglian Water reservoir. Permits are needed for horse riding, bird watching and fishing. These can be obtained from Pitsford Fishing Lodge.
LOCATION: Off the A5199.
OPEN: Walks can be taken at most times.
ADMISSION: No charge for walking. *TEL:* 01604 781350.

ISE VALLEY VAGABONDS

FACILITIES: The Walking Club was formed in 1988 with a number of aims, including producing a programme of non-competitive walking, and there is a partner club in Germany. A number of walks in the area, as well as in other parts of the county. Events like the Danetre Dawdle, Danetre Doddle and the Six Lakes Walks are organised. The Vagabond Times is published regularly.
LOCATION: The group meets in The Star, High Street, Wellingborough.
OPEN: Ring for details.
ADMISSION: There is a subscription fee. *TEL:* 01933 410834.

NEWBOTTLE SPINNEY

FACILITIES: Nature trail through this area of woodland.
LOCATION: On the Kings Suttton and Charlton road.
OPEN: Can be walked at most times.
ADMISSION: Free - leaflet from Brackley TIC. *TEL:* 01280 700111.

NORTHAMPTON ARM GRAND UNION CANAL

FACILITIES: This is a spur of the Grand Union canal, starting at Gayton Junction and falls 109 ft as it passes through 17 locks, before joining the River Nene 5miles away at South Bridge in Northampton. Interesting sites encountered along the way include Rothersthorpe (which featured in the Domesday Book), Express Lifts Tower, Carlsberg Brewery and one of the old green lanes.
LOCATION: Starts at Gayton Junction off the A43, and continues to Northampton Town centre.
OPEN: Can be walked at most times.
ADMISSION: Charge for leaflet.
TEL: 01604 237220 (Countryside Centre).

NORTHAMPTON AND DISTRICT GROUP OF THE RAMBLERS

FACILITIES: Arranges walks in the Northampton area and further afield.
LOCATION: Various venues.
OPEN: See programme.
ADMISSION: Membership fee. *TEL:* 01604 492265 (General Secretary)

PITSFORD WATER

FACILITIES: Excellent views of water, sailing, wildlife and countryside. Walk around the reservoir perimeter from any car park. Permit required for nature reserve area.
LOCATION: Various car parks around the reservoir. Fishing Lodge for permit Brixworth Road, Holcot.
ADMISSION: Charge for permit for nature reserve.
OPEN: Can be walked at most times.
TEL: 01604 781350.

RAVENSTHORPE RESERVOIR

FACILITIES: Birdwatching can be undertaken by permit obtained from Pitsford Fishing Lodge.
LOCATION: Off the A5199 north west of Northampton.
OPEN: Most times.
ADMISSION: Charge for permit.   *TEL:* 01604 781350.

STOKE BRUERNE

FACILITIES: Two pleasant walks alongside the canal. One goes to Blisworth Tunnel, the other to the flight of seven locks. The tarmac walk to the Tunnel is suitable for pushchairs. The other walk is well kept along the towpath.

LOCATION: Canal towpath, Stoke Bruerne.

OPEN: Can be walked at most times.

ADMISSION: No charge.   *TEL:* 01604 862229 (Canal Museum).

STOKE BRUERNE

FACILITIES: The growth of the village, and its former 'livelihood', was due to the canal which was built as the result of a 1793 Act of Parliament. The idea was to shorten the distance between the Midlands and London by some 60 miles. The River Tove, Canal Museum, Stoke Bruerne tunnel entrance, and tunnel airshafts can all be seen.

OPEN: Can be walked at most times.

LOCATION: See map for details.

ADMISSION: Charge for leaflet.

TEL: 01604 237220 (Countryside Centre).

SULBY RESERVOIR

FACILITIES: Walk between the two small lakes which supplies water for the Grand Union Canal.

LOCATION: Reached from the A5199 (Northampton-Leicester road) between Welford and Naseby. The Welford-Sibbertoft footpath starts a few hundred yards along the Welford-Naseby road and crosses between the two small lakes.

OPEN: Always.

ADMISSION: No charge.   *TEL:* N/A.

THRAPSTON GRAVEL PITS

FACILITIES: There are a number of walks around this area. The best place to start is from the layby on the A605, just north of Thrapston.

LOCATION: Close to A605 Thrapston-Oundle road.

OPEN: Can be walked at most times.

ADMISSION: No charge.   *TEL:* N/A.

WALKS AROUND EVERDON

FACILITIES: Twelve walks in and around this west Northamptonshire village.

LOCATION: All walks start outside the Field Studies Centre in the centre of the village, reached off the A45 between Weedon and

Daventry. Copies of the booklet from Everdon Field Studies Centre, Everdon, Daventry, NN11 3BL. Cheques payable to NCC.

OPEN: Can be walked at any reasonable time.

ADMISSION: £1.25 (inc postage) for booklet.

TEL: 01327 361384 - office hours (Field Studies Centre).

WATERLINE WALKS

FACILITIES: Take place along the canal towpaths, and organised to cater for all the family.

LOCATION: Starting points at various places along the Grand Union Canal covering places as far apart as Rothersthorpe and Watford.

OPEN: Ring for details.

ADMISSION: Ring for details.   **TEL:** 01788 890666.

WATFORD

FACILITIES: The village was mentioned in the Domesday Day, and its long history is immortalised in the many earthworks around the village. The walk takes in some interesting villages, including Welton, Ashby St Ledger (of Gunpowder Plot fame), the Parish Church of St Peter and St Paul, as well as the Watford locks.

LOCATION: See leaflet for details.

OPEN: Can be walked at all times.

ADMISSION: Charge for leaflet.

TEL: 01604 237220 (Countryside Centre).

WELFORD

FACILITIES: Welford was already in existence before the Domesday Survey. This tour takes in the deserted village of Downtown, of which little is known, the Manor House, Congregational Chapel and the Church of St Mary.

LOCATION: See leaflet for details.

OPEN: Can be walked at all times.

ADMISSION: Charge for leaflet.

TEL: 01604 237220 (Countryside Centre).

WELLINGBOROUGH AND DISTRICT GROUP OF THE RAMBLERS ASSOCIATION

FACILITIES: Arranges a programme of walks and talks for members.

LOCATION: See programme.

OPEN: See programme.

ADMISSION: Charge for membership.   **TEL:** 01933 680032.

WHISTON LOCKS TO EARLS BARTON

FACILITIES: A circular walk along this part of the Nene Valley. There are maps at the locks which highlight the path.

LOCATION: Whiston Locks/Earls Barton Locks - see maps.

OPEN: Can be walked at all times.

ADMISSION: No charge.   *TEL:* 01604 236633.

WOODFORD - LANDSCAPES FROM THE PAST

FACILITIES: The leaflet has been produced by Northamptonshire Heritage. A circular walk which explores a variety of interesting aspects of the village and the parish, including Three Hills (Tumuli), site of windmill, ridge and furrow, etc.

LOCATION: The village is in the Nene Valley between Irthlingborough and Thrapston. Cars can be parked in the village centre, but avoid obstruction. No parking on the Village Green.

OPEN: Can be walked at most times.

ADMISSION: No charge.

TEL: 01604 237272 (Northamptonshire Heritage).

YARWELL MILL

FACILITIES: Riverside walks.

LOCATION: Yarwell Mill Caravan Park, Yarwell, on an unclassified road to the north east of Oundle.

OPEN: Ring for times.

ADMISSION: Ring for details.   *TEL:* 01780 782344.

WATER SPORTS

BODDINGTON RESERVOIR

FACILITIES: Dingy racing, cruising and windsurfing operated by Banbury Sailing Club. Public open day and beginners, sailing courses, etc.

LOCATION: Reached off the A361 at the second mini-roundabout in Byfield. The club is about 1.5 miles ahead on the left.

OPEN: Ring for details.

ADMISSION: Charge.   *TEL:* 01926 498368.

BRITISH SUB-AQUA CLUB

FACILITIES: Diving.

LOCATION: Ring for details.

OPEN: Ring.

ADMISSION: Charge.   *TEL:* 01933 318521.

CORBY BOATING LAKE

FACILITIES: Boating in season.
LOCATION: Cottingham Road.
ADMISSION: Charge for boats.
OPEN: Ring.   *TEL:* 01536 400093.

BUBBLES DIVING

FACILITIES: On-site swimming pool, classrooms, etc. Courses arranged for beginners to instructor level.
LOCATION: 1 St Edmunds Road, Northampton.
OPEN: Tues-Sat 1000-1800.
ADMISSION: Charges.   *TEL:* 01604 636338.

COSGROVE PARK

FACILITIES: Private leisure complex with facilities for a wide range of water-based activities over eight lakes. These include wind surfing, water-skiing, and jet-skiing.
LOCATION: Cosgrove village, off the A508 east of Stony Stratford.
OPEN: Mar-Oct: ring for details.
ADMISSION: Charge.   *TEL:* 01908 563360.

CRANSLEY RESERVOIR

FACILITIES: Sailing for members of Cransley Sailing Club. Youth open day and public open day.
LOCATION: From Kettering, turn left into Thorpe Malsor, then take left fork. Continue along road to gated entrance on the right. There is a club park.
OPEN: Ring.
ADMISSION: Charge.   *TEL:* 01536 710943.

DRAYTON RESERVOIR
See Middlemore Reservoir

EARLS BARTON RIVERSIDE PICNIC SITE

FACILITIES: Canoe launch site.
LOCATION: Station Road.
ADMISSION: Free.
OPEN: Usually accessible.   *TEL:* 01604 237220 (Countryside Centre).

GRENDON LAKES WATER SKI CLUB

FACILITIES: Water skiing and wind surfing. Club room, restaurant, bars and corporate hospitality.
LOCATION: Main Road, Grendon, east of Northampton, off either A45 (Earls Barton turn), or A509.

328

OPEN: Apr-end Sept - Fri, Sat, Sun - 1000-2100.
ADMISSION: Charge.   *TEL:* 01933 665305.

HIGHAM FERRERS CANOE CLUB
FACILITIES: Canoeing for all stages.
LOCATION: Ring.
OPEN: Ring.
ADMISSION: Club fee.   *TEL:* 01933 622124.

HOLLOWELL SAILING CLUB
FACILITIES: Sailing for members on the 130 acre Hollowell Reservoir.
Courses organised, including 'Start sailing', 'Better boat handling', etc.
Public open day.
LOCATION: Just off the A5199 on top of the hill leaving Hollowell for
Guilsborough.
OPEN: Ring.
ADMISSION: Charges.
TEL: 01933 652735, Clubhouse - 01604 740328.

MIDDLE NENE CRUISING CLUB
FACILITIES: Ring for full details,
LOCATION: Titchmarsh Mill.
OPEN: Ring.
ADMISSION: Membership fee.   *TEL:* 01832 720380

MIDDLE NENE SAILING CLUB
FACILITIES: Situated on the west bank of Thrapston Lake, and
adjacent to the River Nene. The Clubhouse has a well appointed club
room with a refreshment counter which is staffed at busy times. There is
also a licensed bar and lounge. Ample car parking. A signposted walk is
part of the Nene Way. A variety of courses is organised including 'Start
to Sail', 'Junior start to sail', etc. Windsurfing and canoeing also
available.
LOCATION: Can be reached via Chancery Lane from the centre of
Thrapston.
OPEN: Ring for details.
ADMISSION: Membership fee.   *TEL:* 01933 460220 (Secretary).

MIDDLEMORE (DRAYTON) RESERVOIR
FACILITIES: Sailing for club members - Rugby Sailing Club. Organises
'Beginners' Sailing courses, and has a public open day.
LOCATION: Ashby Road, 2 miles north of Daventry town centre, on the
A361, the reservoir is on the left opposite Hotel.

OPEN: Ring.
ADMISSION: Charge.　　*TEL:* 01203 333795.

NASEBY SAILING CLUB
FACILITIES: Sailing for members. Public open days held.
LOCATION: Naseby Reservoir, 2 miles south of Welford on the A5199 on the left.
OPEN: Ring.
ADMISSION: Charge.　　*TEL:* 01858 575711.

NORTHAMPTON BOAT CLUB
FACILITIES: A range from beginners to advanced.
LOCATION: Weston Mill Lane, Weston Favell, Northampton.
OPEN: Ring.
ADMISSION: Membership fee.　　　*TEL:* 01604 630583.

NORTHAMPTON CANOE CLUB
FACILITIES: Provides a variety of courses for all stages.
LOCATION: River Nene in Northampton.
OPEN: Ring for times.
ADMISSION: Fees charged.　　*TEL:* 01604 831183/493375/766660.

NORTHAMPTON ROWING CLUB
FACILITIES: Provides courses for individuals from the age of 14. Rowing and sculling, women's session, men's squad training.
LOCATION: River Nene, Bedford Road, Northampton.
OPEN: Sat starts 1400; Suns from 1000 (sculling and rowing); 1400-1600 (squad training).
ADMISSION: Charges made.
TEL: 01327 341730 (Sat session/women's session); 01604 845949 (Sun session); 01604 791946 (squad training).

NORTHAMPTON SAILING CLUB
FACILITIES: Meets at Pitsford Water with a wide range of activities.
LOCATION: Off A508 at the turning for Brixworth Country Park, and enter gate by the dam.
OPEN: Ring.
ADMISSION: Charge.　　*TEL:* 01858 431313.

NORTHAMPTON SUB-AQUA CLUB
FACILITIES: Experience scuba-diving. Courses include 5 pool sessions. 5 lectures, 4 open water dives.
LOCATION: 43b Abbey Road, Far Cotton.
OPEN: Courses to suit - Mon-Fri, Sat/Sun, etc. Ring.

ADMISSION: £50 per course, Unemployed and student fees.
TEL: 01604 453333.

NORTHAMPTON WATER SKI CLUB LTD
FACILITIES: Facilities for water-skiing.
LOCATION: Delapre Lake.
OPEN: Ring.
ADMISSION: Charge.   *TEL:* 01604 709440/412303.

NORTHAMPTONSHIRE SCHOOLS SAILING AND CANOEING ASSOCIATION
FACILITIES: Meets at Pitsford Water and provides in-term courses for Northamptonshire schools and for the general public. Includes dinghy sailing, windsurfing and canoeing for adults and children - from 8 years upwards. Also race training, all ladies courses and activity holiday weeks. More details in a separate brochure. There is a large classroom, rescue boat, and the use of changing rooms and showers.
LOCATION: Pitsford Water - take the road off the roundabout on the A508 sgnposted Brixworth Country Park, and enter the gates by the dam.
OPEN: Ring for leaflet/brochure.
ADMISSION: Charges.   *TEL:* 01604 880801 (answerphone).

OUNDLE BOAT CLUB
FACILITIES: Cruising.
LOCATION: Riverside Buildings.
OPEN: Ring.
ADMISSION: Charge.
TEL: N/A. Contact Mr P Hanley, 3 Southbridge Ct, Oundle, PE8 4DH.

POWERBOAT RACING
FACILITIES: Over the county border, but operated from Northamptonshire. Formula 0, 0.500, T850, Osy400, J250, HR100.
LOCATION: Ring.
OPEN: Ring.
ADMISSION: Charges.
TEL: 01327 842121 (evenings), 01604 617845 (day).

YARWELL MILL
FACILITIES: Slipway for launching boats.
LOCATION: Yarwell Mill Caravan Park, Yarwell, on an unclassified road off the A605 or A1, to the north east of Oundle.
OPEN: Ring for times.
ADMISSION: Charge.   *TEL:* 01780 782344.

See also Nature Reserves

BUCKNELL WOOD
FACILITIES: Forest Enterprise 500 acre mixed woodland with waymarked trails. Picnic places and car parking.
LOCATION: Off the A43 Silverstone to Abthorpe Road.
OPEN: All year round.
ADMISSION: Free.   *TEL:* 01780/444394 (Forest Enterprise).

CHARTER WOOD
FACILITIES: The wood was established by the Major of Northampton (Malcolm Lloyd) to mark the 800 Anniversary of the Charter granted to Northampton Borough by Richard I. The woodland covers 8ha and consists of 800 oaks planted during 1989/90. The trees were sponsored and each sponsor received a vellum.
LOCATION: The wood is in Delapre Park (behind Delapre Abbey), one of Northampton's Public Open Spaces. and is maintained by Northampton Borough Council.
OPEN: When the Park is open.
ADMISSION: Free. *TEL:* 01604 233500 (Northampton Boro' Council).

CHERRY LAP/MOUNTERLEY
FACILITIES: Covers 124 ha, and is owned by the Forest Enterprise. Woodland walks.
LOCATION: Near brigstock.
OPEN: Every day.
ADMISSION: No charge.   *TEL:* 01780 444394 (Forest Enterprise).

DRAYTON ESTATE WOODLAND
FACILITIES: The wood was planted in the mid 1980's for cuttings which could be used to fuel a 1 million BTU wood burner in Drayton House. Plans are in hand to harvest coppiced timber in some of the semi-natural woodlands. Not normally open to the public but visits are arranged at various times.
LOCATION: From Islip, near Kettering, take the road to Slipton. Limited parking at Slipton Grange Chip Store.
OPEN: Ring for details of pre-planned visits.
ADMISSION: Ring. *TEL:* 01832 732405 (L G Stopford Sackville).

EVERDON STUBBS
FACILITIES: This ancient piece of woodland is owned by the Woodland Trust. The 72 acres includes a mixture of hardwoods, including

pendunculate and sessile oak, hazel, rowan, hornbeam, sycamore and silver birch. Famed for its bluebells in the spring, but a delight at any time of the year, with many wild flowers, birds, butterflies and other insects. Small car park and well-worn paths (not waymarked). A booklet about the wood can be obtained from Everdon Field Studies Centre, Everdon, Daventry, NN11 3BL, price £1.25 including postage (Tel 01327 361384).

LOCATION: Situated on an unclassified road, and reached via the A45 Weedon to Daventry road, at the Dodford turn, signposted Upper Weedon and Everdon. At the T-junction at the end of this road, turn left and the wood is about half a mile along the Farthingstone road.

OPEN: All year round.

ADMISSION: Free, but the WT would welcome your membership.

TEL: 01476 74297 (Woodland Trust).

FIELDSIDE COVERT

FACILITIES: Covering 15.8 acres the area is owned by the Woodland Trust.

LOCATION: Yelvertoft is on an unclassified road off the A428 to the north of Crick.

OPEN: Access usually available.

ADMISSION: Free, but the WT would welcome your membership.

TELEPHONE: 01476 74297 (Woodland Trust).

FINESHADES WOODS

FACILITIES: A large area of woodland (475ha), which was once part of Rockingham Forest, it has a high conservation value. It is rich in plants and animals, including many rare species, like the wild service tree. There are fallow deer and muntjac, together with a wide variety of woodland butterflies. Educational facilities. Woodland walks. Parking, picnic areas, together with leaflets. Special cycle route. Also HQ of the Northants Forest District.

LOCATION: Off the A43 Stamford-Corby road near Duddington.

OPEN: All year.

ADMISSION: No charge.

TEL: 01780 444394 (Forest Enterprise).

GRAFTON PARK WOOD

FACILITIES: On the Boughton Estate, it is an area used for shooting and game rearing. Picnic areas, waymarked walks, car parking. Group visits can be pre-booked seven days in advance

LOCATION: North east of Kettering, off the A43/A604.

OPEN: Most of the year, but by appointment only, because the wood may be in use for shooting or forestry operations. A roadside notice board gives details of when walks can be taken.
ADMISSION: Free, but there is a charge for group visits.
TEL: 01536 515731 (The Director, The Living Landscape Trust).

HARLESTONE FIRS

FACILITIES: Owned by the Althorp Estate Woodland Trust, the area mainly consists of coniferous plantations. It is a working wood and the timber is harvested at regular intervals. There is a sawmill on the site (not open to the public). There are many footpaths and bridleways, but visitors are asked to keep to these. There is only one official Right of Way through the Firs.
LOCATION: On the A428 Northampton to Rugby Road before Harlestone village, and parking is in the layby opposite the entrance and by Harlestone Garden Centre.
OPEN: Can be walked at most times.
ADMISSION: No charge. TEL: 01604 751346.

HARRY'S PARK

FACILITIES: 186ha owned by the Forest Enterprise
LOCATION: Near Brigstock.
OPEN: Always.
ADMISSION: Free. TEL: 01780 444394 (Forest Entrprise).

HAZELBOROUGH FOREST

FACILITIES: A mixed woodland covering 407ha, the area is owned by Forest Enterprise. It is part of the original Whittlewood Forest. Parking, walks and picnic places. 2km Forest Trail.
LOCATION: Off A43 south of Silverstone.
OPEN: Can be used at most times.
ADMISSION: Free.
TEL: 01780 444394(Forest Enterprise). Trail available from Brackley TIC (01280) 700111.

IRCHESTER COUNTRY PARK

FACILITIES: 81ha of planted woodland within the country park. Walks and leaflets available covering plants and animals (see also Country Parks section). Free parking.
LOCATION: Gypsy Lane, on the B570, Little Irchester to Irchester road, and off the A509 south east of Wellingborough
OPEN: Park's facilities always open, including out of hours parking. Some facilities closed at certain times.

ADMISSION: Free.   *TEL:* 01933 276866.

LINGS WOOD

FACILITIES: An area of mixed woodland, it is a nature reserve owned by Northampton Borough Council and managed by the Wildlife Trust for Northamptonshire. There are walks (not waymarked) through the area, which also houses the Trust's offices. Car parking at entrance to wood. Playscheme Activity and Watch group meetings.
LOCATION: On Lings Way off the A4500 4 miles east of Northampton.
OPEN: All year round.
ADMISSION: Free.   *TEL:* 01604 405285 (Wildlife Trust).

THE NUTTERY

FACILITIES: The area was originally a commercial cob nut orchard, which covers 1.5 acres and has been donated to the Woodland Trust. Coppicing is taking place to restore the nuttery to production. It is advisable to take care in the spring when the ground is covered with snowdrops.
LOCATION: Situated in Manor Lane, Newnham, not far from the Nene Way.
OPEN: Access usually available.
ADMISSION: Free, but the WT would welcome your membership.
TEL: 01476 74297 (Woodland Trust).

ROTARY WILDLIFE CORRIDOR

FACILITIES: Covering 4ha the area was planted during National Tree Week in November 1993 by Rotary International, with help from Lord Northampton (whose land it is on), 400 members of the public and with assistance from Northamptonshire County Council, The Nene Valley Project and South Northamptonshire Council. Trees planted include 280 field maple, 250 oak, 175 each of birch, crab apple. hazel and alder, together with 600 ash, and 3000 hawthorn to provide the roadside hedge. Although the trees are young, it is worth visiting the area regularly to see how they are doing.
FACILITIES: A car park. Dogs must be kept on a lead. Access is available to the main central footpath linking the area to the Nene Way.
LOCATION: Take the Grendon road off the A45 Northampton to Wellingborough road. At the T-junction turn west towards Cogenhoe. Car park is about 1 mile along this road.
OPEN: All times.
ADMISSION: Free.   *TEL:* 01604 696839.

SALCEY FOREST

FACILITIES: Covers 500ha and is owned by the Forest Enterprise, it is an ancient hunting forest and a piece of woodland with some very old oaks. Waymarked walks (Lesser Spotted and Great Spotted Woodpecker Trails), orienteering course, nature trails, guided walks at various times, picnic area, car parking, some play equipment, toilets, information boards, Ranger service.

LOCATION: Off the B526 between Northampton and Newport Pagnell.

OPEN: All year round.

ADMISSION: Charges for some activities including parking.

TEL: 01780 444394 (Forest Enterprise).

SOUTHEY WOOD

FACILITIES: An ancient woodland site, there has been continuous woodland cover in the area for many centuries. Although the trees are not as old as the site, the ground and the shrub flora have changed little over the centuries. Plants found include lords and ladies, bluebells, wild garlic (ransoms), and wild service tree, wild privet and guelder rose. A trail leaflet shows what to look for. Easy access trail. Car park.

LOCATION: On a minor road from Helpston and the A47 near Wansford.

OPEN: Can be visited at most times.

ADMISSION: No charge.   *TEL:* 01780 444394 (Forest Enterprise).

STOKE WOOD

FACILITIES: The present wood is a remnant of the once extensive Rockingham Forest, covering 26.9 acres with a wide variety of trees, birds, wild flowers and butterflies. It is owned and managed by the Woodland Trust.

FACILITIES: Car parking and walks (not waymarked).

LOCATION: Between Stoke Albany and Desborough, off the B690.

OPEN: All year.

ADMISSION: Free, but the WT would welcome your membership.

TEL: 01476 74297 (Woodland Trust).

WAKERLEY GREAT WOOD

FACILITIES: Owned by the Forest Enterprise and the Marquis of Exeter, the wood was once part of the extensive Rockingham Forest, and covers 361ha. Waymarked walks, car parks, toilets, orienteering course and picnic area.

LOCATION: North east of Corby near Wakerley and off the A43.

OPEN: All year round.

ADMISSION: Free.   *TEL:* 01780 444394 (Forest Enterprise).

WHISTLEY WOOD

FACILITIES: Consists of remnants of the former Royal hunting forest of Whittlebury, which covered around 20000 acres. An excellent place for birds, and - apart from the traffic - also the dawn chorus.
LOCATION: Off A43 about 0.75 miles beyond Syresham. Take the turning for Crowfield. Entrance to the wood on the left.
OPEN: Access normally available.
ADMISSION: Free. **TEL:** 01780 444394.

WOOD BURCOTE (Land at)

FACILITIES: Covers 9.5 acres and has been planted. It is owned by the Woodland Trust.
LOCATION: Wood Burcote 2 miles south of Towcester and on an unclassified road from the end of the Towcester bypass (A43).
OPEN: Access at most times.
ADMISSION: Free, but the WT would welcome your membership.
TEL: 01476 74297.

YOUTH CLUBS

BECTIVE YOUTH CENTRE

FACILITIES: Wide range, including Campaigners - Gymnastics, Music Factory, Gym Club, Tap and Dance, Youth Club, Jugglers, Octopus After School Club.
LOCATION: Whiston Road, Northampton.
OPEN: Mon-Sun - various times for various activities - ring for details.
ADMISSION: Charges for some activities.
TEL: 01604 712924.

BRIXWORTH YOUTH CLUB

FACILITIES: General youth club activities, and a social meeting place for teenagers. Visits and trips organised.
LOCATION: By the Church.
OPEN: Fri for youth group. Other nights for different youth organisations.
ADMISSION: Charge. **TEL:** 01327 877022 (Daventry office).

JOHN CLARE CENTRE

FACILITIES: Organises events for different groups. Bangladeshi Boys group and All Nations Youth Group.
LOCATION: John Clare Centre, Kettering Road, Northampton.

OPEN Bangladeshi Boys Group - Tues/Thurs 1530-1830; All Nations Youth Group Tues/Fri 1930-2000.
ADMISSION: Ring for details.   *TEL:* 01604 630849.

THE CONNAUGHTY CENTRE

FACILITIES: Mainly aimed at young people, but there are a number of facilities for adults. Coffee bar from 1100-1530 serving drinks, snacks and meals. Computer video games, counselling rooms/service, large hall with stage, bar football table, clinic room, meeting rooms, outdoor cafe/barbecue/picnic area, pool table, satellite tv, sports hall marked out for various team games, showers, changing room, table tennis.
LOCATION: Cottingham Road, Corby.
OPEN: Coffee bar 1100-1530; sports hall and other facilities 0900-2000; other users ring for details.
ADMISSION: Some groups have a membership fee.
TEL: 01536 204258.

DAVENTRY AND DISTRICT YOUTH TEAM

FACILITIES: Support for village youth groups, exchange visits involving young people from other countries, Girls and Young Women's groups, Young Mums Group, Training courses for volunteer youth workers, Pegasus Rural Youth Work project visiting smaller villages. Duke of Edinburgh's Award, opportunities for young people with disabilities, sports and outdoor pursuits, personal mailing, arts events, subsidised use of school premises by youth groups, Dino's - Town Centre Drop in Cafe, Go-for-it Club - Leisure/Socials for young people, hire of equipment - and lots, lots more!
LOCATION: Office: Abbey Centre, Market Square Daventry. Activities arranged for the Daventry District area.
OPEN: Ring for further information - from 0900-1300 - Mon-Fri.
ADMISSION: Charges for some activities.   *TEL:* 01327 877022.

DREAMS YOUTH CLUB

FACILITIES: Various activities.
LOCATION: Connaughty Centre, Cottingham Road, Corby.
OPEN: Wed & Fri 01930-2000.
ADMISSION: Charges for various activities.   *TEL:* 01536 204258.

DUSTON FOLK CENTRE

FACILITIES: General activities, including soccer, pool and table tennis.
LOCATION: Duston Upper School.
OPEN: Tues afternoon 13 year olds; Wed evenings 14+.
ADMISSION: Charge.   *TEL:* 01604 751303.

EARLS BARTON YOUTH CLUB
FACILITIES: Ring for details.
LOCATION: Recreation ground.
OPEN: 1900-2130 Wed.
ADMISSION: Ring. *TEL:* 01604 812177.

EAST NORTHANTS AREA YOUTH TEAM
FACILITIES: Organises a range of activities for youth groups, etc. in the East Northants area.
LOCATION: Based at the Youth Centre, Moor Road, Rushden.
OPEN: 0900-1300 (Mon-Fri) for enquiries.
ADMISSION: No charge for this service.   *TEL:* 01933 314077.

ECTON BROOK YOUTH CLUB
FACILITIES: General club activities for 14+.
LOCATION: Ecton   Brook   Community   Centre,   Ecton   Brook, Northampton.
OPEN: Fri starts at 2000.
ADMISSION: Ring for details.   *TEL:* 01604 648221 (for information).

FARM YOUTH CLUB
FACILITIES: General club activities.
LOCATION: Rickyard Road, Arbours, Northampton.
OPEN: Mon/Wed/Thurs 1930-2200 Open Club for 14+.
ADMISSION: Charge.   *TEL:* 01604 405253.

HESKETH CENTRE
FACILITIES: Cafe Deja Vu for 13-17 year olds.
LOCATION: Lodge Farm, Goldings.
OPEN: Mon/Wed evenings.
ADMISSION: Charge for drinks. *TEL:* 01604 648221 (for information).

KINGS HEATH ADVENTURE CLUB
FACILITIES: Arranges activities for various age groups, there is also a girls group.
LOCATION: North Oval.
OPEN: Girls Group Tues 1900-2000; General Youth Club 2000-2200; Thurs 13 years and under 1800-1930; 13 and over 2000-2200.
ADMISSION: Ring.   *TEL:* N/A.

KINGSTHORPE UPPER SCHOOL YOUTH WING

FACILITIES: A range of activities, which includes D of E Group for 13-25 year olds; D of E training during winter; Swimming Club for mentally and physically disabled young people and able bodied. General youth club activities, and self-programming activities, including gym, swimming, photography, keep-fit. Also Asian Girls Night.
LOCATION: Kingsthorpe Upper School.
OPEN: Mon/Wed/Thurs.
ADMISSION: Charge.   *TEL:* 01604 711953.

OUNDLE YOUTH CLUB

FACILITIES: Activities for 9-21 year olds, including sports, computer games, discussions, trips, discos.
LOCATION: The Drill Hall, Benefield Road.
OPEN: Tues/Fri 1900-2200.
ADMISSION: Small charge.   *TEL:* 01832 272767.

PHOENIX YOUTH CENTRE

FACILITIES: Wide range of activities.
LOCATION: Ashby Road, Daventry.
OPEN: Ring.
ADMISSION: Charge.   *TEL:* 01327 703864.

RECTORY FARM HOUSE

FACILITIES: General Club activities.
LOCATION: Rectory Farm Community Centre, Rectory Farm, Northampton.
OPEN: Mon 1930-2000.
ADMISSION: Ring for details.   *TEL:* 01604 648221 (for information).

RUSHDEN YOUTH CENTRE

FACILITIES: Wide range of activities.
LOCATION: The Youth Centre, Moor Road.
OPEN: Ring for times.
ADMISSION: Ring.   *TEL:* 01933 314077.

THORPLANDS YOUNG PEOPLES ASSOCIATION

FACILITIES: Youth Club for 13+, also after-school activities for 9-13 year olds.
LOCATION: Ring for details.
OPEN: 13+ Mon/Thurs 1930; 9-13 Tues 1530-1730.
ADMISSION: Ring for details.   *TEL:* 01604 648221.

WOODFORD HALSE YOUTH CLUB

FACILITIES: Social meeting place for teenagers, with general club activities. Programme of visits and trips.

LOCATION: Behind the village school.

OPEN: 13+ Mon/Thurs 1930; 9-13 Tues 1530-1730.

ADMISSION: Ring.   *TEL:* 01327 877022 (Daventry office).

STOP PRESS

March 1998:   Planet Quaser Laser Gun   Page 203 is now closed.

GET OUT!

FUTURE REPRINTS

Do you know of an organisation etc. not mentioned in this edition? Do you wish to be included in future editions? Have details of organisations altered?

If you wish alterations or inclusions then return, or photocopy this page with details.

Name of Organisation ....

Details ....

....

....

....

....

Telephone number for contact ....

Return to:
Ron Wilson
c/o Jema Publications
40 Ashley Lane
Moulton
Northampton
NN3 7TJ

FOR YOUR OWN NOTES